Against Moral Responsibility

Against Moral Responsibility

Bruce N. Waller

The MIT Press
Cambridge, Massachusetts
London, England

KH

For information about special quantity discounts, please email special_sales@ mitpress.mit.edu.

This book was set in Stone Sans and Stone Serif by Toppan Best-set Premedia Limited. Printed and bound in the United States of America.

Library of Congress Cataloging-in-Publication Data

Waller, Bruce N., 1946–
Against moral responsibility / Bruce N. Waller.
    p.   cm.
Includes bibliographical references (p.   ) and index.
ISBN 978-0-262-01659-9 (hardcover : alk. paper)
1. Responsibility. 2. Ethics. I. Title.
BJ1451.W275   2011
170—dc22

2011010112

10 9 8 7 6 5 4 3 2 1

9/19/12

Contents

Preface

Against Moral Responsibility is an assault on the moral responsibility system: a system that is profoundly entrenched in our society and its institutions, deeply rooted in our emotions, and vigorously defended by philosophers from Aristotle to the present day. Such an assault might seem foolhardy, or at best quixotic. But in fact, the results from extensive psychological, sociological, and biological studies have caused major problems for defenders of moral responsibility, and there are serious flaws in the moral responsibility system. Furthermore, the philosophical defenders of moral responsibility—though they are numerous, imaginative, insightful, and committed—are in no position to offer a unified defense of the moral responsibility citadel. Instead, in their reactions to the scientific advances challenging the moral responsibility system, philosophers have proposed a great variety of different and conflicting defenses of moral responsibility. There is such controversy among the defenders of moral responsibility that moral responsibility abolitionists might carry the day by sitting back safely while the defenders demolish one another's arguments.

The basic claim of this book is that—all the extraordinary and creative efforts of contemporary philosophers notwithstanding—moral responsibility cannot survive in our naturalistic-scientific system. Moral responsibility was a comfortable fit among gods and miracles and mysteries, but the deeper scientific understanding of human behavior and the causes shaping human character leaves no room for moral responsibility. The second claim is that when we look carefully at the moral responsibility system and at what would actually remain when that system is abolished, it is clear that what we really want—natural *non*miraculous human free will, moral judgments, warm and meaningful personal relationships, creative abilities, and the opportunity to make our own decisions and exercise effective control—can survive and flourish without moral responsibility, and that what is lost—"just deserts," blame and punishment, righteous retribution, special reward—we are better off without. Finally, there is the question of whether it is actually possible to reject the moral responsibility system and replace it with something else. Obviously, that will not be easy on either a personal or societal level, but the final claim of the book is that it is socially and psychologically possible and that we are already making progress toward that goal. In short, the total abolition of moral responsibility is both desirable and possible.

Acknowledgments

In writing this book, I have been remarkably fortunate in the kind and generous support of my family, my friends, and my colleagues, and I have been very lucky to live in an era when so many remarkable philosophers and psychologists are making such insightful contributions to the questions of free will and moral responsibility.

George Graham has marked my path through the psychological literature, often alerting me to important psychological studies that I would otherwise have missed. His work on abnormal psychology and its philosophical implications is a striking example of what can be accomplished by scientifically knowledgeable contemporary philosophers.

My good friend Richard Double, through his published work and our conversations, has long been my guide through the maze of issues surrounding free will and moral responsibility. The remarkable clarity of his views and his ability to map all of the connections and intersections of these tangled questions have been invaluable.

Twenty-five years ago I had an opportunity to write a review of Robert Kane's early book, *Free Will and Values* (1985). Before starting to read the book in preparation for writing the review, I was prepared to scoff: just another in a long line of failed libertarian fantasies, I assumed. Reading only a few pages put a quick end to my scoffing; and though I did not stay to pray, it was soon clear that Bob had developed a libertarian account that was something entirely new: rigorous, never straying anywhere close to miracles or mysteries, carefully argued, scientifically informed. Though we have never been able to reach agreement on the basic issues—Robert Kane remains a resourceful defender of the moral responsibility system that this book attacks—his work, and a number of very enlightening conversations with him, have deepened my understanding of all the issues surrounding free will and moral responsibility (though obviously not quite to the depth that Bob would like) and have been a major stimulus to my musings on the subject.

In recent visits to Tallahassee, I have had the pleasure of luncheon discussions with Randy Clarke, Al Mele, and Mike McKenna; those lively luncheons not only were a great pleasure, but also gave me a much clearer picture of several key issues (I fear they will conclude that my picture is still quite muddled, but at least it is clearer than it was).

I have developed the strongest attacks I can muster against a great variety of defenders of moral responsibility. But it will be obvious to any philosopher that it is the extraordinary richness, variety, and rigor of the arguments in *favor* of moral responsibility that have been the greatest stimulus to my own work, and I am indebted to all of the philosophers who have made the current debate so lively and interesting.

Recently, I completed my second decade in the Department of Philosophy and Religious Studies at Youngstown State University. Youngstown, deep in the heart of the northeast Ohio rust belt, is not a scenic paradise, but if you scratch beneath the surface, it is a beautiful city with beautiful people. My students are from every ethnic background, the children of every wave of immigrants that arrived to work in the now-abandoned steel mills. They do not always have splendid educational backgrounds, but they have a tremendous respect for education and a remarkable capacity for hard work: often taking classes after finishing a midnight factory shift, then getting kids fed and off to school, checking on an aging parent, and still arriving in class eager to learn. For twenty years, they have made my classes stimulating, enjoyable, fresh, and profoundly satisfying. We are also fortunate to have a large and energetic group of superb majors: on a recent Friday afternoon, more than thirty of them converged on a local coffee shop for several hours of reading and discussing John Locke's views on religious tolerance; there would have been more, had they been able to rearrange their demanding job schedules. I am especially indebted to the students in my recent free will seminar, who probed that question with great passion and deep insight.

I am particularly lucky to be working with such stimulating, productive, and congenial colleagues. Every person in the department is actively engaged in fascinating areas of research, ranging from the nature of ritual to the philosophical and religious poetry of Iqbal to the ethics of robotic warfare. People are eager to discuss ideas, share insights, suggest articles and books, consider arguments (no matter how strange), and read works in progress. My indebtedness to my friends and colleagues—Tom Shipka, Brendan Minogue, Linda "Tess" Tessier, Chris Bache, Victor Wan-Tatah, Gabriel Palmer-Fernandez, Mustansir Mir, Deborah Mower, Mark Vopat, and Alan Tomhave—is greater than I can describe. We are also fortunate to have a wonderful group of people who teach a variety of courses with us, including Julie Aultman, Eric Boynton, Walter Carvin, Sister Nancy Dawson, Martina Haines, Zoreh "Z" Kermani, Jeff Limbian, Sarah Lown, Bernie Oakes, Joseph Schonberger, Donna Sloan, Arnold Smith, and Andrew Stypinski. Jeff Butts, who is a research associate in our Islamic Studies Center, is a very valuable and patient resource for all things technical. The vital center of the department, who adds much to its welcoming warm friendliness and everything to its orderly efficiency, is our remarkable departmental administrator, Mary Dillingham, ably assisted by our talented and congenial student worker, Gina Ponzio.

I have been department chair for the past five years, and frankly, it's a pretty soft job: Mary and Gina do all the work. But it is made much more pleasant and satisfying by the presence of a supportive and helpful dean, Shearle Furnish; an associate dean, Jane Kestner, who with remarkable patience manages to straighten out all my mistakes; and a provost, Ikram Khawaja, who is a person of complete integrity and strongly supportive of our department.

There are many people around the university and the city and elsewhere who are wonderful friends and very engaging company. Homer Warren is a frequent lunch companion who loves discussing free will and moral responsibility and who brings to those discussions a unique perspective that is invariably insightful. Many others have enriched my understanding and enlarged my curiosity on a tremendous variety of subjects from politics to environmental issues to poker strategies; they include Howard Mettee, Charles Singler, Fred Alexander, Lauren Schroeder, Luke Lucas, Richard White, Chris Raver, Jack Raver, Paul Sracic, Keith Lepak, Stephen Flora, Lia Ruttan, Gary Salvner, Joe Mosca, Tom Henricks, Judy Henricks, Nawal Ammar, and Robert Weaver.

I am particularly grateful to three MIT Press referees, who read an earlier draft of the book and offered many superb suggestions for its improvement, and to my editor, Phil Laughlin, who found the excellent referees and guided the book safely into the hands of Kathleen A. Caruso, the manuscript editor, who was cordial, clear, precise, and efficient at every step of the editing process. Thanks also to Nancy Kotary for a superb copyediting job, and to Margarita Encomienda, who created the perfect cover image.

Thanks to the editors of *American Philosophical Quarterly* and *Social Theory and Practice*, who allowed me to develop some of my arguments in their pages, and for their permission to include that work here.

Special thanks to the friendly folks at the Beat Coffee Shop, next door to campus, for all the warm smiles, wonderful lunches, and magnificent coffee. Without them, my gears would have long since rusted and ground to a stop.

My richest source of joy and support is my family: my wife, Mary, with her great kindness, patience, warmth, and affection, as well as her very helpful expertise in clinical psychology; my sons, Russell and Adam, who are wonderful math and music students, respectively, and who are the greatest source of pure joy and pride in my life; and my delightful and brilliant daughter-in-law, Robyn, who is deeply engaged in her own very promising philosophical studies.

I am grateful to all of the wonderful people who have made it possible to complete this book and helped me avoid many mistakes, though they deserve neither praise nor reward for their generous efforts. The many flaws that remain in the book are the result of my arrogance and obstinacy, for which I sincerely apologize, and for which I deserve no blame.

1 Moral Responsibility

T. S. Eliot (1943, 37) speaks of "what was believed in as the most reliable—and therefore the fittest for renunciation." Eliot could have been describing moral responsibility. It is believed in fervently. As Cicero (44 BCE/1923, 119) noted, philosophers are willing to entertain almost any hypothesis: "There is nothing so absurd but some philosopher has said it." But even philosophers find it difficult to contemplate the renunciation of moral responsibility. Peter van Inwagen is typical: "I have listened to philosophers who deny the existence of moral responsibility. I cannot take them seriously" (1983, 207). And Peter Strawson insisted that "we cannot take seriously" (1962, 74) the rejection of moral responsibility and the radical changes that it would involve.

Commitment to moral responsibility is based in visceral emotional reactions and locked in place by a far-reaching theoretical system. But the moral responsibility belief system is fighting a running retreat against scientific research that renders this system less and less plausible. The purpose of this book is to show that the key arguments for moral responsibility fail, that moral responsibility is fundamentally inconsistent with our naturalistic world view, that we would be better off if we rejected moral responsibility, and that the abolition of moral responsibility is a genuine possibility; in short, that belief in moral responsibility is a widely held doctrine that is indeed "fittest for renunciation."

What the Moral Responsibility Debate Is About

The dispute over moral responsibility is an old one, with many twists and turns. Some of those twists have involved disputes over exactly what is involved in saying that someone is *morally responsible*. The moral responsibility that is my target is the moral responsibility that justifies special reward and punishment. Moral responsibility provides the moral justification for singling an individual out for condemnation or commendation, praise or blame, reward or punishment. If Susan justly deserves punishment, she must be morally responsible for the wrong she committed. Various philosophers offer a variety of grounds for Susan's moral responsibility: Chisholm and Campbell would say she could have done otherwise, Frankfurt that she reflectively approved of her own will, Fischer that she could exercise guidance control, Dennett that she passed a basic competence threshold. But whatever the conditions required for moral responsibility, it is meeting those conditions that makes punishment (and reward, blame, and praise) fair and just.

The purpose of this book is the abolition of the moral responsibility system, root and branch: we should *never* hold *anyone* morally responsible. It is essential to be clear about what that does not involve. As will be argued in subsequent chapters, it does not involve the rejection of all moral evaluations: Joe may do something that is morally wrong, Joe's immoral behavior may stem from his deeply flawed character, and it is important to recognize and examine those wrongs and flaws, but Joe does not deserve blame or punishment. And it may be useful to blame or punish Joe (though I very much doubt it), but Joe does not justly deserve such blame or punishment. As I use the phrase in this book, "moral responsibility" is the essential (necessary, if not sufficient) condition for justified blame and punishment. Michael McKenna states that "what most everyone is hunting for . . . is the sort of moral responsibility that is desert entailing, the kind that makes blaming and punishing as well as praising and rewarding justified" (2009, 12). What McKenna describes is precisely what I am hunting for as well; the difference is that rather than trying to preserve it and justify it, my goal is to kill it and drive a stake through its heart. But the present point is that when I take aim at moral responsibility, what McKenna describes is my target. That is the dominant way in which "moral responsibility" is understood, both in philosophical and popular use. For example, it is the concept of moral responsibility adopted by Galen Strawson: "responsibility and desert of such a kind that it can exist if and only if punishment and reward can be fair or just without having any pragmatic justification, or indeed any justification that appeals to the notion of distributive justice" (2002, 452). And it is the account given by Randolph Clarke:

If any agent is truly responsible . . . that fact provides us with a specific type of justification for responding in various ways to that agent, with reactive attitudes of certain sorts, with praise or blame, with finite rewards or punishments. To be a morally responsible human agent is to be truly deserving of these sorts of responses, and deserving in a way that no agent is who is not morally responsible. This type of desert has a specific scope and force—one that distinguishes the justification for holding someone responsible from, say, the fairness of a grade given for a performance or any justification provided by consequences. (2005, 21)

I am not claiming proprietary rights to how "moral responsibility" is used; rather, this is only a statement of how it will be used in this book.

So exactly what is this deep philosophical controversy over moral responsibility really about? First, it is not about the conditions for moral responsibility in our current system of holding people morally responsible. That is an important question, certainly, and lawyers and justices and legal scholars have joined philosophers in that debate. This internal debate concerning the proper details of our system of moral responsibility and justice includes difficult questions. Who is competent? What is the age of responsibility? Do addictions destroy moral responsibility? What excuses are legitimate in the moral responsibility system? What is the appropriate legal standard for insanity, and can one be insane and still be morally responsible? A brief perusal of the legal literature on insanity shows how difficult and controversial such questions can be. Those are questions within the system of moral responsibility—difficult questions that have occupied many astute and insightful thinkers. But those are not the questions being examined in this book.

My concern is not with the details of our moral responsibility system, but with the system itself. When philosophers such as C. A. Campbell, Robert Kane, John Martin Fischer, Alfred Mele, Derk Pereboom, Michael McKenna, Saul Smilansky, Susan Wolf, Daniel Dennett, and Randolph Clarke wrestle with the question of moral responsibility, their basic concern is not the details of when our given moral responsibility system justifies and excuses from moral responsibility. Their question is more fundamental: is it ever morally justifiable to hold anyone morally responsible? Rather than the internal details of our system, they are struggling with the question of whether our system of holding people morally responsible is itself morally justified. Is our overall system—or any system—of moral responsibility and "just punishment" really fair? Can our system, or any moral responsibility system, withstand close scrutiny? Can any system of just punishment be morally and rationally justified? That is, they are wrestling with the basic external question of moral responsibility.[1]

It is important to distinguish the internal debates from this fundamental external debate, because too often the lines get crossed. If someone argues, for example, that miscreants who suffered an abusive childhood are morally responsible and justly deserve punishment because our system of moral responsibility does not recognize a harsh childhood as a legitimate exemption from moral responsibility, that's fine; someone else may argue that given the precedents within our system, consistency requires extending excusing conditions to such unfortunate individuals. That is a fascinating internal argument, and it may be pursued with great vigor and insight and resourcefulness. But if someone takes that argument and moves it to the external controversy, then the argument begs the question by assuming the very system of moral responsibility that is in external dispute. That is, if someone argues that murderers who suffer abusive childhoods are not excused from moral responsibility and justified punishment (in our system) and that therefore, at least some people *are* morally responsible, and moral responsibility itself is (externally) justified, then such an argument fails: it assumes what (at this external level) it is supposed to be proving. This distinction means that data on how "moral responsibility" is commonly used—though certainly fascinating—cannot settle the basic external question concerning moral responsibility. I doubt that there is an internal ordinary language usage of "moral responsibility" that is consistent,[2] but there is no doubt that within our culture, people do make claims and ascriptions of moral responsibility. Within the moral responsibility system are frequent assertions of moral responsibility; the external question is whether that system is justified. "Moral responsibility" is in common use and typically understood within that system, but that usage no more justifies the system itself than the common use and understanding of "witch" justified the brutal system that consistently identified and executed witches.

Second, the external debate over moral responsibility is not a debate over whether anyone ever does anything morally wrong or morally right. If no one ever did anything morally right or wrong, the question of moral responsibility would be reduced to a very abstract intellectual exercise. The question is not whether anyone ever does wrong, but whether those wrongdoers justly deserve punishment, whether those who do wrong (and those who do right) are morally responsible for their vicious or virtuous behavior. (Some claim that without moral responsibility there could be no judgments of right or wrong, virtue or vice; that claim will be considered in due course, but I trust that it does not reveal too much of the plot to say that I believe the claim to be false.) Furthermore—and this argument will raise heated objections, which must be considered in later chapters— the basic external debate over moral responsibility is not a question of whether people can have vicious or virtuous characters. The claim here is that they can, but that they do not deserve praise or blame for their characters, or for the behavior which flows from their character traits. No one is morally responsible for being bad or behaving badly—but this does not mean that no one has a character with profound moral flaws.

Third, the debate is not about the efficacy of moral responsibility practices. If someone asserts that the moral responsibility system works well in preventing crime and improving character, there would remain the more basic question: yes, but is it really just? If we could keep a wonderful system of law and order by sacrificing one person chosen at random every year, that might be a tempting tradeoff; indeed, if God offered us such a system, we might well sign on (especially when we consider that otherwise more people will be wrongly killed each year). But we would still have the question: yes, but is it really just? Did the punished person genuinely deserve punishment? Perhaps the larger benefits of this system would outweigh the injustice done to the innocent person who is sacrificed, but that would not change the fact that the innocent person is punished unjustly. The practice of moral responsibility is not an effective way of producing either a safer society or better behaved individuals. To the contrary (it will be argued): moral responsibility blocks implementation of much better systems and causes enormous suffering. But even if the practice of moral responsibility were effective in making a better society, this effectiveness would not prove that the system is just. The point here is only that (unless one is a narrowly doctrinaire utilitarian) it is one thing to determine that a system is efficient—and quite a different process to decide whether it is just.

Accountability and Moral Responsibility

Moral responsibility views that shift the focus away from morally justified punishment and reward fail to capture our basic notion of moral

responsibility. Some claim that moral responsibility is about applying punishment and reward where they will produce the greatest social benefit.
Others claim that moral responsibility involves only the making of moral
judgments: when we say that Beverly did something morally wrong, that
necessarily involves the judgment that she is morally responsible for her
bad behavior. Several of those competing standards for moral responsibility
will be examined and critiqued in the course of this book. But one such
position is quite elegant and will get immediate attention: the view that
moral responsibility is about *accountability*. If you are morally responsible
for an act, then (on the accountability model) it is legitimate to require
you to give an account or justification for your act. When we say that
Cassandra is morally responsible for an act, we mean that she is accountable for that act: she must be capable of giving an account of why she
acted.

Accountability, however, fails as a standard for moral responsibility. In
the first place, people often give an account of why they did something—a
sincere and honest account—that is completely mistaken. There are many
social psychology experiments in which people act under the influence of
factors outside of their awareness, factors that they would vigorously deny
having influenced their behavior. In one famous experiment (Isen and
Levin 1972), people who found a dime in a phone booth almost all stopped
to help a stranger who had "dropped" a set of papers, and those who did
not find a dime seldom helped. Yet the helpers were blissfully unaware—
and would certainly deny—that finding a dime could and did strongly
influence their behavior: it would not be part of any account they would
give of their helping behavior. Even more striking are the experiments in
which part of the brain is externally stimulated, causing people to respond,
but they give an account (in terms of their own motives and reasons) for
why they "acted" as they did. José Delgado, a neuropsychologist, discovered that electrically stimulating a specific region of a patient's brain caused
the patient to turn his head from side to side, as if looking for something.
When Delgado asked his patient to "give an account" of his behavior, "the
patient considered the evoked activity spontaneous and always offered a
reasonable explanation for it" (Delgado 1969, 115).

Even in cases in which an individual gives a correct account of why she
acted badly (or well), that does not establish that she is morally responsible
for that act. Suppose that Ann makes a bad decision and commits a morally

bad act because she decides hastily and fails to consider important moral factors that (had they entered into her deliberations) would have led her to a better choice. If we ask Ann for an account of her bad act, she might accurately report that she chose badly because she is a "cognitive miser" (Cacioppo and Petty 1982) who can deliberate, but who has never developed the capacity for sustained deliberation; indeed, she might regard her cognitive impetuosity as a moral flaw. But is Ann *morally responsible* for her cognitive shortcomings or for the flawed choices that stem from those limitations? Those are questions that still remain after Ann has given an account of her flawed behavior. Thus the capacity to give an account of one's acts is not the same as being morally responsible for those acts.

This view—to be morally responsible is to be subject to the demand to give an account—is appealing because it associates moral responsibility with the special powers of rational account-giving capacity: powers often treated as transcending the histories that shaped us and the limited rational powers we actually enjoy. As tempting as such a view is, as long as we restrain rationality within naturalistic limits, it cannot justify moral responsibility—or so I argue in the forthcoming chapters. Thus if one insists on redefining "moral responsibility" in terms of "accountability," the original question of moral responsibility will still be there after the accountability question is settled: Ann is accountable for (can give an account of) her behavior, but is she morally responsible (justly deserving of blame) for what she did?

Whatever the merits or faults of other views of moral responsibility, this book focuses on what I take to be the core concept of moral responsibility: moral responsibility is what justifies blame and praise, punishment and reward; moral responsibility is the basic condition for giving and claiming both positive and negative just deserts.

The Deep Belief in Moral Responsibility

My goal in this book is to show that claims and ascriptions of moral responsibility (in the robust sense specified previously) cannot be justified, that there are strong arguments to show that—absent miracles—the system of moral responsibility and "just deserts" is fundamentally unfair, and that we will be better off when belief in moral responsibility is utterly eliminated. But belief in moral responsibility is so deep and pervasive—among philosophers and nonphilosophers alike—that it is necessary to pause for a moment and insist that my goal truly is the complete denial and rejection of moral responsibility. It is necessary to insist on that denial because many people (including many philosophers) find it difficult to imagine that anyone genuinely denies moral responsibility.

If we examine why so many regard moral responsibility as immune from serious challenge, then the basis of that belief does not seem nearly so solid and attacking moral responsibility may appear less quixotic. Moral responsibility has many dedicated defenders, but few of them would claim that compelling reasoned arguments have placed moral responsibility beyond challenge. Many philosophers believe that there are good arguments to support moral responsibility, but they do not regard the arguments as so conclusive that they are beyond doubt. Thus the unshakable certainty of many philosophers concerning moral responsibility must have some emotional source independent of rational argument. Perhaps that deep and widespread emotional commitment to moral responsibility is positive and defensible, but we are sadly familiar with many deep emotional commitments—to racism, sexism, jingoism, xenophobia—that examination reveals to be harmful and irrational. Of course some of our deep emotional commitments—our love for our children, for example—still look worthwhile after close scrutiny. But when we recognize that moral responsibility is rooted in emotions rather than reason, it should be less difficult to take seriously the possibility of rational philosophical challenge to the system of moral responsibility. At that point, we can carefully examine the actual arguments for moral responsibility, as well as the case against moral responsibility, and judge them on their merits.

The philosophical literature is replete with a wide variety of very sophisticated arguments in favor of moral responsibility, ranging from exotic varieties of libertarian speculation to mundane claims of pragmatic benefit. But those arguments do not purport to discover moral responsibility; rather, they are put forward to justify a visceral and universal emotional reaction: the basic retributive impulse, the deep desire to strike back when we are harmed. Legal philosopher and scholar Michael S. Moore describes this retributive desire quite clearly:

Of course Dostoyevsky's nobleman [who has his dogs kill a small child in front of the child's mother] should suffer for his gratuitous and unjustified perpetration of a terrible wrong to both his young serf and that youth's mother. As even the gentle

Aloysha murmurs in Dostoyevsky's novel, in answer to the question of what you do with the nobleman: you shoot him. You inflict such punishment even though no other good will be achieved thereby, but simply because the nobleman deserves it. The only general principle that makes sense of the mass of particular judgments like that of Aloysha is the retributive principle that culpable wrongdoers must be punished. This, by my lights, is enough to justify retributivism. (1997, 188)

Whether Jew or Gentile, courtly or common, Elizabethan or contemporary, the words of Shakespeare's Shylock resonate: "I am a Jew. Hath not a Jew eyes? hath not a Jew hands, organs, dimensions, senses, affections, passions? fed with the same food, hurt with the same weapons, subject to the same diseases, heated by the same means, warmed and cooled by the same winter and summer as a Christian is?—if you prick us do we not bleed? if you tickle us do we not laugh? if you poison us do we not die? and if you wrong us shall we not revenge?" (Shakespeare 1596–1598/1993, 3.1.58–68). Many philosophers seem to have a similar visceral commitment to retributive just deserts. Robert C. Solomon states: "Sometimes vengeance is wholly called for, even obligatory, and revenge is both legitimate and justified. Sometimes it is not, notably when one is mistaken about the offender or the offense. But to seek vengeance for a grievous wrong, to revenge oneself against evil—that seems to lie at the very foundation of our sense of justice, indeed, of our very sense of ourselves, our dignity, and our sense of right and wrong" (2004, 37).

Even Daniel Dennett, who has developed an incredible variety of sophisticated arguments to support moral responsibility, has recently rested his case for moral responsibility on our deep retributive desires:

We ought to admit, up front, that one of our strongest unspoken motivations for upholding something close to the traditional concept of free will is our desire to see the world's villains "get what they deserve." And surely they *do* deserve our condemnation, our criticism, and—when we have a sound system of laws in place—punishment. A world without punishment is not a world any of us would want to live in. (2008, 258)

Among contemporary philosophers, Peter French is the most outspoken in celebrating vengeance as a virtue, and he is brutally frank concerning the emotional roots of this view: "Personal and vicarious moral anger can be and ought to be placated by hostile responsive action taken against its cause. Wrongful actions require hostile retribution. That, despite its seeming lack of fit with the body of moral principles upheld in our culture, is actually one of the primary foundations of morality. It is a foundation that is settled in passions, attitudes, emotions, and sentiments, not in reason" (2001, 97). Thus the source of fervent belief in moral responsibility is feelings: the powerful feeling that those who do wrong and cause harm should suffer. That feeling is rooted in an even deeper feeling: when we are harmed, we should strike back.

Perhaps those feelings can, ultimately, be justified by rational argument. I think not, and most philosophers think so; the immediate point is not whether such rational justification can be provided, but that the profound and common belief in moral responsibility is not the product of rational deliberation. Thus, regardless of whether the arguments to justify moral responsibility work, we should not be surprised to find widespread strong belief in moral responsibility. But that almost universal belief cannot itself be used to justify moral responsibility, any more than widespread belief in the existence of God or the justice of subordinating women can justify those beliefs. The strong and common feeling of male superiority was no justification of that view; even if one imagines that the widespread masculine sentiment in favor of female subordination is evidence that it once had some survival value, it is clear that what may have been useful at one stage of development is now maladaptive. The same may be true of belief in moral responsibility: even if one grants that at earlier stages of development, retributive practices were of some benefit (in terms of either group or individual selective pressures), it may be that in our present state they are maladaptive (just as human aggressive tendencies have become severely problematic in an era of handguns, not to mention nuclear weapons), as well as being morally and rationally unjustified and unfair.

When we examine the origins and nature of our retributive emotions, we may conclude that those emotions are not as attractive and virtuous as we had once imagined. Their roots are in a strikeback response that attacks whatever is near. When rats are placed in a cage with an electrified floor and then shocked, they attack one another. When a rat is hurt, its immediate desire is to strike back at *something*: its assailant, or an innocent bystander, or a gnawing post if nothing else is around. Rats that are shocked, but that can vent their rage against another rat (or a gnawing post), suffer fewer problems than rats with nothing to attack: they have less increase in adrenal hormone and blood pressure levels and develop fewer stomach ulcers (Virgin and Sapolsky 1997; Barash 2005). In monkey colonies, a subordinate who suffers an attack from a higher-ranking monkey typically seeks out an individual lower in the hierarchy for attack (Kawamura 1967). Veterinarians warn that a gentle but territorial pet cat may become disturbed by the smell or sound of another cat in the vicinity, and if unable to attack the "intruder," it may redirect its aggression by attacking a family member.

We might imagine ourselves well beyond such primitive reactions, but we understand perfectly when Curly hits Moe, and Moe then strikes Larry. A cartoon shows a boss berating a subordinate man, the man coming home to yell at his wife, the wife reprimanding the child, who then kicks the unoffending dog; a little funny and a lot depressing, but we need no explanation to see the sad humor. When layoffs and economic stresses increase, we reliably expect a corresponding increase in abuse of spouses and children. When the United States was hurting from the September 11, 2001, attacks, the assailants were either dead or elusive; Iraq, which had nothing to do with the attack, bore the brunt of U.S. strikeback anger. A nineteenth-centry British jury, in the farmlands of Devonshire, once returned the following note when it found a young man guilty of stealing hay: "We don't think the prisoner done it, but there's been a lot taken hereabouts by someone" (Brown 1899, 513). And so *someone* has to suffer for it: the thief if handy, but an innocent if no one else is available. Unscrupulous prosecutors have long realized that if the case against a defendant is weak, then grisly photos of the crime scene and the murder victim and graphic descriptions of the brutal murder can be an effective substitute for the missing evidence: when jurors are outraged by a criminal act, their desire to strike back at somebody can easily overwhelm their concern about whether the defendant is the appropriate target of their wrath.

Analyze This is a film comedy about a mob boss who seeks psychological treatment. The mob boss, Giotti, is furious with a rival mobster who had attempted to kill him, and Giotti's psychologist is offering counsel on anger management: "You know what I do when I'm angry? I hit a pillow. Just hit the pillow, see how you feel." Whereupon Giotti pulls out a pistol and fires several slugs into the pillow. When the psychologist regains sufficient composure to ask "Feel better?" the mobster responds, "Yeah, I do."

He does indeed feel better, and there's a good reason for that: when someone (human, chimp, or rat) is attacked or threatened or harmed, they experience "subordination stress": they suffer from chronically overactive stress responses. But if the attacked individual is able to attack someone else, his hormonal levels are then reduced and the stress is eliminated (Virgin and Sapolsky 1997).

How did this unattractive and inefficient emotional reaction become so deeply entrenched? Our ancestors who struck back—or lashed out at someone—when attacked or wronged were more likely to survive and flourish than those who "turned the other cheek" or reacted passively. As David Barash notes, if my attacker is too strong for a successful counterattack, by attacking someone else I serve notice that I am still someone to fear, someone who cannot be attacked (at least by subordinates) without serious consequences: "Evolution would most likely reward victims who—even if unable to retaliate against the actual perpetrator—conspicuously 'take it out' on someone else" (2005, 4). The reciprocal tit-for-tat approach—particularly the punishment of harms—was favored because it worked—not because it worked particularly well (it didn't and doesn't). Retributive impulses are often directed against innocent family members and scapegoats rather than wrongdoers. Even when aimed at an offending target, punitive or retributive responses are grossly inefficient, as behavioral research has long since established; in addition, the side effects (such as blocking inquiry into deeper systemic causes) result in even greater harm. Still, in the many millennia before behavioral science, the strikeback response—crude as it is—was the only available tool for social control and a means of protecting status, and it was better than nothing. Because it sometimes produced positive effects, it became biologically, socially, and psychologically entrenched.

The basic retributive emotion runs deep—much deeper than the history of our species. Belief in moral responsibility is more recent. If we look at early legal codes, moral responsibility is not an important element: an eye for an eye, a tooth for a tooth, and there is little or no distinction between causing harm purposefully or inadvertently. Questions of moral responsibility do not arise: God commands this punishment, and that settles it. No further justification is required, and it would be wicked to ask for one: who are you to question God? We have reports late into the medieval period of animals being executed for having caused a death, and questions of whether the offending animal is morally responsible or justly deserving of punishment are not an issue. But—some exceptions notwithstanding—over the centuries, distinctions were made between wrongs committed purposefully and wrongs that occurred by accident and eventually between wrongs done by competent persons and wrongs committed by the demented or those who have not reached the "age of responsibility" (though in the United States an eight-year-old child was recently charged with murder; perhaps we have not come so far as we might have imagined). And as the system grew more sophisticated, eventually the most basic question emerged: what are the grounds for holding people morally responsible? Attempts at justification come comparatively late, but the fundamental grounding for moral responsibility lurks much deeper in our strikeback desires; we feel those desires so deeply that we are certain they *must* be justified.

The basic belief in moral responsibility is not a product of reason, but of visceral emotion. Obviously, contemporary philosophers who defend moral responsibility do not defend—and would deplore—attacks on scapegoats; to the contrary, the focus of their efforts is to make clearer and more precise exactly who is and is not morally responsible. But the deep belief in moral responsibility—among philosophers and the general public alike—is much stronger and deeper than the arguments for moral responsibility can begin to justify.

Moral responsibility was born on the wrong side of the tracks, in the harsh and undiscriminating strikeback reaction we feel when we suffer harm. That origin doesn't carry much philosophical weight. Its unsavory evolutionary history does not show that the basic emotional reaction underlying moral responsibility is bad. After all, our affection for our children probably has its origin in selfish aggressive genetic advantage; that self-serving history does not undercut the moral worth of our deep affection for our children. Primatologist Frans de Waal makes this point quite effectively:

Even if a diamond owes its beauty to millions of years of crushing pressure, we rarely think of this fact when admiring the gem. So why should we let the ruthlessness of natural selection distract from the wonders it has produced? Humans and other animals have been endowed with a capacity for genuine love, sympathy, and care—a fact that can and will one day be fully reconciled with the idea that genetic self-promotion drives the evolutionary process. (1996, 16–17)

Still, moral responsibility comes with a lot of baggage. Even if we grant that squalid origins do not establish that a value or emotion is wrong, it does not follow that origins are irrelevant to our judgments concerning values. Consider our aesthetic values. Many of us regard diamonds as beautiful, but when we learn that our aesthetic judgment was manipulated by diamond merchants through clever advertising campaigns ("a diamond is forever") and an artificially contrived sense of something rare and wonderful (when in fact diamonds exist in quantities that would destroy their status as precious stones, were the mining not carefully limited), then diamonds lose some of their luster. And when we recognize that the deep and confident belief in moral responsibility is not based on solid rational arguments (because even the most committed supporters of moral responsibility acknowledge that their own belief in moral responsibility is stronger than any argument in favor of moral responsibility), then we may wish to look more skeptically at the primitive and unattractive visceral feelings that provide the ultimate support for tenacious belief in moral responsibility.

The point of noting the dark origins of moral responsibility is to combat the powerful presumption in favor of moral responsibility and encourage genuine scrutiny of that deep belief. Do we have good reasons for believing in the legitimacy of claiming and attributing moral responsibility, or do we instead start from the certainty that it is legitimate and so conclude that we must have reasons? When we look at moral responsibility from a thoroughly naturalistic perspective, do we really find it plausible? Or is moral responsibility an atavistic remainder of our evolutionary history: a remainder requiring miracles and deities that cannot be justified within our contemporary scientific system?

Systemic Belief in Moral Responsibility

The deep and almost unshakable belief in moral responsibility owes much of its strength to our retributive emotions and powerful strikeback desires. But there is another source for the constancy and certainty of our commitment to belief in moral responsibility: it is held securely in place by its central location in a larger system of belief, and challenging moral responsibility requires challenging that larger theoretical system.

C. A. Campbell (1957) attempts to square belief in moral responsibility with our scientific knowledge, but he insists that if that project were a failure, he would renounce his belief in the credibility of scientific research in order to preserve his belief in moral responsibility, as the latter is essential for our lives as practical ethical beings. P. F. Strawson (1962) claims that no argument is required to defend moral responsibility, because it is so central to our belief and value system that it cannot be denied without collapsing the foundation of our moral and emotional lives. Peter van Inwagen suggests that no matter what some philosophers may claim about their denial of moral responsibility, it is very unlikely that anyone genuinely rejects that deep belief. And van Inwagen affirms his unconditional commitment to moral responsibility: his strong doubts concerning compatibilism notwithstanding, if determinism were proved and the libertarian model were unsustainable, he would adopt compatibilism: "To deny the free-will thesis is to deny the existence of moral responsibility, which would be absurd. . . . It is conceivable that science will one day present us with compelling reasons for believing in determinism. Then, and only then, I think, should we become compatibilists" (1983, 223). Van Inwagen prefers to reject determinism and preserve a libertarian basis for moral responsibility, but if faced with problems he is willing to give up his libertarian commitments and embrace the despised compatibilism to save moral responsibility. As Quine made clear in "Two Dogmas of Empiricism," "Any statement can be held true come what may, if we make drastic enough adjustments elsewhere in the system" (1951, 40). And van Inwagen is willing to make whatever adjustments are necessary for the preservation of moral responsibility. But such a commitment to moral responsibility sounds more like a statement of faith than a reasoned conclusion: any possibility of rejecting moral responsibility is "absurd," and no doctrine is too implausible for acceptance if it saves moral responsibility.

Nick Trakakis and Daniel Cohen offer an interpretation of Wittgenstein according to which "belief in free will [and moral responsibility] begins to look more like a religious commitment than a theoretical or scientific belief" (2008, xvii). That is an interesting interpretation of belief in moral responsibility—as an article of faith—because it leads to the second reason why so many people (and perhaps especially philosophers) find the denial of moral responsibility too absurd to take seriously. Like religious doctrine, belief in moral responsibility is a central element of a complex and comprehensive system of belief. That system frames the way we pose the questions and colors the way we see the arguments, and the assumptions of that system make it difficult to develop opposing arguments. The questions concerning moral responsibility are typically asked from within the framework of moral responsibility, so that rejection of moral responsibility soon leads to absurdity. Thus in order to challenge moral responsibility, one must challenge the vast moral responsibility legal and philosophical system; for those operating deep within that system, any challenge to the system is difficult to take seriously. From within that system (criminal justice is only one of its elements), the denial of moral responsibility does seem absurd; in such a rich system, it is always possible to save moral responsibility by making adjustments elsewhere in the system: for example, by significantly lowering the standards for justified blame until moral responsibility becomes a necessary truth, as Dennett proposes: "If no one *else* is responsible for your being in state A, you are" (2003, 281), or by ruling deeper inquiry into causal history out of order, or—as suggested by Stephen White—by starting from the assumption of justified moral responsibility and redefining what we mean by "could have done otherwise," so that "an agent could have done other than he or she did just in case the ascriptions of responsibility and blame to that agent for the action in question is justified" (1991, 236).

Understanding the emotional and systemic sources of the almost universal belief in moral responsibility opens the way to careful consideration of the argumentative case in support of moral responsibility as well as the case that can be made against moral responsibility. There are, of course, arguments for moral responsibility; indeed, a multitude of conflicting arguments. The remainder of this book attempts to show that those arguments don't work. But before examining the range of arguments in more detail, it should be noted that the great variety of arguments in support of moral responsibility is evidence of both the powerful emotional appeal of moral responsibility and the weakness of the philosophical arguments to support it. Many philosophers offer arguments to justify moral responsibility, each believing that the other arguments fail. If twelve jurors are convinced that the defendant is guilty, but each juror bases his or her guilty verdict on a single item of evidence that the other eleven jurors reject, that is not good grounds for conviction: for each element of evidence, eleven out of the twelve regard it as faulty. Ultimately, we would be convicting on evidence that is almost unanimously rejected. The rich variety of arguments in favor of moral responsibility may remind us of the rich variety of arguments for the existence of God and may prompt the same response to that large collection: if there were really *a* good argument for God or for moral responsibility, would there be so *many*? In contrast to the multitude of arguments in support of moral responsibility, there is one basic argument against moral responsibility—though it is available in a number of different styles and colors. That argument is the subject of the next chapter.

2 The Basic Argument against Moral Responsibility

The best account of moral responsibility was given more than five centuries ago by a young Italian nobleman, Count Giovanni Pico della Mirandola. In his "Oration on the Dignity of Man," Pico della Mirandola explained the origins of the uniquely human miraculous capacity for moral responsibility. In the process of creation, God gave special characteristics to every realm of His great cosmos, but when His work was finished, God "longed for someone to reflect on the plan of so great a creation, to love its beauty, and to admire its magnitude," so He created humans for that role. But all the special gifts had already been bestowed on other elements of His creation, and there was nothing left for humans. So God decreed that humans "should share in common whatever properties had been peculiar to each of the other creatures"; that is, only humans would have the special power to make of themselves whatever they freely chose to be:

The nature of all other beings is limited and constrained within the bounds of laws prescribed by Us. Thou, constrained by no limits, in accordance with thine own free will, in whose hand We have placed thee, shalt ordain for thyself the limits of thy nature. We have set thee at the world's center that thou mayest from thence more easily observe whatever is in the world. We have made thee neither of heaven nor of earth, neither mortal nor immortal, so that with freedom of choice and with honor, as though the maker and molder of thyself, thou mayest fashion thyself in whatever shape thou shalt prefer. Thou shalt have the power to degenerate into the lower forms of life, which are brutish. Thou shalt have the power, out of thy soul's judgment, to be reborn into the higher forms, which are divine. (Pico della Mirandola 1496/1948, 224–225)

This is a marvelous account of moral responsibility, which meets all the essential requirements: we make ourselves, by our own independent ab initio choices; past history, the genetic lottery, social circumstances, and cultural influences play no part. It might be hard to understand how such special choices work—after all, *who* is doing the choosing?—but with miracles, anything is possible; besides, such miraculous events are not supposed to fall within the range of human understanding.

The delights of Pico della Mirandola's moral responsibility account notwithstanding, it does have one problem: it requires miracles. And although that was one of its charms for Pico della Mirandola and his contemporaries, it is a daunting problem for those devoted to a naturalistic world view that has no room for gods, ghosts, or miracles. The basic claim of this book is that moral responsibility belongs with the ghosts and gods and that it cannot survive in a naturalistic environment devoid of miracles. Roderick Chisholm has the right idea: "If we are responsible, and if what I have been trying to say is true, then we have a prerogative which some would attribute only to God: each of us, when we really act, is a prime mover unmoved. In doing what we do, we cause certain events to happen, and nothing and no one, except we ourselves, causes us to cause those events to happen" (1982, 32). But because—in the naturalistic system—we do not have such miracle-working powers, then (by *modus tollens*) it follows that we are not morally responsible.

Once we adopt a naturalistic world view and give up miraculous self-creating powers, it would seem an easy and obvious conclusion that we must also give up moral responsibility. But the moral responsibility system was too entrenched and the emotional underpinnings of retributive "justice" were too powerful: giving up moral responsibility was—and for many still is—unthinkable. So most philosophers pushed the argument in the opposite direction. The original argument (as Pico della Mirandola might have framed it) claimed that miraculous ultimate self-making powers are a necessary condition for moral responsibility—we do have moral responsibility; therefore, we must have miraculous self-making powers. Naturalists who reject moral responsibility agree that miraculous self-making powers are necessary for moral responsibility and conclude that because naturalism leaves no room for such powers, it thus leaves no room for moral responsibility. Those who embrace naturalism but refuse to abandon moral responsibility take a different line: we *know* that we are morally responsible, so—because miraculous self-making powers do not exist (in our natural world)—we must have been mistaken about the powers necessary for moral responsibility. Those powers were not special miraculous powers of ultimate control, but significantly more modest powers that can fit within a naturalistic system. Thus Dennett insists that "skepticism about the very possibility of culpability arises from a misplaced reverence for an absolutist ideal: the concept of total, before-the-eyes-of-God Guilt. That fact that *that* condition is never to be met in this world should not mislead us into skepticism about the integrity of our institution of moral responsibility" (1984, 165).

Carlos Moya admonishes us not to make ultimate control a condition for moral responsibility, because doing so "is to lose sight of our ordinary practice of moral responsibility ascriptions and to look instead for an unattainable myth" (2006, 91). Later chapters examine various compatibilist efforts to lower the bar for what sort of control powers suffice for moral responsibility, but before making that examination, it is important to note the plausibility of the original—naturalistically unattainable—standard for moral responsibility.

The Case against Moral Responsibility

The traditional question is whether determinism is compatible with moral responsibility; however, the more basic issue—and the question as it is posed in most contemporary philosophical discussions—is whether moral responsibility is compatible with a naturalism devoid of miraculous powers. Bernard Williams makes it clear that it is naturalism (rather than determinism) that poses the challenge for moral responsibility:

There may have been a time when belief in a universal determinism looked like the best reason there was of expecting strong naturalistic explanations of psychological states and happenings, but, if that was once the case, it is no longer so. It now looks a great deal more plausible and intelligible that there should be such explanations than that the universe should be a deterministic system, and it is the possibility of those explanations that itself creates the problem. (1995, 7)

There have been many arguments why moral responsibility does fit within naturalism/determinism, and those arguments are examined in subsequent chapters. But first, it is worth noting that there are powerful grounds for supposing that moral responsibility is fundamentally incompatible with naturalism. It is particularly worth noting—because the contemporary philosophical fashion is to look disdainfully at those who believe that moral responsibility is incompatible with our naturalistic world view. It is implied that anyone who understands the sophisticated philosophical position of compatibilism will abandon the naïve notion that there is a conflict between determinism/naturalism and moral responsibility.

Arguments for compatibilism are legion and wonderful in their rich variety; the argument for the *in*compatibilism of moral responsibility and naturalism comes in several models, but it is constructed from a common foundation. The fundamental naturalistic argument against moral responsibility is that it is unfair to punish one and reward another based on their different acts, because their different behaviors are ultimately the result of causal forces they did not control, causal factors which were a matter of good or bad luck. For Lorenzo Valla, God "created the wolf fierce, the hare timid, the lion brave, the ass stupid, the dog savage, the sheep mild, so he fashioned some men hard of heart, others soft, he generated one given to evil, the other to virtue, and, further, he gave a capacity for reform to one and made another incorrigible" (1443/1948, 173).

So although some are genuinely virtuous while others are evil, and some reform their evil characters and become virtuous while others lack the resources for such reform, in all cases, the capacities for good or bad behavior are ultimately the result of their good or bad fortune, and thus there are no grounds for moral responsibility for acts or character (some may reform themselves, but that does not make them morally responsible, as the capacity for such reform is a matter of luck and not something over which they have ultimate control). Spinoza (1677/1985), Holbach (1770/1970), and Schopenhauer (1841/1960) argue that once we trace all the causes in detail, we recognize that all our acts can be traced back to earlier sources that we did not control. Thomas Nagel's problem of "moral luck" is based on the recognition that—under close scrutiny—luck swallows up the ultimate control required for moral responsibility: "If one cannot be responsible for consequences of one's acts due to factors beyond one's control, or for antecedents of one's acts that are properties of temperament not subject to one's will, or for the circumstances that pose one's moral choices, then how can one be responsible even for the stripped-down acts of will itself, if *they* are the product of antecedent circumstances outside of the will's control?" (1979, 34)

Peter van Inwagen developed his *Consequence* argument to show that moral responsibility will require a special libertarian break in the determinist/naturalist world: "If determinism is true, then our acts are the consequences of the laws of nature and events in the remote past. But it is not up to us what went on before we were born, and neither is it up to us what the laws of nature are. Therefore, the consequences of these things (including our present acts) are not up to us" (1983, 16).

Derk Pereboom (2001, 2007) constructed his Four Cases argument to show that contrived cases in which we obviously lack adequate control for moral responsibility are (when we look closely) relevantly similar to ordinary cases in which moral responsibility is commonly assumed: in all the cases, the subjects lack the sort of control that moral responsibility requires. Galen Strawson's Basic Argument (2010) is designed to undercut the ultimate causal control necessary for moral responsibility: you do what you do because of the way you are, and so to be ultimately responsible for what you do, you must be ultimately responsible for the way you are. But you can't be ultimately responsible for the way you are (because your genetic inheritance and early experience shaped you, and ways in which you subsequently change yourself are the result of that genetic inheritance and early experience, and you are certainly not responsible for those), so you can't be ultimately responsible for what you do. All of these arguments, fascinating as they are in their detail and structure and inventiveness, are variations on a single theme. Sometimes it is presented in terms of luck; sometimes the focus is on the impossibility of making ourselves from scratch, without being limited by our raw material and our self-making skills; it may be offered in terms of basic fairness; in some versions, the focus is on the inevitability of the result given the initial capacities, but all are based on the claim that our characters (and the behavior that stems from our characters) is the product of causal forces that we ultimately *did not control*. Indeed, the argument is a naturalized version of the ancient arguments for the incompatibility of God's omnipotence with human moral responsibility, with God taking the place of nature. Some have a capacity for reform, Valla (1443/1948, 173) notes, and some don't: having or not having that capacity was not under our control.

Comparative Unfairness

I prefer to frame this fundamental challenge to moral responsibility in terms of a *comparative unfairness* argument. It is just another way of presenting the same basic argument against moral responsibility, or—more precisely—the same basic argument to show that claims and ascriptions of moral responsibility to humans (humans who lack godlike miraculous powers of originating self-creation) are unfair. This comparative unfairness argument—which is a variation on a very old theme—goes like this. Consider two people, Karen and Louise, performing an act of moral significance: as an example, they are confronted with a situation in which their supervisor is about to make an overtly racist hiring decision, and they must object or acquiesce, knowing that a strong objection will probably block the racist decision but will also have a chilling effect on their career advancement prospects. Both Karen and Louise are intelligent persons, capable of deliberation; both are ambitious; both find racism morally repulsive; both are competent; and both are aware that the hiring decision is racist and that challenging it will be personally risky. Karen takes a courageous strong stance against this racist act, and Louise meekly acquiesces. Karen behaves in a morally upright manner, and Louise's act is morally bad. (Some may doubt that we can call an act morally good or morally bad until we know whether the actors are morally responsible; that is an issue that will be discussed later.)

Why did Karen act virtuously and Louise act vilely? There are four possibilities. One possibility is that the difference was a result of *chance*: the dice rolled, and this time Karen came up the moral winner and Louise the loser, but if we play the same case out tomorrow, the result could just as easily be the opposite. But if the result is just a matter of chance, then—as David Hume (1748/2000) so effectively argued—then neither can be morally responsible, because the events of resistance and acquiescence do not seem to belong to Karen and Louise at all: they are fortunate and unfortunate events in the world, but not the acts of Karen and Louise. Robert Kane (1985, 1996, 2002, 2007) has developed a very sophisticated argument to show that indeterminism might play some role in morally responsible acts, but he would agree that if the results were simply attributable to chance, then there is no basis for moral responsibility. A second possibility is that the different results were the product of the miracle-working powers of Karen and Louise: they make choices that are *first causes*, they act as *unmoved movers*, they originate choices through a miraculous power that transcends all natural causes and boundaries. If one offers that as an explanation of their different actions, then there is nothing more to say. With miracles, you can "explain" anything, but the price you pay is abandoning the naturalistic-scientific framework and abandoning any hope of explaining the difference in a manner that is accessible to human inquiry and scientific investigation. The third possibility is that Karen and Louise are actually in very different *situations* (and that had their situations been reversed, their acts would also have been reversed). Thanks to the intriguing results from situationist psychological research, we now understand that seemingly insignificant differences in environmental circumstances—an admonition to hurry (Darley and Batson 1973), a lab-coated researcher urging "please continue the experiment" (Milgram 1963), finding a dime in a telephone booth (Isen and Levin 1972)—can have a profound impact on behavior: it can make the difference between stopping to help and rushing past a person in distress, and that difference (between callous disregard and kind assistance) is a significant difference indeed. And as the infamous Milgram (1963) authority experiment and the Stanford Prison Guard experiment (Haney, Banks, and Zimbardo 1973) teach us, in the right situation, most of us would perform acts of cruelty that we fervently believe we would never do under any circumstances. But if the difference between Karen's courageous act and Louise's dastardly acquiescence is the product of a difference in their situations—situations they neither made nor chose—then it is difficult to believe that they justly deserve the profoundly different treatments of reward and punishment, praise and blame. Or finally, we can insist that there is something in Karen and Louise—some strength or weakness of character—that accounts for their behavioral divergence, for if their characters and capacities—including rational capacities—were the same, and they were in identical situations, and neither chance nor miracles intervened, then Karen and Louise would perform identical acts and there would be no basis for distinguishing between their just deserts. But if we look carefully and thoroughly at the way their character traits were shaped, we recognize that ultimately they were shaped by influences and forces that were not under their control. If Karen tries harder, thinks more effectively, deliberates more thoroughly, or empathizes more deeply than Louise, then Karen's superior powers (like Louise's inferior qualities) resulted from causes far beyond her control. Or perhaps Karen worked hard to develop her own superior thinking skills, and Louise exerted no such efforts, but in that case, Karen's fortitude, as well as her strong commitment to self-improvement—qualities that certainly *do* facilitate self-improvement—ultimately can be traced back to

Karen's good developmental fortune and not to her own choices and efforts. Likewise, the inferior fortitude and commitment of Louise (which led to meager or abortive efforts toward self-improvement) were due to forces that were not under her control.

It may be tempting to say that everyone can always try harder and that therefore it is Louise's own fault that she exerted less effort toward cognitive self-improvement, so—when she does something bad because of her inferior critical thinking abilities—she justly deserves opprobrium. But that is to push this account over into the miracle-working model: it detaches *effort-making* from any causal or conditioning history, so that in the area of effort-making we are first causes or unmoved movers. When we think carefully about it, few of us imagine that our capacities to exert effort and show fortitude are under our pure volitional control: if we have great fortitude, it is because that fortitude was *shaped* and strengthened over a long and fortunate history (had we spent our younger years in circumstances in which all our efforts were failures that produced nothing of benefit—and perhaps even brought punitive responses, possibly in the form of ridicule— then we would not have the degree of fortitude we now *fortunately* enjoy: we can no more choose to exert effective sustained efforts than we can choose—at this point, with no training—to be an effective marathoner). If we refrain from appeals to miraculous powers—whether they are powers of sustained effort-making or rational deliberation—then careful comparison of the acts of Karen and Louise leaves no room to justify claims of significant differences in their just deserts.

When we look deeper and longer at exactly how their characters (including both strengths and flaws) were shaped, we find (if we renounce miraculous self-forming powers) that their characters were the product of causal forces that neither woman controlled or chose. Karen is more reflective, and perhaps more deeply committed to her nonracist values; she has a much stronger sense of positive self-efficacy:[1] self-confidence in her own ability to effectively produce positive results. Furthermore, she has a strong sense of internal locus-of-control (Rotter 1966, 1975, 1979, 1989): she believes that her *own efforts*—rather than external forces—are vitally important in shaping outcomes. All these factors are important and valuable, and they enable Karen to stand up against her racist supervisor. And Karen isn't "just lucky" to have those characteristics; she has nurtured them through her own efforts. But her capacity to nurture them and the rudimentary powers that were there for the nurturing and further development were not there by Karen's choice and were not under her early control. Suppose Karen had recognized in herself a harmful tendency toward external locus-of-control and successfully worked to develop a stronger sense of internal control: her capacity for sustained reflection and careful self-scrutiny and her strong sense of self-efficacy to undertake self-improvement projects made such self-modification possible; those valuable resources were ultimately not of her own making or choosing, and neither those qualities nor the results that flow from them are a legitimate basis for moral responsibility. Even the example is problematic: if Karen has a strong sense of external locus-of-control (a character trait she developed at a very early age and without choice or reflection), then it is very unlikely that it will occur to her that her sense of control might be reshaped by her own powers. Now compare Karen and Louise, with the deep understanding of how their vices and virtues were shaped. Is it fair to treat Louise worse and to subject her to blame and perhaps punishment for an act she could not have avoided? Of course, if she had been a different person with different capacities and a different history, then she would have acted differently. If she had exactly the same history and resulting character as Karen, she would have acted as Karen did. In a different world, there would have been a different result, but that fact has no relevance whatsoever for the question of whether Louise justly deserves blame or punishment in the world in which she actually lives and acts and which shaped her in every detail. Louise does have flaws; does she deserve blame for them?

It is obvious that we do not make ourselves: ultimately, we are the products of an elaborate evolutionary, genetic, cultural, and conditioning history. So whether I am vile or virtuous, I am not so by my own making. It is doubtful that we can make sense of the idea of having made ourselves or chosen our own characters. Certainly, any ultimate self-making would have to occur outside the natural world: if it makes sense at all, it could only be in a world of miracles. However, some philosophers have suggested that such ab initio self-making is not required for moral responsibility and that some intermediate level of self-construction might suffice. For example, Daniel Dennett states:

I *take* responsibility for any thing I make and then inflict upon the general public; if my soup causes food poisoning, or my automobile causes air pollution, or my robot runs amok and kills someone, I, the manufacturer, am to blame. And although

I may manage to get my suppliers and subcontractors to share the liability some-what, I am held responsible for releasing the product to the public with whatever flaws it has. Common wisdom has it that much the same rationale grounds personal responsibility; I have created and unleashed an agent who is myself; if its acts produce harm, the manufacturer is held responsible. I think this common wisdom is indeed wisdom. (1984, 85)

Obviously, Dennett—whose naturalist credentials are not in doubt—does not suppose we make ourselves "from scratch" in some miraculous manner. Instead, once we reach a certain level of competence, we begin to shape ourselves. But this "intermediate level" of self-making cannot support moral responsibility. If you "make yourself" more effectively than I do, it is because you have better resources for self-making; those are resources that you did not make yourself, but resources that you are lucky to have and that I am unlucky to lack. If Jan makes a better product than Kate, but Jan has the use of better raw materials, higher quality tools, and a superior work environment, then it is unfair to ascribe moral responsibility to Jan and Kate and to reward Jan while punishing Kate for their very different outputs. Perhaps at some earlier point, Jan thought carefully and chose to develop her cognitive capacities through vigorous cognitive exercise, but that added step leads back to the same destination: her beneficial cognitive exertions were the result of differences in cognitive capacities that were products of good luck and that cannot justify assertions of moral respon-sibility. This argument is only a preliminary sketch of one that requires much more discussion (see chapter 8), but the immediate point is that squaring moral responsibility with naturalism will not be an easy task and that there are good reasons behind the "naïve" view that naturalism/ determinism is incompatible with moral responsibility.

The Unfairness Argument against Moral Responsibility

The central claim of this book is that claims and ascriptions of moral responsibility are unfair: it is fundamentally unfair to give special praise and reward to some and to blame and punish others. It is unfair because the differences in our characters and behavior are the result of causal forces that we ultimately did not choose and did not control. To examine that claim from a different angle, and to put flesh on the comparative unfairness argument sketched previously, consider the arguments of two of the clearest and most forceful participants in the debate over moral responsibility: Galen Strawson's "regress" argument against moral responsibility and Albert Mele's critique of that argument.

Galen Strawson (1986, 28–29) formalized a well-known argument against moral responsibility: the regress argument. In its essentials, the argument goes like this. If one is to be truly responsible for how one acts, one must be truly responsible for how one is, morally speaking. To be truly responsible for how one is, one must have chosen to be the way one is. But one cannot really be said to choose (in a conscious, reasoned fashion) the way one is unless one already has some principles of choice (preferences, values, ideals) in the light of which one chooses how to be. But then to be truly responsible on account of having chosen to be the way one is, one must be truly responsible for one's having *those* principles of choice, but then one must have chosen them, in a reasoned, conscious fashion. But that requires that one have principles of choice. And thus the regress.

Alfred Mele develops a powerful critique of Strawson's regress argument, focusing on a vital premise of the argument: to be truly responsible for how one is, one must have *chosen* to be that way. He offers a charming example to support his critique: the case of Betty, a six-year-old child with a fear of the basement. Betty knows that no harm has come to herself or others when they have ventured into the basement, and she recognizes that her older sister has no fear of the basement. Betty decides that her fear is "babyish," and that she will take steps to overcome it. Her plan is simple but effective: she will make periodic visits to the basement until she no longer feels afraid there. As Mele states, "If Betty succeeds in eliminating her fear in this way, this is an instance of intentional self-modification" (1995, 223).

Clearly such cases of "intentional self-modification" are possible; as Mele argues, there is no reason to suppose that they stem from "an infinitely regressive series of choices":

Betty's choice or decision to try to eliminate her fear need not rest on any attitude that she *chooses* to have. Desires and beliefs of hers might ground her choice—and her judgment that it would be best to try to eliminate the fear—without her having chosen to have any of those desires (or beliefs). Can she nevertheless be "truly responsible" for her choice and her behavior? If it is claimed that *true responsibility* for any choice, *by definition*, requires that the agent have chosen "in a conscious, reasoned fashion" an attitude that grounds the choice, it is being claimed, in effect, that the very definition of 'true responsibility' entails that possessing such responsibility for any choice requires having made an infinitely regressive series of choices. (1995, 223–224)

But Mele insists that we "should want to have nothing to do with *this* notion of responsibility, nor with any corresponding notion of free action" (1995, 224). So what sort of freedom *should* we find desirable? Mele's answer is as follows:

In ordinary practice (at least as a first approximation), when we are confident that self-reflective, planning agents have acted intentionally, we take them to have acted freely *unless* we have contrary evidence—evidence of brainwashing, compulsion, coercion, insanity, or relevant deception, for example.

In the same vein, we take Betty to have freely tried to eliminate her fear. Our learning that she did not choose to have any of the attitudes on the basis of which she chose or decided to make the attempt will not incline us to withdraw the attribution of freedom, unless we are inclined to hold that free action derives from choices made partly on the basis of chosen attitudes or, at least, that any action etiology that includes no such choice is a freedom-blocking etiology. Those who have this latter inclination are, I suggest, in the grip of a crude picture of the freedom of an agent with respect to an action (or "practical freedom," for short) as a *transmitted* property—a property transmitted from above by earlier free behavior, including, of course, choice-making behavior. It is impossible for such a picture of practical freedom to capture the freedom that it is designed to represent, for reasons that Strawson makes clear: the picture requires an impossible psychological regress. And it ought to be rejected. Practical freedom, if it is a possible property of human beings, is, rather, an "emergent" property. It must be, if some of us are free agents (i.e., agents who act freely, in a broad sense of 'act' that includes such mental actions as choosing) and none of us started out that way. (1995, 224–225)

This passage is a superb description of how the capacity for "practical freedom" develops. The development of that capacity requires nothing mystical, and it does not result in a vicious regress. As Mele makes clear, most of us do develop that capacity and become free agents, and "none of us started out that way."

Mele gives a marvelous account of "free agency/practical freedom" and its emergence. But its virtues notwithstanding, the account does nothing to establish moral responsibility; to the contrary, careful examination of Mele's excellent account of freedom and its enriched development soon undercuts any claims of moral responsibility. Place alongside Betty her six-year-old twin brother, Benji, who also suffers from fear of his basement (and who, like Betty, knows that no harm has befallen those who venture there). Benji also regards this fear as "childish" and wishes to get beyond it. But Benji is a little—just a little—less self-confident than his sister. Rather than taking bold steps to deal with his fear, Benji decides to wait it out: maybe I'll grow a bit bolder as I grow older, Benji thinks; besides, Mom is plenty strong and courageous, so there's no need for me to make an effort that might well fail. Betty has thought up a good plan, Benji recognizes, but well-planned projects often come to a bad end, like that well-thought-out plan to stand on a chair to reach the cookie jar. Benji is not quite as strong as his sister, in some very significant respects. He does not have her high level of self-confidence (or sense of self-efficacy); his sister has a strong internal locus-of-control, but Benji is inclined to see the locus-of-control residing in powerful others. And although Betty is well on her way to becoming a chronic cognizer (to be discussed shortly), Benji has developed significant tendencies toward cognitive miserliness (the abysmal failure of that well-thought-out campaign to liberate the cookie jar left a deep mark); that is, even at this tender age, Betty and Benji already have significant differences (not of their own making or choosing) in what psychologists call "need for cognition" (Cohen, Stotland, and Wolfe 1955).

Cognitive misers (Cacioppo and Petty 1982; Cacioppo et al. 1996) do not enjoy thinking—especially careful in-depth abstract thinking—and they tend to make decisions more quickly, with less deliberation, and with less attention to all the significant details; in contrast, *chronic cognizers* take pleasure in thinking, eagerly engage in careful extended deliberation, and reflect in more detail and at greater depth before making decisions. Like their differences in self-efficacy and locus-of-control, this early difference in need for cognition is likely to have profound effects: those with a weaker need for cognition (the cognitive misers) are more likely to be dogmatic and closed-minded (Cacioppo and Petty 1982; Fletcher et al. 1986; Petty and Jarvis 1996; Webster and Kruglanski 1994), and they are more likely to avoid or distort new information that conflicts with their settled beliefs (Venkatraman et al. 1990). In contrast, those who are fortunate enough to be shaped as chronic cognizers tend to have greater cognitive fortitude (Osberg 1987), stronger curiosity (Olson, Camp, and Fuller 1984), be more open to new experiences and new information and more careful in evaluating new information (Venkatraman et al. 1990; Venkatraman and Price 1990; Berzonsky and Sullivan 1992), and more successful in solving complex problems (Nair and Ramnarayan 2000, 305). That's not to say that Benji is doomed to a terrible fate, or that he will never reach a level of competence, or that he will never be capable of making his own decisions (and, overall, benefit by doing so). But it is to say that Benji's incipient "relatively sophisticated intentional behavior" will have fewer resources to draw upon than those available to his sister.

One of the best parts of Mele's argument is his very plausible account of the long-term results from six-year-old Betty's intentional self-modification:

Agents' free choices and actions have significant psychological consequences for them. By choosing and acting as we do, we affect our psychological constitution—sometimes, even, *intentionally* affect it, as young Betty did. Further, successes like Betty's may have important consequences for agents' psychological constitutions well beyond the immediate present. Betty's success in conquering her fear may, for example, enhance her self-esteem, expand her conception of the range of things she can control, and contribute to her deciding to try to conquer other fears of hers. Her successful effort at self-modification regarding her fear of her basement may lead to bigger and better things in the sphere of self-modification as a partial consequence of its relatively proximal effects on her psychological condition; and given that the effort was freely made, a *free* action of Betty's will have contributed to the psychological changes. Of course, the more proximal bigger and better things may lead to more remote ones that are bigger and better yet. Seemingly minor successes at self-modification may have, over time, a major impact on one's character. (1995, 229)

Both Betty and Benji make free choices, and those choices have significant impact on their formed characters and their subsequent choices stemming from those qualities of character. Mature Betty has a strong internal locus-of-control, believing that she herself has significant control over the most important events in her life; Benji believes that much of what happens to him is outside his power to control, being in the hands of powerful others (perhaps God). Betty has a powerful sense of confident self-efficacy for most of the projects that are important to her: she believes that she is very good at acting and controlling (including acting to change herself, should she find faults that need changing). Benji's sense of self-efficacy is substantially weaker: he is not very confident that he can carry out his valued projects successfully (including any self-improvement projects). Mature Benji wants to stop smoking, and he might try to do so—but he doesn't really believe that he has the resources to succeed (and because one of the needed resources is a strong sense of self-efficacy, he is probably correct in expecting failure). Betty's strong resources give her a very generous measure of freedom. Benji also chooses and acts freely, though without the rich freedom resources enjoyed by Betty. And as Mele makes clear, those differing resources—though to a significant degree self-made—were shaped by initial resources "that she did not choose to have."

The initial resources, and the early choices that stem from them, are of great importance. As Mele notes:

One's earliest or most primitive free choices are not themselves made on the basis of freely chosen attitudes. It cannot be otherwise; the earliest free choices of an agent cannot themselves be made, even partly, on the basis of *other* free choices of the agent. But this does not preclude one's developing into a person like Betty: a self-conscious, self-reflective, self-assessing agent who can intentionally and freely undertake to eliminate or foster an attitude in herself—and succeed. Success in such endeavors can have consequences for the agent's developing character. The same is true of *failure*. (1995, 230)

So Betty, with her somewhat stronger resources, attempts to eliminate her basement fear and succeeds. Benji takes a more passive path in dealing with his "babyish" fear, and his lesser efforts are a failure. And as Mele notes, both the success and failure "can have consequences for the agent's developing character" (1995, 230), as Betty waxes in self-confidence and cognitive fortitude, while Benji wanes. Twenty years pass, as both continue their divergent development paths. Both have grown up as members of the privileged race in a profoundly racist society, and both have enculturated the racist values of their society, and both have employed their powers of self-assessment to question those racist values. Both Betty and Benji wish to change, but Betty—due to her early success—has more resources and is more successful. She really does change, and she changes because she chooses to do so, and because she exerts the effort and the intelligent planning to succeed. Benji does not, because he is more acquiescent, or less self-confident, or less reflective, or less self-assessing; in short, because his tools for further self-development are not as good. Betty has better resources, and she uses them more effectively, but whether she deserves credit and Benji deserves blame is a very different matter.

Benji does have some powers of reflection and self-assessment—not powers as robust as his sister's, but to a lesser degree. But Benji's reflective self-assessment may result in his becoming resigned to and even contented with his lot: like Eliot's J. Alfred Prufrock, Benji concludes that "I am not Prince Hamlet, nor was meant to be," and I'm not really equipped to undertake major changes or challenges: "I know I'm a racist, and I know that's not good. But so are my friends, and that's who I am, and change is very hard for me. Besides, I'm not very good at giving up bad habits: look at my failed attempts to stop smoking. Changing racism is beyond my powers, anyway; it will have to be done by our leaders. Better not to think too hard about it." Betty is now a civil rights campaigner and is morally very good; Benji is a racist who acquiesces in the racist status quo and is morally bad. Both make free choices (though Betty's are freer than Benji's). Both want and need the freedom to make their own choices (Benji cannot make choices and carry them through as effectively as Betty does; that doesn't mean that he does not wish to make his own choices, and he would deeply resent Betty trying to run his life for him). Both can and do exercise *take-charge* responsibility (the responsibility—distinguished from moral responsibility—for making one's own decisions concerning one's life) as discussed in greater detail in chapter 6; though again, Betty—with her stronger sense of self-efficacy and greater cognitive fortitude—exercises it much better than does Benji. They do act freely, but that freedom does not establish moral responsibility and just deserts. Betty questions and challenges the system, and Benji acquiesces (as noted earlier, Benji's tendency toward cognitive miserliness leads him to avoid new information that would upset his settled beliefs and require him to think carefully about his views). This difference may be a very serious one indeed, if they are both growing up in a viciously racist society. Betty really is a stronger person, indeed a better person, but whether she deserves credit for her better character (much of it self-formed) and her superior behavior is a different question altogether.

Mele offers a clear and valuable reminder of something Aristotle (350 BC/1925) emphasized long ago: our choices today shape our choices and our characters of tomorrow. If you want to be a person of integrity tomorrow, then do not lie and cheat today. Studying the history that shaped us and how we emerged as free actors making our own choices is very important, and that includes the study of the critically important *initial capacities* in our earliest choices and how those capacities are fostered or inhibited. But studying that history with the hope of finding grounds for moral responsibility is a futile hope.

Timothy O'Connor recognizes the important influence of our early unchosen reflective powers and propensities, but he seems to think we can "grow out of" those influences:

We come into the world with powerful tendencies that are refined by the particular circumstances in which we develop. All of these facts are for us merely "given." They determine what choices we have to make and which options we will consider (and how seriously) as we arrive at a more reflective age. However, presuming that we are fortunate enough not to be impacted by traumatic events that will forever limit what is psychologically possible for us, and, on the positive side, that we are exposed to a suitably rich form of horizon-expanding opportunities, the structure of our choices increasingly reflects our own prior choices. In this way, our freedom *grows* over time. (2005, 219–220)

Our characters and our subsequent choices do reflect "our own prior choices"; as we develop, our characters thus become more our own. But whether our own characters are good or bad, strong or weak, we are not morally responsible; unless our choices can miraculously transcend our causal history, our characters and subsequent choices are shaped by given backgrounds that set the direction of further development. Our freedom may grow (along with a stronger sense of self-efficacy and internal locus-of-control and cognitive fortitude), as in the case of Betty, or we may become less confident and more rigid and less reflective, as does Benji. When we look carefully at the differences in their developed characters, we recognize—unless we trust in miracles (such as a power of reason to transcend causal histories), or attribute the difference to chance events they did not control—that those differences were the product of early differences in capacities or in circumstances which they did not control and for which they are not morally responsible. And absent such ultimate control, it is unfair to reward one and punish the other, or praise one and blame the other; that is, it is unfair to treat them in dramatically different ways. Their characters and behavior are their own, but that does not make Betty and Benji morally responsible.

Kane's Argument for Ultimate Responsibility

Robert Kane has made a remarkably innovative and thorough effort to establish room for moral responsibility within a thoroughly naturalistic world. Kane faces the challenge squarely: he refuses to take refuge in attempts to block examination of how our characters were shaped and the differences in our histories, and he rejects facile notions that we can somehow make ourselves without regard to the self-making capacities from which we start. To the contrary, Kane insists that moral responsibility requires genuine *ultimate control*: the "before-the-eyes-of-God" ultimate control that many defenders of moral responsibility dismiss as too strong a requirement. No one has confronted more directly, or struggled more vigorously, with the problem of justifying moral responsibility without compromising naturalism. Kane's remarkable efforts to establish ultimate grounds for moral responsibility without miracles or mysteries are worthy of examination on their own merits; examination of his strong and straightforward arguments offer a clear setting in which to bring the basic argument against moral responsibility—the comparative unfairness argument, as I have framed it—into clearer focus.

Kane attempts to establish naturalistic ultimate control by incorporating a crucial element of indeterminism (he insists it is not chance) into his impressive account of crucial self-forming acts. No brief discussion can do justice to the subtlety and sophistication of Kane's libertarian theory, but the crux of his position is this: our freedom and moral responsibility require the existence of "self-forming acts," in which we genuinely will both of two different open alternatives that cannot both be fulfilled; in the course of this incompatible willing, our neural networks create the right conditions for a genuine indeterminism (in which the random movement of a subatomic particle is amplified by the chaos created by conflicts of neural networks) such that either of these willed events can occur, but whichever event actually occurs, it is an act that we willed, an act for which we have reasons (reasons that we endorse), an act that is not coerced, an act that we acknowledge as our own and for which we take responsibility, an act which results from our own effort of will; that is, for both the genuinely possible acts, we have *dual-control* responsibility (Kane 2002).

In applying a comparative unfairness critique to this model, consider (instead of Betty and Benji) Betty and Barbara: Barbara is identical in all relevant respects to Betty (identical in levels of need for cognition, cognitive abilities, sense of self-efficacy, locus-of-control, rational and empathetic capacities), and they confront identical situations. Both Betty and Barbara are striving to overcome their developed racist characters, and they are also striving to hang onto their comfortable racist beliefs that are endorsed by their friends and community. At a crucial point, the result is indeterminate: Betty and Barbara are identical persons exerting identical efforts, an element of genuine indeterminism enters the equation, and Betty chooses to reject racism while Barbara chooses to remain a racist (of course Barbara will not describe the result as "remaining a racist"; she might describe it as "preserving cultural heritage"). In both cases, the choices are their own (and Kane does a superb job of making a case for dual ownership of either act), but is it really fair to blame one and praise the other? Certainly, one is now good and the other bad, but do they justly deserve differences in treatment for their different character traits? Remember, the difference in outcome is not due to differences in cognitive fortitude or curiosity or openness to new ideas or sense of self-reliance (all of which can be traced back to causes for which Benji and Betty and Barbara clearly are not morally responsible); rather, the difference must stem from indeterminism—ultimately, in Kane's model, to the amplified motion of a subatomic particle. Thus the difference between Betty and Barbara—which is now profound—is not the result of their control, but is the result of an indeterminate random roll of a subatomic particle. Both Betty and Barbara can rightly acknowledge their resulting characters as their own, but the question is not whether their characters and acts are their own, but whether they are morally responsible for them.

Barbara remains a racist, and Betty has renounced racism; both Barbara and Betty now endorse (Kane 2007, 33) those views (both of them were willing the result they now endorse while also willing the opposite result). And both are happy to "take responsibility" (41) for their resulting different characters. All of these factors contribute to an important and psychologically healthy sense of ownership of one's own character and control over what one does and what one becomes (the benefits of that sense of control is discussed in subsequent chapters, particularly chapter 6). The sense of control is not only healthy, but also legitimate: Betty and Barbara (and to a lesser but important extent, also Benji) really do exercise important control over their choices and development. But when we focus in on whether they have the ultimate control (that Kane acknowledges as essential for moral responsibility), we face a very different question. What is the difference between Betty and Barbara, for which the former deserves praise and the latter blame? The difference is that one rejects and the other embraces racism, which is a very significant difference that is likely to lead to even more significant differences (for example, Barbara is likely to become more dogmatic and closed-minded as she struggles to preserve her racist beliefs in the face of countervailing evidence). But although there is much that Betty and Barbara did control, they did not—in Kane's indeterminist scenario—control the development of that difference. The difference between otherwise identical Barbara and Betty at that crucial indeterminate moment is that a subatomic particle bounced one way in Betty and a different way in Barbara, which is what resulted in their now different characters (different characters they both endorse and with which they identify); that key difference is not one they ultimately control, and not one for which they legitimately can be blamed or praised.

Drawing Conclusions Concerning Betty and Benji

When we encounter Betty and Benji, we have a number of possibilities. First, we can willfully ignore the detailed differences in their capacities, insist that everyone is equal on the same plateau and thus is morally responsible: there are no relevant differences among us (an argument that will be critically examined in chapter 12). Second, we could argue that once Betty and Benji have emerged to that level (regardless of how they did it), they have special rational powers that transcend all differences in details, and they can go in any direction and develop any capacities of unlimited strength. But naturalists know too much about how we are shaped—and the psychological factors affecting our rational powers—to draw any such conclusion concerning godlike powers of reason. Third, we can insist that we do have magical self-construction initial powers, as the existentialists claim: that somehow we choose ourselves, or make ourselves ab initio, that we are self-caused in some absolute (nonnatural) manner. Fourth, we could reject mysterious initial self-creation, but insist—with C. A. Campbell (1957)—that along the way we have the special miraculous power of making choices using powers of special contracausal free will that cancel out the effects of our differing initial conditions. Fifth, we can admit that we don't have such magical powers of initial or intermediate self-creation, but claim that the initial starts were generally fair and so the results are fair: as Dennett (1984) attempts for roughly equal starts, and Sher (1987) proposes for overall equal talents (a line of argument critiqued in chapter 7). Sixth, we can attempt to find space for moral responsibility in special instances of indeterminism (Kane's model). Or finally, we can look carefully at how we were shaped and the differences in our starting abilities and in our situations, reject mysteries and miracles, and deny moral responsibility.

The story of Betty and Benji requires no nefarious neurosurgeons and no peremptory puppeteers—or any kind of devious or coercive intervener. Mele's story of Betty is a mundane, plausible, psychologically sound account of the development of Betty's capacity for practical freedom; the account of Benji's development has the same features. The accounts do not require science fiction; they require only that we look closely at the details of how our capacities are formed (including the full process of self-formation), and at how differences in those capacities result. If we start with differences, then (barring differences in racing luck, or a positive intervener—the proverbial kindly priest or concerned coach—or some other factor for which we are not responsible) we end differently. That conclusion doesn't mean that we are not largely self-made, or that we cannot exercise effective choice, but it does mean that we are not morally responsible. Betty isn't just lucky to be so strong and virtuous—after all, much of her strength and ability was shaped by her own successful efforts. But Betty (as compared to Benji) is lucky to have had the start that enabled her to become the person she is, and Benji is unlucky to have had fewer initial developmental powers. The question is not whether Betty can develop so, employing her own developing abilities; she can, as Mele insightfully describes. Nor is it a question of whether Betty can accomplish much (she can) or whether her accomplishments flow from her own strong and resourceful character (they do). The question is whether she deserves special credit and Benji deserves special blame (they don't). Once we recognize that freedom can be distinguished from moral responsibility, and that having good (or bad) qualities of character can be distinguished from being morally responsible for those character qualities, then it is clear that our best account of the development of freedom is not an account that justifies claims and ascriptions of moral responsibility.

Benji is somewhat free (he certainly should not be denied the opportunity to make his own decisions); Betty is much freer. But neither can claim ultimate responsibility; unless they have ultimate, "before-the-eyes-of-God" moral responsibility, then moral responsibility is unfair. It may also be "unfair" that Benji starts with less capacity for free will than Betty does;

it's also "unfair" that some are born sound and others with severe disabilities. Those are differences that we wish to mitigate (not by handicapping the advantaged, obviously, but by improving the opportunities for the disadvantaged), but there is no question of blaming/praising for those critical initial differences. Life is not fair, true enough, but just deserts must be fair, and the natural lottery of genetic traits and early conditioning is not a fair manner of distributing just deserts. Just deserts and moral responsibility require a godlike power—the existentialist power of choosing ourselves, the godlike power of making ourselves from scratch, the divine capacity to be an uncaused cause—that we do not have. Moral responsibility is an atavistic relic of a belief system we (as naturalists) have rejected, for good reason. Freedom—and its enhancement—fits comfortably with our natural world and our scientific understanding of it; moral responsibility does not.

The basic problem for any naturalistic defense of moral responsibility is that we are each different in our capacities and talents and cognitive abilities and fortitude; careful comparisons of those differences in character and history soon undercut any claims or ascriptions of moral responsibility. Those differences make it unfair to blame one and reward another for their differences in behavior. On the naturalist—nonmiraculous—view, if there is a difference in behavior, then there must be a difference in circumstances, influences, or abilities. This view is not intended as a conclusive argument against moral responsibility. But it should serve to establish that the burden of proof rests on those who claim that moral responsibility is compatible with naturalism. Absent such proofs, it is difficult to see how moral responsibility can fit within the naturalistic worldview. Furthermore, as Richard Double has argued (2002) the burden of proof falls heavily on those who claim there is moral responsibility, because they are proposing that we blame and punish people for their misdeeds, and justifying such painful special treatment requires a very strong proof that it is being imposed fairly. This book is an effort to show that—as naturalists—we should reject all claims and ascriptions of moral responsibility. The moral responsibility system has long since outlived the very limited advantages it offered, and it should be replaced—in law, government, education, philosophy, and common belief—by a system that will greatly reduce both physical and psychological harm and will open paths to individual and social progress.

The goal of this book is to show that moral responsibility cannot be justified, that the major arguments in support of moral responsibility fail, that the moral responsibility system is severely flawed, and that the world would be better if belief in moral responsibility vanished from the Earth. But I am not claiming that development and further refinement of the moral responsibility system was altogether bad. To the contrary, the initial development of the moral responsibility system was beneficial: it certainly is an improvement over the more primitive impulse to simply strike back (whoever slays a man shall be slain): we must have justification for striking back, and with the justification comes a wide range of exceptions and exemptions that lessened the extent of harmful punishment. Our system of retributive justice (though I believe it has outlived its early usefulness) was an enormous step forward from lynch mobs and personal vendettas.

Furthermore, I am certainly not suggesting that the rich and fascinating range of arguments in support of moral responsibility have been useless. Though I believe they fail to support moral responsibility, they have provided important insights into questions of personal identity, ethics, free will, and many other areas. Daniel Dennett and John Martin Fischer fail (I claim) to establish grounds for moral responsibility, but in the course of their efforts they have drawn a much clearer picture of the many important varieties of control, their value, the distinctions among them, and their enormous psychological significance. Harry Frankfurt and Gerald Dworkin have not established grounds for moral responsibility, but they have developed a vitally important account of the deeper psychological levels of human desire and will and have therefore greatly improved our understanding of human freedom and constraint. If Alfred Mele's work does not justify moral responsibility, it loses none of its subtle insights into the complex development of human character. And even if Robert Kane's extraordinary model of ultimate self-forming acts fails to support moral responsibility, it is a remarkably clear and honest guide to the conditions required for genuine moral responsibility.

Finally, although some people insist on moral responsibility as a means of justifying greed and exploiting desires for vengeance (some politicians spring to mind), I do not believe that those are the motives of most of the philosophical defenders of moral responsibility. Though the motives for defense of moral responsibility have been many, some of the most dedicated proponents of moral responsibility are certainly not motivated by greed and vengeance; instead, many of them—such as Dostoyevsky (1864/1961), William James (1890), and William Barrett (1958)—want to protect a power of special creativity: the power to be the genuine author, the original source, of something distinctively new—the desire to refute Solomon's depressing insistence that "there is nothing new under the Sun." Robert Kane, though he wants moral responsibility, wants it for much more than a justification of striking back or claiming reward; he wants to be a genuine starting point, an *originator* who is more than a link in a deterministic chain (Kane 1985, 177–178). This issue is examined in chapter 14, but the immediate point is this: at least some of those who have struggled to support a workable account of moral responsibility in the face of scientific challenge have been motivated by goals far more attractive than vengeance and greed.

The case against moral responsibility is a powerful one, on both moral and pragmatic grounds. As the scientific understanding of human behavior expands, the case against moral responsibility grows stronger, while serious flaws are exposed in the arguments supporting moral responsibility. Substantiating those claims is the task of the remainder of this book. But before going into that work, it is essential to examine free will. There is no plausible naturalistic account of free will that can support the weight of moral responsibility: that is the focus of the chapters after the following chapter. The examination of free will in the following chapter makes three claims: the traditional close linkage of moral responsibility to free will is a mistake; the effort to concoct an account of free will that can bear the burden of moral responsibility has resulted in a severely deformed account of free will; and there is a naturalist account of free will that is more empirically plausible, does not support moral responsibility, and can flourish in the absence of moral responsibility.

3 Rescuing Free Will from Moral Responsibility

As noted in the first chapter, many philosophers regard the denial of moral responsibility as nonsense, but if denying moral responsibility is nonsense, denying moral responsibility while endorsing free will is "nonsense on stilts." In an earlier work (Waller 1990), I sketched a case against moral responsibility, and was not surprised that the rejection of moral responsibility would be regarded with skepticism, but I also suggested that free will could survive the demise of moral responsibility, and that was typically thought to be ludicrous: one reviewer (Hocutt 1992) suggested that the title of the book—*Freedom without Responsibility*—was more appropriate for a condom advertisement than a philosophical monograph.

No doubt it was philosophically naïve to suppose that the attempt to sever free will from moral responsibility would not be greeted by philosophical incredulity. After all, free will and moral responsibility have long been regarded as inseparable. C. A. Campbell thinks it axiomatic that any legitimate account of free will must support moral responsibility: "It is not seriously disputable that the kind of freedom in question is the freedom which is commonly recognised to be in some sense a precondition of moral responsibility. Clearly, it is on account of this integral connection with moral responsibility that such exceptional importance has always been felt to attach to the Free Will problem" (1957, 159).

Willard Gaylin regards the connection as so obvious that it need only be stated: "Freedom demands responsibility; autonomy demands culpability" (1982, 338). Walter Glannon, in his writings on bioethics, makes the same confident claim: "Autonomy and responsibility are mutually entailing notions" (1998, 45). Janet Radcliffe Richards notes the centrality of that assumption: "Free will is thought of as the capacity to be genuinely responsible for actions and genuinely deserving of praise or blame for the choices that are made" (2000, 136). In specifying the parameters of an argument, Michael McKenna starts with this definition: "I understand *free will* as satisfying all that is required for the control condition for morally responsible agency. Persons are morally responsible only if they are able to control their conduct. Free will is just the capacity that gives persons the relevant sort of control required for morally responsible agency" (2008, 187–188). James Lenman maintains that "a central aspect of the free-will problem is the problem of explaining how it can even make sense to hold people morally responsible for what they do. To this extent, in this context, the most important sense of 'free' is perhaps just this: someone is free insofar as they satisfy whatever conditions need to be satisfied for this to make sense with respect to them" (2006, 8). And Peter van Inwagen asserts: "If we do know that moral responsibility exists, then we should have no doubt about whether we have good reason to believe we have free will. . . . It is as adequate a defence of the free-will thesis as has ever been given for any philosophical position to say, 'Without free will, we should never be morally responsible for anything, and we are sometimes morally responsible'" (1983, 209).

This common view of the binding connection between free will and moral responsibility is rarely argued; rather, it forms the unquestioned framework for most of our arguments concerning free will and moral responsibility. Libertarians insist that their libertarian theories can support both free will and moral responsibility; compatibilists believe that determinist views can accommodate both free will and moral responsibility, and hard determinists maintain that determinism marks the demise of both free will and moral responsibility. But the basic shared assumption is that free will and moral responsibility must stand or fall together.[1]

The unbreakable link between free will and moral responsibility is an article of philosophical faith, and dissent from that orthodoxy requires explanation. Still, the explanation is not complicated, and I find it difficult to understand why such a position—one that affirms free will while denying moral responsibility—should be regarded as a philosophical curiosity or even as a philosophical monstrosity. For there is really nothing new in this position; to the contrary, it simply combines elements of two positions that are widely held among philosophers. First, it affirms a compatibilist account of free will: that determinism (or naturalism) is compatible with a rich and humanly satisfactory account of freedom and free will.

This view is held by David Hume, G. E. Moore, A. J. Ayer, Harry Frankfurt, Daniel Dennett, and a multitude of other philosophers. Second, it claims that moral responsibility is not compatible with determinism/naturalism (and thus that compatibilist accounts of free will fail to justify claims and ascriptions of moral responsibility), which is a position championed by such philosophical stalwarts as Lorenzo Valla, Immanuel Kant, C. A. Campbell, Peter van Inwagen, Timothy O'Connor, Carl Ginet, Robert Kane, and Derk Pereboom. So why should it be regarded as strange to claim both that we can give a perfectly adequate compatibilist account of free will and that it is impossible to square moral responsibility with determinism/naturalism? Surely, it is because free will accounts were developed primarily to support moral responsibility: to support the claim that it is fair and just to punish and reward, that it is fair and just that some should suffer special detriments while others gain special benefits. As noted previously, Campbell insists that that is precisely why the question of free will has long been such a prominent issue: "It is not seriously disputable that the kind of freedom in question is the freedom which is commonly recognised to be in some sense a precondition of moral responsibility. Clearly, it is on account of this integral connection with moral responsibility that such exceptional importance has always been felt to attach to the Free Will problem" (1957, 159).

The special attention to devising an adequate account of free will has its roots in an ancient and continuing effort to justify moral responsibility, but that is no reason to suppose that we cannot now examine free will apart from the question of moral responsibility. In particular, why shouldn't someone reasonably hold that the compatibilists have developed an excellent account of free will, but—as libertarians and hard determinists concur—that it will not support claims and ascriptions of moral responsibility? The roots of chemical science can probably be found in the alchemists' hope of transmuting lead into gold; that the transmutation goal was not accomplished does not lessen the value of the science of chemistry that eventually resulted from those failed initial goals. And just because the major impetus for accounts of free will may have been the justification of moral responsibility, it does not follow that the free will account that eventually developed is not a substantial and worthwhile account, even if it fails to support moral responsibility. Philosophers and theologians endeavored to develop an account of free will that would justify moral responsibility; they failed, or at least they failed to contrive a naturalistic account of free will that would justify moral responsibility (so I—and many others, from Spinoza to Pereboom—have concluded), but it does not follow that the improved understanding of free will brought about by the efforts of Hume, Frankfurt, Dennett, Wolf, and Mele have no value. Thanks to brilliant work by many philosophers (and many psychologists and biologists), we can construct a very good naturalistic account of free will; that this account will not support claims and ascriptions of moral responsibility does not make that accomplishment less significant. To the contrary (so the remainder of this book argues), the very fact that such a rich and substantial account of free will cannot support claims of moral responsibility is one of the most significant contributions of the development of this free will account: not only can we have a substantial and satisfactory account of free will in the absence of moral responsibility, but also the failure of this vigorous naturalistic free will account to support moral responsibility is some evidence that moral responsibility cannot be justified within the naturalistic framework. But before looking further at the plausibility of a naturalistic free will account that is independent of moral responsibility, it is useful to consider some of the problems caused by the traditional insistence on linking free will with moral responsibility.

The Free Will Distortions Generated by Moral Responsibility

The assumption that any satisfactory account of free will must support moral responsibility distorts our understanding of free will. Perhaps the clearest case of that distorting effect can be seen in the work of Richard Taylor, who fashions a very implausible account of free will—an account he himself acknowledges "is strange indeed, if not positively mysterious" (1963, 49)—because he believes that such an account is essential for the sort of first cause agency that moral responsibility requires. Along similar lines, Campbell (1957)—following Kant's lead—is prepared to renounce our best scientific account of humans and human behavior in order to make room for a power of human free will that can preserve moral responsibility.

The assumed link between free will and moral responsibility leads some philosophers—typically libertarians, such as Campbell and Chisholm—to propose implausible accounts of free will that are designed to support moral responsibility. But the strong belief in the free will–moral responsibility connection sometimes works in the opposite direction, especially for naturalists who are not willing to embrace the "strange" and "mysterious" and even miraculous free will powers that would make free will the foundation for moral responsibility. Instead of starting from moral responsibility and fashioning an implausible account of free will to support it, these philosophers start from a more modest naturalistic account of free will and then insist that the conditions for moral responsibility must be understood as whatever their naturalistic free will account can justify. Nowell-Smith recognized that humans have no miraculous powers of self-creation or transformation, but he believed that some human behavior is modifiable through punishment and reward (yet other behavior and capacities—such as native intelligence—are not); then, rather than starting from some view of moral responsibility that requires implausible mysterious powers, he shifted the conception of moral responsibility to fit what can be accommodated in a naturalistic account of human behavior and its shaping: "A man is not punishable because he is guilty; he is guilty because he is punishable, that is to say, because some useful result is supposed to accrue from punishing him" (1948, 58). Stephen White develops this approach in more detail, redefining the concept of free will and "could have done otherwise" in accordance with the demands of moral responsibility: "An agent could have done other than he did just in case the ascription of responsibility and blame to that agent for the action in question is justified" (1991, 236). That is, when human behavior is such that holding people morally responsible—punishing and rewarding them—may yield beneficial effects and thus be pragmatically justified, then we should count that behavior as free.

Dennett, inspired by White, recommends the same approach: "Don't try to use metaphysics to ground ethics . . . ; put it the other way around: Use ethics to ground what we should mean by our 'metaphysical' criterion" (2003, 297). That is, start from the assumption of moral responsibility—the assumption that people justly deserve reward and punishment—and use that to fix what we mean by "could have done otherwise" and by our concept of free will. Start from the assumption that moral responsibility is justified, and then work backward: moral responsibility claims and ascriptions are justified, and free will is the basis for that justification, so whatever plausible naturalistic account of free will we can work out must be adequate to justify moral responsibility. We can't do otherwise in the sense that the miracle-working libertarians would require; therefore, that account of free will cannot be the requisite justification for moral responsibility (because moral responsibility *is* justified, and miraculous powers of free will do not exist and thus could not provide such justification). The resulting account of free will takes this form: we are acting freely when our behavior is such that it is subject to modification by punishment or threat of punishment. We do have that sort of freedom, so that freedom must be an adequate justification for moral responsibility (because we already know that moral responsibility is justified, and such freedom is the only freedom available to provide the justification). The result is an anemic account of moral responsibility joined to a shallow account of free will. Furthermore, such an approach attempts to eliminate by definition a question that should be faced squarely, a question that bubbles up no matter how diligently one tries to suppress it: are blaming and punishing really fair? It also chokes off investigation of another pressing question: are punishment and blame really useful—are they genuinely beneficial to society and its members? The special definitions proposed by Dennett and others don't answer those questions; rather, they bury them. It is much better to break the assumed link between free will and moral responsibility, examine both carefully, and then draw our conclusions concerning their connections and relations.

Separating Free Will from Moral Responsibility

Why should it be assumed that free will must be linked with moral responsibility? Moral responsibility is a concept of moral fairness; free will need have nothing to do with that, especially if we are seeking a naturalistic account of free will that explains the fitness benefits of free will. A naturalistic understanding of free will must involve understanding what such a power could contribute to our survival and our success, how such a power could have evolved, and what benefits or detriments result from exercise of such a power. The question of whether such a power can justify ethical judgments—concerning justice and fairness, punishment and reward, moral responsibility—is a different question altogether.

As noted earlier, we could stipulate a definition of free will that makes its connection with moral responsibility unbreakable: free will is the capacity that makes one morally responsible for one's behavior. This stipulative approach has its charms; Daniel Dennett recommends that in thinking about free will, we should start from this principle: "Free will is whatever gives us moral responsibility" (2008, 254). But using a definition to establish the link between moral responsibility and free will is not an attractive procedure even for advocates of moral responsibility. After all, Harry Frankfurt has endeavored to establish that we can be morally responsible even though we lack the traditional free will power of choosing among open alternatives. And when Peter van Inwagen argues that because we are sometimes morally responsible we can conclude that we do have free will, he is claiming to have established something more than an analytic, definitional truth.

So why should it be impossible for an individual to have free will, and to live and act freely, without also being morally responsible? Why suppose that any adequate account of free will must be one that justifies moral responsibility? For the answer to that question, we must delve into the deep, dark, and continuing history of moral responsibility.

Moral responsibility is rooted much deeper than philosophy, deeper than reason. The desire—indeed, the visceral biological *need*—to strike back at trouble can be found in chimpanzees and rats. It existed long before humans, and long before concern with free will or moral responsibility. It is based in a profoundly irrational strikeback inclination (discussed in chapter 1) that targets wrongdoers only by chance. As Michael Potegal notes, "From the perspective of a theoretical distinction between provoker and target, redirected aggression is not a special case; in most cases aggression just happens to be directed at the object that provoked it" (1994, 88). If someone else is handy, the "retributive" aggression is released on the convenient target. In monkey colonies, a subordinate who suffers an attack from a higher ranking monkey typically seeks out an individual lower in the hierarchy for attack (Kawamura 1967). When two rats are placed in a cage with an electrified floor and subjected to shock, they attack each other (Ulrich and Azrin 1962). The same behavior is evident in humans. In the terrible "mourning wars" among some tribes of eastern North America, whenever a tribe member died (whether from disease, or falling off a cliff, or in war), tribal members felt morally obligated to kill a member of some other tribe, resulting in a spiral of strikeback violence (Richter 1983). And William Ian Miller notes that traditional "honor" cultures (which approved and promoted retributive violence) "were as likely to visit the revenge on a relative of the wrongdoer as on the wrong-doer himself" (2006, 147). It may well be that in games such as Prisoners' Dilemma, the best strategy is "tit-for-tat": cooperate when the person with whom you are playing reciprocates that cooperative treatment, and strike back when the other player harms you. But such artificially arranged game-playing strategies carry no weight in showing that a "tit-for-tat" strategy is genuinely useful in the natural environment. In the artificial game-playing setting, the person who wronged you is the only available target, whereas in our natural environment the strikeback response is likely to be aimed at an innocent bystander.

When humans began to feel a need to justify the strikeback impulse, the early answers came easy: God commands it. "Whoso sheddeth man's blood, by man shall his blood be shed" (Gen. 9:6), and it is worth noting that God often visited His wrath upon future generations along with the actual offenders. But when God's orders were not enough, the concept of moral responsibility and just deserts entered the picture, and questions of how to justify special benefits and punishments became a challenge. Why does Diane deserve punishment for her misdeeds—why is she morally responsible?

Though there were those—notably Aristotle, but also theologians—who wrestled with the question of moral responsibility much earlier, the issue of moral responsibility did not really come into focus until the Renais-sance—though Schopenhauer claims that "the one who was the first to come to the heart of the matter was, to all appearances, Thomas Hobbes" (Schopenhauer 1960, 76), and not until the Enlightenment did it become a major philosophical issue. In the Hebraic tradition, humans are God's creatures, clay in the hands of the divine potter, and the potter can do with them as He wishes: and who are you to ask for an explanation from God? In the words of the Prophet Isaiah: "Woe unto him that striveth with his Maker! . . . Shall the clay say to him that fashioneth it, What makest thou?" (Isa. 45:9). Paul makes this position painfully clear: "Nay but, O man, who art thous that repliest against God? Shall the thing formed say to him that formed it, Why hast thou made me thus? Hath not the potter power over the clay, of the same lump to make one vessel unto honour, and another unto dishonour?" (Rom. 10:20–21).

So why does one do evil, and receive harsh (even eternal) punishment, while another is virtuous and favored by God? It is purely God's choice, and human free will is nonexistent: "So then it is not of him that willeth, nor of him that runneth, but of God that sheweth mercy" (Rom. 10:16).

In case anyone should miss the point, consider the story of poor Job. God Himself calls Job "a perfect and an upright man, one that feareth God, and escheweth evil" (Job 1:8). But in a rather silly cosmic dare, God sanctions the destruction of Job's fortune, the killing of his children, and the agony of "sore boils from the sole of his foot unto his crown" (Job 2:7). When Job sought an explanation—why should such suffering be the fate of an upright man that escheweth evil?—God swiftly puts Job in his place: "Where wast thou when I laid the foundations of the earth? declare, if thou hast understanding. . . . Shall he that contendeth with the Almighty instruct him? he that reproveth God, let him answer it. . . . Wilt thou also disannul my judgment? wilt thou condemn me, that thou mayest be righteous? Hast thou an arm like God? or canst thou thunder with a voice like him?" (Job 38:4, 40:2, 8–9). In short, almighty God will do as He wishes with His human creatures, and questions of justice do not apply.

Martin Luther found this model deeply disturbing, but not daring to question the ways of a wrathful God, Luther sought refuge in abject faith:

This is the highest degree of faith—to believe that He is merciful, who saves so few and damns so many; to believe Him just, who according to His own will makes us necessarily damnable. . . . If, therefore, I could by any means comprehend how that same God can be merciful and just who carries the appearance of so much wrath and iniquity, there would be no need of faith. But now, since that cannot be comprehended, there is room for exercising faith. (1823, section 24)

The Islamic tradition embraces the same model of unavoidable fate, as in the famous story of the road to Samarra. The story tells of a merchant who traveled to Baghdad and then sent his servant to the marketplace to buy supplies. The servant returned, pale and terrified: while he was in the marketplace, he was jostled by an old woman; when he turned to look, the old woman was Death, and she glared at him. "Now lend me your horse," the servant pleads, "that I may ride to Samarra and escape my fate." The master lends the servant his horse, and the servant flees Baghdad as fast as the horse will run, on his way to Samarra. Later, the master goes to the market to buy the supplies that his terrified servant had forgotten, and at the market he encounters Death. "Why did you glare at my servant?" asks the master. Death replies: "I didn't glare at him; that was an expression of surprise. I was surprised to see him here in Baghdad, for I have an appointment with him tonight in Samarra." You may ride fast or slow, strive for virtue or embrace vice, but your fate is set: moral responsibility, just deserts, and free will don't enter into it.

The Greek story of Oedipus is more elaborate, but the point is the same: Oedipus may strive to be honorable and virtuous and use all his wit and energy to avoid his fated wrongdoing, but his efforts and his virtues avail him nothing: his fate is sealed, and his efforts to avoid it only propel him toward his fate. The moral of these stories: you have no real control over your destiny, and considerations of justice and moral responsibility don't apply. You are a pawn in God's unfathomable game, and who are you to question God, you puny worm?

By the Renaissance, and certainly in the Enlightenment, the worm has turned; humans believe that they can understand and even control the world, and they demand fair treatment and justice, not the caprice of God or of God's divinely appointed ruler. Of course, the deep desire to strike back when harmed remains—including the desire for retribution against those who cause harm, but now there must be justification for acting on this deep-felt impulse, and the justification must be more than "God (or God's divinely chosen ruler) commands it." How can we be justified in causing special harm to a wrongdoer? Because the wrongdoer justly deserves to suffer harm; that is, the wrongdoer is morally responsible for the wrong done. It is no accident that demands for just treatment and just punishment emerge together with a sense of greater human powers. It was an era when science and magic intermingled, and the powers of humans to control the world and make themselves gods seemed almost within grasp—just a few more secrets to be unlocked by the astrologers and the astronomers, the Hermetics and the magicians, the scientists and the alchemists. And even if humans do not quite become gods, at least we have the godlike powers to choose, to legislate, to reason.

So free will was traditionally linked with moral responsibility because we were seeking a justification for moral responsibility, and free will seemed like a convenient peg. After all, free will is supposed to be a uniquely human power, and humans are the only ones who are morally responsible. And free will is a special divine miracle-working power to make ourselves; so if anything can support moral responsibility, free will seems the best candidate. Pico della Mirandola saw free will as a divinely given power to make ourselves, with our options entirely open and ranging from the bestial to the divine: "You shall be able to descend among the lower forms of being, which are brute beasts; you shall be able to be reborn out of the judgment of your own soul into the higher beings, which are divine" (1496/1948). Chisholm's account of free will is more modest, but not by much: "If we are responsible . . . then we have a prerogative which some would attribute only to God: each of us, when we really act, is a prime mover unmoved. In doing what we do, we cause certain events to happen, and nothing and no one, except we ourselves, causes us to cause those events to happen" (1982, 32).

When the power of free will was initially proposed as a justification of moral responsibility, it was a godlike power of self-making and free choice. It certainly was not free will within the confines of naturalism. But once these powers become less than godlike, does the moral responsibility justification remain? We make choices, of course, but those choices are more like those of our fellow animals than the absolute choices of the deities. And we have powers of reason, but not superrational unlimited powers. So even if a miracle-working power of free will is good grounds for moral responsibility, it is not at all clear that any plausible naturalistic account of free will can support moral responsibility.

This conclusion will hardly be a shock to contemporary naturalists. After all, the key question of the contemporary free will debate is whether we can find a naturalistic justification for free will and moral responsibility. But the underlying assumption of those inquiries has been that if we can give a satisfactory naturalistic account of free will, then we will have automatically given an adequate justification of moral responsibility as well; that is, the assumption that free will must provide support for moral responsibility has remained intact, though the account given of free will has radically changed. But once we embrace naturalism and put away miracles, is there any reason to suppose that an adequate free will account must support claims and ascriptions of moral responsibility?

Natural Free Will without Moral Responsibility

Is it plausible to bind our naturalistic concept of free will so closely to the burden of moral responsibility? The problem is that by insisting that free will serve as a foundation for moral responsibility, we twist and distort our understanding of natural freedom and its value. Rather than examining closely what is most basic in freedom—that which we share with other closely related species—we focus on what sets us apart: moral responsibility is a uniquely human characteristic, so the capacities that support it must also be unique to humans. Thus we emphasize elements of free will that are rather marginal, and neglect the opportunity to expand our knowledge of free will by examining it writ large in the behavior of other animals—animals with which we have much more in common than with gods.

What is free will? When most people think of free will, they think of the free choice among alternatives. That, obviously, is why determinism is commonly thought to undermine free will: it threatens our ability to choose among open paths, to choose among alternatives. But if we can genuinely make our own free choices among open alternatives, then we can exercise free will. (Obviously many philosophers would dispute that claim, Harry Frankfurt and Susan Wolf being among the most obvious. That will be discussed later. At this point I am not claiming this is the correct philosophical account of free will, only that it is commonly thought to be a—perhaps *the*—key element of free will.)

Suppose we ask: why do you want free will? Why do you want to be able to make your own choices among genuine alternatives? The answers are likely to be rather weak, and often circular. I want freedom because I don't want to be forced to follow a rigid path; I like to make my own choices; I don't want to be enslaved. The weakness of those answers does not imply that this belief in open alternatives free will is weak; rather, it is an indication that the desire is so deep, so fundamental, that it is difficult to give any further justification. One might say, "I want to have open alternatives, because that is the best way to test my beliefs and ideas and hypotheses"; that is, one might develop John Stuart Mill's *On Liberty* (1869) arguments, and those are excellent arguments. But that justification is not what actually motivates the desire for open alternatives, for that attraction is much more basic and primitive. It would be like asking someone, "Why do you want sexual relations?" One might—like the Catholic Church—find some rationalization in terms of wanting to procreate and continue the species, but the sexual desires of most people are more basic than any rationalization they could offer. Likewise with the desire for open alternatives: when such alternatives are denied—whether in prison, or in constrained repetitive assembly line work, or as a patient in badly managed hospital wards, or as a resident in a rigidly controlled long-term care facility—psychological damage results (Waller 2001).

Such damage is not surprising. The desire for open alternatives is deeply ingrained and existed long before humans evolved. It is a deep desire that we share with many other species. J. Lee Kavanau successfully trained feral white-footed mice to negotiate a maze to gain a reward, but was frustrated by the fact that even after the mice had mastered the correct path, they continued to occasionally make mistakes and follow the wrong path. But Kavanau's frustration eventually resulted in insight:

Investigators sometimes are puzzled by the fact that once an animal has learned a discrimination well, it nonetheless still makes some "incorrect" responses. Actually, these responses are incorrect only from the point of view of the investigator's rigidly prescribed program, not from that of the animal. The basis for these responses is that the animal has a certain degree of variability built into many of its behavior patterns. This variability is adaptive to conditions in the wild, where there are many relationships that are not strictly prescribed. (1967, 1628; see also Kavanau 1963)

The white-footed mouse needs to learn which path currently leads to food, but food sources are not eternal and unchanging. The bountiful berry patch will soon be barren. By keeping options open, and occasionally exploring other paths, the mouse discovers new food sources that are available when the current best source disappears, and a variety of paths may make the mouse less vulnerable to predators. As Kavanau summarizes the benefits, "The habit of deviating fairly frequently from stereotyped 'correct' responses, together with a high level of spontaneous activity, underlie the remarkable facility with which white-footed mice can be taught to cope with complex contingencies" (1967, 1628).

And what works for mice also works for humans. If one never explores the less than optimum path to work, then highway construction and traffic jams leave one stuck. The investment strategy that was optimum in a bull market may be disastrous in an economic downturn, and the investor who explores options other than the current optimum investment strategy is better equipped to take advantage of emerging opportunities. The researcher who is open to new possibilities is less likely to become locked into a failed research program. This strong inclination toward exploring other options is part of what psychologists and biologists study under the heading of "sensation-seeking." It has been observed in many species (including, obviously, humans), and it takes many forms.[2]

Dostoyevsky claims that spontaneous—unreasonable, less than optimum—choices are the downfall of any systematic naturalistic explanation of human behavior: "So one's own free, unrestrained choice, one's own whim, be it the wildest, one's own fancy, sometimes worked up to a frenzy—that is the most advantageous advantage that cannot be fitted into any table or scale and that causes every system and every theory to crumble into dust on contact" (1864/1961, 110).

But in fact the value of pursuing "one's own whim" is a key element of the naturalistic system: whether white-footed mouse or investment analyst, one's own "free, unrestrained choice" is valuable, and rather than requiring mysteries or miracles, it is best explained in naturalistic terms.

The natural need for open alternatives—found in white-footed mice, Bengal tigers, assembly line workers, and scientific researchers—is an important element of freedom. But exactly what does it involve? First, it involves a need for "spontaneous behavior." This need is not for some miraculous first cause power of behaving with no antecedent causes or conditions; such powers may be required to be godlike, or to establish moral responsibility, but they are not part of either mouse or human natural freedom. Rather, it means that there is a natural desire to occasionally take a different path, try something new, or deviate from the pattern. It is an evolved tendency toward occasional spontaneity: animals that kept their options open and tried new paths were more likely to find food resources and discover escape routes and were thus more likely to survive and procreate and pass such tendencies to their offspring. And it involves the opportunity to change behavior and change paths in response to a changing environment.

For those libertarians (such as C. A. Campbell) who wish to use "choices among alternatives" to support moral responsibility, that is not enough; that one could choose differently *if* circumstances were different, or that one could have acted differently *if* one had chosen to take a different path, leaves open the question of whether one is choosing with no constraints whatsoever, choosing in such a radical manner that "nothing determines the act save the agent's doing of it." Such absolute power of choice—if such can be conceived—might be useful for supporting moral responsibility, but it is not so helpful to the white-footed mouse, who needs freedom to respond differently when environmental conditions change and whose natural inclination toward preserving open alternatives was shaped and determined in a way that makes mouse behavior more adaptive to its changing natural environment. Such open-alternatives freedom works fine for white-footed mice, but they are neither striving to be gods nor struggling to justify moral responsibility. It also works fine for humans, within the same limitations. If we are seeking a naturalistic account of freedom, it should look more like that of a white-footed mouse than that of a god.

Open alternatives are a key element of natural free will, but not the only one: the following chapter examines an important authenticity complement to natural open alternatives.

4   Hierarchical Free Will and Natural Authenticity

It is not difficult to give an account of how open alternatives contribute to natural free will, but it has proved very difficult indeed to develop a naturalistic account of open alternatives that supports moral responsibility (though Robert Kane, Carl Ginet, and Randolph Clarke—among others—have made heroic efforts). Those difficulties have pushed many philosophers toward a new account of free will: an account that does not require choices among open alternatives, but focuses instead on choices that are one's *own* choices. In this approach, the focus moves from alternatives to authenticity. The question is not whether I could have chosen differently, but whether my choice is genuine, reflects my true commitments, and is authentically my own. In contemporary philosophy, Harry Frankfurt is one of the most inventive and influential advocates of the authenticity approach to free will and moral responsibility. In Frankfurt's account, the question is not whether I could have made a different choice, but whether the choice I made is one that I approve and endorse at a higher reflective level.

Frankfurt's Hierarchical Authenticity

This "hierarchical authenticity" approach to free will offers important insights, which are celebrated in later pages. But it fails as a justification for moral responsibility, and its failed struggle to support moral responsibility results in a distorted model of free will. The problem is evident in one of Frankfurt's most provocative and creative examples (1971): the willing addict, who has no alternative to taking drugs but is nonetheless free and morally responsible because he reflectively approves and endorses his drug desire and drug addiction. The case of the willing addict has prompted new scrutiny of our approach to freedom and responsibility, but close examination of the case reveals the fatal flaws in this hierarchical reflection model.

Instead of the abstract philosophical entity of a willing addict who carefully reflects and deeply approves his life of addiction, consider the actual psychological state of a deeply committed willing addict. The *un*willing addict is easy enough to understand; indeed, almost all of us have experienced strong—perhaps even addictive—desires that we deeply disapprove: for tobacco or alcohol, perhaps, or for sweets or video games. The unwilling addict toys with drugs, believing himself fully in control of their use ("I can stop anytime I wish"), but then finds himself trapped in an addiction that he despises: an addiction that is wrecking his health, his career, and his family life. This unwilling addict is not free, as Frankfurt clearly notes. But although the path to unwilling addiction is obvious, the path to willing addiction has tricky turns. Consider the psychological process of embracing addiction—becoming a willing addict. The unwilling addict continues to slide into deeper difficulties, losing his family and friends, destroying his career, and suffering physical and psychological problems. At some point, he has nothing left except his addiction, his only desire is for drugs, and at that point he deeply approves of his addiction, clinging to it desperately. He has now become a willing addict, and when he reflects on his situation, he is glad to be an addict (any other pleasures or satisfactions are now unimaginable). But having lost the desire to escape his addiction, has he now gained freedom and moral responsibility?

Consider Jamal, a fiercely independent warrior who is captured by slavers, painfully shackled, locked in the dark stench of a slave ship for months, and transported in chains to a plantation, where he is whipped, branded, and abused. Through this horrific process, Jamal keeps his commitment to freedom, striking back at his captors at every opportunity and seizing every remote chance of escape. Jamal is an unwilling slave, and—as Frankfurt would rightly acknowledge—Jamal is not free, nor is he morally responsible for his condition of servitude. But eventually even Jamal's spirit is broken: every attempt at escape results in heavier chains and greater suffering, every act of defiance is severely punished, every element of control is lost, every hope extinguished. After a long struggle, Jamal "accepts his fate," embraces his life of slavery, and loses any desire for freedom: now he wishes only to serve his master faithfully, is glad that he is a slave, and reflectively approves of his enslavement. And now Jamal is free; he has free will and is morally responsible for his own slavery. Or so we must conclude, if we accept Frankfurt's model.

Imagine Eve, a strong and independent young woman born into a religious culture that demands that all women be meek and compliant, accept the authority of their male superiors without question, and embrace the subservient role that is their only path to virtue and righteousness. Eve rejects those values, asserts her right to her own ideas, fiercely defends her own independence, and insists that she be respected as fully equal to anyone else rather than as fit only for meekly following orders. Denied the right and opportunity to pursue her own goals and dreams, Eve has no freedom in her oppressive culture. She continues her struggle, but her years of struggle bring a steady stream of failure, condemnation, and psychological and physical abuse. Worn down, Eve finally begins to accept the subservient role prescribed to her, and in so doing she suffers less abuse and even gains approval and reward. Under such relentless pressure, Eve eventually succumbs, loses her desire for freedom and independence, and embraces her role as meek and subservient and her status as inferior. She now reflectively approves of her subservient role, desires to remain subservient and avoid thinking independently, regards her earlier passion for equality and independence as willful and impious pride, and strives to teach her own daughters to fully accept the subservient role she now affirms. Eve is now free: she has the will she wants to have, and she is morally responsible for her deep allegiance to meek subservience, or so Frankfurt's model implies.

The unwilling slave is not free, but the willing slave is even less so: in Simone de Beauvoir's phrase, the willing slave exemplifies "the most consummate and inacceptable form of oppression" (1948, 141). If anyone has less freedom than a willing addict, it is the unwilling addict who has lost even the hope of better alternatives and clings desperately to addiction. In Martin Seligman's (1975) experiments on learned helplessness, dogs were placed in a restraining harness, and in that helpless and immobilized state, they were repeatedly shocked. After several such episodes, they were placed in the electrified side of a shuttle box, in which a low barrier separated the dog from escape into the shock-free side of the box. When dogs that had not been shocked experienced painful shocks from the floor of the box, they immediately leaped the barrier and escaped the shock; the dogs that had been subjected to repeated inescapable shocks cowered, endured the shocks, and made no effort to escape. When the dogs were shocked in the restraining harness, they initially struggled desperately but unsuccessfully to escape the painful shocks, but were not free to do so. The dogs that cowered in the shuttle box and accepted the shocks while making no effort to escape did not gain freedom by their helpless acquiescence; rather, they were even more profoundly unfree than the dogs when they were initially shocked in the restraining harness. Eve, struggling against her oppressive and controlling culture, was not free, but Eve, finally acquiescing in her harsh culture, is even further from freedom. Eve is not insane. She retains rational powers: she now tells her children all the reasons why they should embrace subservience, gives detailed arguments—based in the religious doctrines she now embraces—for why this view is correct, and replies persuasively (from within that system of thought) to her children's questions and objections. She has rational reflective powers, and she reflectively affirms the religious and cultural tradition she once loathed. But none of that changes the fact that she is not free and that she is at a much greater distance from freedom (having internalized the oppressive principles of her culture and religion) than she was when she was unfree but struggling.[1] Why would anyone, much less such an insightful philosopher as Harry Frankfurt, suppose otherwise? He does so because he is trying to save moral responsibility: he wants to hold the *willing* addict (and the subservient Eve, and the satisfied slave) morally responsible, so he must have an account of free will that counts them as free and thus responsible.

"Happy slaves"[2]—and "contented peasants" and "satisfied mindless workers" and "patients who don't want to choose" and Southern blacks who were "happy with their lot until outside agitators stirred them up"— have a long and horrific history. Certainly I am not suggesting that Frankfurt approves such abominable systems. But when a theory implies that such vile systemic mistreatment can engender free will, that raises severe questions about the plausibility of that theory.

When we add flesh and bone and psychological substance to the willing addict of abstract philosophical example, then its plausibility disappears, along with the plausibility of this hierarchical reflection account of freedom and its justification of moral responsibility. True, Frankfurt's willing addict "has the will he wants to have," but this is a will that has become so exhausted and narrow that it can no longer function well as a free exploring option-enhancing will; if it is now the will he *wants*, in his sad state, then he no longer wants a *free* will that can meet the natural needs of white-footed mice, chimpanzees, and psychologically healthy humans. Free will is not a philosophical construct, but a basic power of animals like ourselves for whom open options are advantageous; if that is lost, then what we are talking about may have charms, and it may work as philosophical fancy, but it will not work as animal free will. Open alternatives have gotten a bad reputation because of their association with magical libertarian powers, but when we bring open alternatives back to earth, they have solid benefits for animals like ourselves. Indeed, it is that solid animal value that made them a target for misappropriation by miracle-working libertarians.

The problem of willing addicts and happy slaves has led some who embrace authenticity to impose additional conditions on free will. It is not enough to have the will one currently favors; in addition, that favoring must meet some additional conditions: conditions related to rationality and deliberation, or the absence of coercion, or freedom from deception. Thus Gerald Dworkin, a champion of hierarchical authenticity free will, revises his own authenticity condition with the following proviso: "I now believe that . . . it is not the identification or lack of identification that is crucial to being autonomous, but the capacity to raise the question of whether I will identify with or reject the reasons for which I now act" (1988, 15).

So it is not enough to simply favor and approve, at a higher-order reflective level, my basic desires and character; genuine free authenticity requires that I be able to reflectively evaluate the reasons for my actions. In addition, Dworkin requires that all higher order evaluations meet (what he calls) the condition of *procedural independence*, which involves "distinguishing those ways of influencing people's reflective and critical faculties which subvert them from those which promote and improve them" (1988, 19). This is a nice point: surely it is better to have one's higher order evaluations shaped by education and broader access to accurate information than by the brutal coercion of slavery, or the numbing conditions of learned helplessness, or the stifling forces of a bigoted culture. But it raises problems. First, although it seems clearly desirable, it is harder to say why it is desirable; that is, how does it fit into a systematic explanation of free will? The happy slave and the willing addict and the subservient woman are not free, Frankfurt's arguments notwithstanding. But now it seems that the hierarchical level is not doing much of the work: we are freer when we are acting on the basis of good information and better understanding and less free when our values are the product of abuse or coercion or profound psychological and social pressure. But we can make that point without invoking a hierarchical model, and although the claim certainly garners our immediate approval, it is not clear *why* such conditions enhance free will, and that was the basic reason for invoking hierarchy.

Dworkin notes (1988, 19) that without the concept of hierarchy we cannot draw some important distinctions, and that is true; it is a useful concept for understanding human capacities and human behavior. But it is not clear that it adds anything to our understanding of human free will. Second, once we start along this path of setting standards for rationality and accurate information, it is difficult to find a stopping point—or, rather, it is difficult to find a stopping point this side of perfect rationality and perfect knowledge. Dworkin suggests the condition that our beliefs and values not be shaped by "manipulation," but what if the "manipulation" is not the planned manipulation of some human controller, but instead the fortuitous manipulation of the natural environment, in which it happens that one's first experience in a casino involves a remarkable run of luck at the dice table (the dice were not loaded and there was no conspiracy by the casino management or the croupier), thus shaping a powerful attraction to gambling. The long-term effects for this dedicated gambler are likely to be as debilitating as they would be if the dedication to shooting dice had been contrived by human malevolence, so why should the shaping by fortuitous contingencies not undercut freedom if the same shaping by planned contingencies does?

Dworkin also suggests that we must be able not merely to reflect on and approve of our character and desires: "This seems too passive a view. Autonomy should have some relationship to the ability of individuals, not only to scrutinize critically their first-order motivations but also to change them if they so desire" (1988, 16). But the formerly assertive and now subservient woman can meet all those conditions. She is badly damaged, but she still has critical rational faculties; obviously they are not perfect, but perfect rationality sets a standard well beyond what Dworkin wants to adopt. Her critical capacities reflect on and approve of a commitment to subservience that most of us abhor, but unless we wish to say that all who are committed to subjecting themselves totally to the will of their God or their ruler or their commander have lost their rational capacities, then there is no reason to suppose that she has lost hers. Indeed, Dworkin would insist on that point: "But a person who wishes to be restricted in various ways, whether by the discipline of the monastery, regimentation of the army, or even by coercion, is not, on that account alone, less autonomous" (1988, 18). Furthermore, if the subservient woman wished to change, it is possible that she could, but she has absolutely no wish to change and abhors that sinful alternative. Finally, it might be supposed that if one's deepest (or highest level) values were shaped by manipulation or coercion, then one could not reflectively approve of the process by which one's values were shaped, and thus one would not be free. But to the contrary, it is likely that the subservient woman would reflectively approve of the harsh process that shaped her strong value of subservience: she might well be grateful for and approving of even the harshest and most demeaning coercive measures, especially if she is now convinced—perhaps correctly— that only such harsh measures could have "liberated" her from her willful and sinful assertiveness.

The subservient woman and satisfied slave are, sadly, plausible cases with real-world counterparts. But the force of those cases might be better appreciated with a more fanciful example. You and your nine departmental colleagues—gentle, nonviolent, law-abiding citizens all—are holding an early morning department faculty meeting. Coffee is served, and each person drinks a cup. Unfortunately, one of the cups—selected at random— was drugged by a nefarious scientist who is testing a newly devised potion that instantly transforms gentle philosophers into murderous thugs: an irreversible transformation that is so deep and thorough that the drug-transformed ruffian despises his or her past life, deeply embraces new values of vicious crime, reflectively approves of this new orientation (your colleague who this morning was warm and friendly now sounds like some brutal combination of Al Capone and Friedrich Nietzsche), and is very happy to have drawn the "lucky" coffee cup. This newly minted thug has a deeply brutal character and vicious motives and acts on those motives. Had you drawn the unlucky cup, you would now have that vicious character and would willingly and eagerly and reflectively commit vicious acts. Your colleague certainly is vicious, but do you find it plausible—do you consider it fair—to blame that person for the vicious behavior that now flows from his or her own deep character?

The coffee example—unlike those of the satisfied slave and the subservient woman—is not very plausible. But the moral of the story goes back to very real, everyday cases: analogously to drawing the unlucky coffee cup, had you drawn the unlucky early influences, you would be a violent criminal, deeply and reflectively committed to your violent values and violent behavior. The fact that the latter process takes longer does not change the plausibility or implausibility or attributing moral responsibility to those who are ultimately lucky or unlucky—which includes all of us.

If you believe that the subservient woman and the satisfied slave are free—and not only free, but morally responsible for their approval of subservience and enslavement—then we have reached an impasse. Gerald Dworkin seems to find that view plausible; I find it extremely implausible. The satisfied slave is at the opposite pole from freedom, and the idea of blaming the satisfied slave for his acquiescence in slavery seems to me morally repugnant. True, I find the idea of blaming anyone morally problematic, but blaming the satisfied slave makes that problem so glaring that it is difficult for me to imagine that any thoughtful observer would have a different reaction. Indeed, I suspect that only a desperate desire to save moral responsibility at all costs could lead one to blame the subservient woman and the satisfied slave. But although some may be willing to champion the moral responsibility of the satisfied slave, I think—I fervently hope—that most will balk. Unfortunately, the effect of that balking is typically not to give up moral responsibility, but to set further conditions on freedom and moral responsibility. The problem with setting more conditions is that there is no clear stopping point; no clear stopping point, that is, until we follow this process to its logical conclusion, as Susan Wolf (1980, 1981, 1987, 1990) has done with unswerving dedication. That stopping point is in *perfect* rationality and *perfect* knowledge: the only genuine freedom is the freedom that is achieved by steadfastly following the True and the Good, and this freedom can quickly become such a powerful capacity that it escapes the limits of naturalism and compatibilism altogether and becomes a miraculous unlimited power.

Susan Wolf's Perfectly Rational Freedom

Susan Wolf argues that real freedom is following the right path for the right reasons: the only genuine freedom is the freedom of the narrow path that tracks the True and Good. This view has a long history, first in the Greek tradition and continuing through Christianity as it incorporated Greek thought. True freedom is living in accordance with one's true nature (as a rational being); genuine freedom can be realized only through accurate pursuit of the True; real freedom means living in accordance with the way God designed you; true freedom is found only in perfect obedience to God. Susan Wolf develops a fascinating contemporary version of this approach to free will (which, obviously, emphasizes perfect obedience to reason rather than abject obedience to God). For Wolf, genuine human freedom requires an objective True and Good that humans have the capacity to track: "We can state the condition of freedom and responsibility more directly by referring outright to the ability to act in accordance with (and on the basis of) the True and the Good" (1990, 73). And for Wolf, anything less than single-track devotion to the one true path is a deviation from genuine freedom, and is not desirable: "To want autonomy [in the open alternatives sense], then, is not only to want the ability to make choices even when there is no basis for choice but to want the ability to make choices on no basis even when a basis exists. But the latter ability would seem to be an ability no one could ever have reason to want to exercise. Why would one want the ability to pass up the apple when to do so would merely be unpleasant or arbitrary?" (1990, 55). That would be an ability to act *ir*rationally, and that—Wolf argues—"is a very strange ability to want, if it is any ability at all" (1990, 56). Supposing that it is better to have such an ability would be like supposing a train is better when it can occasionally jump the tracks. Wolf's account of true freedom is exactly right—exactly right, that is, for the angelic hosts who live in a perfect and immutable environment. But for white-footed mice in environments where food sources disappear, where predators discover habitual trails, and where formerly barren tracks become fruitful paths—and for their human cousins, who share a common changing world and have analogous needs—the straight and narrow path has fatal disadvantages. The ability to jump the tracks and pursue other options is very valuable. Options that are not currently optimum may become so under changing conditions, and—as Karl Popper (1959, 1963) taught us—even failed options can be a very valuable part of our exploratory process.

Combining Open Alternatives with Authenticity

Why then does the concept of an "authentic true path" have such undeniable appeal as an account of human freedom, when (like the white-footed mouse) our need to keep open alternatives and available options is so deep and powerful? Actually, its appeal is quite natural. It is beneficial to occasionally pursue new paths, even when we know that our currently advantageous path offers more consistent rewards. But it is also important not to abandon useful paths too easily. Our commitment to authenticity keeps old paths open and available, and thus enlarges our options. Just as narrow devotion to a single true path prevents us from exploring important alternatives and blocks the discovery of new opportunities, foods sources, and escape routes; so the quick abandonment of a hitherto beneficial path closes off an option that might well become beneficial at some future point—beneficial to the fox, when the farmer replenishes his supply of geese; beneficial to the black bear, when the berry patch ripens once again; beneficial to the commuter, when the construction project is completed. A behavioral pattern that has yielded significant benefits—whether to a pigeon pressing a bar for food or a gambler pressing the slot machine lever for coins, a commuter following a convenient route or a white-footed mouse taking an optimum maze path to reward—is not abandoned when it turns up empty. The gambler, commuter, pigeon, or mouse will continue to take that path or press that lever on many failed attempts. After a long series in which the path has yielded no rewards, the path will be tried much less often, but it will not be abandoned entirely for a long time. If—during the period when the animal is trying that path only rarely—the path again yields benefits, then the behavior of following that path will be swiftly restored to a very strong level. Clearly, this approach isn't always good: after a long string of losses, a single win can quickly raise to fever pitch the gambler's devotion to games of chance; lives ruined by undying devotion to a false love is the stuff of country music legend, and a useful tendency—which keeps options open—can be transmogrified by philosophers or prophets into close-minded devotion to a single true path, to the Good and True, to the One True God. Thus this generally useful tendency can be counterproductive when it becomes exaggerated, but that counterproductiveness does not change the fact that in its natural state, it serves the useful function of preserving a wider variety of alternatives.

Most of the preceding discussion has challenged the hierarchical account of freedom, but in fact—when seen from a consistently naturalistic perspective—higher-order reflection can be a very valuable power. Do I really want to continue my pattern of working in the family business? I like going out clubbing every night, but do I genuinely approve of this way of life? I desire to continue my drug use, but do I really want to be psychologically dependent on drugs? Such reflective questions can prompt us to scrutinize the habits and desires we are settling into and lead us to consider other paths and possibilities that we had not explored. That is, such reflective questions can shake us out of our ruts and open options we might otherwise not discover. That is a special ability—one we do not share with white-footed mice and chimpanzees—but an ability to expand our possible paths is valuable for reasons that also apply to the somewhat less sophisticated, but strongly analogous exploratory behavior of other species. That is not to say that opening new possible paths is the only importance of hierarchical reflection, but viewing it from the perspective of a naturalistic account of free will helps us understand at least one important aspect of its value. Hierarchical free will is not a challenge to the naturalistic free will account proposed here; to the contrary, the naturalistic account of free will can help explain why we find this special higher-order reflective capacity valuable.

When thinking of human free will, we cannot neglect the importance of human reason. Not the perfect reason that tracks the True and the Good, but a reason that helps us explore our capacity to imagine and study reports of alternative paths, opens options without exposing us to dangers, and allows us to explore many more options than we could physically pursue—and does so more safely. As Popper (1977) says, "While an uncritical animal may be eliminated together with its dogmatically held hypotheses, we may formulate our hypotheses, and criticize them. Let our conjectures, our theories, die in our stead."

As naturalists, we can bring together both the open alternatives and the hierarchy-authenticity views, show how they fit together rather than conflict, see what is important and worth preserving in each, and understand how they could be part of a natural evolved process: not angelic powers to follow the one true unchanging path or godlike powers to choose alternatives with no causal antecedents. And we can see the benefits of higher order reflection: it opens radically new alternatives that might not otherwise have been considered, and it can shake us out of deep habits.

Degrees of Natural Free Will

The philosophical tradition has insisted on a clear distinction between having and not having free will: Hume, Kant, Frankfurt, Kane, and Dennett offer dramatically different accounts of free will, but they concur in setting a clear boundary between who does and does not have free will and under what circumstances free will does and does not operate. This point of agreement among such differing accounts did not occur by coincidence. The insistence on this well-marked boundary results from two demands: that free will and moral responsibility must go together and that there must be a clear standard for who is and who is not morally responsible. The naturalistic free will model proposed in this chapter breaks away from that tradition: there is no clear line between free will haves and have-nots and no clear standard for when one genuinely exercises free will and when one does not.

Free will (in this naturalistic model) is a matter of degree, and it can be enhanced or inhibited by circumstances, training, development or atrophy of skills, and strengthening or weakening of cognitive fortitude and cognitive abilities. Naturalists should regard that as a virtue of the theory, rather than a strike against it. What Michael Ruse notes concerning morality applies equally to free will: "Darwinism insists that features evolve gradually, and something as important as morality should have been present in our (very recent) shared ancestors. Furthermore, if morality is as important biologically to humans as is being claimed, it would be odd indeed had all traces now been eliminated from the social interactions of other high-level primates" (1986, 227).

So the white-footed mouse does enjoy some degree of free will—a free will that can be substantially reduced by a broken leg. If free will entails moral responsibility, then that claim concerning white-footed mouse rudimentary free will would imply that the mouse also has some degree of moral responsibility. Severing the assumed link between free will and moral responsibility allows us to look more clearly at degrees of free will and processes that enhance and inhibit free will—in mice, chimps, and humans—without having to drag along the burden of ascribing moral responsibility.

Was Benji morally responsible for his acquiescent racism? Was the nonreflective and easily led German shopkeeper morally responsible for acquiescence in the Nazi horrors? Was Patricia Hearst morally responsible for her postbrainwashing participation in armed robbery? Was Hinckley morally responsible for his assassination attempt? Those questions demand clear black-and-white answers, because the answers determine whether the people in question will or will not be subject to blame and punishment. (We may bring up Hearst's special circumstances in mitigation, after she has been found guilty, but prior to that finding, we need a clear line determining whether she is morally responsible.) The problems with drawing such a clear line are indicated by the notorious and continuing difficulties the courts have had in establishing a clear standard for not guilty by reason of insanity. And that difficulty is an indication that there is not a clear line between being and not being morally responsible, because there is no clear line dividing free will from the absence of free will. The demands of moral responsibility nonetheless require that such a line be drawn, even if its arbitrariness is painfully obvious.

Without moral responsibility, we can recognize that there is no fixed marker between having and not having free will, we are freed from the obligation to draw such a dubious boundary, and we can look more clearly at the multitude of factors that strengthen and weaken free will. Greater knowledge, less deception (including self-deception), a stronger sense of internal locus-of-control, more robust cognitive fortitude, a more substantive sense of self-efficacy, a supportive environment that offers a rich but not overwhelming range of alternatives, greater self-awareness, a substantial capacity for higher-order reflectiveness: all of these contribute to a stronger and healthier free will. Betty's level of free will is significantly superior to that of Benji, and it is important to recognize this superiority and carefully study the factors that nurture the development of a rich and robust free will. We can do that more effectively if we are not hamstrung by unanswerable questions concerning the exact necessary and sufficient conditions for free will.

Natural Free Will and Moral Responsibility

So we have a coherent naturalistic account of free will that integrates both alternatives and authenticity into a workable whole and shows how they work together (rather than compete). True, this account makes human free will more similar to that of the white-footed mouse than to a miracle-working deity or a being of perfect knowledge and unerring rationality, but (for naturalists) this similarity should be a strength rather than a weakness. And above all, we have an account of free will that is not twisted and tweaked to make it support moral responsibility. With this naturalistic account of free will in place, we can ask: is there a justification for moral responsibility? And we can distinguish that question from a very different query: do we have free will, and what does it look like?

The foregoing account of free will is quite plausible for naturalists. First, it incorporates the elements that have traditionally been central to free will: open alternatives and deep authenticity. Second, it harmonizes those elements, whereas other free will views present them as opposed. Third, it provides an important role for reason as well as for second-order reflection, both of which figure prominently in contemporary free will accounts. Fourth, it does all this while remaining within a naturalistic framework and makes clear how this account is closely related to behavior that is also valuable for other species (rather than making free will a uniquely human capacity and thus suspect from a naturalist evolutionary perspective). And fifth, it shows why the various elements of free will are genuinely valuable to animals like ourselves. The purpose of this is not only to sketch a more satisfactory account of free will, but also to show that without the burden of supporting moral responsibility, it is possible to develop a plausible account of free will: an account demonstrating that free will can and should be considered independently of the question of moral responsibility.

It is also important to note what is not being claimed: I am not claiming that this is *the* correct account of free will and that because this account does not support moral responsibility, moral responsibility therefore has no legitimacy. I do claim that it is a plausible naturalistic account of free will, but I do not claim that if this account does not support moral responsibility, then moral responsibility is insupportable. After all, there have been many naturalistic accounts of free will, and those accounts have been offered to justify moral responsibility. So one cannot offer *a* naturalistic account of free will, argue that this account does not support moral responsibility, and then conclude that there is no moral responsibility. Instead, I must attempt to show that alternative naturalistic accounts fail to support moral responsibility. That is the task of the following chapters, and the basic strategy will be twofold: first, to show that some of the proposed naturalistic accounts fail in their effort to support moral responsibility, and second, to show that others of the purported naturalistic free will accounts actually smuggle in a miracle working nonnatural power, and although they may support moral responsibility, they are not *naturalistic* foundations for moral responsibility. At that point, it can be concluded that no naturalistic account—at least, no naturalistic account that has been proposed—can support moral responsibility. The final task will be to convince naturalists that rather than mourning the demise of moral responsibility, we should dance on its grave; we shall inherit most of the goods that moral responsibility claimed, while being freed from its oppressive constraints.

Does the naturalistic account of free will proposed here support moral responsibility? I shall argue that it does not, but the immediate point is that whether this is a plausible account of natural free will does not depend on whether it can support moral responsibility. Finally, I maintain that this is a plausible and palatable naturalistic account of free will (that can flourish in the absence of moral responsibility) and that it will provide human animals with all we really want in the way of free will: naturalistic free will can swim while moral responsibility sinks. But if that project is a failure—if this is not an adequate account of free will—that does not alter the case against the naturalistic plausibility of moral responsibility. Moral responsibility still sinks, regardless of whether free will goes down with it.

5 Moral Responsibility in the Gaps

Pico della Mirandola was perfectly comfortable with miracles: the bigger the better. After all, if you accept the idea of almighty God miraculously creating the cosmos in all its splendor, then you aren't likely to flinch at allowing humans to miraculously create themselves. But the centuries rolled by, and scientists from William Harvey and Isaac Newton to Charles Darwin and B. F. Skinner expanded our naturalistic understanding of humans and our world, and as naturalistic explanations waxed, enthusiasm for miracles waned. Rather than full-scale unlimited creation of the self—with the open possibilities ranging from bestial to divine—the self-defining choices became smaller and smaller. As biologists and psychologists enlarged the areas explicable by causal forces outside our ultimate control, the space available for special acts of free will was squeezed tighter. Under pressure from the natural sciences, the miraculous powers of the deities retreated into obscure corners, and Almighty God became a "god-of-the-gaps" whose powers were confined to "whatever science cannot yet explain." In similar fashion, the advance of biological and psychological science has narrowed the power of miracle-working free will down to human powers that science has not yet explained or has not yet reduced to straightforward causal accounts.

Of course compatibilists—who insist that moral responsibility is compatible with naturalism (and with determinism)—insist that the advance of natural science poses no problem for moral responsibility, but their actual practice and their proposed accounts indicate otherwise. Before examining the compatibilists, however, consider the career of the *in*compatibilists, particularly the traditional libertarians, who maintain that the special human freedom essential for moral responsibility must be independent of natural explanation and natural causes. Pico della Mirandola represents the high-water mark of libertarian thought: God grants us the miraculous godlike power of fashioning ourselves in any form we choose with no restrictions on powers or possibilities. By the twentieth century, libertarian free will—buffeted by the increasing success of natural science explanations—had become much more modest.

Campbell's Minimized Free Will

C. A. Campbell, a twentieth-century libertarian of great subtlety, proposes a fascinating small-scale account of the libertarian free will that props up moral responsibility. Campbell understands and acknowledges the fundamental challenge that our knowledge of biology and psychology poses for moral responsibility:

If we are mindful of the influences exerted by heredity and environment, we may well feel some doubt whether there is any act of will at all of which one can truly say that the self is sole author, sole determinant. No man has a voice in determining the raw material of impulses and capacities that constitute his hereditary environment, and no man has more than a very partial control of the material and social environment in which he is destined to live his life. Yet it would be manifestly absurd to deny that these two factors do constantly and profoundly affect the nature of a man's choices. (1957, 160–161)

Campbell's solution to this problem is to radically reduce the scope of the vital free will operation. Rather than "making ourselves from scratch," we make small but decisive choices that are the basis of our moral responsibility. In Campbell's account, our special power of making free choices between "genuinely open alternatives"—choices "of which the person judged [to be morally responsible] can be regarded as the *sole* author" (160)—operates within a very limited space: only when we experience conflict between desire and duty do we have the special power to exert or withhold the moral effort required to combat our desires and rise to duty.

Campbell's own version of libertarian free will has few contemporary champions, but his legacy endures, for Campbell marked the path that many contemporary libertarians have followed: minimal free will. This is a free will of the gaps. Campbell acknowledges that science may explain how our desires were shaped and the causes of much of our character and behavior. But science has no causal account of the inner act of exerting or withholding will power, and that leaves a gap for the exercise of "contra-causal free will," in which a special human creative activity of willing chooses which path will be taken, and in such cases "nothing determines the act save the agent's doing of it" (1957, 178).

Conscious Will

The problem with placing free will in a small gap in our scientific knowledge is that such gaps often close. In Campbell's case, the gap closed swiftly. Psychologists discovered that one's capacity to "exert will power" depends on several subtle but identifiable psychological factors, including one's internal or external locus-of-control (Rotter 1966, 1975, 1979, 1989), one's sense of self-efficacy (Bandura 1997), and one's degree of learned helplessness (Seligman 1975). As noted earlier, Martin Seligman (1975) demonstrated that in many cases it appears that an individual *could* exert an effort of will (to escape a tormentor, or tackle a math problem, or resist abuse), but repeated experiences of ineffectual effort have rendered the individual profoundly incapable of exerting any effort whatsoever. Such "learned helplessness" can be deep and lasting. Even more problematic is Campbell's reliance on the internal perspective, the direct inner knowledge of "free choice": "Reflection upon the act of moral decision as apprehended from the inner standpoint would force him [the determinist] to recognise a . . . *creative activity*, in which . . . nothing determines the act save the agent's doing of it" (1957, 178). There are obvious problems with the reliability of special inner knowledge that reveals remarkable (even miraculous) psychological powers, but in the case of Campbell's "inner knowledge" of free uncaused choice, that gap has been closed by a wide range of psychological and neuropsychological studies. Clearly, we do have the sense of a conscious free will power that causes our acts and choices, but there is strong evidence that this sense of an efficacious conscious unconstrained will is not reliable, whether it is Campbell's introspective observation of making an effort of will or Ginet's insistence on the "actish phenomenal quality" (1990, 1997) of our determinism-transcending free actions. The case against special introspective knowledge of a creative activity of will comes from a variety of sources, but one of the best summaries of the evidence can be found in Daniel Wegner's aptly named *The Illusion of Conscious Will* (2002).

First, there are the cases in which we have a strong sense of consciously willing an action when in fact we have performed no action at all. Wegner and Wheatley (1999) ran an experiment with a device similar to a Ouija

board in which both an experimental subject and a member of the experimental team (thought by the experimental subject to be another subject)
both placed their fingers on the board and caused it to move a cursor to
different points on a monitor, then chose where and when to stop the
motion of the cursor. At varying times, the experimenter controlled the
cursor and the stopping point, but the experimental subject nonetheless
believed that he or she had intentionally willed and performed the action
of stopping.

Second, there are many cases in which one performs an action but
experiences no sense of special willing. What psychologists call "automa-
tisms," often associated with "occult" powers, provide dramatic examples:
obvious cases are table turning and Ouija boards (Wegner 2002, 108–113).
Another striking example (not mentioned by Wegner) is the "facilitating"
practices of some volunteers working with autistic children: volunteers
convinced that they are merely responding to the direction imposed by
autistic partners (who also have their hands on the planchette device),
when in fact they are moving the indicator themselves. The "facilitators"
sincerely deny having controlled the board, when in fact they are in total
control. In experiments in which the autistic child is shown an image of
a ball and the facilitator is shown an image of a dog, "dog" is invariably
spelled out on the planchette, though the facilitators are certain that they
are being guided entirely by the hand pressure of the autistic child, with
no active willing on their own part (Smith, Haas, and Belcher 1994; Jacobson, Mulick, and Schwartz 1995; Mostert 2001).

Third, there are cases in which one has a strong sense of having freely
chosen and willed an act (entirely from one's own unimpeded volition),
when in fact the choice was clearly under the control—or at least very
strong influence—of external factors. In working with one of his patients,
José Delgado discovered that electrical stimulation at a certain point in the
brain caused the patient to turn his head from side to side, as if looking
for something. As Delgado reports, "The interesting fact was that the
patient considered the evoked activity spontaneous and always offered a
reasonable explanation for it. When asked "What are you doing?" the
answers were, "I am looking for my slippers," "I heard a noise," "I am
restless," and "I was looking under the bed" (1969, 115–116).

In another experiment, Brasil-Neto et al. (1992) exposed volunteers to
transcranial magnetic stimulation of the brain, which has been found to

have brief influence on brain activity. Subjects were told to move their right or left index finger, freely choosing which one. Subjects were much more likely to move the finger corresponding to the magnetic brain stimulation area, but they still perceived themselves to be making free uncontrolled choices.

Direct manipulation of the brain is one way of controlling choices that feel totally spontaneous, but that are in fact under experimental control; however, manipulating the subject's environment produces equally dramatic results. Social psychologists have devised a wide range of ingenious experiments that reveal the powerful but unrecognized influence of the situations in which we make our choices, and they have shown that trivial factors—such as finding small change in a phone booth, being encouraged to hurry (Darley and Batson 1973), experiencing a pleasant smell (Baron and Bronfen 1994; Baron 1997)—can have profound effects on our choices and behavior. In one famous experiment (Isen and Levin 1972), one group of experimental subjects found a dime in a phone booth and other subjects did not, as mentioned previously. As each subject left the phone booth, one of the experimenters walked by carrying papers (the experimental subjects didn't know that this person was part of the experiment) and dropped the papers. The subjects who had found a dime almost invariably stopped to help pick up the papers, but most of the subjects who had not found the dime walked on by. Obviously, finding a dime is a trivial factor, but the point is that even a trivial factor, which introspectively one would be unlikely to recognize as an influence, had a profound effect on the choices made by the subjects. In fact, social psychologists have consistently found that subtle situational factors have a much greater effect on our choices and behavior than does "underlying character." The common belief that our choices come from our own deep independent choices (rather than from the situations in which we find ourselves) is recognized by social psychologists as a widespread introspective mistake that is so common they have labeled it the "fundamental attribution error" (Ross 1977). Like the neuropsychological experiments, the even more extensive social psychology research poses a significant challenge for those who place their faith in an introspectively known experience of free choice. That is not to deny that those who found a dime and stopped to help were making a "free choice," but given the results of the experiment, it is difficult to suppose that the free choice was the product of some independent act of will. The "introspective evidence" of free uncontrolled willing—based on introspection that is blissfully unaware of the powerful influence exerted by the details of the situation—is very weak evidence indeed. Pereboom's evaluation of such evidence seems an accurate assessment:

It is sometimes claimed that we have significant phenomenological evidence for the broader thesis that we have libertarian free will. . . . However, the Spinozan response to this claim, that we believe our decisions are free only because we are ignorant of their causes, has not been successfully countered. The lesson to draw from Spinoza is that the phenomenology apt to generate a belief that we have libertarian free will would be just the same if decisions were instead causally determined and we were ignorant of enough of their causes. For this reason, the phenomenological evidence for our having libertarian free will in not especially impressive. (2007, 113)

On the basis of the experimental results described earlier, Wegner proposes an *epiphenomenal* account of our conscious experience of willing: the decision to act first occurs nonconsciously, and the conscious awareness of willing is a by-product of that unconscious decision (the consciousness of the decision occurs a fraction of a second later) that informs us that the willed action is our own. Timothy O'Connor (2005) is not convinced by the experimental results that Wegner cites or the theory that Wegner proposes. According to O'Connor, "much of the evidence that Wegner adduces underwhelms" (224), and O'Connor's considered conclusion regarding Wegner's empirical evidence is that it does not prove what Wegner supposes it proves: "Taken cumulatively, the cases considered . . . do not justify Wegner's extraordinary conclusion that, quite generally, our experience of freedom is illusory—rather than being reflective of an actual self-determination of one's own decisions, the experience is epiphenomenal, caused by processes quite separate from the actual mechanisms of agency" (225).

It is amusing to hear O'Connor call Wegner's epiphenomenal account "extraordinary": Wegner, after all, is merely proposing that our conscious experience of willing serves the useful feedback function of informing us that a behavior was our own and not the result of an external causal force (the movement of my arm came from my own brain operations, rather than from some external force pushing or pulling my arm), and although that may be a shocking idea to some philosophers, it is hardly as "extraordinary" as O'Connor's claim that such experiences of conscious willing signal an "ontologically basic" causal power that "can share a common metaphysical core" with divine freedom (2005, 208). But the important point is that Wegner does not deny that we act freely (though certainly the freedom that Wegner acknowledges will not satisfy a godly libertarian like O'Connor); rather, he denies that the "experience of conscious willing" is evidence of some special power of free will that is the source of our behavior. More important still, Wegner does not count the evidence he offers as *proving* that there is no case of deep reflectiveness and accurate reasoning in which our experience of conscious efficacious willing gives us a true picture of our special power of active will. Rather, Wegner gives a wide range of cases to show that such an experience of conscious efficacious willing is often and clearly *unreliable*: that it often leads us to believe that we acted through an unimpeded and uninfluenced power of will when in fact our choices were controlled by factors of which we were completely unaware. Thus the supposed evidence of an "ontologically basic" power of conscious willing that gives us "ultimate control over what we do" (16) is unreliable. Although such a remarkable power might still exist in some small niche, there is no earthly reason to believe that it does: perhaps heavenly reasons remain.

The wide range of experimental evidence cited by Wegner makes an impressive case against the veridical status of our sense of conscious free efficacious willing, and it is strengthened by the added results from decades of social psychology research. But if we reflect honestly, most of us are well aware that such introspective experiences prove little about the ultimate uncontrolled freedom of our choices. I deliberate carefully about whether to spend my holidays at a favorite ski resort or join some friends who are driving down to Key West. I think carefully, consider all the factors quite objectively, then gather my powers and make a perfectly free uncontrolled unimpeded choice to go skiing at my favorite resort. It certainly feels like a perfectly free act of will, but my friends have long since made their plans without me, knowing full well that I shall "freely will" to go skiing, under the powerful influence of an unrequited passion for a lovely ski instructor who has long since dumped me. "That had no bearing whatsoever on my free choice," I angrily protest, and sincerely believe, but my friends know better—and so does Daniel Wegner, and so do social psychologists, and so do most of us, when we consider it independently of any desire for untrammeled godlike ultimate freedom. A convincing case for such ontologically basic freedom will have to rest on a stronger foundation than our notoriously unreliable sense of freely efficacious willing.

Libet and Conscious Will

The evidence against the reliability of our small niche of "inner experience" of creative free will is strong, and it is strong even without adding what O'Connor calls Wegner's "ace in the hole": the neuropsychological experiments of Benjamin Libet and his colleagues. Those experiments have drawn much interest, as well as extensive criticism. Rightly or wrongly, many have regarded them as the nail in the coffin for traditional free will accounts that rely on an inner experience of creative free choice. In my view, there is more than sufficient empirical evidence to destroy the traditional view, whatever one's conclusion concerning Libet's experiments. But because Libet's work has been the subject of so much attention, it is useful to look at the experiments, their implications, and some of the key criticisms.

In the classic version of his experiment, Benjamin Libet and his colleagues (Libet et al. 1983) examined the phenomenon of free choice, concentrating on what happens in your brain when you make a free choice to move your hand. In this experiment, subjects were asked to "flick their wrists" or "flick their fingers" whenever they chose to do so. This was an experiment explicitly designed to study the "inner feeling" of making a free choice. As Libet describes the essential experimental conditions: "First, there should be no external control or cues to affect the occurrence or emergence of the voluntary act under study; i.e., it should be endogenous. Secondly, the subject should feel that he/she wanted to do it, on her/his own initiative, and feel he could control what is being done, when to do it or not to do it" (1999, 47).

In Libet's experiment, subjects made a free choice of when to flick their wrists, and they also noted (by observing a large "clock" face that marked time through a flashing light that revolved around the clock face once every 2.56 seconds) precisely when they became conscious of the decision to flick their wrists. By observing subjects' brain activity (recorded by means of electrical readings taken on the scalp) along with the consciousness of the choice to move their wrists, Libet discovered that the brain processes leading to the decision to move their wrists occurred prior to the subjects' conscious awareness of their choice. The electrical readings showed that a "readiness potential" (RP) occurred in the brain approximately 550 milliseconds prior to the onset of muscle movement, but the conscious awareness of an urge/intention to flex did not occur until 200 milliseconds prior to muscle movement; that is, the nonconscious brain activity occurred prior to consciousness of the urge/intention to move. "Clearly, the brain process (RP) to prepare for this voluntary act began about 400 msec. before the appearance of the conscious will to act (W)" (Libet 1999, 51). In fact, the nonconscious brain activity probably starts earlier; as Libet notes, "the actual initiating process in the brain probably starts before our recorded RP [readiness potential], in an unknown area that then activates the supplementary motor area in the cerebral cortex" (51). The moral of the story, according to Libet: the actual choice occurs nonconsciously in the brain well before we become consciously aware of such a choice; our "conscious choice" is only the later awareness of a choice that actually occurred as a nonconscious brain activity.

When we reflect on it, this is hardly surprising; we know that we are not conscious of all our brain activities (we "consciously try" to remember a name, without success, and an hour later it suddenly "comes to us" without any conscious intervening effort). And unless you are a dedicated mind-body dualist, you don't believe that your conscious thoughts and decisions somehow operate independently of the physical brain. If you have a conscious thought, something must be happening in the brain, and at least some part of the neurological initiating of such conscious thought must be occurring prior to consciousness. Descartes believed that you have a thought, and the thought then stimulates the waiting brain into energetic activity, but very few in the contemporary free will debate—and none who embrace naturalism—will find that a plausible position.

Libet himself—unwilling to give up belief in some special power of free will that can preserve moral responsibility—adopts the "gap" approach to saving moral responsibility, even though his own research left that gap considerably smaller:

The initiation of the freely voluntary act appears to begin in the brain unconsciously, well before the person consciously knows he wants to act! Is there, then, any role for conscious will in the performance of a voluntary act? . . . To answer this it must be recognized that conscious will (W) does appear about 150 msec. before the muscle is activated, even though it follows onset of the RP. An interval of 150 msec. would allow enough time in which the conscious function might affect the final outcome of the volitional process. (Actually, only 100 msec. is available for any such effect. The final 50 msec. before the muscle is activated is the time for the primary motor cortex to activate the spinal motor nerve cells. During this time the act goes to completion with no possibility of stopping it by the rest of the cerebral cortex.)

Potentially available to the conscious function is the possibility of stopping or vetoing the final progress of the volitional process, so that no actual muscle action ensues. *Conscious-will could thus affect the outcome* of the volitional process even though the latter was initiated by unconscious cerebral processes Conscious-will might block or veto the process, so that no act occurs. (1999, 51–52)

This account wedges the conscious act of special free will into a very small corner indeed: it must occur within one tenth of a second, and it is reduced to a veto power that is unable to initiate acts of will. But even if we suppose that this minimalist conscious veto power is sufficient for moral responsibility, the account has its problems. After all, if the "conscious decision" to move your hand is triggered by a prior nonconscious brain event, then why wouldn't the conscious veto decision also have a prior nonconscious trigger? Libet struggles with that question, and offers this solution:

I propose . . . that the conscious veto may *not* require or be the direct result of preceding unconscious processes. The conscious veto is a *control* function, different from simply becoming aware of the wish to act. There is no logical imperative in any mind-brain theory, even identity theory that requires specific neural activity to precede and determine the nature of a conscious control function. And, there is no experimental evidence against the possibility that the control process may appear without development by prior unconscious processes. (53)

But what this comes down to is the cold comfort that it is *logically possible*—there is "no logical imperative" blocking the possibility—that such a very special conscious power, quite different from what we observe in other choices, exists. Even if it remains a logical possibility, it is difficult to see it as a genuine physical possibility, and it is even more difficult to see such an ad hoc proposal (the only virtue of which is that it might save a dubious notion of free will) as an empirically plausible neuropsychological account.

Rather than trying to squeeze moral responsibility into the gap of a veto power that is supported only by the claim that "there is no experimental evidence against the possibility" (and by the desire to save moral responsibility no matter what), some have attempted to undermine the credibility of this neuropsychological research. A philosophical leader of the attack is Timothy O'Connor. O'Connor defends a free will account that is explicitly designed to support moral responsibility: an account that relies heavily on the very notion of conscious will that Libet's experiment threatens.

Perhaps such a process "need not be understood as something mysterious," but it seems on the face of it considerably more mysterious than processes initiated by brain behavior which then emerge into consciousness. But consciousness is such a disputed concept that it is difficult to draw any definite conclusions concerning degrees of mystery. In any case, what remains undisputed is that a very significant element of our choice making process—the *urge* to act—occurs in the brain *non*consciously, though it certainly seems to us that the entire process is open to and indeed initiated by conscious thought. Thus, even on the most charitable interpretation, this experiment strikes another blow against our common belief that we are consciously aware and consciously in control of our choice-making process. Even if we accept Mele's interpretation, that will squeeze the special power of choice into a time slot of less than one-fifth of a second, continuing the trend of making free choice very small indeed.

Wegner's Epiphenomenalism

As noted earlier, the conclusion Wegner draws—from Libet's experiment, and the many others cited earlier—is that the experience of "conscious willing" is *epiphenomenal*; that is, the actual causal event occurs nonconsciously in the brain, and the conscious experience is an *epiphenomenon*, or a side effect of the nonconscious causal process that is not itself causally efficacious. The sense of conscious willing informs us that the behavior initiated comes from us, and was not caused by some external force. My sense of consciously willing my arm to move indicates that my arm was not pushed or pulled by some force outside of me, but instead the movement was my own. Just as fever is a symptom of infection rather than the cause of illness, the introspective experience of conscious willing is a symptom of choice, not the choice itself.

Not surprisingly, many are uncomfortable with this epiphenomenal neuropsychological account of our conscious experience of free will. Objections from Timothy O'Connor and Alfred Mele have already been noted. John Searle, a leading philosopher of mind, argues that the neuropsychological account runs counter to the most plausible evolutionary explanation. Why would such a complex conscious sense of free will evolve if it is not really involved in causing our free choices? As Searle describes it, on this neuropsychological account one

O'Connor acknowledges as much. In discussing the work of neuroj
chologist Daniel Wegner (who pulls together a variety of studies, includ
Libet's), O'Connor states: "If Wegner is right, my foregoing effort to cla
the nature of human freedom has been futile" (2005, 220). O'Conn
criticism focuses on the mundane nature of the choice Libet studied:
choice to flick your wrist is not the sort of profound choice that we usu
identify as involving our special resources of free will (Campbell wo
agree: the choice to flick your wrist does not rise to the level of a m
struggle between duty and desire). As O'Connor correctly notes, Lil
experimental setup disallows the richest choices. But it does signal
most plausible explanatory account of such cases, and to suppose that
account is false because set up experimentally is too convenient: it sou
rather like the "mentalists" who insist that they do have powers of me
telepathy, but the experimental setting is so austere that it tempor
blocks their powers. If the "inner experience" is false in small things,
casts significant doubt on its veracity in large things.

Alfred Mele has developed an extensive critique of Libet's experin
and of Libet's interpretation of that experiment. Mele argues (2006, 2
that Libet fails to draw some crucial distinctions, running together
cepts such as urge and intention that must be differentiated. Exactly
is it that occurs nonconsciously, some 400 milliseconds before consc
ness? Mele argues that what occurs is not a choice or intention, but ins
only an *urge*. Because not all of our urges to act result in intentioi
decisions to act, it is possible that the actual intention or choice to act
not occur until the onset of consciousness; that is, the actual choi
intention may indeed occur in consciousness, simultaneously with l
activity. That occurrence is a possibility, and Mele offers a subtle
detailed argument for that possibility. But it does raise some difficult i
tions: exactly how does my conscious thought simultaneously caus
brain activity? The brain causing conscious thoughts (with a small
delay) is difficult enough, but the conscious thoughts simultanei
manipulating the brain seems much more difficult to explain. Mele ii
that "a process that is initiated by an unconscious urge may have a s
quent part that is directly initiated by the conscious formation or acc
tion of an intention. The 'conscious self'—which need not be unders
as something mysterious—might more proximally initiate a voluntai
that is less proximally initiated by an unconscious urge" (2006, 42).

has the experience of free will, but there is no genuine free will at the neurobiological level. I think most neurobiologists would feel that this is probably how the brain actually works, that we have the experience of free will but it is illusory; because the neuronal processes are causally sufficient to determine subsequent states of the brain, assuming there are no outside stimulus inputs or effects from the rest of the body. But this result is intellectually very unsatisfying because it gives us a form of epiphenomenalism. It says that our experience of freedom plays no causal or explanatory role in our behavior. It is a complete illusion, because our behavior is entirely fixed by the neurobiology that determines the muscle contractions. On this view evolution played a massive trick on us. Evolution gives us the illusion of freedom, but it is nothing more than that—an illusion. (2007, 62)

So why would evolution play "a massive trick on us"? Neuropsychologists answer: it doesn't. Our experience of freedom doesn't cause our choices, but it does perform an important function: it signals to us that the action we have initiated—the moving of our arm or hand—is our *own* behavior, that it comes from our own choices rather than being the product of some outside force. If your arm moves because it is pulled by a rope (or even because of a sudden seizure), that is a very different experience from the experience of freely choosing to move your arm. Your conscious "free choice" experience is an important feedback mechanism that informs you the movement of your body was initiated *by you* (that's the explanation favored by neuropsychologist Daniel Wegner). Your movement is initiated nonconsciously, but it is still your *own* movement rather than some external force. Evolution didn't play a dirty trick in giving us a conscious sense of free choice; rather, it gave us a useful tool for distinguishing our own motions from those initiated outside of us. If some philosophers insist on misinterpreting that useful conscious experience as a special power of free will that consciously produces our choices, that's not the fault of Mother Nature.

Dennett, Minimum Free Will, and Cognitive Misers

It is not surprising to find libertarians such as Campbell and O'Connor squeezing the crucial element of uncaused or nondetermined choice into a small safe place, but it is interesting that many compatibilists—who profess the view that free will and moral responsibility are perfectly compatible with a thoroughgoing naturalism—propose theories that slip in small but crucial elements of nonnatural free choice. When we carefully scrutinize those small gaps and offer naturalistic explanations to fill them in, we discover that the explanations may leave us with a perfectly workable account of freedom, but an account that will not carry the weight of moral responsibility.

Consider an account of free will developed by Daniel Dennett, one of the most insightful and psychologically sophisticated of contemporary compatibilists:

> The model I propose points to the multiplicity of decisions that encircle our moral decisions and suggests that in many cases our ultimate decision as to which way to act is less important phenomenologically as a contributor to our sense of free will than the prior decisions affecting our deliberation process itself: the decision, for instance, not to consider any further, to terminate deliberation; or the decision to ignore certain lines of inquiry.

> These prior and subsidiary decisions contribute, I think, to our sense of ourselves as responsible free agents, roughly in the following way: I am faced with an important decision to make, and after a certain amount of deliberation I say to myself: "That's enough. I've considered this matter enough and now I'm going to act," in the full knowledge that I could have considered further, in the full knowledge that the eventualities may prove that I decided in error, but with the acceptance of responsibility in any case. (1978, 297)

So the crucial grounds for the legitimacy of "accepting responsibility" is that "I could have considered further," but instead chose to stop deliberating: the option window is very small, but it opens just far enough to allow a free choice that gives grounds for responsibility. However, when we subject "could have considered further" to careful scrutiny, the window quickly closes: people often do act freely when they choose to stop or continue deliberating, but on those occasions of free choice, they are not poised between the two with an open and unimpeded power to choose either way. Such a power is not required for free behavior, but it is required for moral responsibility, which is why even compatibilists tend to slip it into their models. When "after a certain amount of deliberation" I choose to continue (or stop) deliberation, that choice—though certainly mine—is under the influence of powerful factors that psychologists have studied extensively (Waller 1999).

Some people enjoy careful deliberation, find it satisfying, engage in it eagerly, and sustain their cognitive concentration through arduous deliberative efforts; psychologists call such people *chronic cognizers* (Cacioppo and Petty 1982). In contrast, *cognitive misers* do not enjoy careful

deliberation, resist lengthy cognizing, and find careful sustained deliberation oppressive. Differences between cognitive misers and chronic cognizers are shaped by their conditioning histories: Ann, a cognitive miser,
learned early that careful thought is counterproductive. When she hesi-
tated, her coach berated her: "Just throw the damned ball!" When she
deliberated about which choice to make, her impatient parents deprived
her of both options. When she thought carefully about whether to have
cake or ice cream, her greedy siblings left her nothing. In short, Ann was
rarely reinforced for sustained careful thinking, and thus never developed
the required fortitude and capacity for extensive deliberation. Barbara, in
contrast, was encouraged to think carefully, to "look before leaping," to
consider all her options and all the consequences, and she was praised for
her deliberative efforts. Soon the natural benefits of deliberation took hold
and aided in shaping Barbara into a chronic cognizer: "Children who learn,
through observation and experience, that they can cope with their problems through reason and verbal influence rather than through physical
force or flight should tend to develop higher levels of need for cognition
because of the demonstrated import of good problem-solving skills in
charting a course through the hazards of life" (Cacioppo et al.1996, 246).

It is philosophically tempting to imagine that we can "always deliberate
more," because if there is one trait (other than arrogance) common to
philosophers, it is surely that we are chronic cognizers. But our deliberative
powers and deliberative fortitude are not magical, they do not offer a path
that transcends our natural world, and they are not (according to those of
us who are naturalists) independent of our finite and conditioned powers.
Whatever it may seem to us, it is not true that even chronic cognizers can
"always deliberate more," and when we throw cognitive misers into the
mix, the claim becomes even more obviously false.

Dennett adds that "the decision to ignore certain lines of inquiry" is
also a contributor to the legitimacy of ascribing and accepting responsibility. But such decisions—though again, they are our own—provide no
support for moral responsibility. *Why* does Jane ignore certain lines of
inquiry, while Judith considers them? From the naturalist perspective, we
cannot stop with "she just chose to ignore them"; miracle-embracing libertarians are free to treat such decisions as miraculous ab initio choices,
but naturalists are not. Jane was shaped as a cognitive miser and lacks the
capacity for extensive consideration of multiple "lines of inquiry." Or

perhaps Judith had the good fortune to develop excellent philosophical skills of inquiry, and Jane lacked that opportunity; if so, then Jane—like the great majority of people—will find it difficult and unnatural to consider alternative perspectives; as psychologists Jonathan Haidt and Fredrik Bjorklund note, "If you are able to rise to this challenge, if you are able to honestly examine the moral arguments in favor of slavery and genocide (along with the much stronger arguments against them), then you are likely to be either a psychopath or a philosopher. Philosophers are one of the only groups that have been found spontaneously to look for reasons on both sides of a question" (2008, 196). And the "decision to ignore certain lines of inquiry" is very likely to be controlled by social psychological *situational* factors: in an experiment with students at Princeton Theological Seminary, Darley and Batson (1973) instructed one group of experimental subjects that the experiment was running late, and asked them to hurry across campus to a different building where the last phase of the experiment would occur. A second group were given the same instructions, but with no admonition to hurry. A person appearing to be in considerable distress was placed along the subjects' path. The hurrying Princeton theological students avoided careful consideration of the plight of the unfortunate person they encountered in rushing across campus; their more leisurely classmates took the time for further inquiry. Thus a seemingly insignificant situational factor ("please hurry") can have a large impact on our behavior, including our decisions to think further or consider more carefully. Dennett knows all this, but the temptation to preserve a small space that will allow moral responsibility is a powerful temptation, and Dennett's need for such an unexamined small space of special choice indicates that without that space, even compatibilists such as Dennett find it hard to justify moral responsibility.

The idea that "we can always deliberate more" takes various forms in efforts to preserve a *small* space for a special free will that can support moral responsibility. Charles Taylor rejects libertarian "radical choice" as grounds for moral responsibility, and seeks a basis for moral responsibility in the open capacity for self-evaluation: "Because this self-resolution [deep self-evaluation] is something we do, when we do it, we can be called responsible for ourselves; and because it is within limits always up to us to do it, even when we don't—indeed, the nature of our deepest evaluations constantly raises the question of whether we have them right—we can be called responsible in another sense for ourselves whether we undertake this radical evaluation or not" (1976, 299).

But like Dennett's choice to cease or continue deliberation, the idea that it is always open to us to undertake radical self-evaluation of our values and motives—regardless of whether we do so—ignores the different capacities we bring to our deliberative and reflective tasks. The fact that chronic cognizers—indeed, *professional* philosophical chronic cognizers—like Dennett and Taylor find it easy and inviting to undertake cognitively challenging tasks does not mean that such options are always open to those shaped as cognitive misers (or even as modest cognizers). One might be tempted to say that it is then open to the cognitive miser to reflect deeply on whether she really values being a cognitive miser, but that argument spins in such a small circle that it resembles a top. Or perhaps all this is wrong. Perhaps in this situation, I really could choose either way, through some special power that transcends and transforms my powers of cognitive fortitude. But as naturalists, that path is closed; instead, we require a naturalistic explanation of why Judith deliberates further and Jane does not. Certainly, the choice to deliberate further or not (or radically evaluate or not) is mine; indeed, we could agree that I made the choice freely. But when we examine how that choice was shaped by early conditioning forces far outside of our control, then it seems an implausible prop for the heavy weight of moral responsibility.

Automaticity and Conscious Deliberation

Recent research on psychological *automaticity* (Bargh 2008; Bargh and Chartrand 1999; Bargh and Ferguson 2000; Wilson 2002) raises even deeper concerns about relying on conscious deliberation as grounds for moral responsibility. This extensive body of research squeezes the range of conscious deliberative activity—even for the most chronic of cognizers—into an increasingly narrow space. Much of the behavior we had assumed to be controlled by conscious reflective choice is (so this research indicates) in fact under the control of nonconscious processes. John Bargh and Tanya Chartrand claim that "most of a person's everyday life is determined not by their conscious intentions and deliberate choices but by mental processes that are put into motion by features of the environment and that operate outside of conscious awareness and guidance" (1999, 462).

Automaticity theorists generally consider that a positive thing: "The mind operates most efficiently by relegating a good deal of high-level, sophisticated thinking to the unconscious. . . . The adaptive unconscious does an excellent job of sizing up the world, warning people of danger, setting goals, and initiating action in a sophisticated and efficient manner" (Wilson 2002, 6–7). And John Bargh insists that such automaticity findings—though initially surprising—are in fact exactly what we should have expected:

The extensive documentation of unconscious controls from our distant and recent past and our present seem surprising and controversial. But reversing the causal assumption and recognizing the substantial role played by unconscious forces of evolutionary design, cultural assimilation in early childhood, and our minds as wide open to environmental priming influences, makes these and other similar findings much less controversial and more understandable. The lines of priming research . . . show how action and motivational tendencies can be put into motion and cause us to behave in a certain way, without our being aware of the source of those tendencies. (2008, 147)

The claims of automaticity theorists are hardly undisputed, but if they are even partially true, they leave much less room for conscious reflective control, including conscious reflective control over how consciously and deeply reflective we choose to be.

Fischer's Guidance Control

John Martin Fischer is the most enthusiastic and self-consciously minimalist moral responsibility advocate going. Most minimalists are pushed back into that corner only reluctantly, but Fischer eagerly embraces a minimalist guidance-control model of moral responsibility. Fischer's views are creative and intriguing and well worth examination. Whether they can secure a small safe place for moral responsibility is another matter.

One thing that makes Fischer's minimalist position interesting is his attempt to recast the whole history of the debate over moral responsibility, accusing those who reject moral responsibility of being the advocates of metaphysical excess. Fischer does not have a monopoly on this approach; Dennett takes a similar line in some of his writings: "Skepticism about the very possibility of culpability arises from a misplaced reverence for an absolutist ideal: the concept of total, before-the-eyes-of-God Guilt. The fact that *that* condition is never to be met in this world should not mislead us into skepticism about the integrity of our institution of moral responsibility" (1984, 165).

But Fischer embraces this perspective with special fervor, insisting that it is the critic of moral responsibility who is committed to metaphysical excess, and that the defenders of moral responsibility hold more modest metaphysical commitments: "I am thus not 'ultimately morally responsible.' And yet this does not in itself seem to expunge or etiolate my agency and my moral responsibility. To suppose that we must be ultimately morally responsible, in the way imagined by [Galen] Strawson, seems to be a wild extrapolation from the quite legitimate desire to be the initiator of one's behavior in some genuine and reasonable sense. It seems to be a kind of metaphysical megalomania" (2006b, 116).

Are those who reject moral responsibility guilty of "metaphysical megalomania"? Consider how these metaphysical excesses actually developed: we wanted to *justify* holding people morally responsible and subjecting them to blame and punishment (or favoring them with special reward). But after careful consideration, we recognized that people are shaped by forces that are not within their control: their fortitude, rational powers, and virtuous or vicious characters are ultimately a matter of good or bad luck. Obviously, we do make choices that influence our subsequent development, but those choices are ultimately traced to influences that were a matter of good or bad fortune, not something we controlled. Thus when we looked closely, it seemed unfair to punish people for character traits or acts that were ultimately not within their control. Rather than give up moral responsibility, we invented miraculous powers that could make sense of such ultimate buck-stopping causal control. But such powers are an embarrassment for contemporary naturalistic philosophers. Unfortunately, rather than acknowledging that moral responsibility is indefensible within the naturalistic framework, they have taken a different tack: they revert to simply holding people morally responsible without looking closely. Don't look at the ultimate causes; rather, focus on the immediate choice or immediate act—Jane didn't try hard enough, so she deserves blame; Joe didn't think carefully enough, so he deserves punishment; Julia acted from her own greedy desires, so she deserves retribution—and don't look deeper at why Jane is weak in fortitude, why Joe is a cognitive miser, and why Julia is deeply avaricious. Among naturalists, both moral responsibility advocates and moral responsibility abolitionists reject miraculous

powers of self-creation: neither side is guilty of "metaphysical megalomania." But the difference is that abolitionists insist you can't justify moral
responsibility without such metaphysical excesses, and the advocates insist
you can—if you just stop looking deeply at how character and behavior
are shaped. Fischer is a leader in the latter movement.

In short, the situation is this: we *want* to hold people morally responsible, and we especially *want* to punish them for their wrongdoing—we
feel a powerful urge to strike back at them. When we reflect deeply and
carefully, we recognize that the behavior and characters of those we want
to blame and punish were shaped by forces beyond their control, and it
seems fundamentally unfair to punish people for their bad luck in being
misshapen. We invent special miraculous powers of self-creation in order
to save the moral responsibility that we know "intuitively" that we must
have: as Jonathan Haidt notes (Haidt 2001; Haidt and Bjorklund 2008;
Haidt 2008), we are very good at finding rational justifications for the
moral judgments that we make nonrationally or intuitively. But as our
understanding of our natural world increases, the plausibility of those
miraculous powers decreases. At that point, one might expect that having
rejected the "metaphysical excesses" that we regarded as the essential
foundation for justifying moral responsibility, the next step would be a
rejection of moral responsibility. But that expectation underestimates the
mesmerizing power of our belief in moral responsibility. Instead of giving
up moral responsibility, believers conclude that they must have set conditions for moral responsibility too high. Fischer thus writes:

Life is extraordinarily fragile, and (from a certain perspective) we are remarkably
lucky to be agents at all, or the particular agents we are (with the particular dispositions, values, and psychological propensities we actually have). Intuitively speaking,
I am not "ultimately responsible" for my particular psychological traits or even for
my very agency. We are not "ultimately responsible" for "the way we are," and yet
it just seems crazy to suppose that we are thereby relieved of moral responsibility
for our behavior. (2006b, 113)

When one is in the powerful grip of the moral responsibility system, it
"just seems crazy" to consider rejecting belief in moral responsibility:
that belief is held firmly in place by its centrality to our justice system
as well as by our basic psychological inclinations. But when we examine
carefully (from a thoroughly naturalistic orientation) the causes and resultant differences in "the particular dispositions, values, and psychological

propensities we actually have," then we recognize the basic unfairness of the moral responsibility system. To block that recognition requires that we block the careful detailed inquiry and insist on a shallower view of moral responsibility and of human behavior. Fischer offers an intriguing model of such an approach to saving moral responsibility: a model that places crucial behavioral details and histories (examination of which would undercut moral responsibility) beyond the limits of legitimate inquiry.

The cornerstone of Fischer's model is his distinction between *regulative* control (which we generally do not have) and *guidance* control (which we do enjoy, and which suffices for moral responsibility). Regulative control is the control that enables us to pick out the path of our life by making open choices among genuinely open alternatives: my choice, and only my choice, sets the course among various open possibilities. Libertarians insist on this freedom of open alternatives, but Fischer is doubtful that we have such powers; in any case, he does not believe that regulative control is needed for a free will that can satisfy the demands of moral responsibility. In contrast to regulative control is the more modest guidance control: "Guidance control—the sort of control exhibited when I guide my car to the right, even though I could not have caused it to move in some other direction, and, more generally, a sort of control that does not require alternative possibilities—is all the freedom required for moral responsibility" (Fischer 1994, 160). At the close of *The Metaphysics of Free Will*, Fischer summarizes his position:

Even if there is just one available path into the future—I may be held accountable for *how I walk down this path*. I can be blamed for taking the path of cruelty, negligence, or cowardice. And I can be praised for walking with sensitivity, attentiveness, and courage. Even if I somehow discovered there is but one path into the future, I would still care deeply how I walk down this path. I would aspire to walk with grace and dignity. I would want to have a sense of humor. Most of all, I would want to do it my way. (216)

Fischer draws the regulative control/guidance control distinction effectively, and he makes interesting use of it, but the distinction is hardly new: the great Stoic philosopher, Epictetus, marked it many centuries earlier: "Remember that you are an actor in a drama of such sort as the Author chooses—if short, then in a short one; if long, then in a long one. If it be his pleasure that you should enact a poor man, see that you act it well; or a cripple, or a ruler, or a private citizen. For this is your business, to act well the given part, but to choose it, belongs to another" (107/1865). Epictetus had good reason to believe that the details, but not the greater destiny, were under individual control: the fates controlled your destiny, and human powers were helpless against them; however, the cosmic fates couldn't be bothered with the details, so humans could have control over those. But Fischer has no grounds for such a distinction: as a contemporary naturalist, he cannot plausibly claim that nature is careful about the big picture but careless of the details; to the contrary, the details are what ultimately shape the larger picture, in evolution as in physics.

Fischer's idea seems to be something like this: not all paths are open to me. I couldn't be a physicist or engineer because I can't pass calculus, I couldn't be a soldier or police officer or fire fighter because I'm cowardly, I couldn't be a baseball player because I can't hit a curve ball, and I don't have the manual dexterity to be an electrician or the physical strength to be a construction worker, so in fact I did not exercise regulative control over becoming a philosopher, because it was the only path open. But I do have wonderful guidance control over how I carry out my philosophic role: I can do it with fortitude or with laziness, be gracious or surly toward my philosophical colleagues, teach my classes well or ill, and so forth. But why should we make such a distinction and insulate guidance control from the same causal factors that shape all our behavior? My degree of cognitive fortitude was largely shaped long before I entered the academy; my sense of philosophical self-efficacy or self-confidence—which is crucial to how confidently and well I philosophize—was and is heavily influenced by factors outside my control (including many in my early childhood), and so on. Of course, many of these factors do depend on my own choices, but the nature and results of those choices are shaped by forces that do not support claims or ascriptions of moral responsibility. It is as if Fischer concludes that because we can't be morally responsible for the large causal factors, we must be morally responsible for the smaller ones. But he gives us no reason whatsoever to believe that is true. He gives us a model of what it would look like to have moral responsibility within those limits, but no reason to believe that we have moral responsibility for either the chosen path or the style of travel.

Fischer's focus on the often neglected details of control is a valuable addition, for that delicate control can be very important. In settings where sense of control is often at risk, small elements of personal control can be of great importance: "The exercise of choice is of special significance in environments that are normally inhospitable to the perception of control (i.e., hospitals, nursing homes, etc.) because it can decrease morbidity and possibly even sustain life itself" (Perlmuter, Monty, and Chan 1986, 113). Medical psychologists know that in maintaining patient fortitude and preventing patient depression, the small elements of control exercised by patients are often more significant than the large scale control of their disease. Cancer patients cannot control the fact that they have a life-threatening disease, but those patients who feel that they can exercise intelligent control over their treatment choices suffer less depression (Thompson et al. 1993). Morris and Royale (1988) found that breast cancer patients who made their own treatment choices and felt in control of the treatment process suffered less anxiety and less depression. Studies (Devins et al. 1981; Devins et al. 1984) show the vital importance of maintaining a sense of control for patients suffering from end-stage renal disease. Margaret Wallhagen and Meryl Brod discovered that in chronic diseases, perceived control over symptoms has a greater impact on patient well-being than do beliefs concerning overall control of the disease itself: "Data from the current study suggest that more specific, situational beliefs about one's ability to control the symptoms that are experienced on a daily basis have a greater influence on well-being than more global, long-term beliefs about one's ability to control the progression of the disease" (1997, 27).

Thus even when regulative control is clearly impossible, guidance control can be of great importance to both the physical and psychological well-being of patients. When a disease overmatches the resources of medical science and neither the course of the disease nor the symptoms can be effectively managed, that loss of control often can be effectively offset by patient control of seemingly minute matters—such as what the patient wears and eats, when visitors are admitted, and even control of end-of-life plans. Shelley Taylor's research (Taylor 1983; Taylor et al. 1991) confirms the importance of detailed "guidance control" for patients facing terminal untreatable illnesses: when patients cannot control the course of their disease, they may still be able to control their reaction to the disease, their choice of how to spend their remaining time, their process of leave taking.

Perhaps the most dramatic evidence of the importance of guidance control for psychological well-being is found in research conducted in long-term care institutions. Residents of those institutions often have a strong sense of losing control over their lives and choices: a loss of control accompanied by severe depression, reduced immunity, and higher mortality rate (Schulz 1976; Schulz and Hanusa 1978; Langer and Rodin 1976; Rodin and Langer 1978; Rodin 1986; Waller 2001; Waller 2002). But small opportunities to exercise limited control—such as control over visits from undergraduate students (Schulz 1976; Schulz and Hanusa 1978), control over the arrangement of furniture in one's room and control over caring for houseplants (Langer and Rodin 1976; Rodin and Langer 1978), or even control over a bird feeder (Banziger and Roush 1983)—can have dramatic effects in preventing depression, reducing sickness, and lengthening life.

But valuable as it is—for all of us, from the healthy to the terminally ill—guidance control does not support moral responsibility. If Joan handles her untreatable cancer with grace and dignity and fortitude and a sense of control, she will be better off—will more likely avoid depression (Thompson et al. 1993), endure pain better (Bowers 1968; Reesor and Craig 1987; Hill et al. 1990), and be less vulnerable to opportunistic infections (Rodin 1986; Wiedenfeld et al. 1990), and certainly she will be more attractive (and her friends will be more likely to visit her) and admirable, but whether Joan is morally responsible for her effective guidance control and whether Joe is morally responsible for exercising his guidance control very badly indeed and becoming cross and self-pitying are very different questions. Some people have the resources to close the final chapter of their lives with dignity and grace and at least some measure of control; others do not. Fischer is right about the importance of guidance control, but he is right for the wrong reasons: it cannot support moral responsibility.

In his more recent work, Fischer's space for guidance control shrinks almost to invisibility. I don't have regulative control over whether I am a philosopher or physicist (or homeless wanderer), but neither do I have open alternatives when it comes to philosophizing with good humor or grumpiness, grace or clumsiness. Instead, guidance control reduces to self-expression. It is important in the construction of our life narratives, and remains important even if the narrative could not differ in even the tiniest details:

What one wants to say, I believe, is that the value of acting so as to be morally responsible consists in *unhindered* or *unimpaired* self-expression of the relevant sort. Perhaps another way of saying the same thing is to note that when one engages in unhindered or unimpaired self-expression of the relevant kind, one is *freely* expressing oneself. I will then suggest that the value of acting so as to be morally responsible consists in one's freely expressing oneself. We value freely—in the sense of not being hindered or impaired in certain ways—writing the book of our lives. (Fischer 2006a, 118)

Certainly we do value "freely expressing" ourselves, "freely . . . writing the book of our lives." But why should this expression provide grounds for moral responsibility? Consider again Lorenzo Valla's *Dialogue on Free Will*, in which Valla imagines Apollo (the Roman god of knowledge) addressing the following speech to young Sextus Tarquinius, who had asked Apollo to tell his future:

Jupiter as he created the wolf fierce, the hare timid, the lion brave, the ass stupid, the dog savage, the sheep mild, so he fashioned some men hard of heart, others soft, he generated one given to evil, the other to virtue, and, further, he gave a capacity for reform to one and made another incorrigible. To you, indeed, he assigned an evil soul with no resource for reform. And so both you, for your inborn character, will do evil, and Jupiter, on account of your actions and their evil effects, will punish sternly, and thus he has sworn by the Stygian swamp it will be. (1443/1948, 173)

Sextus lives his own life, expressing his own character, constructing his (inevitable) life narrative. He chooses evil acts because of his own character (no one holds a sword to his throat and forces him to do evil), and through his own process of guidance control, he constructs the (prophesied) narrative of his own evil life. But why should we suppose that Sextus is morally responsible—and deserving of Jupiter's stern punishment—for the acts he chooses and the narrative he constructs? Perhaps he is responsible and deserving, but nothing in this narrative model gives any reason whatsoever to justify such a moral responsibility claim.

Consider *A Christmas Carol*, the story of Ebenezer Scrooge. Scrooge has sharp intelligence and great fortitude: he makes his own choices and resolutely follows the miserly pattern he favors. Scrooge certainly does not have regulative control, for Dickens shows us how early poverty marked him with a terrible fear of the way the world treats the impoverished: "there is nothing on which it [the world] is so hard as poverty," Scrooge insists (1843, 44). His early love, Belle, watches as Scrooge—through the guidance control of expressing his self—makes the choices that shape his subsequent character: "I have seen your nobler aspirations fall off one by one, until the master passion, Gain, engrosses you" (44). But Scrooge is unwavering in favoring his path of miserliness: "'What then?' he retorted. 'Even if I have grown so much wiser, what then?'" (44). For Fischer, there is no question of either Sextus or Scrooge changing the path or pursuing other alternatives: it is enough that they are themselves making the choices and writing the narrative, even though the choices and narrative are set and grooved. Scrooge makes his own choices, following out his own narrative as a miser. He could not have chosen or been otherwise, but it is still his *own* miserly character that is expressed by his miserly behavior. But why should we suppose that either Sextus or Scrooge is morally responsible for the ugly narratives of their lives? The lives are their own, and they are morally bad lives—on that everyone agrees. And morally good or morally bad, in most cases people do value not being coerced or interfered with in "freely writing the book of their lives." But why do you then deserve special credit for writing a good narrative, while I deserve special blame for writing a bad one? You write a good life narrative because you have better resources or because I have been shaped by fear of poverty; these are our own narratives, but we do not have open alternatives for making them different, in neither the plot nor the details. Just at that point, when one would expect Fischer's argument for moral responsibility to start, the argument ends. It ends with no grounds whatsoever for supposing that Sextus, Scrooge, or anyone else is morally responsible for their lives or choices or narratives.

Perhaps the last sentence of Fischer's *Metaphysics of Free Will* (1994), echoed in the title of his more recent book, reveals what Fischer really wants: he wants to do it "my way," he wants to place his own individual stamp on his life, write his own unique narrative without interference or coercion. Fischer does do it his way, with grace, style, and ingenuity. But he was fortunate to have the talents, background, and environmental history to weave those elements into a positive narrative. That doesn't make it any less the unique story and product of John Martin Fischer. It is Fischer's own distinctive style, it is uniquely Fischer's work, but the question of whether he is morally responsible for that unique narrative is a question that remains to be answered, and the uniqueness and style points do nothing to answer that question. If Scrooge is a miserly individual who exercises guidance control to pursue his miserly miserable course, the question still remains: does Scrooge deserve blame for being such a miserly individual pursuing miserly policies? Does Fischer deserve credit for the gracefulness and fortitude with which he exercises guidance control on his much more agreeable tasks stemming from his much more agreeable person and character? That's where the debate starts. Fischer's gracefulness and Scrooge's miserliness were shaped by factors well beyond their control. Scrooge is a miser and Fischer truly is warm and generous, but whether they deserve credit or blame for their very different path-walking abilities and propensities—or any of the details of their narrative journeys—is a question that Fischer's account leaves unanswered.

John Doris and Small Deliberative Space

John Doris is perhaps the most intriguing advocate of saving a small space for moral responsibility. Having developed a powerful account of the subtle situational forces that shape our paths and choices without our conscious knowledge or control, Doris suggests that we plan carefully to avoid bad situations: "We should try, so far as we are able, to avoid 'near occasions for sin'—ethically dangerous circumstances" (2002, 147). That's excellent advice, and a good example of learning and benefiting from experimental results rather than dismissing them. But then Doris suggests that if we bear this point in mind, "condemnation for ethical failure might very often be directed not at a particular failure of the will but at a certain culpable naiveté or insufficiently careful attention to situations. The implication of this is that our duties may be surprisingly complex, involving not simply obligations to particular actions but a sort of "cognitive duty" to attend, in our deliberations, to the determinative features of situations" (148). But even when we understand the complexity of our "cognitive duty," that will not justify holding people morally responsible, and it will not justify "condemnation for ethical failure." After all, if we have a strong capacity for careful planning, we did not make it ourselves, or if we did (to some degree), then that self-improvement capacity was the product of a shaping process independent of our choices and efforts. Careful reasoning may indeed guide us to wiser decisions and safer situations, but one's capacity as a "chronic cognizer" or "cognitive miser" is itself a matter of good or bad fortune. And many of the crucial shaping processes occurred in situational contexts that preceded any capacity or opportunity for cool careful detached deliberation. (In fairness to Doris, he clearly recognizes how difficult carrying out such "situationally sophisticated" cool deliberation would be.)

Moral Responsibility Is Not in the Details

Controlling details is important, as Fischer makes clear, but whether one exercises such control well or ill is a function of one's cognitive fortitude and sense of self-efficacy, which were—at crucial points—not self-made. In sum, the moral responsibility supported by "free will of the gaps" is confined to very small gaps indeed. And when we look closely, even the small gaps of "reasoned choice" and "guidance control" and "acts of will" are closed off by explanatory accounts that leave no room for moral responsibility.

There is a strong temptation to preserve moral responsibility by appeal to a special power that exempts some small but crucial element of human behavior from natural forces: a temptation to which even compatibilists can succumb. But most contemporary philosophers maintain that such an exemption is not necessary for moral responsibility, because moral responsibility is not incompatible with a thorough naturalism: both humans and human moral responsibility (they claim) can flourish in a completely natural environment that is devoid of miracles and mysteries. The argument of the following chapters is that these compatibilists are half right: humans can indeed flourish in the thoroughly natural environment that shaped us, but moral responsibility cannot. And human flourishing will be enhanced once humans give up the idea that we can transplant moral responsibility from its native habitat of miracles and mysteries and make it survive in the natural nonmiraculous world.

6 Taking Responsibility

While some try to discover moral responsibility in small corners not yet explored by science, there is another defense of moral responsibility that is more aggressive. Rather than trying to *find* responsibility in some scientifically inaccessible niche, these bold spirits *take* responsibility. Consider this claim by Harry Frankfurt: "To the extent that a person identifies himself with the springs of his actions, he takes responsibility for those actions and acquires moral responsibility for them; moreover, the question of how the actions and his identifications with their springs is caused is irrelevant to the questions of whether he performs the actions freely or is morally responsible for performing them" (1975, 122).

So your past doesn't matter; once you take responsibility, the responsibility is yours by virtue of your act of accepting and identifying with and acknowledging the responsibility as your own. In a similar vein, Daniel Dennett emphasizes the importance of taking responsibility:

One often says, after doing something awful, "I'm terribly sorry; I simply never thought of the consequences; it simply didn't occur to me what harm I was doing!" This looks almost like the beginning of an excuse—"Can I help it what occurs to me and what doesn't?"—but healthy self-controllers shun this path. They *take* responsibility for what might be, very likely is, just an "accident," just one of those things. That way, they make themselves less likely to be "accident" victims in the future. (1984, 143–144)

And taking responsibility is, for Dennett, a key element of being an agent: "We want to be in control of ourselves, and not under the control of others. We want to be agents, capable of initiating, and taking responsibility for, projects and deeds" (169). Dennett continues to push the importance of taking responsibility in *Freedom Evolves*: "Since there will always be strong temptations to make yourself really small, to externalize the causes of your actions and deny responsibility, the way to counteract these is to make people an offer they can't refuse: If you want to be free, you must *take* responsibility" (2003, 293).

Robert Kane, a dedicated libertarian, finds little common ground with Frankfurt and Dennett, but even Kane cannot resist the siren song of taking responsibility, though he places it in a very different context. In Kane's wonderfully inventive account of ultimate responsibility, when we are morally responsible for our "self-forming choices"—and act with ultimate responsibility—we are choosing between two courses of action, we are in a state of indecision in which we have good reasons (of which we reflectively approve) for either course, and we are actually willing both of these incompatible options, then an indeterminate force (the amplified effect of the random motion of a subatomic particle) tips the balance one way or the other and we choose a path that we have good and sufficient reasons for choosing (even though a key element of the choice involves a random event). One objection to Kane's model—which Kane himself regards as "perhaps the most telling" (2007, 41)—is that such undetermined choices would be arbitrary; as Kane states the objection: "A residual arbitrariness seem to remain in all self-forming choices since the agents cannot in principle have sufficient or conclusive reasons for making one option and one set of reasons prevail over the other" (41). Kane's answer to this objection turns on taking responsibility:

There is some truth to this objection . . . but . . . I think it is a truth that tells us something important about free will. It tells us that every undetermined self-forming free choice is the initiation of what might be called a value experiment whose justification lies in the future and is not fully explained by past reasons. In making such a choice we say, in effect, "Let's try this. It is not required by my past, but it is consistent with my past and is one branching pathway in the garden of forking paths my life can now meaningfully take. Whether it is the right choice, only time will tell. Meanwhile, I am willing to take responsibility for it one way or the other." . . .

Suppose we were to say to such persons [who take responsibility for their self-forming choices]: "But look, you didn't have sufficient or conclusive prior reasons for choosing as you did since you also had viable reasons for choosing the other way." They might reply: "True enough. But I did have good reasons for choosing as I did, which I'm willing to stand by and take responsibility for. (41–42)

So from Kane to Dennett to Frankfurt—a very broad philosophical spectrum—taking responsibility plays a prominent role in the justification of moral responsibility: *I* am responsible, because I *take* responsibility.

There is much to like about taking responsibility: taking responsibility for your own acts and choices—indeed, for your own life and your own projects—is healthy and valuable, and Dennett in particular has done a great service in showing how valuable and psychologically beneficial the taking of responsibility really is. But although there is real value in taking responsibility, it is essential to distinguish between two very different types of responsibility, only one of which can be taken (and only one of which is worth taking). Taking responsibility is psychologically healthy and beneficial, but the responsibility taken is not moral responsibility. Moral responsibility cannot be taken, and the genuine benefits of taken responsibility do not apply to moral responsibility. To the contrary, claims and ascriptions of moral responsibility are impediments to the valuable process of taking responsibility.

Though even very astute and perceptive philosophers confuse taken responsibility with moral responsibility, it is not difficult to mark the basic difference. You can take responsibility for many things, from the mundane to the vitally important. You can take responsibility for teaching a course, arranging a symposium, and planning the department picnic, and you can take responsibility for making your own health care decisions ("I value my physician's advice, but I will make my own choices about what medications to take or treatments to have") or choosing a career ("You can't tell me what to major in, or whether to take over the family business; I make my own career decisions, and I take responsibility for them: the decisions are up to me"). But the responsibility taken is profoundly different from the moral responsibility that would justify blame and punishment, praise and reward. Suppose that the symposium you organized is a complete failure: the keynote speakers don't arrive, and no one attends. "I took responsibility," you assert, "so I deserve blame for the failure." Someone might well respond, "That's ridiculous; of course it was your (taken) responsibility, but given the terrible blizzard, there was nothing you could do; you certainly don't deserve blame." Or suppose the failure of the symposium—for which Ed took responsibility—is the product of Ed's own flaws, and Ed says, "I procrastinated, and I was lazy, and I didn't get things organized in a timely manner." One might respond, "Yes, it was your responsibility, and you messed up, but you aren't really to blame, because your laziness is part of your genetic inheritance from your father." One might doubt that genetic analysis, and one might insist that Ed is morally responsible and deserves blame, but the point is that such a claim is different from the claim that Ed took responsibility. We can agree that Ed took responsibility and still dispute whether Ed is morally responsible, so clearly these are very different concepts. Or, from the other side, suppose that Ann takes responsibility for organizing the symposium, and it runs splendidly. Ann says: "I took responsibility for the symposium, and it was great, so I justly deserve special credit." Someone might say, "Well, yes, it was a great symposium, and you took responsibility for it, but in fact the department secretary did all the work, so you don't deserve any special credit, you aren't morally responsible." Ann might dispute that statement and claim that she does deserve credit and is morally responsible for the successful symposium. But clearly that question is a different one from the question of whether she took responsibility. Or suppose that Ann is claiming moral responsibility for the symposium success, and someone responds, "No, you don't deserve special credit; you took responsibility, and did a great job, but you are just lucky to have a strong gene for responsibility taking and another strong gene for symposium organizing, so you don't deserve special credit for taking responsibility for the symposium or for running it well." Again, Ann might dispute that denial of her moral responsibility, but she cannot do so by asserting that she took responsibility. Everyone agrees that she took responsibility, but there remains the separate and distinct question of whether she is morally responsible.

Hart's Role Responsibility

The distinction neglected by Dennett, Frankfurt, and Kane stems from a distinction drawn by H. L. A. Hart. The responsibility that one can take might be called *take-charge responsibility*. It is similar to the *role* responsibility described by H. L. A. Hart:

A sea captain is responsible for the safety of his ship, and this is his responsibility, or one of his responsibilities. . . . A sentry [is responsible] for alerting the guard at the enemy's approach; a clerk for keeping the accounts of his firm. These examples of a person's responsibilities suggest the generalization that, whenever a person occupies a distinctive place or office in a social organization, to which specific duties are attached to provide for the welfare of others or to advance in some specific way the aims or purposes of the organization, he is properly said to be responsible for the performance of these duties. . . . If two friends, out on a mountaineering expedition, agree that the one shall look after the food and the other the maps, then the one is correctly said to be responsible for the food, and the other for the maps, and I would classify this as a case of role-responsibility. (1968, 212)

Hart's role responsibility is very different from moral responsibility; after all, it makes perfectly good sense to say that the sentry was (role) responsible for sounding the alert, but—given the overwhelming exhaustion resulting from three days of nonstop battle followed by an all-day march—he should not be blamed (is not morally responsible) for failure to meet his genuine role responsibility. And the same point applies in the other direction: Captain Aubrey is role responsible for his ship, and he does a great job fulfilling that responsibility, but he deserves no praise or reward for his good work, because he was lucky to have had wonderful early training that taught him to be an excellent captain; or because he has a superb first lieutenant who keeps the ship running smoothly; or even because he has the ship captain's gene, and was therefore merely lucky in the natural genetic lottery. Someone might wish to dispute that claim: Captain Aubrey *is* morally responsible, and deserving of special reward, just because he fulfills his duties so admirably; it doesn't matter what historical circumstances equipped him to be a superb captain, so Captain Aubrey is not only role responsible, but also morally responsible. For the moment, we can set aside the question of whether that moral responsibility claim is correct: the point is that establishing Captain Aubrey's moral responsibility will be an additional claim, beyond the question of his role responsibility. If we can agree that Captain Aubrey is role responsible but still have an argument about whether he is also morally responsible, then it is clear that role responsibility and moral responsibility are distinct.

Take-Charge Responsibility

Although inspired by Hart's distinction, take-charge responsibility (Waller 1998) designates the broader taking of responsibility—including taking charge of one's own plans and projects and life—that must be distinguished from moral responsibility. Just as a captain may have role responsibility for a ship, so you may have take-charge responsibility for your projects, your values, your goals, your *life*. Will you pursue a career in philosophy, or accounting, or safe cracking? Take up distance running, or join a bowling league, or devote your leisure time to needlework? It's your life, and the choices are your own. It's not that no one could manage your life better than you do; to the contrary, there are probably legions of superior life managers. But you have take-charge responsibility for your own life, which is a responsibility you deeply value and enjoy exercising, and you would rather exercise it badly than turn it over to someone else who could run your life better. And (in most circumstances) there is great psychological benefit from exercising your own take-charge responsibility.

A captain may have role responsibility for his ship without being morally responsible for exercising that role responsibility well or ill; likewise, the fact that you have take-charge responsibility for your life does not imply that you also have moral responsibility. Barbara exercises her take-charge responsibility well, but she was lucky to have a loving and supportive family, a superb education, encouragement to think carefully and develop as a chronic cognizer, the support to develop a strong sense of self-efficacy, a (perhaps genetic) internal locus-of-control. But whether she takes responsibility well or ill, it does not follow that she is morally responsible. Perhaps she is, but because there are cases in which take-charge responsibility is clear and moral responsibility is problematic, it is obvious that they are distinct and that establishing take-charge responsibility does not establish moral responsibility.[1]

With the distinction between take-charge responsibility and moral responsibility in hand, the basic problem for the "taking responsibility" model of moral responsibility becomes obvious. I can indeed take responsibility. It is healthy to do so, and we are generally happy to have take-charge responsibility. But that has no bearing on moral responsibility, for I obviously cannot legitimately *take* that. Daniel Dennett takes responsibility for his own life and work. That's a good thing, and his strong capacity for taking responsibility and exercising it well has resulted in marvelous books and a wonderful career. But is Dennett morally responsible— deserving of special reward or credit—for his splendid work? Perhaps someone might argue that Dennett's strong sense of self-efficacy, his splendid fortitude, and his powerful cognizing are wonderful characteristics that enhance his superb take-charge responsibility and make him a great philosopher, but he was lucky to have a fortunate formative history. That is, Dennett achieves great things because he has great resources, but he does not deserve special credit: he is not morally responsible. Dennett is wonderfully take-charge responsible, but he is not morally responsible for his splendid take-charge responsibility capacities or the positive results that flow from them. Dennett might reply: "Yes, I *am* morally responsible: I *take* responsibility for that capacity." But such a reply proves nothing. Obviously, he has take-charge responsibility; the question is whether he has moral responsibility.

There are no doubt cases in which advocates of moral responsibility would argue that someone who has take-charge responsibility *is* morally responsible: "You took the responsibility for reserving the lecture hall; you are to blame for the failure to reserve it." As a moral responsibility abolitionist, I believe that no such claim could ever be justified. But the immediate point is that if you suppose there are times when take-charge responsibility results in moral responsibility, that supposition will require further justification, for there are obviously times when take-charge responsibility does not entail moral responsibility, and the two are clearly distinct. When responsibility advocates appeal to taking responsibility to justify moral responsibility, that is a result of confusing take-charge responsibility with moral responsibility.

The Pleasures of Taking Responsibility

Because Dennett thinks it is moral responsibility that people are taking, he supposes that we must coerce them into acceptance: "Since there will always be strong temptations to make yourself really small, to externalize the causes of your actions and deny responsibility, the way to counteract these is to make people an offer they can't refuse: If you want to be free, you must *take* responsibility" (2003, 292).

But when we recognize that what is taken is take-charge responsibility, then the need for coercion disappears. Take-charge responsibility is not the price we pay for freedom, but is instead a vital element of living freely and exercising free control. It is very satisfying to take responsibility for my own life, my own decisions, my own projects, my own health care choices. Or it is at least usually very satisfying. Unfortunately, in some circumstances it is not at all satisfying, but instead profoundly distressing. When one has the knowledge and confidence to exercise control effectively, then exercising control is healthy and invigorating. In those circumstances, patients who exercise take-charge responsibility for their own health care decisions recover faster and follow rehabilitation regimens with greater fortitude (Rodin 1982; Wallston 1993; Waller 2001). As noted in the previous chapter, long-term care residents who have the opportunity to exercise effective control are less vulnerable to infection, less likely to suffer from depression, and more involved in their residence community. Workers who exercise more control over their work environment and more involvement in making plans not only find greater satisfaction in their work and work more efficiently, but also are less likely to become depressed (Karasek 1979; Spector 1986) and less likely to develop serious illness (Marmot et al. 1978; Karasek et al. 1981; Karasek 1990; Hammar, Alfredsson, and Johnson 1998; Netterstrom et al.). But if one is placed in a position of making an important decision or carrying out a vital task, and one lacks the confidence that one has the knowledge and ability to make the decision effectively or complete the task successfully—that is, if one lacks what psychologist Albert Bandura (1997) calls *self-efficacy*—then instead of finding the control satisfying and invigorating, the control becomes a frightening burden (Rodin, Rennert, and Solomon 1980). When the elderly are surveyed, many say they would prefer not to make their own health care decisions, but instead leave them up to their physicians (Schneider 1994, 1995); however, when asked if they had sufficient knowledge and understanding to confidently make their own medical decisions whether they would prefer to make the decision themselves, then the number of elderly patients preferring to decide for themselves greatly increases (Woodward and Wallston 1987).

Those who have a strong confident sense of self-efficacy—whether the task is making a decision concerning medical treatment, or making career choices, or carrying out a work project, or teaching a course—find great satisfaction in making their own decisions, carrying out their own plans, and exercising take-charge responsibility. They don't have to be coerced into taking such responsibility; to the contrary, they value and welcome take-charge responsibility and fear its loss. Rather than coercing people into taking responsibility, the better course is to foster those conditions—of adequate knowledge, self-confidence, sense of self-efficacy—in which people naturally embrace and enjoy the taking of responsibility. In those favorable circumstances, people are eager to have take-charge responsibility and gain substantial benefits from its exercise.[2]

The Right Conditions for Take-Charge Responsibility

Unfortunately, when take-charge responsibility is confused with moral responsibility, the conditions that foster the effective taking of take-charge responsibility are neglected—and not merely neglected, but actively hidden from view. When we wish to hold people morally responsible and blame them individually for their bad acts or characters, doing so requires that we *not* look closely at the forces that shaped them, for if we look closely, it becomes painfully obvious that we are blaming and punishing people for flaws and misdeeds that are the product of their unfortunate history. Dennett seems to be aware of this problem and counsels not looking carefully in order to maintain our practices of holding people morally responsible: "Instead of investigating, endlessly, in an attempt to *discover* whether or not a particular trait is of someone's making—instead of trying to assay exactly to what degree a particular self is self-made—we simply *hold* people responsible for their conduct (within limits we take are not to examine too closely)" (1984, 164).

So don't investigate how one's character was shaped, and take care not to examine too closely how responsibility works. Dennett is right. If we want to keep the system of moral responsibility functioning, it is essential that we not look closely. The sad consequence of that moral responsibility myopia is that the conditions that foster and undercut the effective exercise of take-charge responsibility must be ignored in order to sustain the moral responsibility illusion. If we want people to take responsibility—take-charge responsibility, the only kind they can take and the only kind worth taking—then it is essential to look carefully at the cultural and psychological conditions that foster (and often impede) the effective exercise of take-charge responsibility. For those who enjoy at least a minimal level of sense of self-efficacy (who have adequate confidence in their ability to manage their own lives and make their own decisions), the opportunity to exercise take-charge responsibility for their own lives and choices is both inherently satisfying and developmentally sound, and those deprived of this opportunity are likely to suffer severe depression and a sense of profound helplessness.[3] With the right support, even those weak in sense of self-efficacy can learn to make their own choices, do so with some effectiveness, and gradually enhance both their sense of self-efficacy and their skill at exercising their own take-charge responsibility.

We should make sure people really do have the opportunity to become confidently self-efficacious, but nothing is gained by persuading a severely deprived person to accept responsibility if that person is unable to do so effectively; to the contrary, we cause great harm. We gain much more if we set up the right conditions under which people naturally want to take and exercise effective control. Doing so will not require offering incentives (with nasty alternatives) for taking take-charge responsibility; it will require only the opportunity to act freely. Rousseau believed that man is born free and that he is everywhere in chains. He was right about the latter, but not the former. We aren't born free, but must develop the capacity for freedom. And we are in chains, but they are the chains of substandard education, hierarchical authoritative religions, standardized jobs that require obedience rather than thought, and a consumer culture that encourages and rewards mindless conformity. These destroy our sense of self-efficacy, and deprive us of freedom as surely—and perhaps even more thoroughly—than do chains. And forcing "responsibility" on people under those circumstances adds injury to injury. Change the conditions to enhance the sense of confident self-efficacy and people will be eager to freely exercise take-charge responsibility.

Frankfurt and Taking Responsibility

When Dennett insists that one can take moral responsibility, he is confusing take-charge responsibility with moral responsibility, and when he then praises the advantages of take-charge responsibility, he supposes that he is providing justification for moral responsibility. But another great advocate of taking or claiming moral responsibility—Harry Frankfurt—pursues a different path. Recall the passage from Frankfurt quoted at the beginning of this chapter: "To the extent that a person identifies himself with the springs of his actions, he takes responsibility for those actions and acquires moral responsibility for them; moreover, the question of how the actions and his identifications with their springs is caused is irrelevant to the questions of whether he performs the actions freely or is morally responsible for performing them" (1975, 122). Frankfurt's source for moral responsibility is one's deep identification with her character and traits and actions: that is how one "takes responsibility for those actions and acquires moral responsibility for them." For Frankfurt, the strong identification with and approval of one's character and actions and motives is the very process of acquiring moral responsibility for them. Frankfurt's case of the willing addict (described in chapter 4) makes his position clear. Suppose that Robert is addicted to drugs (and thus strongly desires to take drugs) and—under the iron grip of his addiction—does take drugs, but Robert hates his addiction and longs to be free of this overwhelming drug desire. In that case, Robert does not act with free will: he does not have the will he wishes to have. Robert may successfully act on his desire for drugs, but he cannot banish the hateful desire though he wishes he could: Robert's will is not free, he does not have the will he wants and approves, he does not identify with his will, does not take responsibility for it, and is not morally responsible. But if Robert should become a willing addict—an addict who deeply and reflectively approves of his drug addiction, who identifies with his addictive desire for drugs—then Robert makes his addiction his own, takes responsibility for it, and becomes morally responsible for his addiction. This analysis is insightful. Though the notion of a "willing addict" has an air of paradox, Frankfurt's account offers a dramatic picture of the *authenticity* model of moral responsibility: this is my true self, my authentic self, the self of which I reflectively and profoundly approve, and thus I claim and take moral responsibility for my own self.

Frankfurt's hierarchical account of freedom is impressive, but closer scrutiny reveals its failure as a justification of moral responsibility. Moral responsibility cannot be taken, either by asserting a claim to it or through deep identification. Examining the actual psychological process of becoming a willing addict shows that Frankfurt's willing addict has moved farther from freedom, not closer, and although the unwilling addict is clearly not morally responsible for an addiction that he despises, the moral responsibility of the willing addict is even less plausible. The unwilling addict is not free, as Frankfurt recognizes, but the willing addict is even more distant from freedom: his will has not become free, but has instead been as profoundly enslaved as his desires.

An unwilling drug addict takes drugs because of his addiction, but his addiction is alien to him, and he longs to be free of it. His addiction is not really his own; he is coerced by his addiction and is not morally responsible for taking drugs. (To avoid the Aristotelian complications of whether he is morally responsible for starting to take the drug, and thus responsible for the addictive outcome, suppose that this unwilling addict was initially given the addictive drugs without his knowledge.) But eventually the unwilling addict evolves into a willing addict: he now approves of his addiction, identifies with it, and deeply favors his own enslavement to drugs. At this point, Frankfurt would regard the drug addiction as profoundly—authentically—the addict's own, and Frankfurt is correct. But Frankfurt also regards the willing addict as having gained moral responsibility for his addiction (and Frankfurt insists that how the willing addict's identification with his addiction came about is irrelevant to whether he is morally responsible), and on that point, Frankfurt is wrong.

Robert is an unwilling addict who hates the addiction that is destroying his marriage, thwarting his desire to become a competitive marathoner, and ruining his career. All Robert's affections and hopes and plans are being undercut by a drug addiction that he longs to escape. As Robert's life of addiction continues, he gradually loses almost everything: his wife leaves, his body atrophies to a point at which marathons seem ridiculous, and he loses his job and his career prospects. What remains is his drug addiction: It is his only source of pleasure, his only comfort, and provides his only community. Without his drug addiction, Robert would have nothing at all. Now he desperately clings to his addiction, deeply approves his addiction, cannot imagine life without his addictive desire for drugs, and fears the emptiness that would replace a lost desire for drugs. Robert has become a willing addict and is certainly more profoundly addicted than he was as an unwilling addict.

Robert's life, and the profound drug addiction with which he identifies, are certainly his *own*, and Robert can and does have take-charge responsibility for his drug-addicted life. As Frankfurt notes, "he identifies himself with the springs of his actions, he takes responsibility for those actions" (1975, 122). But the responsibility he takes is not moral responsibility. Rather than this deep authentic addiction carrying moral responsibility along with it, the two pull in opposite directions. Robert's take-charge responsibility has shrunk to a single point, his freedom is a cruel parody of any genuine natural alternatives freedom, and holding Robert (or the profoundly enslaved Jamal or the deeply acquiescent Eve) morally responsible is fundamentally unfair.

Belief in moral responsibility blocks us from looking closely at the causes, and thus hamstrings efforts to develop and enhance healthy take-charge responsibility. In sum, take-charge responsibility is positive and beneficial, and moral responsibility is not only a different sort of responsibility (that cannot be justified by the existence and the desirability of take-charge responsibility), but also a severe impediment to the development and exercise of take-charge responsibility.

7 Responsibility for the Self You Make

Chapter 6 rejected taking responsibility as grounds for moral responsibility: taking responsibility is generally good and psychologically healthy, but the responsibility taken is not moral responsibility, and even strong identification with one's own authentic character cannot support claims of blame and just deserts. But some moral responsibility advocates have gone further, arguing that you don't just take moral responsibility for the character you happen to have; rather, you gain moral responsibility for yourself because you make yourself.

The notion that we are morally responsible because we make ourselves has long been appealing. As noted in chapter 2, Pico della Mirandola's famous Renaissance oration on "The Dignity of Man" suggests that God grants humans the special power of unlimited and unconstrained self-making; Pico della Mirandola has God address "his last and favorite creation" thus:

The nature of all other beings is limited and constrained within the bounds of laws prescribed by Us. Thou, constrained by no limits, in accordance with thine own free will, in whose hand We have placed thee, shalt ordain for thyself the limits of thy nature. We have set thee at the world's center that thou mayest from thence more easily observe whatever is in the world. We have made thee neither of heaven nor of earth, neither mortal nor immortal, so that with freedom of choice and with honor, as though the maker and molder of thyself, thou mayest fashion thyself in whatever shape thou shalt prefer. Thou shalt have the power to degenerate into the lower forms of life, which are brutish. Thou shalt have the power, out of thy soul's judgment, to be reborn into the higher forms, which are divine. (1496/1948, 225)

In a more contemporary vein—and equally miraculous, though without recourse to God—Jean Paul Sartre (1946/1989) insists that our *existence* precedes our *essence* and that we humans are self-conscious self-creating "being-for-itself" with the free power—indeed, the necessity—to make ourselves; we are different in kind from entities with their own given natures, the unfree "being-in-itself." The echoes of Pico della Mirandola are not coincidence. All other creatures are "limited and constrained within the bounds of laws prescribed by Us," constrained by natural causes, but humans are uniquely self-creating "being-for-itself," and we make ourselves, unconstrained by natural causes or natural processes.

So moral responsibility based on special self-making powers has a long and dramatic history, but naturalists, eschewing such miracle-working resources, have been reluctant to embrace self-making as grounds for moral responsibility. After all, the notion of "making myself" is a bit tricky: exactly who is doing the making? If it's a miraculous process (as in Pico della Mirandola), or if it defies natural understanding (as in Sartre), then fine, but then it's clearly not something we can fit into a naturalistic system of thought.

Recently, however, some committed naturalists have taken the leap and offered self-making as grounds for moral responsibility. Dennett is at the forefront of that effort:

I take responsibility for any thing I make and then inflict upon the general public; if my soup causes food poisoning, or my automobile causes air pollution, or my robot runs amok and kills someone, I, the manufacturer, am to blame. And although I may manage to get my suppliers and subcontractors to share the liability somewhat, I am held responsible for releasing the product to the public with whatever flaws it has. Common wisdom has it that much the same rationale grounds personal responsibility; I have created and unleashed an agent who is myself; if its acts produce harm, the manufacturer is held responsible. I think this common wisdom is indeed wisdom. (1984, 85)

But for a naturalist, problems with self-making as grounds for moral responsibility soon emerge. Pico della Mirandola may suppose we make ourselves with miraculous powers granted by God, and Sartre may insist that as "being-for-itself" we are not confined to natural powers, but naturalists have no such recourse. And the problem is that even though there is a perfectly legitimate sense in which we do make ourselves—the hard-practicing basketball player makes herself into a better shooter, the hard-working student makes himself into a better writer, the diligent hobbyist makes herself a better woodworker—it is clear that the basketball player and the student and the hobbyist start with different resources and capacities. We are both making birdhouses, and mine is misshapen and so badly constructed that no bird would be foolish enough to call it home. Your birdhouse is beautiful, solidly constructed, soundly designed. Do I deserve blame for the lousy birdhouse I constructed, while you receive special credit for your charming result? If I start with flimsy materials, poor tools and little knowledge of construction principles, while you have the benefits of superb materials, excellent tools and strong carpentry training, then it is still true that you made a superior birdhouse, but it does not follow that we are distinctly different in just deserts for our very different results. The same point applies if the question is self-making: if you have a better early education, a better draw in the "genetic lottery," and better support for your efforts, then you are likely to fashion a superior self; if I start from the opposite extreme—very limited native abilities that have been damaged by early abuse or neglect—then the self I fashion is likely to have serious flaws, but it is not at all clear that I deserve blame for those flaws.

Dennett and Sher on Equal Opportunity

Dennett offers a clever answer to that objection.

Suppose—what certainly seems to be true—that people are born with noticeably different cognitive endowments and propensities to develop character traits. . . . Is this "hideously unfair" . . . or is this bound to lead to something hideously unfair? Not necessarily.

Imagine a footrace in which the starting line was staggered: those with birthdays in January start a yard ahead of those born in February, and eleven yards ahead of those born in December. Surely no one can help being born in one month rather than another. Isn't this markedly unfair? Yes, if the race is a hundred-yard dash. No, if it's a marathon. In a marathon such a relatively small initial advantage would count for nothing, since one can reliably expect other fortuitous breaks to have even greater effects. . . . Is it fair enough not to be worth worrying about? Of course. After all, luck averages out in the long run. (1984, 95)

This is a charming metaphor, but Dennett's race goes badly off track. He is right, of course, that we start with "noticeably different cognitive endowments and propensities to develop character traits," but the supposition that those with disadvantaged starting points will be compensated by later good fortune—"after all, luck averages out in the long run"—is absurd. The young student with a "small initial advantage" is placed in gifted classes, receives more attention from her teachers, enjoys greater academic success, and thus increases both her fortitude and her self-confidence. Jan is a young basketball player who starts with a small advantage in athletic ability over Kate; Jan receives somewhat more playing time and more attention during practice and develops greater skill and "court savvy" and fortitude and confidence. Next year Jan plays on the varsity team and gets better coaching and more games; on the junior varsity team, Kate plays fewer games against worse competition under inferior coaching, and the gap between Jan and Kate widens, rather than "evening out." The initial advantage is much more likely to be cumulative, rather than offset by subsequent bad breaks. Contrary to Dennett's cheery claims of equal luck, the dark words of Jesus of Nazareth are much closer to the truth: "For he that hath, to him shall be given: and he that hath not, from him shall be taken even that which he hath" (Mark 4:25).

The same sort of dubious equality claim can be seen in Sher:

Even if M is initially stronger or more intelligent than N, this difference will only entail that M does not deserve what he has achieved relative to N if the difference between them has made it impossible for N to achieve as much as M. However, differences in strength, intelligence, and other native gifts are rarely so pronounced as to have this effect. The far more common effect of such differences is merely to make it more *difficult* for the less talented person to reach a given level of attainment. He must work harder, husband his resources more carefully, plan more shrewdly, and so on. (1987, 31–32)

As in Dennett's case for equal luck, this claim of equal *overall* resources is obviously false. In Sher's model, Ann's superior athletic ability is balanced out by Barbara's greater "court savvy," Carla's superior fortitude, and Dianne's stronger self-confidence. But in fact, Barbara's superior athleticism results in more playing time and more attention from her coaches and greater athletic success, which brings with it enhanced knowledge of the game, greater endurance and fortitude, and stronger athletic self-confidence.

Dennett and Sher both know that it is false that "luck balances out" and false that our weaknesses in one capacity are compensated by strengths in another. Initial advantages tend to be cumulative, and talents and strengths—as well as weaknesses—typically bunch together. Politicians may pretend that "every child in our country has an equal opportunity," and "every child can make him or herself whatever she wishes," but philosophers as clear-sighted as Dennett and Sher know that it isn't true. We start with different tools and different raw materials in different workshops, which is a fatal problem for attempts to base moral responsibility on self-making. One little pig makes his house out of straw, because that's the only building material he has; his brother—with better materials and tools and superior construction knowledge—builds his house out of bricks. Both built their own houses, but it hardly seems fair to blame the first little pig when his house blows over and conclude that he justly deserves to be eaten by the big bad wolf. In the naturalist view—with no appeals to miraculous powers—if George and Harshad build different selves, then there must be differences in their starting abilities or their formative circumstances; those are differences not of their making, and results that stem from those differences cannot justify claims of just deserts and moral responsibility.

In his later work, Sher abandons the attempt to show that differences in self-making results are fair, but (as discussed in chapter 9) rather than abandoning blame, Sher opts to abandon fairness. Dennett also seems to abandon his claim that unequal starts are fair (because luck balances out) and instead argues that uneven results stemming from uneven starts do not undercut moral responsibility because we need only reach a plateau of responsibility, so finishes can be quite uneven and luck need not balance out. And like most plateau theorists, Dennett doesn't seem to care how people reach the plateau, whether by do-it-yourself or ready-made talents. Plateau arguments will be examined in chapter 12, but there are other versions of the self-making argument for moral responsibility, and they must also be considered.

Choosing Yourself

One popular variation of the self-making argument appeals to self-choosing, which doesn't carry quite as much baggage as self-making. There are many things I can choose that I can't make: making a car is far beyond my skills and resources and capacities, but choosing one is something I can manage. Choices, however, are fraught with peril for naturalists; it is very easy for choices—especially those that are supposed to prop up moral responsibility—to transcend the natural world and natural causes, transfigured into the traditional libertarian mysterious choices that can go in various ways under precisely the same natural circumstances: the choices of gods and miracle workers and unmoved movers. This temptation toward transcendence is strong among those who emphasize self-choosing as grounds for moral responsibility; if their choices remain grounded in the naturalistic framework, then such choices have great difficulty in supporting the weight of moral responsibility.

Charles Taylor gives an interesting account of the "radical evaluation" by means of which we can reevaluate and choose our deepest values, and thus become responsible for ourselves:

This radical evaluation is a deep reflection, and a self-reflection in a special sense: it is a reflection about the self, its most fundamental issues, and a reflection which engages the self most wholly and deeply. Because it engages the whole self without a fixed yardstick it can be called a personal reflection . . . ; and what emerges from it is a self-resolution in a strong sense, for in this reflection the self is in question; what is at stake is the definition of those inchoate evaluations which are sensed to be essential to our identity.

Because this self-resolution is something we do, when we do it, we can be called responsible for ourselves; and because it is within limits always up to us to do it, even when we don't—indeed, the nature of our deepest evaluations constantly raises the question whether we have them right—we can be called responsible in another sense for ourselves whether we undertake this radical evaluation or not . . . . And it is this kind of responsibility for oneself, I would maintain, not that of radical choice, but the responsibility for radical evaluation implicit in the nature of a strong evaluator, which is essential to our notion of a person. (1976, 299)

Taylor avoids the "radical choice" of libertarian miracles, but only a philosopher would suppose that it is "always up to us to do it" when the question is one of deep and careful and sustained deliberation. Philosophers are chronic cognizers, moving in crowds of chronic cognizers, and indeed, it may seem to philosophers that we—and all the other chronically cognizing philosophers in our midst—can always freely choose to make deep, sustained, radical self-evaluations. But obviously, not everyone is a philosopher, and certainly not everyone is a chronic cognizer who can readily engage in deep, lengthy, demanding cognitive reflection. And although philosophers may readily engage in chronic cognizing about epistemological contextualism or new versions of utilitarianism or the nature of time, it is not at all clear that for philosophers—or anyone else—it is "always up to us" to engage in the deep and deeply personal self-evaluation on which Taylor bases his self-choosing claim of moral responsibility. A readiness to cognize about epistemology or the philosophy of science does not imply that we are equally ready to explore the sometimes painful nature of our deepest values and commitments: it is much easier to ponder the strengths and weaknesses of virtue theory than the strengths and weaknesses and flaws of my own value system. Is my deep commitment to a life of philosophical reflection really a commitment to a life of academic ease and safety? Is such philosophical reflection on esoteric philosophical questions a worthwhile way of spending my life and my energies when I could instead be working to relieve hunger and cure devastating illnesses and prevent global warming? And if the questions touch on particularly sensitive spots—do I really think this philosophical question is worthwhile, or am I merely pursuing a topic that might lead to publication and promotion? Is my commitment to pacifism really just knee-jerk rebellion against my father's military career and military values?—then deep reflection may be psychologically impossible, rather than "always available." But even if it were always available, such deep reflection and evaluation is not godlike; rather, it occurs in a context of values and is influenced by a wide range of forces. The radical reevaluations that lead Arnold to devote his life to finding a cure for malaria and Bryan to join a terrorist cell may well be their own, but whether they are grounds for moral responsibility is a very different question.

Jonathan Jacobs offers an account of moral responsibility that, like Taylor's, is based in "self-making" through choice, but Jacobs avoids the reliance on deep reflectiveness that raises difficulties for Taylor, opting for a much more modest process of self-making choice. According to Jacobs, the choices and activities that establish my character need not be the product of careful reflection:

It need not be the enactment of an identification that I settle on after a critical assessment of my desires. I may be that sort of person because I have *not* undertaken that sort of assessment. That inattention, or, if you will, that sort of neglect of the ethical features of our dispositions, is not inattention or neglect that makes the states and the actions they give rise to less than voluntary. This is true of characteristics such as being submissive to authority, or resenting authority, aiming to ingratiate oneself, or being a person of one's word, among others, on a very long list. In exhibiting these characteristics we are typically acting voluntarily, and the entrenchment of these dispositions occurs largely through voluntary action. We have many policies and strategies of action and reaction for which we are responsible not by virtue of having legislated them, except in the thin sense of ratifying them by enactment. We do not determine practical identities for ourselves by each reasoning our way into one. Instead, as a result of habituation, circumstance, and natural temperament we accept certain sorts of desires and considerations as reasons, certain sorts of passions as apt, and we are able to deploy reason in order to work with those character contents with a view to acceptance, adjustment, or rejection. (2001, 120–121)

Something like that process is probably a reasonably accurate account of how our characters develop, but then the critical question is exactly how we "work with those character contents with a view to acceptance, adjustment, or rejection." If it is not through some power of reflection that transcends our characters and conditioning, then the "acceptance, adjustment, or rejection" comes from the character formation that has occurred in our history, and those are the resources we bring to bear. If Louise and Martha are both arrogant and self-centered, and Louise accepts those character traits while Martha considers and rejects them, then we must examine why they had such different evaluations and engaged in such different processes. That is where the quest for a naturalistic explanation for moral responsibility for character must begin, not where it can legitimately conclude.

The Capacity for Self-Reform

One challenge for those who favor self-making as grounds for moral responsibility is that it is quite clear that sometimes people lack the capacity to improve or reform themselves: persons who are profoundly lazy or settled into alcohol abuse may not be able to make themselves either industrious or sober. The classic answer to that challenge was given by Aristotle, who claims they are still morally responsible because they made the earlier choices that shaped their incorrigibly lazy or drunken characters:

But perhaps a man is the kind of man not to take care. Still they are themselves by their slack lives responsible for becoming men of that kind, and men make themselves responsible for being unjust or self-indulgent, in the one case by cheating and in the other by spending their time in drinking bouts and the like; for it is activities exercised on particular objects that make the corresponding character. This is plain from the case of people training for any contest or action; they practice the activity the whole time. Now not to know that it is from the exercise of activities on particular objects that states of character are produced is the mark of a thoroughly senseless person. Again, it is irrational to suppose that a man who acts unjustly does not wish to be unjust or a man who acts self-indulgently to be self-indulgent. But if without being ignorant a man does the things which will make him unjust, he will be unjust voluntarily. Yet it does not follow that if he wishes he will cease to be unjust and will be just. For neither does the man who is ill become well on those terms. We may suppose a case in which a man is ill voluntarily, through living incontinently and disobeying his doctors. In that case it was then open to him not to be ill, but not now, when he has thrown away his chance, just as when you have let a stone go it is too late to recover it, but yet it was in your power to throw it, since the moving principle was in you. So, too, to the unjust and to the self-indulgent man it was open at the beginning not to become men of this kind, and so they are unjust and self-indulgent voluntarily, but now that they have become so it is not possible for them not to be so. (350 BC/1925, III.5)

Jonathan Jacobs adopts a similar defense of ascribing moral responsibility to the "ethically disabled agent" who lacks resources to act virtuously or reform: "Our views about the nature and acquisition of virtue and about the fixity of character go together in a way that relates the objectivity of ethical considerations to the fact that they are inaccessible to some agents. The inability of the ethically disabled agent to overcome that condition is not exclusively a matter of bad constitutive luck. It is something the agent has brought about and for which the agent bears ongoing responsibility" (2001, 80–81). And Daniel Dennett offers a plain statement of the same grounds for ascribing moral responsibility to persons of profoundly bad character: "Can they help being despicable? They *may* not be able to help it *now*, for they may be too far gone (like the drunk who is responsible for having made himself drunk), but . . . one can be as responsible for one's character as for any other artifact arising from one's past efforts" (1984, 167). So you can't make or remake yourself *now*, given your depraved or despicable character, but that character was made by you, and in its formative stages it was more malleable, and at that point you could have formed it differently, so you are to blame for this lousy artifact you produced.

George Sher offers a powerful critique of this Aristotle/Jacobs/Dennett argument:

An immature, unformed agent is unlikely either to know much about what he must do to become a good person or to care much about doing it. Thus, whether a child's character develops in the right way depends largely on whether he is lucky enough to receive a sound moral education. If he is not, we can hardly blame him for not seeking one out. Even when a child is able to do various things that would in fact result in his receiving the requisite moral instruction—even when, for example, it is within his power to study a simplified version of Aristotle's ethics or talk his way into a military academy—these are not steps that someone whose picture of the world is not yet formed, and who has had little experience or guidance, can reasonably be expected to take.

Thus, if someone whose character is now bad could ever reasonably have been expected to take steps to prevent his own corruption, the time at which this expectation was reasonable could not have come until after he had achieved a degree of maturity. However, by that time, the person's bad traits were already partly in place. . . . Thus, by the time a miscreant-in-training has already achieved a degree of maturity, the expectation that he will display the insight, flexibility, and persistence that are needed to arrest or reverse his incipient corruption may well be unreasonable. (2006, 54–55)

Sher is giving this argument not to challenge moral responsibility (in which he fervently believes), but as part of his effort to establish that even though one's bad traits may be outside of one's control, one can still deserve blame for those traits. Setting that aside (until chapter 9), consider Sher's argument that moving back to an earlier formative stage—before bad habits and bad character are firmly established—will *not* justify claims that the individual in question has special control over her development. Jacobs attempts to revive the Aristotelian line of argument that although we may not be able to change our established character, at an earlier stage, the individual may well have had sufficient control to shape her character along a different and more virtuous path by her own choices. And in the course of that argument, Jacobs considers an objection very similar to the argument given by Sher. Jacobs formulates that objection thus:

It could be objected that maybe *mature* agents can reason about policies of action and select ends and projects, but all of that activity is undertaken by a character *already* formed, over which the agent had very little control. Thus, the account may seem problematic in the following way: It holds that we are most responsible for our characters and the actions that flow from them at that time of life when character is most fixed and least susceptible to revision. But, earlier, when there is the *most* plasticity in our characters, and they are being formed, we are least able to exercise control over what dispositions we acquire because we are not yet critical, experience-informed practical reasoners. How can those claims be reconciled? How *can* we be responsible for our characters? (2001, 31)

Jacobs offers the following solution to that problem:

A person can have beliefs, values, motivational tendencies, and so forth, that is, characteristics, without those constituting a stable, established character. As a person matures, it is reasonable to expect more capacity for practical reasoning and evaluation of one's ends and motives, and more awareness of the influence of one's own actions on character. One is better able to see that what one does and the ways in which one is motivated make a difference to what sort of character is settled into. The account acknowledges the number and variety of influences at work in forming character. However, that formation is taking place in an agent who is increasingly able to make his own judgments, acknowledge his responsibility for his acts and their outcomes, and to consider and revise his motives and aims. There is no time during which the individual does not have characteristics, though there is a role for voluntariness with respect to the formation and content of mature character. (2001, 31–32)

Certainly it is true that a "person can have beliefs, values, motivational tendencies, and so forth, that is, characteristics, without those constituting a stable, established character." But how do we then proceed to that established character? Consider Isaac and Jeremiah, two individuals in their formative stages who later develop very different established characters. If they have different resources, then those weren't resources of their own making. If they have the same resources, but different subsequent environments and situations and influences, then those also are a matter of good or bad moral fortune. If different choices result from exactly the *same* resources and circumstances, then we have fallen into either the realm of luck or the realm of miracles, and neither offers much hope for naturalistic moral responsibility.

Someone might claim that this begs the question against moral responsibility, but the question here is whether *this* account can give grounds for moral responsibility within a naturalistic framework. Of course people choose, but they choose with different resources of chronic cognizing, different resources in self-efficacy, different experiences of the broadness of open possibilities, different temperaments. Jeremiah, at an early age, makes a better moral formative choice than does Isaac because Jeremiah has greater cognitive fortitude, or greater self-confidence, or broader experience. Robert Harris was a notoriously brutal and callous murderer, who kidnapped and murdered two sixteen-year-old boys and laughed about his crime. He made choices during his formative years; they were his own choices, from his own "characteristics," and they resulted in a deepening of those characteristics into a settled brutal character. The differences between the characteristics of Robert Harris (whose brutal childhood led to development of a brutal murderer) and the characteristics of a child from a loving and supportive family in a safe and caring environment are profound, and that makes them obvious, but the point is that if there is a difference in choices—and we are turning to neither miracles nor chance—then there must be (from the naturalistic perspective) a difference in history or characteristics or circumstances, and none of those are my choice. That difference in history doesn't mean that Robert Harris made no choices, but it does mean that he did not make choices of the sort that would justify moral responsibility. Or if he did, or if anyone does, there must be justification of that claim. The referral to the formative stage fails to provide that justification.

Jonathan Jacobs does a wonderful job with "ethical disability" and why such individuals are not outside the moral realm, though it may well be impossible for them to reform. But on the question of whether they could have shaped themselves differently at an earlier formative period, his argument is sketchy—indeed, it is almost nonexistent. And on the question of why even the severely "ethically disabled" can often still be held morally responsible, his argument has severe problems; indeed, it seems to carry the seeds of its own destruction within it. Consider the "severely ethically disabled" individual whom Jacobs describes so well. Jacobs does a marvelous job of showing that we can still make ethical evaluations of such an individual and still consider this individual rational, part of the moral community, and indeed a candidate for some reactive moral participant attitudes (Strawson 1962). But why should we regard this individual—who is incapable of reform or of acting differently—as morally responsible? It is because this individual can be a legitimate subject of moral evaluation and is thus "blameworthy" and morally responsible. But the conclusion does not follow from the premise. Granted that the incorrigible individual is a legitimate subject of moral evaluation, why should it follow that this individual deserves blame and should be held *morally responsible* for the misdeeds that flow from her own vile character?

One might suppose that at this point Jacobs would lean on the argument that the incorrigible individual "made herself" at some earlier formative stage, but in fact, Jacobs does not rely on this weak reed. Instead, he places the weight on the fact that we can make legitimate moral evaluations of the incorrigible individual. But the problems in that conclusion are evident. Consider an individual who is profoundly incorrigible and had no chance of escaping that terrible character: Robert Harris (Watson 1987b) is a clear example. By adulthood, he is surely morally incorrigible if anyone is (he murders two young men on a whim, then eats the hamburgers they had bought and laughs about it), and he shows no indication whatsoever of wishing to change his character. But Robert Harris's brutal character was forged by his almost unimaginably brutal childhood and adolescence. Harris is certainly morally vile, but it does not follow that he deserves blame or is morally responsible for his vicious nature. So from the fact that Harris is morally horrific and that we can legitimately describe Harris and his behavior as morally bad, it does not follow that Harris is morally responsible for his morally flawed character and acts. So if Jacobs is going to make a case for anyone being morally responsible for his character, he will have to rest that case on some claim that we really do "fashion ourselves" and that we do it through our own free choices. Certainly, we do, to some extent. But when we look carefully at those free choices, we see that they were shaped by forces that we did not control. And unless free deliberative choice has a power to transcend such causes—and Jacobs does not want to make such a claim, as that would undercut his claims concerning incorrigible but rational "ethically disabled" individuals—then it is difficult to see how moving the process back makes it any more effective as a support for moral responsibility; except that it makes it a bit hazier, and that is always an advantage when trying to justify claims of moral responsibility. (There is, or course, an ongoing debate concerning the power of rational deliberation to transcend past causal history, but that is a debate that has been often discussed, and regardless of what verdict non-naturalists might reach about that—for example, if humans have special mysterious miracle-working powers of reason, then transcending the causes that shaped us will be as easy as turning water into wine or transubstantiating wine into blood—for naturalists, reason can be quite wonderful, but it cannot embrace such transcendent powers.)

In sum, self-making fails as justification for moral responsibility. We do to some degree make ourselves, and we often make our own choices, which in turn may develop into habits and shape our formed character. Robert Harris, like all of us, makes choices, and Robert Harris made choices as a youth that were important elements in forming his brutal adult character. Likewise, Sean is a young person from a loving and supportive family who attends an excellent school and has every advantage that Harris so conspicuously lacked and who also made choices that were important in the shaping of his subsequent adult character. But their choices notwithstanding, it is difficult to imagine that anyone—other than, perhaps, one who supposes that we all possess the power of making miraculous first-cause transcendent choices that have no connection with our earlier cumulative shaping history—could suppose that the choices made by Robert and Sean can be a sound foundation for claims and ascriptions of moral responsibility. It would be like saying to Robert and Sean, at age eighteen, "Okay, your past histories don't matter, now we start even, and your current choices and behavior are up to you." The past is not so easily erased. Suppose Sean said, "*I* made good choices and became successful and virtuous, while Robert made bad choices and became horrific and vicious; therefore I justly deserve praise for my success, and Robert deserves blame for his vicious failure." That would be evidence of Sean's shallow and myopic arrogance, not of his wisdom. So whatever else we might say about the value of youthful choices, we cannot make them support moral responsibility. Even without the starkly contrasting cases of Robert and Sean, the point is a simple one: when I make my own choice—a choice that shapes my further character development—that choice is not made in a vacuum, nor is it the product of some miraculous power that transcends my causal and social and genetic history (at least naturalists cannot claim such transcendent choices). For the issue of moral responsibility, the key self-making question is whether it is fair to punish or reward for the results of choices that are themselves the product of vastly different conditions that ultimately were not the product of choice. Perhaps it is fair, but if so, those who champion moral responsibility have given no reason to believe that it is, and there is powerful evidence to show that it is not.

Murphy and Brown on Self-Choosing

Nancey Murphy and Warren S. Brown (2007) base their account of free will and moral responsibility on the uniquely human rational value choices that give us the freedom to choose our own paths and shape our own character. Murphy and Brown are thoroughly naturalistic in their approach, but they also insist that contemporary psychological and neurobiological naturalism is not a crude industrial model; instead, it involves the use of reason and evaluation and feedback mechanisms:

The one who is able to evaluate that which moves her to act . . . on the basis of reason . . . especially moral reasons . . . ; who is furthermore not unduly influenced by the judgment of others . . . nor prevented from acting according to that evaluation by weakness of will or overpowering emotions . . . is indeed an agent, the primary, top-down cause (agent causation) of her own actions. Our suggestion, then, is that free will be understood as being the primary cause of one's own actions; this is a holistic capacity of mature, self-reflective human organisms acting within suitable social contexts. (305)

Another element of the Murphy/Brown model is the power of "self-transcendence," which is the capacity to reevaluate one's values and goals in light of reflection on one's earlier acts and their effects and on the imagined future of such acts. Perhaps we don't engage in such self-transcendence on a regular basis (indeed, for most of us it may be quite rare), but it does happen, and (as Murphy and Brown emphasize) it is neither mysterious nor mystical.

Murphy and Brown offer an interesting model of someone who is acting freely, but they carry it too far, claiming, "There is no limit, other than lack of imagination, to the ability of the agent to transcend earlier conceptions" (2007, 258). But of course it is not only "lack of imagination" that limits such self-transcending abilities; there are also limits imposed by lack of cognitive fortitude (cognitive misers cannot suddenly decide to be chronic cognizers) or by lack of the necessary self-confidence to challenge comfortable beliefs and explore unknown and unsettling alternatives. A supportive community may provide the necessary support for such explorations, but a comfortable supportive community may, on the other hand, make it more difficult to genuinely challenge the basic set of beliefs one shares with that community. It is tempting to suppose that we all *could* engage in radical self-transcending at any time, challenging our deep values and goals, but supposing that we could do so assumes a power of cognitive fortitude with which few are equipped. And as psychologists note, it is in fact very difficult—and very *un*common—for people to genuinely consider alternatives to their values and goals (Haidt and Bjorklund 2008).

Murphy and Brown start from a natural model of human agency, but it begins to spin out of natural control when they describe it thus:

The important point is that it is not a linear process, since the feedback from the environment *and from the person's own higher-order evaluative processes* is constantly restructuring the structuring causes themselves. We have to imagine countless iterations of such causal loops, the consequence of which is that the structural causes are to a greater and greater extent the consequences of prior actions and *evaluations* of the organism. . . . The really interesting cases appear in conscious organisms, and especially in humans, whose imaginations and symbolic abilities allow them to imagine future scenarios, evaluate them, and shape their behavior accordingly. Language allows us to build up elaborate models of possible futures, which, along with finely modulated and flexible descriptions of motives, provide "final causes" for behavior. (2007, 290–291)

But the "final causes" of Murphy and Brown are far from final, in either Aristotle's or the contemporary sense of being ultimate. Why does Tamara self-modify more effectively than Veronica? Why does Tamara do so readily, but Veronica engages in such activities reluctantly, if at all? Why is Tamara's self-modification guided by careful deliberation, and Veronica's is slipshod and shallow? Certainly, we do shape ourselves, in important ways, but the shaping never transcends the causal history that set our starting points and structured the resources we bring to our own subsequent shaping. Murphy and Brown seem to think that if we "imagine countless iterations of such causal loops, the consequence of which is that the structural causes are to a greater and greater extent the consequences of prior actions and *evaluations* of the organism" (290), then we can ignore the fact that those prior actions and evaluations were shaped by capacities and causes and advantages and disadvantages—differences in starting resources and abilities—that resulted in very different "prior actions and evaluations," which in turn shaped differing subsequent actions and evaluations. "Veronica could always do a transcendent self-evaluation and decide that she is too shallow and that she should work to think more carefully and develop greater cognitive fortitude, more self-confidence, and greater willingness to honestly consider alternatives." But such an answer would abandon any pretense of being a naturalistic model, plunging headlong into self-creating powers that are true final causes and unbounded by natural history. That's not surprising: when a model of human agency asks us "to imagine countless iterations of such causal loops," we may suspect that the model is becoming unhinged from natural forces and flying off in the direction of mysterious moral responsibility.

So we do—by our own decisions and evaluations—play a very important role in shaping ourselves: we are ourselves part of the shaping process, not helpless pawns of fate. But the way the shaping proceeds (in accordance with our own values and choices) and its results can still be traced to initial differences in starting capacities and opportunities, together with differences in circumstances and situations, that were a matter of each agent's good or bad fortune. Thus if Luke shapes a better character than does

Matthew—because Luke started with better resources for subsequent shaping and decision-making and choosing, which resulted in better choices, which in their turn led to better choices, it is unfair to blame Matthew for the faulty character he shaped by his own choices.

Of course, it is always possible to ignore the inconvenient starting points and stipulate that intermediate choice-making is sufficient self-making to sustain claims and ascriptions of moral responsibility in our system. But then the questions are whether that system is fair and whether that system is desirable. And one thing that makes the moral responsibility system undesirable is its systematic blocking of deeper inquiry into the causes that shape our values and our behavior. Once we say that someone is morally responsible, then we stop looking at the details of the behavior—at cognitive fortitude and how it is shaped, at differences in self-efficacy, differences in circumstance and situation, differences in conception of locus-of-control, and differences in distant but vitally important starting points.

8 The Illusory Benefits of Moral Responsibility

When all else fails, the advocates of moral responsibility fall back on practical usefulness. As Daniel Dennett recommends: "Instead of investigating, endlessly, in an attempt to *discover* whether or not a particular trait is of someone's making—instead of trying to assay exactly to what degree a particular self is self-made—we simply *hold* people responsible for their conduct (within limits we take care not to examine too closely). And we are rewarded for adopting this strategy by the higher proportion of 'responsible' behavior we thereby inculcate" (1984, 164). Perhaps we can't give a satisfactory theoretical justification for moral responsibility, or answer all the theoretical arguments against it, but that shouldn't trouble us. We must maintain the system of moral responsibility and just deserts, because it *works*.

The pragmatic justification for moral responsibility goes back at least to Hume: "All laws being founded on rewards and punishments, it is supposed as a fundamental principle, that these motives have a regular and uniform influence on the mind, and both produce the good and prevent the evil actions" (1748/2000, 74). Moritz Schlick—giving credit to Hume—offers a more detailed pragmatic account:

Punishment is concerned only with the institution of causes, of *motives* of conduct, and this alone is its meaning. Punishment is an educative measure, and as such is a means to the formation of motives. . . .

Hence the question regarding responsibility is the question: Who, in a given case, is to be punished? Who is to be considered the true wrongdoer? The problem is not identical with that regarding the original instigator of the act; for the great-grandparents of the man, from whom he inherited his character, might in the end be the cause, or the statesmen who are responsible for his social milieu, and so forth. But the "doer" is the *one upon whom the motive must have acted* in order, with certainty, to have prevented the act (or called it forth, as the case may be).

Consideration of remote causes is of no help here, for in the first place their actual contribution cannot be determined, and in the second place they are generally out of reach. Rather, we must find the person in whom the decisive junction of causes lies. The question of who is responsible is the question concerning the *correct point of application of the motive*. And the important thing is that in this its meaning is completely exhausted: behind it there lurks no mysterious connection between transgression and requital, which is merely *indicated* by the described state of affairs. It is a matter only of knowing who is to be punished or rewarded, in order that punishment and reward function as such—be able to achieve their goal. (1939, 152–153)

Manuel Vargas justifies his revisionist defense of moral responsibility by appeal to the practical benefits of the moral responsibility system: "The responsibility-characteristic practices, attitudes, and judgments are justified inasmuch as they, on the whole and over time, tend to contribute to our better perceiving and appropriately responding to moral considerations. . . . Since they are reasonably effective at doing this, it is plausible to think that the responsibility system is by and large justified" (2007, 155–156). But the clearest statement of that pragmatic justification is offered by J. J. C. Smart:

When in a moral context we say that a man could have or could not have done something we are concerned with the ascription of responsibility. What is it to ascribe responsibility? Suppose Tommy at school does not do his homework. If the schoolmaster thinks that this is because Tommy is really stupid, then it is silly for him to abuse Tommy, to cane him or to threaten him. This would be sensible only if it were the case that this sort of treatment made stupid boys intelligent. . . . The schoolmaster says, then, that Tommy is not to blame, he just *could not* have done his homework. Now suppose that the reason why Tommy did not do his homework is that he was lazy. . . . In such a case the schoolmaster will hold Tommy responsible, and he will say that Tommy could have done his homework. By this he will not necessarily mean to deny that Tommy's behaviour was the outcome of heredity and environment. . . . If Tommy is sufficiently stupid, then it does not matter whether he is exposed to temptation or not exposed to temptation, cajoled or not cajoled. When his negligence is found out, he is not made less likely to repeat it by threats, promises, or punishments. On the other hand, the lazy boy can be influenced in such ways. Whether he does his homework or not is perhaps solely the outcome of the environment, but one part of the environment is the threatening schoolmaster.

Threats and promises, punishments and rewards, the ascription of responsibility and the nonascription of responsibility, have therefore a clear pragmatic justification which is quite consistent with a wholehearted belief in metaphysical determinism. (1961, 302)

Smart offered his pragmatic justification of moral responsibility—and reward and punishment—half a century ago. At that time, our knowledge of human behavior and its causes and shaping was much more limited (and the limits were even greater when Schlick was writing, not to mention Hume). Reward and punishment works, although not very well—indeed, it often does more harm than good—but it works better than nothing. And because for many millennia, reward and punishment (in accordance with the principles of moral responsibility) were the only alternative to doing nothing, our commitment to "justly deserved" reward and retributive punishment became deeply entrenched. Indeed, if we accept the observations of primatologists (de Waal 1982), we must conclude that patterns of reward and punishment (roughly along the lines dictated by moral responsibility) were probably present in our simian ancestors, as they are in our chimpanzee cousins. Thus when an individual does something beneficial or virtuous, we are inclined to reward or reciprocate, and when an individual does something harmful or vicious, we desire to punish or strike back. That very crude means of social control and behavior shaping met with some success, ultimately becoming a deeply entrenched inclination (especially the retributive strike back response); thus when it was not effective or even counterproductive—as caning the stupid boy invariably is, and as caning the lazy boy is very likely to be—the punitive schoolmaster received satisfaction by meting out the "deserved" punishment. Thus the moral responsibility model of reward and punishment became even more firmly fixed. Some obvious problems with "strikeback retributivism" were noted earlier: the target is often an innocent bystander or a spouse or a child (or a "witch"), rather than the source of harm. But the problems with the pragmatic justification of the reward and punishment model of moral responsibility run much deeper and broader. Perhaps that model works better than nothing (which is why it is so deeply entrenched in our society and our psyches), but still it works very badly, it is often more harmful than beneficial, it blocks better policies and deeper understanding, and—its benefits and detriments aside—it is fundamentally unfair.

Why Moral Responsibility Rewards and Punishments Do Not Work Well

When we reward and punish in accordance with just deserts and moral responsibility standards, we sometimes achieve positive results. Rewarding the bright, hard-working, highly successful, and strongly motivated student will sometimes sustain high levels of effort and achievement. However, the traditional pattern of reward and punishment—the pattern dictated by the moral responsibility model—is often ineffectual and sometimes severely detrimental. Consider two students, brilliant Jill and mediocre Laura. Both work hard, but Laura's best efforts still fall significantly short of Jill's accomplishments, and Jill consistently receives the justly deserved rewards while Laura receives few if any. Jill continues to work hard as her efforts are consistently reinforced, but Laura's academic efforts are gradually extinguished. And of course Jill occasionally turns in a subpar effort—but her less-than-optimum work is still far superior to Laura's best, and Jill is rewarded even when she does not do her best work; after all, Jill's work was still much better, and thus more deserving of reward. As a result, Jill may also become rather lazy; at the very least, the just deserts model will not effectively promote Jill's best efforts and best work.

If we become slightly more sophisticated—to the level of Smart's schoolmaster—and focus our rewards and punishments on effort, that will be a modest improvement, but it will still have severe problems, and there will remain many cases in which it causes more harm than benefit. Suppose that Jill is industrious and Laura is lazy (which is not difficult to imagine: as already noted, bright Jill's efforts are likely to be positively reinforced while dull Laura's efforts are ignored and eventually extinguished). If we reward (in accordance with just deserts) on the basis of effort, we will fail to shape even stronger efforts in Jill, and Laura's lethargy will become entrenched. For instance, suppose that one day Jill makes a subpar effort, and Laura's efforts rise well above her low norm. Jill's subpar efforts are still significantly greater than Laura's best, so Jill still deserves reward, yet Laura's (still mediocre) efforts do not. In this manner, Jill's weakest efforts are likely to be encouraged/reinforced, and Laura's stabs at making an effort are extinguished. Under such conditions, Laura may eventually reach the level of "learned helplessness," in which exerting effort becomes impossible.

Recall Martin Seligman's (1975) experiment in which dogs were repeatedly placed in a restraining harness and subjected to painful inescapable shocks. After several such cruel sessions, the dogs were then placed in a shuttle box: a box with an electrified floor grid on one side and a low barrier blocking access to the adjoining shock-free compartment. Dogs that had not been subjected to inescapable shock quickly leaped over the barrier when shocked, but the dogs that had experienced repeated inescapable shock—and had developed profound learned helplessness—made no effort to escape the shock, quickly giving up and cowering. Under the moral responsibility model, the individual who has been reduced to learned helplessness is the perfect candidate for neglect at best and punitive measures at worst. She "won't even try" to help herself, so why should anyone try to help her? She is also the perfect candidate for punishment from Smart's "enlightened" schoolmaster, who spares the stupid but beats the lazy. But that approach not only adds another episode of cruelty to the helpless individual, but is also counterproductive. When Seligman's dogs experienced more shocks, it did not motivate them to leap the barrier; rather, it made them even more profoundly helpless. When the profoundly lethargic boy is beaten by the schoolmaster, the learned helplessness is deepened, not corrected. When the abused woman is abandoned and later abused by a second partner, that does not make her more likely to escape, but more likely to give up and continue giving up. Blaming her is easy, but it is neither effective nor fair. Helping her overcome learned helplessness is not easy: Seligman's dogs had to be pushed across the shuttle barrier many times before they would attempt it on their own. The student who won't try is frustrating; the satisfaction in beating such a student is real; the temptation to abandon such a student is profound ("I'm not wasting my time with someone who won't even try"). It requires a significant understanding of the deeper causes to overcome such temptations and adopt effective methods. The first step in helping the lazy student and the abused woman is recognizing the causal history that shaped them and the problems caused by that harsh history; unfortunately, the widespread allegiance to moral responsibility impedes such inquiry and recognition.

There is some benefit to the practice of rewarding and punishing in accordance with good and bad behavior, and there is some benefit to rewarding and punishing along the lines of moral responsibility and just deserts; unfortunately, there is just enough benefit to hold the practices in place. That is unfortunate, because—their limited and occasional benefits notwithstanding—those patterns and practices often have very harmful results: the extinction of the less energetic student's efforts and the entrenchment of learned helplessness are among the obvious examples. It is doubly unfortunate, because without the blinders of the moral responsibility system, we could look more carefully at patterns of positive reinforcement that would be more effective in shaping desirable character and behavior while avoiding the harmful effects of the moral responsibility system. That is the main problem with allegiance to moral responsibility: maintaining belief in moral responsibility requires that we "not look too closely," that we not scrutinize the details of the individual's causal and environmental history, and that we ignore significant differences in abilities and capacities. The importance of looking closely at differences in abilities is obvious: Joe is minimally competent, but he is severely limited in sense of positive self-efficacy. Recognizing that fact encourages development of programs that would empower Joe to overcome that serious deficiency; ignoring it—and just "holding Joe responsible"—makes things worse.

The Genuine Need for "Reward"

The benefit from rewarding and punishing (in accordance with moral responsibility principles) is that it is important that behavior be connected with results. Long-term sustained efforts do require positive results to avoid the decaying of effort, and when the environment is such that positive behavior is rewarded, then positive behavior becomes more frequent. This is an area studied carefully and insightfully by psychologists, but it is not some esoteric element of psychological theorizing; rather, the psychological theories and studies confirm and expand and add depth and detail to what every thoughtful and observant person has long recognized: behavior that is unconnected with effects is not strengthened and tends to wither away (ignoring a child's tantrums is a good way of reducing the number of tantrums; "giving in" to the tantrums produces the opposite effect). And when "rewards" are not associated with efforts, they tend to disrupt positive behavior: the young person who has been "given everything" with no effort suffers almost as much psychological damage as the person whose efforts never produce beneficial results. The "spoiled rich kid" whose father lavishes upon the lazy child "all the things I never had and worked so hard to obtain" winds up frustrated and lethargic and depressed; the lottery winner—whose sudden fortune bears no relation to effort—is more likely to find misery than happiness. All of this is common knowledge, but we can understand the details much better and eliminate the misunderstandings that plague us if we look carefully and in detail at how behavior and character develop and the vital differences among people. It is precisely such careful analysis that moral responsibility beliefs prevent. So it is important that our behavior be connected with results. But the optimum pattern of connection is not the one guided by moral responsibility; in fact, the best pattern often runs directly counter to the pattern prescribed by moral responsibility judgments (Waller 1989).

There is a grain of truth in the pragmatic justification for moral responsibility—a grain of truth that has unfortunately entrenched moral responsibility practices. The grain of truth is that reward—or better, positive reinforcement—*is* valuable; the problem is that the reward and reinforcement schedules that are genuinely valuable do not fit the moral responsibility model. As already noted, punitive measures are seldom efficient and often disastrous. But rewards—though considerably more valuable than punishments—are badly dispensed if we follow the moral responsibility model. Too often, such patterns shape laziness rather than industry and fortitude. This result is easily overlooked by philosophers, as those who are writing and reading philosophy are among those lucky enough to have avoided the often unfortunate effects of traditional patterns of reward and punishment. Typically, we started with advantages—very early childhood education, strong family support—that resulted in more early rewards, and that pattern of reinforcement shaped strong work habits. Not optimum work habits, certainly, as most of us would acknowledge, but not severe lethargy, either. So positive reinforcement and reward is valuable—and even essential—but it is also essential that such rewards occur in a favorable pattern, in the appropriate relation to our efforts and accomplishments. Indiscriminate positive reinforcement can be almost as destructive as absence of positive reinforcement. If there is no systematic relationship between successful efforts and positive reinforcement—reward or reinforcement is received when one has done nothing—then lethargic purposeless destructive behavior is shaped. But efforts that consistently yield no positive results—no positive reinforcement—also result in lethargy, as effort is extinguished.

This account may sound as if good efforts should be rewarded and substandard efforts should be deprived of reward; that is, it may sound as if the optimum, practical reward pattern is one that matches the guidelines of moral responsibility. But any similarities with the moral responsibility model of punishment and reward are superficial, and the differences are vital. Recall the case of Jill and Laura. Jill—who is brilliant and industrious—makes a significant effort and writes a solid paper, but her effort is well below her usual standard and the resulting paper is quite mediocre by her standards. Laura—who is comparatively dull and lethargic—exerts a (for her) heroic effort and writes a paper that is one of her very best. Jill's effort is still significantly greater than Laura's, and her paper is far superior. By moral responsibility standards (whether they track accomplishment or effort), Jill deserves greater reward than Laura, but such a reward pattern would encourage Jill's slide backward, while failing to support Laura's mild but improved efforts. Pulling someone out of lethargy will require a steadier and more frequent pattern of reinforcement than will sustaining high-quality effortful behavior (though the latter is more justly deserving of reward, by moral responsibility lights). So what pattern of reward and reinforcement works best and avoids harm? Certainly, it is not one in accordance with moral responsibility; rather, it is one that carefully examines the history and the abilities of the individual (a careful examination that commitment to moral responsibility blocks), recognizes the strengths and the problems of individuals, utilizes patterns of reinforcement that sustain our best and most talented efforts, fosters the abilities and energies of those who are weaker in ability and fortitude, and supports the recovery of those unfortunates who have fallen into deep learned helplessness. Following such a pattern will mean that the most energetic and capable individual will sometimes receive less reward (positive reinforcement) than does the profoundly lethargic individual who exerts a very small stumbling effort.

Answering Outrage

At this point, it is necessary to pause for a moment to allow for outraged objections from the hard-working philosophers industriously examining this argument: "Do you honestly claim that the lazy bums who never do any work deserve a bigger reward than I get for my diligent and productive efforts?" No; the lazy do not deserve greater reward than the industrious. The claim is that just deserts and moral responsibility are atavistic remainders from the age of mysteries and miracles, and contemporary naturalists should eliminate them altogether. But there are times when it is beneficial to reward (reinforce) the very small efforts of the profoundly lethargic and to reward them more frequently than the much more energetic sustained efforts of the industrious. Careful examination of the histories and capacities of both the lethargic and the diligent, combined with informed understanding of the optimum methods of sustaining strong efforts and remedying lethargy and learned helplessness, will result in policies that are very different from (and much more effective than) those endorsed by the moral responsibility system.

It is not surprising that those who were nurtured by the moral responsibility system (and who have been rewarded by that system, though not as effectively as they would have been in the alternative system) would be outraged by the proposed rejection of that system, but in this case there is an additional source of that outrage. The notion that the lethargic should receive greater or more frequent "reward" (reinforcement) for their clumsy small efforts—greater reward than that received by the vigorously and consistently industrious—seems outrageous. It seems outrageous because there is a sense that the lethargic already receive their reward: the reward of lethargic leisure, which the industrious forgo. "How can that be fair?" an industrious philosopher might object. "They get the joys of layabout sleep-in lethargy, and then on top of that their slighter efforts get greater reward. It's doubly unfair."

A moment's careful reflection shows the fundamental falsity of that objection. Rest and relaxation after hard work is satisfying and rewarding, but such restorative relaxation should not be confused with deep lethargy, which is more commonly associated with depression than joy. Almost all of us have memories of times when it was especially difficult to work, times when it was hard to get started, hard to get out of bed, hard to exert effort: times when we felt deeply lethargic and accomplished nothing. Those are not pleasant memories, and they have nothing in common with the delightful weekend at the beach following long and exhausting but very satisfying work on a dissertation or book or paper. Lethargy is not its own reward; to the contrary, it is a state that is highly correlated with depression. In contrast, sustained hard work—and the psychological capacity to carry it out—is typically very satisfying in itself, and the direct results from that work (a new insight, a clearer grasp of a fascinating problem, a solution that makes everything fall into place) are especially satisfying. Think of the times when you were working with the greatest energy and fortitude, and contrast those with your periods of comparative lethargy; you don't require psychological studies to know which is the most enjoyable and inherently rewarding.

Beyond Individualism

The claim of pragmatic benefits from moral responsibility runs aground on the fact that the model of reward and punishment it proposes is not optimally effective; indeed, it doesn't come close to the optimum, and even the limited benefits it produces are purchased at the price of significant harms. But there is a second problem with the pragmatic case for moral responsibility. The moral responsibility system focuses attention in the wrong direction—on the individual rather than on the conditions that shaped the individual and the situation in which the individual acts—and thus blocks consideration of potentially beneficial broader policies.

There is a common theme in the pragmatist justifications of moral responsibility offered by Hume, Schlick, Smart, and Dennett: focus on the individual (don't look at the parents, don't look at the past, don't look at the system). And that is the fundamental problem with any pragmatic approach to moral responsibility: it ignores larger causes, and even in its study of individuals, it is adamantly shallow. Recall the passage in which Schlick focuses responsibility on the individual who does wrong: "Consideration of remote causes is of no help here, for in the first place their actual contribution cannot be determined, and in the second place they are generally out of reach. Rather, we must find the person in whom the decisive junction of causes lies. The question of who is responsible is the question concerning the *correct point of application of the motive*" (1939, 153). Narrow focus on the individual malefactor makes it impossible to understand the fundamental problems. Restricting attention to the individual wrongdoer—and inflicting punishment to change his character and behavior—is like supposing that the best way to deal with an epidemic is to concentrate exclusively on the sick individuals and ignore the systemic problems (such as environmental toxins or unsanitary drinking water or plague-carrying rats) that are the root cause of the problem. Perhaps we can focus attention on the suffering patient and find treatments that will heal him, but we will be more effective if we seek out and change the larger systemic causes that are the source of illness. If we are faced with lazy college students (or negligent physicians or unscrupulous bankers), it is important to look deeper: what is wrong with the early childhood education process that saps student cognitive fortitude, or destroys their confidence in their own academic self-efficacy, or stifles their curiosity? Until we take this deeper look, we may manage to academically invigorate and motivate a few individuals, but we will make little or no progress toward solving the bigger problem. It's easier to blame the student sitting in front of us, but that will not deal with the larger difficulty. And even when we do focus on helping the individual, thinking in terms of blame and just deserts will be counterproductive: in order to maintain belief in blame, we must avoid looking carefully at the detailed character and causal history of that individual (and the individual's history may be essential to understanding the current character and abilities of the individual). Thus—like Smart—we blame the lazy boy, but because we fail to look closely at the boy who "just won't try," we fail to appreciate that he has suffered a long string of failed efforts, that he has very limited cognitive fortitude resources, and that he has almost no self-confidence (sense of self-efficacy) in his ability to do the required work. Precisely such careful scrutiny—which allegiance to moral responsibility blocks—is essential to the difficult process of shaping greater self-confidence and stronger cognitive fortitude in the unfortunate student. Blaming and punishing is easier (and more self-righteously satisfying), which explains why it remains popular, its history of failure and minimal success notwithstanding.

Moral responsibility focuses attention on the immediate behavior and tends to ignore—and even insists on ignoring—the causal history or the deeper characteristics of the individual, as well as avoiding consideration of larger systemic causes; as a result, it neglects the most effective ways of improving behavior and shaping character. But there is another way in which the moral responsibility narrow focus on individual behavior results in harm rather than benefits: it blocks our understanding of the key *situational* controlling factors for much of our behavior, and those controlling factors—though frequently invisible and often denied—exert a powerful influence on our choices. It seems obvious to us that finding a dime would have no effect on our subsequent behavior: it would not make us more likely to stop and help someone who had dropped books and papers. But a famous experiment by Isen and Levin (1972) demonstrates the falsity of that "obvious" fact. Of sixteen experimental subjects who found a dime, fourteen stopped to help; of twenty-five subjects who did not find a dime, only one stopped to help. Surely being instructed to hurry across campus to complete a task would not prevent anyone from stopping to help a person slumped on the ground and obviously in distress, but an experiment by Darley and Batson (1973) found that when not told to hurry, 63 percent of subjects stopped to help, and only 10 percent of those told to hurry offered help. It seems incredible that peaceful and decent Stanford students who were placed in the situation of "prison guards" would become brutal and sadistic (Haney, Banks, and Zimbardo 1973) or that two-thirds of people would administer severely painful or even lethal shocks to a stranger just because a lab-coated experimenter told them to proceed (Milgram 1963), but that's what happened. Under the influence of moral responsibility, we focus on the student "guard" who brutally mistreated "prisoners" and blame and punish him. That's the end of the story, no further inquiry is permitted, the problem is regarded as solved: we "find the person in whom the decisive junction of causes lies," assign the sanctions to that individual, and the issue is closed. But the extensive body of situationist psychological research has demonstrated that focus on individual behavior ignores the critical influence of the situation in which the person acted. When we focus on and blame and punish the prison guards—whether in the Stanford experiment, or the county jail, or Angola, or Abu Ghraib—we ignore and leave intact an environment that continues to produce brutal behavior. This is not to deny that the development of individual character is important, but larger situational causal factors are also significant. We overestimate the importance of individual character to behavioral outcome, and underestimate the impact of situational/environmental influences: it is such a common mistake that social psychologists have named it the *fundamental attribution error* (Ross 1977). Under the baleful influence of moral responsibility, we get the fundamental attribution error on steroids.

Dennett's "Creeping Exculpation"

The contemporary philosopher most deeply devoted to the pragmatic justification of moral responsibility, and to maintaining the focus on the morally responsible individual (rather than the individual's situation or behavioral history) is Daniel Dennett, who warns against the dangers of "creeping exculpation" (1984, 156; 2003, 289). As psychology and biology teach us more about the complex and subtle causes of our characters and capacities and behavior, there is a danger we will excuse more behavior that we previously thought of as our own free morally responsible acts. Excuses encompass a greater part of our lives until they swallow up both our moral responsibility and our free selves. As we learn more about the causes of our behavior and how our characters were shaped, there is— Dennett claims—a tendency and temptation to "make ourselves really small" until there is nothing for which we are really responsible and nothing that comes from our own character and our own free acts. To avoid "creeping exculpation," we must keep the focus tightly on the individual, not on the situation or the history or the external causes: "Since there will always be strong temptations to make yourself really small, to externalize the causes of your actions and deny responsibility, the way to counteract these is to make people an offer they can't refuse: If you want to be free, you must *take* responsibility" (Dennett 2003, 292).

So to avoid creeping exculpation and claim your freedom, you must take responsibility for your acts—and because the responsibility buck stops with you, neither the history that shaped your range of abilities nor the situation that strongly influences your behavior can be considered.

Dennett's picture of the bad effects of denying moral responsibility is wrong on two basic points. First, rather than starting from an assumption of moral responsibility and chipping away at it with excuses, moral responsibility abolitionists argue that no one—no matter how skilled, reasonable, self-motivated, self-controlled, and flawless—is ever morally responsible, because moral responsibility has no place in our naturalistic world view. Dennett refers with approval to what he calls the *default responsibility principle*: "If no one *else* is responsible for your being in state A, you are" (2003, 281). If we start from the assumption that everyone is morally responsible and excuse them only when there is clear indication of debilitating flaws or someone else to blame, then "creeping exculpation" does indeed look scary: complete denial of our moral responsibility must be based on our utter incompetence. But that is a false model of the naturalistic denial of moral responsibility: such denial is not an *excuse-extensionist* model (Waller 2006) in which we start from moral responsibility and gradually erode it away through excuses; rather, it starts from the claim that we cannot make sense of moral responsibility within a naturalistic framework. Because there is no moral responsibility, there is no exculpation—creeping, crawling, or cantering—from moral responsibility. This issue is taken up in more detail in chapter 11.

The second mistake of the "creeping exculpation makes us small" peril is the claim that denial of moral responsibility makes us small and insignificant. We make ourselves so small that all causal factors are outside of us: "there will always be strong temptations to make yourself really small, to externalize the causes of your actions and deny responsibility" (Dennett 2003, 292). But the moral responsibility abolitionist is not *making* small, but *viewing* small—that is, viewing the small but significant detailed differences in our capacities that the moral responsibility advocate ignores. Recognizing those differing capacities and the processes that shaped them doesn't make you small, unless "making you small" means making you mortal and natural rather than godlike. Dennett imagines that denying moral responsibility would make us small because he confuses moral responsibility with take-charge responsibility (described in chapter 6): when you can't make choices, exercise control, take charge, that does make you small. But looking small—viewing small, looking at details, studying subtle differences in abilities and how they were caused—does not make us small. To the contrary, viewing small empowers us: by studying the critically important details that the moral responsibility advocate ignores, we learn how to shape ourselves so that we can better exercise control and increase our confidence in taking control. (We aren't morally responsible for wanting to engage in such study or for having or lacking the capacity to carry it out, but that lack of responsibility in no way diminishes the importance of the study or the psychological benefits of having these important control capacities.)

Studying why you act as you do—your resources, as well as the history of their development—does not "externalize the causes of your actions"; when you act skillfully, it is really your own act, not chance. Rather than externalizing, this perspective emphasizes the importance of changing and improving and strengthening character and sense of self-efficacy and fortitude. It rejects the idea that people deserve blame when they have fewer resources and deserve special reward when they have more (it rejects moral responsibility), but it emphasizes—rather than denies or neglects—the importance of strengthening and sustaining take-charge responsibility. Tiger Woods consistently wins golf tournaments because Woods is a superb golfer with wonderful skills, remarkable confidence, and tremendous fortitude. (And there is nothing in the denial of Woods's moral responsibility to suggest that we should handicap Woods until every duffer has an equal opportunity to win the British Open.) Of course there are causes for why Tiger Woods is a superb golfer, but none of those causes lessen the fact that he really is superb, and that he wins golf tournaments as a result of his own efforts and ability and practice. So denial of moral responsibility is not "making yourself small"; rather, it is *observing* small—studying the details and scrutinizing the critically important factors that result in differences of behavior. If you do not "observe small"—if you confine yourself to shallow observation of immediate behavior—then it is easy to suppose that Ann and Barbara have the same capacities, so when Ann acts virtuously and Barbara acts viciously, they both had equal opportunity to act well and thus both justly deserve punishment or reward for their acts. Carefully examining the details undermines moral responsibility, but does not reduce the size or importance of the individual observed.

When we learn more about situationist psychology—about the powerful impact of unrecognized situational factors on our choices and behavior—in one sense, that does make us somewhat "smaller": we learn that our behavior is not as exclusively the product of our own characters as we might have thought. But rather than the futile denial of that fact—and a desperate attempt to avoid "making ourselves small"—it is better to note that fact and to consider carefully how we can design our environments and the situations we face in order to maximize desirable behavior. And although situationist psychological research teaches us that situations have greater influence than we had imagined, that influence does not imply that our characters and histories are irrelevant. Julia and Kate work in a very similar situation as logic professors at State University. Both teach similar classes to similar students, but Julia is an energetic and effective logic teacher and Kate is rather lethargic and dull; Julia is a brilliant logician and Kate is merely competent; Julia is friendly and outgoing with her colleagues and Kate is rather reserved and private; Julia spends her leisure time playing tennis and Kate's leisure is devoted to writing poetry. The fact that their situations often have a profound impact on their behavior does not imply that they do not have distinctive characters and capacities. Denying moral responsibility does not make us small and certainly does not make us insignificant, but it does push us to broaden our perspectives.

In particular, it encourages a deeper and wider perspective than the narrow concentration on immediate behavior required to sustain belief in moral responsibility.

Contemporary medical science has devised better ways of treating cancer, so many who would have died swiftly from cancer now live additional years, and in many cases, treatments produce a full cure. Such treatments are wonderful, and are rightly celebrated. But one environmentalist—disturbed by the rapidly increasing cancer rate that is produced by the problem of increasing environmental pollution—compared our situation to one in which an ever-increasing number of cars are plunging off a cliff and we are becoming better and better at treating those who are injured in the crash, but we do little or nothing to stop cars from going over the cliff. That analogy is only half true when we consider moral responsibility: by focusing on the individual rather than the systemic causes, we do nothing to change the processes (substandard schools, ghettoized housing patterns, lack of employment opportunities, dysfunctional families, domestic violence) that produce flawed individuals; unfortunately, moral responsibility also prevents us from taking effective measures to help the individuals who have been badly misshapen by those forces.

Moral Responsibility Pragmatism

There is a powerful tendency to believe that the moral responsibility pattern works: it is supported by social institutions such as law and religion, it is deeply entrenched, and it is psychologically satisfying in the short term (immediately reinforcing) for those who reward and punish. But that powerful tendency notwithstanding, the moral responsibility system is not efficient—it is only marginally effective (and often causes great harm), it blocks understanding, it impedes the development of better models, and it is grossly unfair. But the pragmatic case for moral responsibility remains popular among contemporary philosophers, even among philosophers very knowledgeable concerning contemporary psychological processes who nevertheless seem to place that knowledge on hold when they offer pragmatic justifications for moral responsibility. Obviously, Hume didn't have such research available to him, and it was not widely known among philosophers when Smart developed his pragmatic justification. Dennett, however, certainly does have knowledge of such research, and one element of his pragmatic justification involves resolutely turning a blind eye to such knowledge and refusing to consider it in the context of moral responsibility. When pushed into a theoretical corner, Daniel Dennett dismisses the theoretical problems, and stakes his case for moral responsibility on its practical benefits:

Why then do we want to hold people—ourselves included—responsible? "By holding someone responsible and acting accordingly, we may cause him to shed an undesirable trait, and this is useful regardless of whether the trait is of his making" (Gomberg 1978, 208). Once again, the utility of a certain measure of arbitrariness is made visible. Instead of investigating, endlessly, in an attempt to *discover* whether or not a particular trait is of someone's making—instead of trying to assay exactly to what degree a particular trait is self-made—we simply *hold* people responsible for their conduct (within limits we take care not to examine too closely). And we are rewarded for adopting this strategy by the higher proportion of "responsible" behavior we thereby inculcate. (1984, 163–164)

As already noted, under the right circumstances—when people have adequate preparation, confidence, and sense of self-efficacy—the opportunity to take and exercise take-charge responsibility is beneficial: people enjoy the sense of being in control and making their own decisions, and by taking such responsibility, they often become better at it as they become more confident and more practiced. But as valuable as such take-charge responsibility is, holding people morally responsible (as recommended by Dennett and Gomberg) is not useful; to the contrary, it typically causes more harm than good, and it blocks the understanding of genuinely effective policies. The key to the problem is in the very process that Dennett recommends: "Instead of investigating" we simply hold people responsible, and we do so "within limits we take care not to investigate too closely." That is, we simply hold people responsible, rather than investigating deeper causes. But that's precisely the problem with holding people morally responsible: it not only operates instead of deeper investigation, but it also precludes careful, deep investigation. When we "simply hold people responsible," we don't check to see whether they have the capacity to successfully exercise (take-charge) responsibility, we neglect the resources that foster the capacity, and—when they fail—we blame them. Blaming them is much simpler and easier than looking deeper into the causes for why they failed and working to change those causes. Refusing to look closely is tempting, but like many temptations, the long-term effects are harmful. When we look closely, we can understand the causes, the circumstances under which one can effectively take responsibility, and the problems that lead to failures; when we look closely, the grounds for "holding people responsible" disappear. The lazy boy really is lazy, but after careful scrutiny, we recognize that "simply holding him responsible" won't work, and "simply holding him responsible" is fundamentally unfair and unjust.

The key problem is that moral responsibility practices block inquiry and militate against understanding (the first step toward changing) the deeply lethargic individual who suffers from learned helplessness or perhaps a severely stunted sense of self-efficacy. "You can always *try* harder": for some miracle-loving libertarians, that statement is an article of faith, but for naturalists who rely on psychological studies rather than miraculous powers, it is clearly false, and it is a false belief that causes enormous damage. As naturalists, we need to study the causal history that shaped degrees of energy or lethargy and levels of self-confidence and self-efficacy, and through understanding those essential details we can find ways to enhance fortitude and prevent deep lethargy (and help those who suffer from it).

It is disappointing when a psychologically sophisticated naturalist like Daniel Dennett recommends that we *not* look too closely, that we "simply hold people responsible for their conduct (within limits we take care not to examine too closely)" rather than carefully study their causal history. It is true that sometimes "we are rewarded for adopting this strategy by the higher proportion of 'responsible'" behavior we thereby inculcate," and indeed the sporadic success of the moral responsibility strategy is a major factor in its stubborn endurance. But such a strategy also causes terrible harm, and it is not as effective as a strategy that rejects moral responsibility patterns. But that insistence on not looking closely is a measure of the stubborn grip of moral responsibility: it cannot survive close causal scrutiny, so its advocates—rather than jettisoning the marginally useful but long-obsolete model of moral responsibility—instead draw careful limits on inquiry.

Dennett writes, "Skepticism about the very possibility of culpability arises from a misplaced reverence for an absolutist ideal: the concept of total, before-the-eyes-of-God guilt. The fact that *that* condition is never to be met in this world should not mislead us into skepticism about the integrity of our institution of moral responsibility" (1984, 165). Rather than "a misplaced reverence for an absolutist ideal," the naturalistic skeptics concerning culpability and moral responsibility have a "reverence" for unlimited inquiry into deeper causes: an inquiry that undercuts claims that the moral responsibility system is fair as well as claims that the moral responsibility system is effective. Consider the moral responsibility abolitionist's insistence on deep, detailed study of causal history and psychological conditioning, and compare it with the moral responsibility advocate's refusal to look closely (in order to maintain the cherished system of moral responsibility), and then decide which one exhibits "a misplaced reverence for an absolutist ideal."

The Impracticality of Moral Responsibility

Arguments for the moral responsibility system come in a variety of shapes and sizes: arguments that we have special powers of will or rationality that make us morally responsible; arguments that we must save moral responsibility in order to preserve ethics; arguments that we are morally responsible because we take responsibility, or that we are morally responsible because we are self-made. Philosophers offer these and other arguments with many fascinating variations and interesting twists. Many of the arguments are remarkably inventive and genuinely fascinating, and attempting to answer them poses daunting philosophical challenges. But the pragmatic argument for moral responsibility falls into a different category. It is almost embarrassing—given the rich development of contemporary psychological and sociological and criminological and biological studies—to be arguing that the moral responsibility model, with its baggage of blame and retribution, is not the optimum model for shaping either effective individual behavior or positive social policies, and that the moral responsibility approach in fact does considerably more harm than good. That is not to say that it does not have enormous influence over us and a strong hold on us, but that unfortunate power is not an argument for the effectiveness of moral responsibility. Instead, it explains the continued popular and philosophical allegiance to a system that is obviously and deeply flawed.

Though contemporary scientific research affords abundant evidence of the shortcomings of the moral responsibility system, the most glaring evidence of that failure—which shines through even the most severe case of moral responsibility myopia—can be found in our system of retributive criminal justice. The United States has the most consistently retributive system of "justice" of any Western industrialized country—with brutal prison conditions, an incarceration rate many times that of other Western democracies, "three strikes" policies of extremely long-term incarceration, psychologically debilitating Supermax prisons, long sentences for minor drug crimes, children tried and imprisoned as adult offenders, and—the ultimate retributive measure, abolished in almost every other Western country—capital punishment. Yet the United States has a more severe drug problem than countries that adopt alternative measures and a violent crime rate that is consistently several times higher than that of similar countries. Within this country, the violent crime rates of states with capital punishment are significantly higher than the violent crime rates of states that have abolished that barbaric retributive practice. Indeed, there seems to be a consistent inverse relationship between allegiance to moral responsibility (and retributive punishment models) and the reduction of violent crime. This is not to suggest, of course, that all advocates of moral responsibility support the brutal excesses of the U.S. retributive justice system: obviously, there are many who favor moral responsibility but reject capital punishment. But the point is that moral responsibility is an essential prop for the harsh retributive justice system, and that the *rejection* of moral responsibility undercuts that essential foundation and opens the way for more effective and humane methods of both preventing crime and reforming criminal characters. Whatever the virtues that moral responsibility advocates can claim for their system, practical effectiveness is one of the least plausible.

Recall the case of the willing drug addict, Robert. Examining the process that leaves Robert deeply devoted to his drug addiction leaves no doubt that Robert is profoundly addicted and that the addiction is his own, but simultaneously, as we understand the powerful addiction that deprives Robert step by step of all other hopes and affections, such an understanding erodes the foundation for Robert's moral responsibility. Robert is profoundly addicted, and the flaw is deep within Robert; that he is morally responsible for that flaw is a different claim altogether. (Of course, some may still conclude that when Robert becomes a willing addict he is morally responsible, but so long as they agree that such a conclusion is a step beyond the conclusion that Robert is a willing addict, the distinction in question is acknowledged.) Robert may insist that his addiction is his own, that he wants no interference, and that he claims take-charge responsibility for his own life, but doing so will not be evidence that he is morally responsible for his life and his choices and his character.

Recall Eve (from chapter 4): a young woman who is independent, inquisitive, and self-directed and who has a healthy confidence in her own decision-making ability and a sturdy desire to mark out her own path and make her own choices. Unfortunately, she is living in a harshly sexist society in which women are expected to be subservient, passive, and acquiescent: they are pressured to follow the directions given to them by men without question or dissent. Independence in women is regarded as sinful arrogant willfulness. Eve struggles to keep her independence and her self-confidence, but all her efforts to follow her own path and make her own decisions are met with hostility and ridicule from her community and family. Her independence draws consistent condemnation; small acts of acquiescence are warmly approved. Eventually worn down by this unrelenting social pressure, Eve's longing for independence and self-determination are extinguished, and she embraces subservience. Indeed, she comes to deeply and reflectively approve of her subservience, regarding her youthful independence as sinful pride, and she strives to teach her daughters the subservient docility she now profoundly values. Eve has become authentically subservient and deeply flawed, but she certainly has not gained free will, much less moral responsibility. In the stifling conditions of her youth, Eve was not free, and by internalizing those oppressive values, she has not gained free will, but has instead moved a giant step further from freedom.

The example in chapter 4 of Jamal also serves to distinguish *being* profoundly at fault from *deserving blame* for one's own fault. Jamal is captured and sold into slavery. He struggles against his enslavement, seeks to escape, and hates being enslaved: he is a very unwilling slave. All of Jamal's escape attempts are in vain, and he is severely punished for his efforts. Eventually, Jamal learns that there is no escape and that his efforts to throw off his shackles are futile. As year follows brutal year, Jamal loses all hope. He begins to accept his enslavement (his years of struggle have accomplished nothing, except to gain him even harsher treatment), and ultimately acquiesces in his enslavement. Jamal now identifies himself as a slave, approves of his servitude, and loses all desire for freedom. Jamal has become a "happy slave," a willing slave whose sincere desire is to serve his master. This cruel process has left Jamal profoundly enslaved, and the fault of passive preference for enslavement is now Jamal's own deep fault. But it is something very different to suggest that Jamal deserves blame for his own flawed preference for enslavement. Jamal is profoundly enslaved, and his enslavement has been deeply internalized, but to suppose that he is to blame for his acquiescence to enslavement is another claim altogether. A happy slave is more completely enslaved, but he does not gain moral responsibility for his enslavement. The fact that he deeply identifies with slavery does not give him a free will—even though it is now the will he wants to have—and it certainly does not make him morally responsible. He is deeply flawed, but is not to blame.

The acquiescent slave is not a fanciful flight of the philosophical imagination. As discussed earlier, psychologist Martin Seligman's "learned helplessness" experiments conditioned dogs to quickly give up and make no effort to escape painful shocks. But their resigned acceptance of their suffering is a mark of their deep helplessness, not their freedom. An abused wife struggles for freedom, but after much suffering and terror, she finally gives up and quietly accepts the abuse. When her abusive husband leaves her, she lacks the confidence to seize the opportunity for freedom and instead marries another abusive spouse and continues the pattern. Someone may say, "Well, she made her choice, it's her own fault." And it is her character fault—the product of her deeply conditioned character flaw—but it is not her blame fault. Less extreme is the case of the student who "just won't try" to learn math. His repeated frustrating failures have extinguished any hope of success, and he has developed the deep fault of helplessness and passivity, but that does not imply that he deserves blame for his genuine faults. Of course, blaming such a student is easy (and perhaps a natural tendency), and if we fail to think carefully about it, it will seem obvious that the student who "won't even try" justly deserves to suffer failure. But when we look closely, it is clear that the profoundly discouraged student—whose repeated earlier efforts met with repeated painful failure, until debilitating learned helplessness set in—no more deserves blame for the deep defeated passivity that is genuinely his own than does the "satisfied" slave or the repeatedly abused woman or Seligman's cowering dogs that "won't even try" to leap across a low barrier to escape.

One might object that this challenge to moral responsibility is based on the history of the willing addict, the subservient woman, the acquiescent slave, and that the history of what shaped their characters is irrelevant to whether they are morally responsible *now*. The history that shaped Robert into a willing addict doesn't matter: what matters is that Robert now chooses—Robert favors and wills and approves and identifies with—his addiction; he is an addict who values an addictive life, and that makes him morally responsible. Viewed very narrowly, it is true that Robert's causal history is irrelevant: if we are judging whether he is now morally flawed, it doesn't matter what process shaped him into a willing addict. Whether he became a willing addict as a result of his own bad choices, or through the machinations of the philosophically famous evil neuroscientist, or through a well-intentioned but terribly flawed drug education program that was supposed to lead him away from addiction, the focal point is the fact that he is now a willing addict.

But even if we adopt that ahistorical perspective, it will not support claims of Robert's moral responsibility for his willing addiction. When we look closely at the capacities of the willing addict and the subservient woman and the acquiescent slave, we see that given who they actually are and the capacities they actually have, they cannot avoid their bad behavior. And even if we accept that their causal histories are narrowly irrelevant, this acceptance does not imply that we should ignore those histories; it is by looking closely at their histories that we can best recognize the limited capacities that they actually have. Robert is not an automaton, nor is he insane or incompetent. He can choose in accordance with his own values. Robert can employ his rational abilities (though—as in all of us—those rational abilities are not transcendent powers that can rise above and step outside of his formed character; if Robert has a special cognitive fortitude that enables him to carry out sustained deliberation and consider other possibilities and contrive means of pursuing a radically new unaddicted path, then that also is one of his special capacities, and he is lucky to have this capacity, which most of his fellow addicts, willing or unwilling, lack). But can anyone suppose that it is fair and just that persons with radically different capacities and characters (which they certainly did not make or choose themselves and which the ahistorical perspective would count as irrelevant even if they had) should be punished and rewarded for the behavioral results that flow from those different capacities? It would be like saying: Beth starts the race with broken ankles, while Carolyn starts physically sound; we don't care how that happened, but only about what they do *now*, and so Beth justly deserves punishment for her lousy performance and Carolyn justly deserves rich reward for her outstanding race. Such a position can work only if one supposes that all that is being asked is whether the individuals are morally corrupt. Robert, Eve, and Jamal *are* morally flawed, just as Beth is now physically impaired and Carolyn is physically sound. But that does not imply that they deserve blame for their moral corruption, or the results that flow from it.

Michael McKenna argues:

What is relevant to moral appraisal is the moral quality of the motive with which an agent acts. The sort of control spotlighted in a Frankfurt example [involving a potential intervener who never actually intervenes], and the demand that we evaluate a person in terms of what she did (even if we cannot say what else we would have had her do), can be organized around a thesis that ties moral responsibility to the quality of an agent's will in acting as she does. (2005, 179)

It's true that what is relevant to moral appraisal is "the moral quality of the motive with which an agent acts": Robert, Jamal, and Eve are truly and profoundly morally flawed. But those moral flaws do not entail moral responsibility.

Being at Fault

The basic problem is in the confusion of being at fault (and the fault being one's own) and being morally responsible for that fault—that is, the confusion between character fault and blame fault. Strong identification (as Frankfurt describes) may be grounds for thinking the fault is my own, but not for concluding that I am morally responsible for the fault. Confusing "being at fault" with "deserving blame for his own fault" is a common mistake. Robert Nozick, for example, says, "I see blaming him for something merely as attributing that to the exercise of a character defect of his" (1981, 396). And similarly in Daniel Dennett's pithy remark, "Who more deserves to be despised than someone utterly despicable?" (1984, 167). But it is one thing to act from one's own character flaw, and another to deserve blame for such actions; it is one thing to have a despicable character, and another to deserve to be despised.

So when we say "John is at fault," or "It is John's fault," the statement is ambiguous. It may mean that John is the source of the bad act, and the act stems from his own character, and John is morally responsible for the act: John has *blame* fault. Or it may mean that the act is John's, and it comes from John's own character faults, but with no implications concerning John's moral responsibility (the desert of blame or punishment) for the act: it is John's own *character* fault. The fault is not in John's stars; rather, the moral fault is in John himself, which may pose its own problems. If the fault is John's drug addiction, but a drug addiction from which John feels alienated—John is not a "willing addict"—then we may hesitate to say that the fault is John's own. But that's a different issue. Even when we agree that the fault *is* John's own, and that John is competent and purposeful, there remains a different question that arises from saying that the failure is "John's fault."

The distinction is between saying that John is at fault for the mess (the fault is in John) and John is a rational person who makes his own—often flawed—decisions, and thus John deserves blame and punishment for his rotten behavior, and, on the other side, agreeing that John is "at fault" for the mess (the fault does indeed lie within John), and John is a rational person who makes his own bad decisions, but John is not morally responsible and does not deserve punishment for his own faulty behavior (perhaps because John was shaped by a genetic and environmental history not of his own making or choosing, or for whatever reason). In both cases, John is at fault: he is reckless, shallow, and short-sighted. And the faults are John's own, and—serious as they are—they are not faults that disqualify him from membership in Strawson's moral community of persons. But there is a further question—and it is on this question that the different classifications pivot—of whether John justly deserves condemnation and punishment for his flawed character and bad behavior.

The first point to note is that there is a clear distinction to draw between these cases. John makes a mess of things because he is lazy and incompetent and lacking in self-discipline and deliberative fortitude. The mess was certainly John's fault: it results from flaws that are John's own, and John is not so flawed—either temporarily or permanently—as to be excluded from membership in the moral community of persons (John can be loved or hated, we can reason with him, and we may have a wide rich range of reactive attitudes toward John). But there remains an important difference between classifying John as deserving blame for his faults and on the other hand regarding him as faulty but not deserving of blame.

An example may elucidate this distinction. John has a deep-rooted gender prejudice—a profound character flaw that he recognizes and perhaps even approves. "Probably women are equal in ability to men," John thinks to himself, "and it's wrong and unjustified to discriminate against women. But that's the way I am, and it's part of me. I'm neither morally nor rationally perfect, but I like the way I am, and I don't want to change." John's discriminatory behavior stems from his own character flaw, and the fault is John's own. John discriminates by purpose, not accident, and although flawed, he is not a maniac or sociopath who must be "permanently excused" and ostracized from the moral community. John's bad behavior stems from his own deep character flaws. One might call John a "willing sexist," comparable in commitment and authenticity to Frankfurt's "willing addict." The fault is in John, not in his stars.

But the question of whether John should be blamed for his own character flaws (and the bad behavior stemming from them) is a different question altogether. It is perfectly meaningful to say: John is competent, and he has deep character flaws that are his own; he does not, however, deserve blame for either the flaws or the behavior. (This lack of blame might be because, for example, John is the product of a sexist culture that shaped him to be profoundly sexist; all his friends are sexist, and he fears that if he changed he would lose his friends and perhaps a vital part of his own identity. John regards himself as a "good old boy," and overcoming sexism would involve a fearful fragmenting of his personality. Though John internalized his sexism from his culture, that does not make it any less his own, but recognizing those cultural forces may raise doubts concerning John's blame for his flaws: "John had the bad fortune to be reared in a profoundly sexist culture; he is a vile sexist, but you can't really blame him for it.") At this point, I am not concerned with whether that is or is not a good reason for denying that John deserves blame for his bad character and bad acts; the point is that the distinction it employs is genuine. If we can argue about whether morally flawed John deserves blame for his own moral faults, then the distinction is established. Because we can meaningfully argue about whether crimson sunsets are beautiful, "beautiful" must have a meaning that is distinct from "crimson sunset," and that will remain the case, even if the class designated by crimson sunsets and the class designated by things of beauty are exactly coextensive.

Sher's Challenge

Although Dennett and Frankfurt neglect the distinction between blame fault and character fault, George Sher seems intent on demolishing it. Sher maintains that "blame is a stance that a person takes toward himself or another on the basis of a judgment that that person has in some way failed to conform to some moral standard" (2006, 7). Thus one whose character or acts fail to measure up is therefore blamed. Blame is finding moral fault, and the question of whether an individual justly deserves blame for her moral faults or morally bad acts is eliminated. As Sher states:

To see how the intimacy of the connection between a person and his bad traits supports the conclusion that we are justified in condemning him for them, we need only remind ourself of how difficult it would be to condemn a person's bad traits *without* condemning him. As we saw, to have a morally bad trait is to be systematically unresponsive to a certain class of moral reasons. It is to be disposed both to see bad acts of the relevant type as live options and actually to perform such acts whenever they seem sufficiently advantageous or attractive. It is, as well, to have a variety of associated cognitive and affective dispositions—dispositions to notice vulnerability and enjoy its exploitation if one is cruel, to discern opportunities for self-advancement and disregard the interests of others if one is selfish, and so on. Taken together, these vice-related dispositions are bound to place their stamp on much of what an agent thinks and does. They are also bound to have their roots in stable patterns of interaction among the desires, beliefs, and finer grained dispositions that together make him the person he is. For both reasons, there is no clear difference between condemning a person's cruelty, manipulativeness, or unfairness, and simply condemning *him*. It is something of an exaggeration, but not much of one, to say that where a person's vices are concerned, it is not possible to hate the disposition to sin but love the sinner because the sinner is in good measure constituted by his dispositions to sin. (2006, 64–65)

Thus for Sher, the difference between character-fault and blame-fault disappears: When we condemn Scrooge's greed, we are condemning Scrooge himself; we are *blaming* Scrooge for his character flaws and the bad acts that stem from them. But—contrary to Sher's claim—the difference between condemning Scrooge's flaws and condemning/blaming *Scrooge* remains a very important difference, no matter how fine-grained our view of Scrooge and his very serious faults. Scrooge (pre-ghosts) is genuinely a miser, his character is one of miserliness, and he reflectively approves of his miserliness: "'What then?' he retorted. 'Even if I have grown so much wiser, what then?'" (Dickens 1843, 44). But once we understand the forces that shaped him—the grinding poverty and the personal indignities that wore away his "nobler passions"—then it is not so clear that we are right to blame or condemn Scrooge, though our negative moral judgment of his character and acts remains strong.

Moving from classic fiction to science fiction, imagine that Carl and David are both warm, generous, honorable college undergraduates, standing in line at the college cafeteria. The mad scientist of gothic novel and philosophical fantasy happens to be conducting an experiment on a vile concoction he has been perfecting: a drug that transforms even the noblest and best individuals into greedy unscrupulous cruel persons who "notice vulnerability and enjoy its exploitation" and who deeply and reflectively approve of their new vicious characters (after taking the drug and being transformed from virtuous to vicious, their response to any admonition to abandon their wicked ways and return to virtue is "Even if I have grown so much wiser, what then?"). The mad scientist drops the tasteless concoction in a glass of orange juice that Carl happens to select and David gets the unadulterated glass beside it. Carl is now profoundly vicious, and glad to be so, but to suppose that he deserves to be condemned or that he deserves blame for his genuinely vicious character and behavior is a different matter altogether. The orange juice example is fanciful, but the extension of the example is not. One infant—say, Robert Harris, a brutal murderer who kidnapped two sixteen-year-old boys from the parking lot of a fast food restaurant, casually murdered them, laughed about killing them, and calmly ate the hamburgers the boys had bought—goes home with his parents to a brutally dysfunctional family filled with violence and rejection; another infant—in an event as much a matter of luck as Carl's selection of the tainted orange juice—goes to a loving and supportive family. Harris becomes brutal and vicious, and the other child becomes kind, generous, and morally upright. But distinguishing and evaluating their genuine moral characters—the former is vicious, the latter is virtuous—is fully consistent with distinguishing that moral evaluation from judgments of blame. Certainly, we could decide to renounce any distinction between character-fault and blame-fault, but losing the distinction would limit and impoverish our moral judgments.

Consider another example, unfortunately also very real. Stanley Milgram's famous social science experiment (1963) on obedience and authority revealed results both surprising and disturbing. I'm glad I was not a subject in the Milgram experiment; as a child of the 1960s, I am devoted to the principle of "question authority," but given my Southern Baptist upbringing and my deep respect for anyone wearing a lab jacket, I fear that I would have been among the two-thirds of subjects who were willing to inflict severe punishment—even lethal punishment—during the course of the experiment. Like many subjects, I might well have been rather unhappy about doing it, but probably I would have continued to flip the switch and administer (what the experimental subjects thought to be) a severe punitive shock. And so I would have learned about myself that I would have likely followed the demands of authority and become a Nazi prison guard or an Abu Ghraib tormentor. Not having been part of that experiment, I can hope that I would have been part of the minority who refused to cooperate, though I fear I would have been one of the large majority who were willing to do awful things if directed by a strong authority. If my fears are correct, then I have a very serious character flaw—a flaw that I share, apparently, with most members of my species, or at least with most members of my culture. But that should not be a surprise. We are a profoundly hierarchical species: we adore kings and presidents and surround them with pomp and ceremony, honor popes and archbishops and prophets, worship gods on our bended knees—and we make them cruel and jealous, and rush to follow their demands to kill heathens, heretics, and witches. We eagerly follow strong leaders into wars and crusades, and when the war is over, we place our military commanders in positions of political power. Many times, this tendency is manifested in a way that is brutal and horrific: the prison guards at Abu Ghraib acted in the same manner as the "prison guards" in the Stanford prison experiment (Haney, Banks, and Zimbardo 1973); "ordinary German citizens" took part in brutal cruelties against Jews, and "ordinary American citizens" followed along in lynch mobs attacking and murdering blacks. All of these are egregious acts, done by people with horrific character traits—sadly, character traits shared to some degree by a large majority of us. Certainly, this is a severe character-fault, but—Sher's views notwithstanding—our blame-fault for this flaw is a very different matter. The flaw is likely the product of a combination of genetic propensities and cultural conditioning, not something we chose. Very few of those who harbor this flaw are even aware of it; when asked, most people vehemently deny that they would go along with the authoritative orders to shock others, though experimental studies show that most of those who sincerely make that denial are honestly but profoundly mistaken. When there is a genuine fault that afflicts most of us and that we certainly did not choose or create and of which most of us are blissfully unaware, it is difficult to suppose that we deserve blame for that fault, but it is not at all difficult to conclude that it is a very severe fault that has— from the Crusades to Abu Ghraib—produced terrible wrongs.

Jeanette is fortunate to come across the social psychology literature on widespread acquiescence to authority, to be sufficiently self-perceptive to now recognize the flaw in herself, to enjoy a high degree of cognitive fortitude and a strong sense of personal self-efficacy, and to have the resources to seek the help of a competent psychologist. She undergoes a sustained and ultimately successful program of therapy that overcomes her tendency toward authority acquiescence. But Jeanette is very fortunate to have that opportunity to recognize her own flaw, as well as the capacities and resources to resolve to correct that flaw and to carry out this program of character modification. The glib suggestion that everyone—no matter what their capacities and resources—could have carried out the same self-improvement (and thus everyone is morally responsible for this character flaw) is both shallow and false. In short, there are genuine faults, but no matter how profoundly they are our own, and no matter how strongly we identify with them and even reflectively approve of them, doing so does not establish that we deserve blame for them or that we are morally responsible for the faults or the behavior that results from them.

It is not only implausible to count us as deserving blame for this authoritarian fault (given our genetic propensities, a culture that promotes conformity, jobs that insist on worker compliance, and religions that demand unquestioning obedience and mindless faith); it is also counterproductive. If we blame people for the fault, they will be less likely to acknowledge and confront it and less likely to seek effective means of eliminating or controlling it. And if we blame the individuals who have genuine character-faults, then our focus will be both too narrow and too shallow, and we will ignore the deeper sources of the problem and the most promising ways of fixing it.

It is vitally important that we study our authoritarian and dominance tendencies, learn about them, recognize their perils, and determine how to offset or control them. Do our authoritarian hierarchical tendencies occur naturally? Are they genetic in origin? Can they be held effectively in check in small groups? In large nation-states? What is the best way of controlling such tendencies or at least blunting their most harmful manifestations? I don't know the answers to those questions. But I do believe that it is better to study them carefully—and to try to learn from what psychologists and biologists and neuroscientists and anthropologists can teach us—than to blame individuals and thus impede further inquiry into the causes of their behavior. Blaming individuals who manifest this character flaw does not help. To the contrary, it harms, by blocking examination of the causes: you are to blame, so we don't want to look too closely at the causes. If we obscure the distinction between blame-fault and character-fault, we block the inquiries that can help us understand why Robert Harris and Nazi prison guards and Abu Ghraib torturers developed awful character traits and manifested morally vicious behavior, and we block the best opportunity to understand how to prevent that from occurring in the future. Or perhaps the focus on character traits itself misleads us. The young people who joined the army and wound up inflicting psychological torture on Abu Ghraib prisoners came from very different backgrounds than did the privileged young people whose families could afford to send them to Stanford, but the Stanford undergraduates who participated as "guards" in the prison experiment apparently inflicted abuse as readily as the Abu Ghraib guards. Perhaps what we need to examine is not character traits, but situations and environments and social pressures. But whether character traits or situations—or both—should be our focus, blaming individuals will not help us answer that question. The prison guards at Abu Ghraib did horrific things, but court-martialing them did not answer the questions, and it did not solve the problem.

Is Blame Unavoidable?

I have argued that we can and should distinguish between character-fault and blame-fault, recognizing the former while rejecting the latter. George Sher is skeptical of drawing such a distinction; so is Paula Hieronymi, for similar but distinct reasons. Hieronymi maintains that certain moral judgments of character—"most centrally, the judgment that a person failed to show proper regard for others" (Hieronymi 2004, 115)—necessarily involve a special force, as an inseparable element of their content, and that this special force carries the blame that follows inevitably from adverse moral judgments of character:

Resentment and indignation are like distrust. Though distrust also carries a special, characteristic and burdensome force or significance, and though it may be unfair that a person has suffered from formative circumstances that render her generally unreliable and so leave her systematically subject to constant distrust, those who interact with her cannot be unjustified in distrusting her on these grounds. The distrust simply marks the fact that the untrustworthiness is known. Its force is inherited from the significance of untrustworthiness. Likewise, it may be unfair that a person is subject to formative circumstances that render her unable to show proper regard for others and so leave her systematically subject to others' resentment and indignation. But, once it is granted that the relations in which she stands are of a certain quality, the attitudes which simply acknowledge those facts cannot be unfair. (2004, 136)

Hieronymi goes on to claim that by being in interpersonal relations with others one is subject to fair application of these negative attitudes, and one is thus morally responsible: "To be morally responsible just is to be a suitable object of resentment and indignation should one show significant disregard for others" (2004, 136). Thus when one who is a competent participant in interpersonal relations shows significant disregard for others, then being subject to such negative forceful attitudes is simply part of our system of holding people morally responsible.

But is it really impossible to make negative moral judgments of a person's character and behavior without directing negative blame attitudes toward that person? Suppose that we have a friend, Jake, who is good-natured, generous, friendly, and courageous, but Jake can't be trusted to keep his promises or honor his commitments. Certainly, one who breaks promises or ignores commitments or otherwise shows disregard for the interests and feelings of others has moral flaws and serious faults, but recognizing those faults is consistent with believing that the faulty person does not justly deserve blame. If you are a slow runner, that fault makes you a poor candidate for center field, and if you are untrustworthy, that fault makes you a poor candidate for anything requiring trust or commitment. It is true that lack of speed is not like lack of integrity, but the point is that one can recognize a flaw, whether physical or moral, and make the appropriate judgment about the fault and its implications ("This guy might be good as a pinch hitter, but we better not play him in the outfield" and "This guy would be marvelous company for a weekend at the beach, but I wouldn't want to marry him") without in any way blaming the person for his or her faults. Suppose the random orange juice potion of earlier discussion had less dramatic effects: instead of turning the unlucky recipient into a brutal killer, it transforms the person into someone who is profoundly unable to keep a promise, someone who is deeply and permanently untrustworthy, and that formerly trustworthy Joan draws the unlucky adulterated glass. In that case, we would certainly take account of the fact that Joan now has this serious moral flaw and adjust our behavior accordingly. "Joan's a warm and friendly person," we might say, "and a hard worker, very creative, the soul of generosity. But unfortunately, you have to always keep in mind that she can't be trusted to keep her promises; if she promises to have important material ready for you on a certain day, or promises to pick you up from the airport, it's essential that you have a backup plan in place. Other than that, she's great. And her inability to keep promises isn't really her fault: she used to be perfectly reliable. But unfortunately, she happened to drink some of that tainted orange juice that the mad scientist was spreading around, and her promise-keeping virtue has become a promise-breaking vice. We have to make the best of it, but we certainly can't blame her for her serious flaw." In that case, "those who interact with her cannot be unjustified in distrusting her," but they would be unjustified in blaming her for her fault.

We might even "think worse" of the tainted orange juice recipient, and that is an accurate assessment of the person's changed character. Certainly, such a result is unfortunate for the person who is "thought worse of," but that person does not justly deserve the reduced moral status that results from this accurate assessment of the person's unlucky new character. Phineas Gage was a respected, congenial, reliable railroad worker until he suffered a severe brain injury in an accidental explosion; as a result of this brain damage, Gage became quarrelsome, unreliable, and lazy (Damasio 1994). Given that radically altered character, negative judgments of Gage's moral character are accurate. But Gage did not justly deserve a much reduced moral status. If the accident causes Gage to become severely quarrelsome and abusive and unpleasant, then social ostracism may well be the result, and such ostracism would come about because of an accurate understanding of Gage's new character, but it is a very different claim indeed to suggest that Gage justly deserves the suffering that would result from such social isolation. With genuine understanding of the faults and their detailed causes, we can still acknowledge them as faults, but that will not carry with it any sense of justified blame. If Professor Andrews develops early-onset Alzheimer's Disease and is no longer the brilliant lecturer and scholar she once was, then our accurate judgment of her will change, and our relation with her will also change, and change for the worse: she will no longer be respected as a brilliant authority, we shall no longer seek her wise counsel, we shall no longer send her drafts of our journal articles and value her advice on how to improve them. Given the change in her capacities, this new assessment of her is fair, but she clearly does not justly deserve to suffer a painful loss of status and respect.

If it is difficult to imagine judging someone to be morally faulty without that involving blame, it is perhaps because we are so deeply immersed in a moral responsibility system in which all competent persons—persons who are full participants in interpersonal relations—are automatically assumed to be morally responsible and to deserve blame for their faults and their faulty behavior. But a citizen of *Erewhon* would have no trouble picturing such a case; in Samuel Butler's (1872) imaginary utopia (or some would say dystopia) moral flaws are not proper objects of blame or opprobrium or punishment, but simply unfortunate characteristics that the society makes every effort to fix. An Erewhonian with a tendency toward theft is certainly not trustworthy, and taking the possessions of others clearly indicates "significant disregard for others," but this fault is recognized to be the product of forces that were ultimately beyond the control of the theft-prone person. Instead of blaming the unfortunate individual, the focus is on finding the cause of this problem and correcting the flaw. Perhaps in a system (like our own) that assumes moral responsibility for all competent persons, it is impossible to recognize a moral fault without also making a moral evaluation that includes attitudes of blame. If that is so, that would reveal a blind spot in our moral responsibility system: it is unable to draw an important and useful distinction. Rather than being evidence in favor of moral responsibility, it would be evidence of the limits and flaws of the moral responsibility system.

Blame and Fairness

It is counterproductive to blame, but the basic problem with blaming is that it is unfair. David has an authoritarian character flaw that was shaped by some combination of genetics and culture. David has no idea that he has such a flaw; to the contrary, he is very confident that he does not (and learning of his flaw in the course of Milgram's experiment would be deeply disturbing to him). David did not choose this character flaw, he had no opportunity to avoid developing the flaw, and—being unaware of it—he could take no steps to eliminate it, but he does have the flaw, it is part of his character, and—in the wrong situation—it might well prompt David to carry out morally bad acts. But because David cannot help having that flaw, it is unfair to blame him for the flaw or its consequences.

That seems obvious, but it does not seem obvious to Sher, and indeed Sher believes that it is false. Sher rejects that fairness principle, claiming that often it is quite legitimate to blame people for what they cannot help. Sher holds that the fairness principle, F, "has, to my knowledge, never been defended. It is, moreover, not at all clear how F could be defended" (2006, 60). On this point, perhaps Sher is correct. It is difficult to think of ways to defend the fairness principle, because it is difficult to think of a principle that is more obvious or more morally basic that could be used to support it. Carl got the drugged orange juice, and David drew the unadulterated. Carl really is bad, but if you think it fair to blame or condemn Carl, then I doubt that any argument could shake you. If that seems fair to you, then we are talking different languages—we are working in different systems of thought. One who finds such a scenario fair is most likely trying to save a system—the moral responsibility system—that can be salvaged only by making very implausible ad hoc adjustments elsewhere in the system. The moral responsibility system is in crisis, as scientific research encroaches on those areas where grounds for moral responsibility were taking refuge. Efforts to save that system take on many different shapes, but none seem successful.

Sher is offering a radical solution: it's fair to blame people for traits and acts that they could not change or control. That is, Sher explicitly rejects (what he names) the F principle: "that it is unfair to blame a person for anything he cannot help" (2006, 60). Sher offers the following objection to F:

There is, on reflection, a good deal that can be said against F. The basic source of the difficulty is that many of the acts over which agents exercise control are themselves manifestations of *traits* over which they *lack* control. When someone performs such an act, his control over it may not go very deep. If it does not, then we may wonder whether it is any fairer to blame him for manifesting his bad trait than merely for having it. If there is no difference in fairness, then anyone who insists that it is not unfair to blame an agent for such an act will indeed have to reject F. (2006, 61)

We may indeed wonder whether it is fairer, and with good reason: indeed, it does not seem "fairer to blame him for manifesting his bad trait than merely for having it." But although Sher concludes that therefore we should forsake the principle of fairness and blame people for both the acts and the traits from which they spring, it is surely just as plausible to conclude that we should reject blaming for either acts or traits. This is an instance of one person's *modus ponens* being another person's *modus tollens*; Sher argues that if blame for acts then blame for traits, and because we blame for acts we must (*modus ponens*) blame for traits. It seems at least as reasonable to argue that if we blame for acts, then we should also blame for traits, but it is fundamentally unfair to blame for traits (such as the trait of submissiveness to authoritarian rules), and thus we should also reject blame for acts. Indeed, if the only grounds for blaming for traits is that such blame—which violates the principle of fairness, as Sher acknowledges—is required by the blame system, then that would seem to be an excellent reason for calling into question our ancient and thoroughly rotten system of blame and moral responsibility and just deserts.

Sher attempts to prop up his rejection of the fairness principle (F) by noting further ways in which it is inconsistent with the blame system:

> As long as any significant number of bad acts are rendered (close to) inevitable by the corresponding traits, there will remain a significant class of agents whom we cannot fairly blame for their bad acts without also blaming them for their bad traits. Thus, as long as we can fairly blame people for bad acts that are the near-inevitable effects of their bad traits, there will be no shortage of counterexamples to F.
>
> And, in fact, blaming people for such bad acts often does seem fair. At a minimum, it appears no less fair to blame someone for a bad act that he performs because he is so selfish that the suffering of others barely registers on his consciousness, or because he is so corrupt that he sees no point in being honest, than it does to blame another who sees the point of being honest perfectly well, but who decides—perhaps after a struggle—to give in to a dishonest impulse. Indeed, if anything, many would actually consider it fairer to blame the thoroughly corrupt person, whose bad decision requires no thought, than the merely imperfect agent whose transgression represents a surrender or a falling away. Yet once we have acknowledged that it is fair to blame people for bad acts that flow automatically from bad traits over which they lack control, we can hardly deny that it is fair to blame them for those bad traits themselves. (2006, 63)

In fact, it's not fair to blame either one, because—episodically or automatically greedy—both were shaped by factors they did not control (one is short on moral scruples and the other on moral fortitude, but neither shaped themselves).

Sher's stronger inclination to blame the unrelentingly greedy individual is revealing. On Sher's view, if Scrooge had been born to relatively comfortable circumstances and not been so cruelly marked by poverty, he would be less to blame than the Scrooge who was early scarred by desperate need. This scenario looks plausible to Sher—and Frankfurt—for two reasons: first, they have not looked closely at the actual process that shapes committed misers and willing addicts and satisfied slaves, and second, the person who is a willing slave—and embraces and identifies with servitude—may well be more profoundly and deeply a slave, just as the person who "is so corrupt that he sees no point in being honest" is more profoundly and thoroughly and "authentically" dishonest than the occasional liar. But when we look carefully at the profoundly flawed "satisfied slave," then the process that shaped the individual calls into question any ascriptions of blame, and the deep commitment to servitude is an indication of the brutal thoroughness of the enslavement process, not a justification for blaming the profoundly enslaved person. The student who never exerts any effort is more "authentically lazy." The dog that invariably cowers when shocked is more deeply passive than the dog that does so on occasion, but when we realize that the former suffered only one episode of restrained shocks and that the latter was placed in the harness on repeated occasions, then it hardly seems fair to blame the deeply passive dog that has been brutalized into learned helplessness (nor the deeply passive victim of repeated abuse).

Gary Watson and Blame

The case of Robert Harris is one that troubles Gary Watson and his commitment to moral responsibility, but Watson—like Sher and Frankfurt and Dennett—is unwilling to renounce that commitment, so he makes adjustments elsewhere: adjustments along the same lines as Sher, with the same degree of plausibility. Watson's doubts about moral responsibility and the legitimacy of retributive emotions are prompted by the disturbing yet moving story of Robert Harris. A constant menace even in prison, the other death row inmates were eager for his execution. Vengeful outrage comes easy when hearing of the horrors committed by Harris. But there is an earlier chapter in Robert Harris's story. Robert's father was a violent and sadistic man who abused his wife and all his children. He seemed to single out Robert, because he suspected that he had not fathered Robert. His suspicions about Robert also caused him to be particularly brutal to Robert's mother, and as a result, his mother grew to hate Robert, never showing him any affection and blaming Robert for all her suffering. One of his sisters described Robert's situation as a small child: "He would just break your heart. He wanted love so bad he would beg for any kind of physical contact. He'd come up to my mother and just try to rub his little hands on her leg or her arm. He just never got touched at all. She'd just push him away or kick him. One time she bloodied his nose when he was trying to get close to her" (Watson 1987b, 273).

In addition to his horrific home life, Robert—who had a speech imped-iment—was mercilessly teased at school. By age fourteen, he was sentenced to a federal youth detention center, where he was one of the youngest inmates and was repeatedly raped.

When we hear the story of Robert Harris's vicious murders, retribution seems an appropriate reaction: Harris deserves severe punishment for his crimes. But when we learn the whole story, Harris's just deserts seem more problematic. Thinking hard about the brutal environment that shaped this brutal person raises basic questions about the fairness of punishing him. As Watson comments on the Harris case, "The case is troubling in a more personal way. The fact that Harris's cruelty is an intelligible response to his circumstances gives a foothold not only for sympathy, but for the thought that if *I* had been subjected to such circumstances, I might well have become as vile" (1987b, 276).

But this is a conclusion that Watson cannot quite accept. Had Watson experienced a similar environment (Watson claims), he would not have been shaped in exactly the same way because Watson's genetic makeup is unique and thus different from that of Robert Harris. And, on this basis, Watson finds room to take credit for his own virtuous character:

There is room for the thought that there is something "in me" by virtue of which I would not have become a vicious person in Harris's circumstances. And if that factor were among my essential properties, so to speak, then that difference between Harris and me would not be a matter of moral luck on my part, but a matter of who we essentially were. That would not, of course, mean that I was essentially good or Harris essentially evil, but that I would not have been corrupted in the same circumstances as those that defeated Harris. To be sure, to suppose that this difference is in itself to my moral credit would be odd. To congratulate me on these grounds would be to congratulate me on being myself. Nevertheless, this difference still might explain what is to my credit, such moral virtues as I may possess. This will seem paradoxical only if we suppose that whatever is a ground of my moral credit must itself be to my credit. But I see no compelling reason to suppose this. (1987b, 279)

Watson is driven to notions of "who we essentially are" because he wants to preserve his virtues as genuinely his own, while acknowledging that "luck" plays a great part in who we are. It is unclear why our genetic makeup has a stronger claim than our early environment in establishing our essence, but my concern is elsewhere. When we recognize the difference between character-fault and blame-fault (or in this case, the corresponding character-virtue and reward-virtue), then the distinction that Watson is trying to establish can be drawn without the need of an essence, genetic or otherwise. Watson is virtuous, Harris vicious; those are deep character traits for each, and there is no need to consult either their genetic or formative histories to draw that conclusion. Harris's vicious crimes were the result of his own character-fault: that is, they spring from faults that are his own and that resulted in purposeful vicious acts (he did not kill his victims by accident, nor was he coerced); likewise with Watson's virtuous character and virtuous acts. But this conclusion does not prove that Harris justly deserves blame for his vicious deeds. Likewise, Watson's moral virtues are his own and are deeply fixed in his character. We need not discover what caused or grounds Watson's moral virtues to recognize that they are his own character-virtues. But we cannot dismiss such questions when deciding whether Watson deserves praise and reward for his moral virtues—whether his virtues are also reward-virtues. (And don't suppose that simply by acknowledging Watson's virtue, we are automatically and rightly praising him. We may be, but it may be just a matter of stating an evaluation: "Watson is virtuous, and lucky to be so"; that is like saying "Watson is handsome, and lucky to be so"—neither implies that he deserves praise for his virtue or his visage.)

Watson has genuine virtues: they belong to him, as a distinctive and unique individual. But it is something quite different to say that he "deserves credit" for them, that he "deserves reward" for the virtues that are indeed his. We may conclude that he was lucky (and thus deserves no reward) for his virtuous character and the self-controlled, virtuous acts that he energetically and self-confidently and effectively performs. When we deny that someone "deserves credit," we are not denying competence and virtue and self-control. We are denying instead that she deserves praise or reward for her splendid, deliberative, courageous, self-motivated, self-controlled character or the behavior that flows from it. One might yet argue that she does deserves reward, but that remains a separate question of her reward-virtue, unresolved by the establishment of her genuine character-virtue.

Michael McKenna, Essential Traits, and Blame

Failing to recognize the distinction between character-fault and blame-fault leaves one struggling with a "deep" or "essential" notion of who the person is who is morally responsible, and it lands us in severe difficulties. Consider Michael McKenna's development of this view; though he criticizes Watson, he does so in the context of defending Watson's essentialism: "But given the fact that I have had the history that I have had, there are certain options which are plainly unavailable to me; these limits reflect features essential to who I now am. I, as I am now, am *not* (to the best of my knowledge) a potential wrong-doer in the way Harris is" (1998, 140). Comfortable in his essential goodness, McKenna follows with this:

No doubt he [Watson] is correct; had many of us had quite different formative years we might be quite different people—possibly morally contemptuous ones. But this thought does not seem to me to have the effect upon our reactive attitudes which Watson suggests it does. The thought that we ought not blame does not seem compelling in these cases since it is hard to take seriously that we might have been like that—for *we are now not anything like that*. Furthermore, for many of us, perhaps most of us, it is *essential* to our present selves that we *could not* be like that. The intuition that we ourselves ought not cast blame seems only to gain a purchase upon our sentiments when the condition of our present selves shares the same kind of moral fault, or minimally, shares the *potential* for the same kind of fault. (To illustrate the kind of potential I have in mind, consider the person who *is* prone to binge eating. She might be *susceptible* to compulsive drinking even though she might never have drunk compulsively. Such a person might easily see how, given her weakness for food, she might find a like weakness for drink.) (1998, 140)

McKenna claims the right to cast blame on Harris because he has—given his essential decent character—no potential for the kind of fault that is glaringly present in Harris. But this leads to a blatantly unfair situation: having had the great good fortune to grow up in a safe community with loving parents, and not subjected to horrific childhood abuse or the tender mercies of the juvenile "justice" system, I cannot even imagine myself becoming the sort of brutal and capricious killer that Harris became (such a person would not be *me*), so I have the right to hold Harris morally responsible and condemn him to severe punishment. David, however, was born on the wrong side of the tracks: he grew up in an abusive home, he ran with a bad crowd as a young man and narrowly escaped arrest on numerous occasions. When David was a freshman in high school, his remarkably dedicated history teacher took a special interest in David, channeled David's energies and anger into more productive paths, and pushed and prodded David toward college. David was very lucky to have had such a wonderful teacher who intervened to turn him from what was likely a path of serious crime. David can well imagine himself continuing along a path that would have ultimately led to brutal murders comparable to those committed by Robert Harris. David is now a respected and talented history professor, but he knows how easily he might have become something entirely different; in fact, David still has some issues with anger management as a result of his brutal childhood, but he has a good therapist and good friends and he keeps his problems under control. But he has no trouble, even now, imagining himself giving in to a brutal and destructive outburst of anger; indeed, it is his acute awareness of this potential that keeps him punctual in his anger management sessions with his therapist. David is now a warm, kind, and affectionate person, beloved by his friends, family, students, and colleagues. But he has no problem imagining himself being very different. And so—by McKenna's lights—David is not entitled to hold Robert Harris morally responsible, and we (who had no such brutalizing history) can confidently and complacently blame Robert to our heart's content.

There is an insightful element in the essentialist claims of Watson and McKenna, but that insight turns bad when it is used to defend moral responsibility. Watson's essentialism is captured in this passage: "There is room for the thought that there is something 'in me' by virtue of which I would not have become a vicious person in Harris's circumstances. And if that factor were among my essential properties, so to speak, then that difference between Harris and me would not be a matter of moral luck on my part, but a matter of who we essentially were" (Watson 1987b, 279). And it is echoed by McKenna: "The thought that we ought not blame does not seem compelling in these cases since it is hard to take seriously that we might have been like that—for *we are now not anything like that.* Furthermore, for many of us, perhaps most of us, it is *essential* to our present selves that we *could not* be like that" (1998, 140).

It may be true that Watson and McKenna could not be like Robert Harris. I am somewhat doubtful of Watson's stronger claim that "there is something 'in me' by virtue of which I would not have become a vicious person in Harris's circumstances": I doubt Watson or McKenna or anyone else is blessed with an "essence of goodness" that would protect him from becoming vicious and brutal were he shaped—from infancy to adulthood—in the almost unimaginably horrific circumstances that Harris endured. But that's another issue. McKenna manages to focus the point more precisely: we are now not anything like that. And if McKenna became a brutal and heartless killer, then that killer would *no longer be McKenna*. Perhaps there are circumstances in which the good and decent person that McKenna now is could be transformed into a sadistic and capricious murderer, but the resultant murderer would not be the same gentle and reflective person who writes insightful philosophy papers. And that is the point McKenna is making when he says that, being who we now are, "it is *essential* to our present selves that we *could not* be like that" (1998, 140).

If the beloved of my youth assures me that she will love me when I am gray and wrinkled, that is a touching and reassuring testimony of devotion. If I want further assurance, I might question further, "Would you love me if I were bald and paunchy?" Again, her positive response is a comfort. But if I push these questions too far, positive answers may become troubling. "Would you love me if I became the leader of a right-wing paramilitary death squad? Would you still love me if an evil witch turned me into a frog?" Affirmative answers to such questions might raise doubts about whether my beloved really loves *me* at all.

I confess to skepticism about essential traits of ourselves, but let that pass. Even if we grant the legitimacy of such essentialism, it does not provide grounds for moral responsibility. Watson and McKenna are confusing two senses of "finding fault" or "assigning credit." Note Watson's remark: "Nevertheless, this difference [between the strengths of Watson and the vulnerabilities of Harris] still might explain what is to my credit, such moral virtues as I may possess. This will seem paradoxical only if we suppose that whatever is a ground of my moral credit must itself be to my credit. But I see no compelling reason to suppose this" (1987b, 279). Certainly, understanding whatever genetic or conditioning forces shaped Watson's good character will help "explain what is to my credit, such moral virtues as I may possess." It will confirm that Watson really is deeply and genuinely good, that his virtuous character is not shallow but instead solidly rooted in who he is. It that sense, it is to Watson's credit (and not the result of whim or external coercion). Watson's good character is genuinely Watson's own. But it is something very different to suppose that Watson is morally responsible for his good character. And doubts about that are not the doubts raised by Watson: "This will seem paradoxical only if we suppose that whatever is a ground of my moral credit must itself be to my credit. But I see no compelling reason to suppose this" (1987b, 279).

Rather, the real doubts are based on recognizing that what is to Watson's credit in the sense of being his own is not the same as being to his credit in the sense that he justly deserves praise or reward for it. Perhaps one really does deserve "just deserts credit" whenever one has "character credit"; that is, perhaps character-virtue and reward-virtue (and character-fault and blame-fault) are coextensive. But that will require substantial argument, and I doubt that any such argument will succeed. After all, it makes perfectly good sense to say that Watson really is deeply and profoundly virtuous (he has character-virtue), but he is not morally responsible for his virtue, as he was simply lucky to have been nurtured in an environment that shaped him to become virtuous (or—even more obviously a matter of good luck—he was blessed with a genetic propensity to virtue that Harris lacked). Perhaps that is false, but it is surely not obviously false, as Watson acknowledges (after all, the Harris case gives Watson pause about the moral responsibility of Harris and the justice of blaming Harris, though there is no doubt of Harris's brutal character).

When the two senses of fault (character-fault and blame-fault) are distinguished, the supposed essentialist grounds for moral responsibility are undercut. Fortunately, however, when the distinction is made, Watson's main reason for wanting moral responsibility also disappears. We can reject blame-fault (and moral responsibility) and still make moral judgments: Harris is vicious and morally bad, and Watson is virtuous. And we can study the histories that shaped Harris and Watson, try to understand those histories and learn how to modify or improve them to produce less vice and more virtue, and keep our reactive attitudes (or at least the ones worth keeping).

Rather than such desperate strategies as essential natures, the distinction between two senses of "finding fault" allows an easy solution: we can indeed find that someone has faults (whether we ourselves are likely to have those faults or not), and that is enough for our valuable reactive attitudes, but it is something quite different to conclude that people deserves blame or punishment for their faults. This conclusion also opens the way to pointing out large-scale or even universal faults: we might be universally (as a species) at fault for our aggressiveness (compared to our primate cousins, the Bonobos), and, as de Waal suggests, that aggressiveness would be worth recognizing and trying to ameliorate. So the distinction is an important one. (After all, in an era of nuclear weapons and belligerent politicians—whose popularity seems to depend on having a forceful profile and a capacity for bellicose speech—it might be well to consider how to deal with this problem, rather than deciding that because it is universal, it is not really a flaw.)

If one rejects naturalism, it is easy to take credit for one's virtue and easy to blame Harris for his vicious character and acts: Harris freely chose the path of crime and cruelty, and we freely chose the path to virtue. No matter what our genetic or formative histories, each of us had the power to make that mysterious godlike choice. But in order to save blame and moral responsibility within the naturalistic framework, we must make severe adjustments elsewhere in the system: in this case, we must blind ourselves to the distinction between being vicious or virtuous and being to blame for those character traits. We can save moral responsibility within naturalism, but it requires twisting the system in ways that oversimplify our moral judgments, or by giving up basic beliefs concerning fairness, and the question then becomes: is such a system worth saving? We must choose between our basic sense of fairness and our myopic system of blame. Other than a deep inertial commitment to preserving the moral responsibility system, whatever its faults, I cannot see why anyone would find this a difficult choice. In order to save the blame system, one will have to make adjustments in the system that seem both ad hoc and implausible: it is legitimate to blame people for acts and character traits they did not and could not control. "If you couldn't do anything about it, you can't legitimately be blamed for it": giving up that principle to keep the moribund system of moral responsibility on life support seems a move born from desperation, not plausibility.

There does remain a difference—a difference that makes a difference—"between condemning a person's cruelty, manipulativeness, or unfairness, and simply condemning *him*" (Sher 2006, 65). Scrooge's flaws are deep, real, and awful, and those flaws result in harmful behavior. But we can recognize that—and be very sad that Scrooge is what he is, and sincerely wish that he were different and that he would become different in the future (we are glad that the ghosts pay him a visit), and examine steps that might reform Scrooge, and study policies to prevent our children from developing similar character traits—without condemning Scrooge or blaming him for his very real faults.

We can take take-charge responsibility, and doing so is a vital element of good psychological health, but we cannot take moral responsibility, and we should not be blamed for failing to take take-charge responsibility. The satisfied slave, the student who "just won't try," the abused spouse who "won't help herself," the dogs that won't make the effort to jump over the shuttle box barrier: they are all deeply flawed, they have very unfortunate faults, but they do not deserve blame for those faults. Or in any case, establishing that some individuals are faulty and that there is one type of responsibility that we can take (take-charge responsibility) does nothing whatsoever to establish that people are ever morally responsible for their characters or behaviors.

10 What Does Not Follow from the Denial of Moral Responsibility: Living Morally without Moral Responsibility

It is widely believed that moral responsibility is a necessary condition for moral judgments and moral evaluations and moral acts. Peter van Inwagen takes that position:

I have listened to philosophers who deny the existence of moral responsibility. I cannot take them seriously. I know a philosopher who has written a paper in which he denies the reality of moral responsibility. And yet this same philosopher, when certain of his books were stolen, said, "That was a *shoddy* thing to do!" But no one can consistently say that a certain act was a shoddy thing to do *and* say that its agent was not morally responsible when he performed it. (1983, 207)

Along similar lines, C. A. Campbell (1957, 167) asserts that denying justly deserved praise and blame means denying "the reality of the moral life." F. C. Copleston claims that without moral responsibility, "there would be no objective moral distinction between the emperor Nero and St. Francis of Assisi" (1965, 488). Susan Wolf insists that without moral responsibility, we must "stop thinking in terms of what ought and ought not to be" (1981, 401). Jeffrie Murphy claims that the demise of moral responsibility would mean the demise of "the moral significance of human beings that is founded upon such responsibility—would, indeed, spell the end of one's own moral significance" (1988, 400). J. Angelo Corlett states the implications of denying moral responsibility: "If causal determinism is true in the hard deterministic sense, then there is no sense to be made of ethics and moral responsibility, and not even moral practices such as forgiving others make much sense" (2006, 123).[1]

This widely held premise—no moral judgments without moral responsibility—occurs in philosophical arguments in two ways: first, in arguments from the existence of moral judgments to the existence of moral responsibility. This is the argument famously developed by Kant: the moral law obligates us to live morally and be better, and therefore "it follows inevitably that we must *be able* to be better men" (1960, 46). The second use of this premise is in arguing that the denial of moral responsibility has grievous implications that moral responsibility abolitionists have failed to recognize. This often includes a secondary argument: because no one who recognizes these egregious consequences can really accept them, we must hold onto moral responsibility at all costs—even including the embracing of illusion (Smilansky 2000) or the refusal to consider the rejection of moral responsibility (Strawson 1962). (The great exception to this trend is Sartre [1946/1989], who argues from the *non*existence of objective moral judgment to the existence of moral responsibility.)

Consider the first argument: if there are moral judgments, then there must be moral responsibility; there are moral judgments; therefore, there must be moral responsibility. The argument is *modus ponens*, so its validity cannot be challenged, but what about its soundness? Is it true that if there are moral judgments, then there must be moral responsibility? Is moral responsibility a necessary condition of moral judgments? If we step back a moment and look at that claim, it hardly seems as obvious as philosophers have generally supposed. Indeed, some noteworthy philosophers have not only denied that it is obviously true, but even claimed that it is obviously false: John Stuart Mill asserted that in the absence of belief in moral responsibility we can still maintain "the highest and strongest sense of the worth of goodness, and the odiousness of its opposite" (1865/1979, 456). More recently, Harry Frankfurt maintained that judgments of moral distaste and even moral contempt are consistent with denial of moral responsibility (1973, 79), and Jonathan Bennett insisted that rejecting moral responsibility and all claims of justified praise and blame would not pose "the slightest threat to the value-system according to which we judge some actions to be good or right or successful and others to be bad or wrong or failures" (1980, 31). Derk Pereboom concludes, "When the assumption that wrongdoers are blameworthy is withdrawn for hard incompatibilist reasons, the conviction that they have in fact done wrong could legitimately survive" (2001, 212). There would indeed seem to be many exceptions to the principle that moral judgments require belief in moral responsibility. Martin Luther (1525/1823) believed that humans have no moral responsibility; we are fashioned by God according to God's unfathomable purposes, and some are made evil with no power whatsoever to reform their evil characters, yet others—by God's gift of grace, and not by any choice or act of their own—become righteous and virtuous. Neither the evil damned nor the virtuous chosen have any moral responsibility whatsoever (the choice is made entirely by God; in the words of Paul, "it is not of him that willeth . . . but of God that showeth mercy" [Rom. 9:16), but the evil are certainly morally bad, and the virtue of the fortunate elect is genuine. However strange Luther's views may seem (especially to a naturalist), there is nothing inconsistent in his claim that one can be morally bad or good without being morally responsible. Robert Harris was shaped by natural forces rather than a divine potter, but the shaping was equally inexorable, and Robert Harris became a vicious person: a claim consistent with the conclusion that he was not morally responsible for the character shaped by those forces so far beyond his powers of control.

Does "Ought" Imply "Can"?

Why do so many astute philosophers regard it as obvious that the denial of moral responsibility entails the denial of moral judgments? One reason—discussed in the previous chapter—is the failure to distinguish blame-fault from character-fault. A second key source is commitment to the famous Kantian principle: ought implies can. This is a principle that Kant considers morally axiomatic: "When the moral law commands that we *ought* to be better men, it follows inevitably that we must *be able* to be better men" (1793/1960, 46). "Ought implies can" is often offered as a philosophical conversation-stopper, a fixed point of ethical theory that marks a clear boundary of reasonable discussion. Ishtiyaque Haji regards it as a central truth of ethics that enjoys "widespread intuitive support" and serves as a basic theorem in and thus is validated by "some of our best theories about the concept of moral obligation" (2000a, 352). Whatever its status as "a basic theorem," there is no doubt that it enjoys wide acceptance both within and without the contemporary philosophical community. But is that support warranted?

Joseph Margolis (Haji 2000b, 368) notes that in Greek tragedy, Antigone is obligated both to bury her brother and to follow the king's law prohibiting the burial. Thus she has conflicting obligations: she ought to do both, but obviously she cannot. To the Greeks, this seemed an unfortunate situation, though certainly not impossible. Haji, however, does consider it impossible: "If your central claim is that on a particular occasion, perhaps due to unlucky personal history, it is possible that some person have both an overall moral obligation to do *A* and an overall moral obligation to refrain from doing *A* . . . then I'd say that according to the theories about the concept of moral obligation that I favor, such situations are impossible: they can't occur" (2000b, 369). But what is behind this confidence—shared by Haji and most contemporary philosophers—that such conflicts cannot occur? And why should the ancient Greeks have held different views?

The ancient Greeks were much less confident that the world was morally well ordered. Their gods were spiteful, arbitrary, and cruel, and the best human efforts could be thwarted by cosmic caprice. (Aristotle held a different opinion, but his theological perspective was not widely shared.) There may be many things that we ought to do and that we may strive to accomplish, yet be unable to achieve. In the centuries that followed, Aristotle's god was integrated into Christianity, and the Aristotelian-Christian notion of a morally well-ordered cosmos triumphed. In such a system, obligations and capacities must coincide: a just God would give no obligations beyond our abilities to fulfill them. But in the natural world, devoid of divine order, there is no such assurance. Having evolved in this world it is hardly surprising that it accommodates us reasonably well, but fitting our moral obligations to our powers is well beyond what natural selection is likely to provide. Whatever one believes to be the source of one's obligations, there is no reason to suppose that the natural world is designed to help us meet them. It is hardly surprising that Kant would hold that ought implies can; after all, Kant designs his ethics to set it apart from the grubby natural world of feelings, making genuine principle-following ethical acts such that only beings with extraordinary rational capacities and influence-transcending powers of will could be ethical actors (thus setting human ethical actors apart from the deterministic world of Newton and the animal emotions of Hume). But it is surprising that naturalists—who have no wish to escape the natural world and its forces—should embrace such a principle. When we look at it closely, "ought implies can" has little to recommend it other than the exalted stature of Kant, the antinaturalist desire to transcend the natural world and set humans apart from other animals, and the belief that some divine force imposes a moral order on the world so that we will never face the misfortune of having a moral obligation we are incapable of meeting. It is obvious why libertarian non-naturalists should cherish this principle, but its charms for naturalists are more difficult to fathom. Jonathan Jacobs—though eager to save moral responsibility—says of the "ought implies can" principle that "there are reasons to think that this is an implausible idealization of moral agency" (2001, 68), which seems to be an accurate assessment of Kant's ethical shibboleth.

A key source for the popularity of ought implies can is the belief that doing wrong or failing morally implies that one deserves blame. Robert Harris ought to have reformed, but could not. As long as we think he therefore deserves blame, then we have problems: how can we blame someone for something he couldn't do, or couldn't avoid? But if we recognize that he is flawed, but does not deserve blame for his faults, then the problem disappears. He ought to have reformed, and he didn't, because he couldn't—but sometimes the world is like that. Not every good thing can be accomplished; the world is not set up to satisfy our moral demands or desires. We shouldn't blame him for the flaw or the failure, but we should recognize the flaw (because we don't want others falling into it, and with help, he might someday change), and we should recognize what is right to do in this case and what he ought to have done.

Consider Jonathan Jacobs's "ethically disabled" individual (2001, 34), who cannot act virtuously. Can we say of such an individual—Robert Harris, for example—that he ought not have killed the two young men? Certainly. Could we say that he was morally wrong to commit such murders? Of course. Even though he could not have done otherwise, what he did was horrifically wrong. And the implausible alternatives are that Robert could have acted differently (an article of faith that leads out of naturalism and into libertarian miracles), or that Robert—in his brutal, purposeful murders—did no wrong. It makes perfect sense to recognize that Harris is severely morally disabled, and that given who he is at this mature stage of life, he could not have resisted committing the murders, and he is incorrigible: far beyond his own powers of reform, and probably beyond the powers of contemporary psychological science. This recognition is very different from saying, "That tornado ought not to have killed that family." Robert Harris is not a tornado, but a person with rational powers (not super rational) who makes choices (though not super "ultimate" choices) and who might be capable of reform (as Jacobs notes, we should be very reluctant to judge someone as beyond reform). It may be somewhat disturbing to recognize that in the real world there are things we ought to do that we cannot do, moral obligations we cannot fulfill. Recognizing that is better than spinning out a "morally ordered" world to suit our moral wishes.

We could stipulate that no one counts as having an obligation if they are unable to fulfill it, but doing so will result in a difficult dilemma: either Robert Harris is not morally obligated to refrain from violence, or he really could have acted morally. The latter is empirically absurd. Ebenezer Scrooge has a moral obligation to help the poor, and Robert Harris has a moral obligation not to harm others, but given their harsh histories and current circumstances, they cannot meet those obligations. The former alternative is possible: we could insist that they do not have such moral obligations. In fact, that option is precisely the alternative favored by David Copp, when he confronts this problem: "But if the kleptomaniac lacks the ability to prevent himself from stealing, then I think he is not morally required not to steal. If he does steal, he would have performed an action of a *kind* that is wrong even though his stealing was not wrong in my view since he did not violate a moral requirement. The requirement he otherwise would have faced was defeated by his inability" (2003, 282).

But why should we narrow our ethics in that manner? It would severely limit the ethical judgments we can make and weaken our system of moral thought, and ethics could not function as well—if at all—for some of the most important things that moral thought does. I ought to repay the money you so kindly loaned to me, but I have suffered severe financial reverses, and I cannot do so. It's absurd to suggest that somehow—through some miracle-working financial power?—I really can. We could (if we are resolved to save "ought implies can" at any costs) stipulate that I do not have such an obligation, as I cannot fulfill it, but doing so will place limits on our system of moral thought that will hamstring important moral judgments. I ought to exert an effort to feed my hungry children, but if I suffer from severe learned helplessness, then I cannot exert such an effort. It is sad to think that the world is such that we sometimes have genuine moral obligations that we have not the power or resources to fulfill; if I believed in a just God, or a divinely well-ordered moral world, then it would be difficult for me to accept that the world can be like that. As a naturalist, I am disappointed—but not surprised—that the world often falls short of my moral ideals. Robert Harris is genuinely bad, and his brutal acts are morally bad, and it's important to note these things so that we can make efforts to prevent him from doing such acts in the future, attempt to reform his character, and—above all—examine the conditions that shaped his vicious character and try to change them so that fewer people like Robert Harris emerge. Saying that Robert doesn't deserve blame for his genuine moral faults does not impair the effectiveness of our system of moral thought; in contrast, we do severely limit our moral system if we must say that (because he could not act virtuously) it was not wrong for him to act viciously and that he was under no moral obligation to refrain from murder. If Rita fails (or succeeds) in meeting her moral obligation to visit her hospitalized friend, then—given the full history of Rita's conditioned character, the full panoply of situational forces acting on her, the full consideration of all the factors that came to bear on the situation—Rita could not have fulfilled her obligation and could not have acted differently. But there is nothing in that claim that precludes the judgment that Rita was morally wrong to forgo the obligatory hospital visit. The denial that Rita is morally responsible and the denial of "ought implies can" maintain a substantive system of moral judgments; the denial that Rita has morally failed in her moral obligation (though she could not do otherwise) leaves an impoverished system.

Leaving theological history aside, is there any good reason to suppose that ought implies can? Of course. After all, it may make perfectly good sense to say that I ought to rescue a child stuck in a tree, because I have the capacity to reach up and rescue the child; however, it would be non-sense to suggest that I ought to rescue the people falling toward Earth in a 747. With the best will in the world, I can't accomplish it. Perhaps Super-man ought to, but not me.

Such cases seem to support the idea that "ought" language applies only when our capacities are equal to our obligations. But that is too strong a conclusion. Consider another case: Sam ought to stop being jealous. Suppose we learn that Sam (because of his conditioning or genetics or other similar reason) cannot presently stop being jealous. It may still make sense to say that Sam ought to stop being jealous: it makes sense, and it may serve several useful functions. First, even if Sam cannot presently stop being jealous, if he believes that he ought to do so (perhaps as the result of being admonished to that effect), he might take steps to make it possible to stop being jealous in the future (for example, he might seek the services of a good psychotherapist). Second, "You ought not be so jealous" may be useful, even if we believe that Sam cannot presently exercise control over his jealousy, and indeed even if there are no steps available to Sam that would lead to gaining such control; even if he cannot stop being jealous, he may come to see it as a character flaw and not something to be acted upon, rather than a virtue that is a good guide to action. Furthermore, he may work to prevent his children from following in his own flawed path. Finally, even if we think that Sam has no chance of reform and that he will never even be capable of seeing his jealousy as a flaw, it may be useful to say that Sam ought not be jealous; such an admonition may help shape others who are currently more malleable to avoid such a character flaw. Of course, if Sam has no resources for reform, then it may be useless to tell *Sam* that he ought not be jealous, but that fact certainly does not make the statement false or incoherent. As Robert Stern notes, "A moral rule that goes beyond our capacities is not ipso facto pointless: for example, it may serve as a source of inspiration, or awe. Many of us admire certain figures or acts which we know we could not follow or even try to follow because of our own incapacities, where nonetheless this admiration gives these exemplars a kind of point" (2004, 50).

Contrast the case of jealous Sam with the earlier case: as we watch a doomed 747 plunge toward destruction, you say to me, "You ought not let that plane crash." Here the "ought" statement really is false; indeed, I shall have trouble even making sense of your statement. I share with Sam an incapacity to perform the action in question: he cannot stop being jealous, and I cannot rescue the airliner. But that common incapacity does not lead to a common result: the "ought" statement addressed to me is false, or perhaps nonsensical; the "ought" statement addressed to jealous Sam is true, useful, and quite intelligible. Thus, when it is not true that one can, it does not automatically follow that one is not a proper object of "ought" language. The difference is that no amount of moral resolve or proper conditioning or ethical admonition will make me into someone capable of rescuing malfunctioning jetliners. But when you say that I ought to avoid jealousy, or I ought to work harder at teaching, or I ought to stop smoking, that is to admonish me to do things that are within the capacities of at least some humans. If my smoking habit is such that I cannot over-come my addiction—perhaps I lack the psychological resources to make a concerted effort to stop, or perhaps even my best efforts will fall short of conquering my powerful addiction—it will still be useful to point out that

I should stop smoking: perhaps not useful to me, though still intelligible, but useful to children whom you are admonishing not to follow my health-hazard example.

The Ambiguity of "Ought"

The previous point leads to a basic distinction that has been sorely neglected in the "ought implies can" controversy. "Ought" is an ambiguous term and can be employed in two distinct senses. There is the admonition use of "ought," and there is also the quite different judgment use. If Uncle John cannot stop smoking—for whatever complicated combination of genetic and conditioning factors—then it would be silly to admonish him to stop. In that case, when you hear me tell John, "You ought to stop smoking," you may well instruct me to "Leave the poor fellow alone; he can't stop smoking, and your admonition is useless." In contrast, the judgment use of "ought" will remain quite useful. Even if we believe that John cannot stop smoking, it may be important to note that "John ought not smoke." I may want my children to understand that their Uncle John's behavior is wrong, and that they should not take up his filthy, dangerous, and bothersome habit. And although it may be rude and sometimes cruel and certainly nonefficacious to admonish John that he ought not smoke, it may be appropriate to use the "judgment" use of "ought" directly in our conversations with John: it may evidence a kindly concern with his flaws. "You ought not smoke," we tell John, even knowing that he cannot stop. "I know I ought to quit," John replies, "but I can't. However, I appreciate your concern." In this case, John is acknowledging his own moral flaw and expressing gratitude for sibling solicitude for his flaw; this is brotherly commiseration over a flaw that can't be fixed, just as the brothers might commiserate over a fatal and inoperable cancer. In the judgment use of "ought," John may meaningfully and rightly acknowledge his own deeply flawed and intractable character: a character that makes it impossible for him to do what he nonetheless ought to do. Even if we decide that John is not morally responsible for his own deep character flaws, we may none-theless note and regret the flaws that make John incapable of meeting the obligations that he should discharge.

Recognizing that ought statements come in two varieties—admonition and judgment oughts—makes it clear that denial of moral responsibility leaves quite sufficient scope for moral judgments. If Pharaoh's heart is hardened by an omnipotent deity, then it will be in vain to admonish Pharaoh that he ought to renounce slavery and free the children of Israel. If Joe's heart is hardened by more mundane processes, and "ought" admonitions cannot penetrate his flinty perspective, then it will also be in vain to urge Joe to meet his moral obligations to the less fortunate. But we may make all manner of legitimate and harsh moral judgments of Pharaoh and of Joe: one who purposefully and knowingly and cold-heartedly enslaves others is doing what he ought not do, and he is deeply flawed, whether the cause of that flawed character is divine purpose or natural forces. Thus it makes perfectly good sense to say that Pharaoh ought to have freed the slaves, though his divinely hardened heart makes such behavior impossible. Pharaoh really is a bad person, with evil purposes and selfish motives; the fact that God made him that way, and that he is incapable of reform, does not change that. But it does of course raise serious questions about whether Pharaoh deserves blame for his rotten character and the acts that stem from it. It will be useless to admonish Pharaoh that he ought to free the slaves, but it may be quite useful to make the moral judgment that Pharaoh ought to free the slaves: it may be part of the moral instruction we impart to our children, just as we teach them that Uncle John *ought* not smoke, notwithstanding the fact that we know Uncle John is utterly incapable of breaking his nicotine addiction.

This also explains why it makes sense to say that Uncle John ought to stop smoking (though he cannot) but does not make sense to suggest that Uncle John ought to rescue the doomed airliner (another feat beyond John's capacities). In neither case is an admonition ought of any use, but a judgment ought serves an important function in the first case, and is useless in the second. No matter how well we instruct our children, we cannot transform them into beings capable of leaping tall buildings and rescuing falling jetliners, but we can teach them about the dangers of tobacco, and thus such judgment oughts may be useful in shaping healthy habits.

The Value of Ought Language without Moral Responsibility

Some may suggest that these considerations and distinctions rescue "ought" language for naturalism-determinism, but leave it so limited that it is hardly worth saving: if "ought" language can no longer be used to admonish, it's not the "ought" language we knew and loved. Such a criticism seems to me misguided, for two reasons. First, judgment oughts are important and useful in their own right, in the absence of admonition oughts. But second, even in a natural world devoid of moral responsibility, there remains an important role for admonition oughts. Not in dealing with Pharaoh, of course: our admonitions won't have much force in changing a heart that has been hardened by almighty God—and perhaps not in dealing with Uncle John's nicotine addiction, either. But admonition oughts are sometimes useful in shaping desirable behavior. If the world is determined, then such ought admonitions will take their place among the other causal forces shaping—determining—character and behavior, and they may play an effective causal role in the shaping environment. We should not exaggerate their effectiveness: my ought admonition that "you ought to work hard at your math" will not be nearly as powerful a causal force in shaping math industriousness as will be the right schedule of reinforcement in which the child has math problems that are not so impossibly difficult that her efforts are frustrated (thus engendering math helplessness) and that are not so easy that she succeeds with no effort and thus fails to develop fortitude in working on challenging problems. But that is not to say that such admonitions are of no use: an environment in which children are admonished to work hard at math because it is valuable and important to do so is more likely to be a positive environment for shaping positive math behavior than would be an environment in which no such "ought" admonitions occur.

When we reject the naturalistically implausible principle that "ought implies can," there is no reason to suppose that denying moral responsibility implies denial of moral judgments, and no reason to suppose that the making of moral judgments implies the existence of moral responsibility. I ought to treat my children affectionately; it does not follow that I can, and that I am morally responsible for failing in affection. And from the other direction, it does not follow from the fact that I cannot act generously or virtuously that I have no moral obligation to do so. Thus with the demise of "ought implies can," there is no problem in affirming the judgment of John Stuart Mill: denial of moral responsibility is perfectly consistent with "the highest and strongest sense of the worth of goodness, and the odiousness of its opposite" (1865/1979, 456).

P. F. Strawson and Morality without Moral Responsibility

The argument path described in the previous section leads to the second way that "no moral judgments without moral responsibility" is used in support of moral responsibility: the claim that denial of moral responsibility has such odious consequences that the abolition of moral responsibility cannot be contemplated. This argument reaches its apex in P. F. Strawson (1962): denying moral responsibility demolishes the whole system of moral judgments, extinguishes our reactive attitudes toward one another, reduces us to emotionally impoverished objective judgments, and banishes people from the moral community. Strawson's arguments have been very influential, but they are also profoundly wrong. Not wrong in a shallow, silly way, but wrong in a way that is very important, wrong in a way that only a deep and insightful philosopher could be wrong, wrong in a way that reveals a great deal about the fundamental conflict over moral responsibility. And wrong in a way that requires careful examination—an examination that will be taken up in the discussion of the competing systems of moral responsibility advocates and moral responsibility abolitionists, and the basic assumptions of the moral responsibility system (see chapters 11, 12, and 13). The remainder of this chapter will be devoted to a closer look at how the denial of moral responsibility—rather than destroying our moral system—actually enhances some important aspects of our moral judgments and moral behavior. To take one salient case: it is widely assumed that the denial of moral responsibility would eliminate sincere apology for wrongdoing. That belief is false. To the contrary, the demise of moral responsibility would facilitate the moral practice of sincere apology.

Alice is a dedicated moral responsibility abolitionist. She firmly believes that no one (including herself) is ever morally responsible, that rewards and punishments can never be justified on the basis of just deserts, and that blaming people for vicious character traits and vile acts is never morally justified. One day, Barbara—Alice's dearest friend—confides to Alice a special secret: a secret that Barbara clearly does not want revealed to others, a secret shared only with a special and specially trusted friend. A week later, Alice—thoughtlessly, in a moment of weakness, without special intent to harm Barbara but with conscious awareness of betraying a deep confidence—tells Barbara's secret to Carl, who spreads the secret to a wide circle. Barbara soon discovers that her secret has been betrayed, and her feelings are profoundly hurt. Can Alice—who denies all moral responsibility—sincerely apologize to Barbara?

Moral responsibility abolitionists can indeed make sincere apologies. The denial of moral responsibility promotes sincere apology, and (it will be argued) insistence on moral responsibility is an impediment to sincere apology. This claim that apology is compatible with the denial of moral responsibility is not based on some attenuated version of apology: the politician's pseudoapology (Davis 2002), in the form of "I'm sorry if anyone took offense at my words," or "I'm sorry if anyone misinterpreted my statement in such a way as to feel insulted." Denial of moral responsibility is consistent with, and contributes to, full *categorical* (Smith 2005) apologies: apologies in which the moral responsibility abolitionist honestly acknowledges having done wrong, sincerely regrets the moral flaw in his or her character, resolves to avoid such wrongful acts in the future, and desires to repair or mitigate the harm caused. Moral responsibility abolitionists can consistently make such categorical apologies, and the denial of moral responsibility will facilitate sincere full apology.

The assertion that denial of moral responsibility is compatible with sincere apology does have some limits. Obviously, if you set the standards for moral responsibility low enough—for example, Dennett (1984) suggests that anyone meeting a very minimal standard of rationality is morally responsible—then it follows that anyone who is not morally responsible is incapable of reasoning, and is thus incapable of recognizing what counts as a wrongful act and incapable of genuine apology for such acts. But the question is not whether the denial of moral responsibility on some grounds would preclude apology, but whether there is something inherent in the denial of moral responsibility that makes sincere apology impossible. The proper test for that question is whether—given the common grounds for denying moral responsibility favored by moral responsibility abolitionists—sincere apology remains viable. This universal denial of moral responsibility is not based on denial of rationality; rather, the claim is that there is no moral responsibility because whatever our talents and flaws, our virtues and vices, they are ultimately a matter of our good or bad fortune: ultimately, they are the product of forces we did not control. Whether that is a good reason to deny moral responsibility is not the immediate question; rather, the question is whether we can deny moral responsibility on those grounds and consistently apologize. The answer is that sincere apology can function and flourish under that standard *universal* denial of moral responsibility.

There is no inconsistency in Alice denying that she is morally responsible for her bad act while also maintaining that the act was her own morally egregious act of betraying a friend's trust. Of course, if Alice were not morally responsible because she is insane, or deeply deranged, or incapable of reason, or driven by the fates and devoid of any control over her own acts, then it would make little sense to think of Alice's act as morally bad any more than we think of the destructive force of a hurricane as morally bad. Indeed, we might doubt that it is Alice's act at all. But Alice is not deranged, not irrational, not the pawn of capricious fate. She is an intelligent, reflective, self-directed person with considerable strength of character. She is not, however, perfect. She sometimes does wrong, and her wrong acts stem from deep flaws in her own character: flaws she acknowledges as her own, faults that—in the words of Shakespeare's Cassius—lie "not in our stars, but in ourselves" (Shakespeare 1599/1998, 1.2.140–141). Alice is at fault, her act flowed from her own flawed character, and the harm caused is due to Alice's intentional bad act. But Alice can acknowledge all of that—sincerely acknowledge to Barbara that the bad act was due to her own fault—and still deny that she deserves blame for either her flawed character or her flawed behavior (because, Alice might insist, both are ultimately the result of causes she did not and could not control). So, employing the distinction from the previous chapter, Alice can recognize and acknowledge her own *character*-fault while denying *blame*-fault.

The distinction between character-fault and blame-fault is essential in examining another requirement for sincere apology: genuine remorse, or "self-reproach" (Davis 2002, 171). For genuine apology, I must acknowledge that I have violated a moral principle that is my own, and that we share. It would make no sense for me (a WASP) to apologize to you because you are offended by the presence of my African-American friends; I might well regret that you are offended, but I can't apologize because I do not share your racist values, and I do not believe I have done anything wrong (Smith 2005, 480–481). But Alice—in betraying her friend's confidence—certainly does believe that she did something wrong, and she might well feel regret at her acknowledged moral transgression and disgust at the character flaw revealed. It is very disturbing to discover that one's character has deep flaws. Imagine you are called before the House UnAmerican Affairs Committee, and under intensive authoritarian pressure you "name names" of your friends. After leaving the hearings, you recognize your vile behavior and the character flaw behind it. This would be a profoundly disturbing revelation, and a source of deep regret, even self-disgust, and would be so even if you firmly believed that you were not morally responsible for the character flaw or the resulting behavior: "I realize that I'm not morally responsible for this flaw in my character; after all, I can see the powerful environmental forces that shaped me to be weak and acquiescent when confronted by figures of authority. But I am very sad to recognize this deep moral failing in my own character." Alice—as a moral responsibility abolitionist—will not blame herself for her bad character, and if "self-reproach" is synonymous with "self-blame," then Alice will not self-reproach or self-blame. But Alice might feel profound and sincere regret at the character and behavior that she acknowledges as her own, which seems quite sufficient to satisfy this condition for sincere apology. Alice might well say to herself, with genuine regret at this painful self-acknowledgment, "Alice, you are weak, you are not worthy of trust, you casually betray your best friend's confidence; you have some serious moral problems, and you need to see what you can do to reform that part of your moral character." But such sincere acknowledgment of moral fault does not imply that she believes herself to be morally responsible for her flawed character. (Alice desires to reform, but she does not count herself morally responsible for that virtuous desire or for her success or failure in achieving reform.)

Of course, Alice might instead seek an excuse for her behavior—an option equally open to those who affirm and those who deny moral responsibility. Alice might insist that the fault lies not in her weak character, but instead in some other quarter: Alice was tricked into betraying her friend's confidence, or she was coerced, or drugged, or demon-possessed. In offering such excuses, Alice is claiming that the fault is not really her own: the event did not flow from her own flawed character, but from some external force. If Alice was forcefully administered a powerful drug that led to the delusional belief that she was talking to Barbara (rather than to Carl), then Alice is excused: her betrayal of Barbara's secret is not the result of Alice's own character flaw. But if instead Alice acknowledges that she wronged Barbara due to Alice's own weak character, that is not an excuse. An excuse claims a special exception: the act was not really my own, it did not come from me, it was not the result of my own purposeful act. But for Alice, the sad truth is that the act *did* come from her own flawed character. If Alice had revealed Barbara's secret under the coercive influence of drugs, Alice would have regretted that Barbara's secret was revealed, but that would be a very different order of regret from the regret she feels when she realizes that she has betrayed Barbara's secret due to her own deep shortcomings. Of course, Alice (as a moral responsibility abolitionist) does not believe that she is morally responsible for her character weaknesses or strengths. But that is not because she believes she meets a special excusing condition; rather, it is because she believes that no one—under any circumstances whatsoever—is morally responsible: that no coherent case can be made for moral responsibility.

Alice—as a moral responsibility abolitionist—acknowledges her own character-fault, but denies blame-fault. Perhaps she is mistaken in her denial, but her position is not incoherent: there is no conceptual inconsistency in acknowledging character-fault while rejecting blame-fault. Thus Alice's denial of blame-fault is no impediment to her sincere apology for an act that she acknowledges as her own act from her own character. Even if Alice is wrong in thinking that she is not morally responsible, there is nothing in her denial of moral responsibility that undercuts sincere apology. Alice can consistently believe that she is not—that she is *never*—morally responsible while offering a sincere apology for her character-faults and the bad acts they produce.

Even if one accepts that a moral responsibility abolitionist could consistently believe that she has done wrong, one might still object to the claim that those who deny moral responsibility can sincerely apologize. After all, as a moral responsibility abolitionist, Alice does not believe that she is morally responsible for her misdeed, so how could it make sense for Alice to apologize for her wrongful act? How can she apologize if she does not believe she is responsible? Almost everyone who examines apology treats accepting responsibility as an essential and obvious condition of sincere apology. Thus Martin Golding (1984–1985) speaks of apology as a case of making moral amends, requiring that we express moral regret in acknowledgment of our responsibility for doing wrong. Louis F. Kort (1975) regards accepting responsibility as a central condition for sincere apology. Trudy Govier and Wilhelm Verwoerd state, "To apologize for an action is to admit that one did it, that it was wrong and harmful to the victim, and that one was responsible for doing it" (2002, 69). Kathleen Gill regards "an acknowledgment of responsibility for the act" as one of five essential elements for an apology (2000, 12).

In the standard cases of apology, it seems obvious that accepting responsibility for the wrongful act is an essential element of sincere apology. I can't sincerely apologize if I was not responsible (or, more precisely, if I do not believe that I was responsible) because without responsibility, there is nothing to apologize for. I'm sorry that Joe treated you badly, but unless I was somehow in control of Joe, or conspired with Joe to do you harm, I can't apologize for the wrong Joe did to you, though I may certainly regret that you were wronged. I can't apologize, because I wasn't responsible. So it appears that even if blame-fault is not essential for sincere apology, the moral responsibility abolitionist is still barred from the most obvious and basic requirement for sincere apology: the acknowledgment of responsibility.

Acknowledging responsibility is an essential condition for sincere apology, but the requisite responsibility is not the moral responsibility denied by moral responsibility abolitionists. There are at least three distinct types of responsibility. We have long realized that being causally responsible is very different from being morally responsible: I might cause something to happen, yet quite obviously not deserve blame or punishment. Having no medical history of such problems, I suffer a sudden seizure that results in my jerking my car into an oncoming vehicle; in that case, I am causally responsible for the other driver's injury, but clearly not morally responsible.

The distinction between moral responsibility and causal responsibility is widely recognized, but the distinction between moral responsibility and take-charge responsibility (noted in chapter 6) is easily overlooked. Alice can take responsibility for planning a symposium, and she can also take responsibility for her own life and her own decisions—and in most cases, taking such take-charge responsibility is satisfying and healthy. But it is something very different to suppose that because one has take-charge responsibility one must also have moral responsibility. We can acknowledge Alice's take-charge responsibility while questioning or denying that she is morally responsible: questioning or denying that she justly deserves blame or praise, punishment, or reward. Take-charge responsibility is very important to us: the belief that we can make effective decisions and exercise control is psychologically healthy, and even when we recognize that perhaps someone else could run our lives better than we can, we prefer to take responsibility for ourselves and our projects. Often we really do take and exercise control. But that we exercise such control (as opposed to being socially or physically or psychologically incapable of doing so) and exercise it well (or poorly) is ultimately the result of our good fortune, and not something for which we are morally responsible. Alice exercises take-charge responsibility for her own life, and usually she does it well; when she betrayed Barbara's confidence, she—by her own acknowledgment—exercised her own take-charge responsibility very poorly. But whether exercised well or ill, this valuable taken responsibility is not moral responsibility.

There may be a case for claiming that take-charge responsibility and causal responsibility are essential for sincere apology, but the present claim is only that if responsibility is essential for sincere apology, the responsibility in question will be taken and/or causal responsibility rather than moral responsibility. So there is no reason to suppose that the moral responsibility abolitionist—who can quite happily claim all manner of take-charge and causal responsibility for her acts and offices and character—cannot sincerely apologize. Or perhaps it really is moral responsibility that is required for sincere apology. But establishing that claim will require substantial argument, and given the argument offered here for why take-charge responsibility will suffice for sincere apology, the burden of proof will rest on those who insist that there is a further requirement of moral responsibility.

When we eliminate the confusions between blame-fault and character-fault and between moral responsibility and take-charge responsibility, there remains no reason to deny the sincere apology of moral responsibility abolitionists. I can take responsibility for a project, fail to discharge that taken obligation due to my own character fault, and not be morally responsible for the failure (and as a moral responsibility abolitionist, not believe myself to be morally responsible for the failure)—and still make a sincere apology for the failure. Alice can honestly and sincerely say to Barbara, "I am sorry that my own flaws resulted in a failure that caused you harm; I am sincerely sorry for my own character flaws and for their harmful effects on you. The harmful act was my own, and I am not a puppet or a pawn: I make my own decisions, and I take responsibility for my own acts and character (I run my own life, no one 'manages' me). I do not deserve blame for my acts or my character, or for how well or ill I manage to take responsibility for myself and my behavior, but the act was my own, it came from my own flawed character and choice, and I am sincerely sorry for what I did and deeply regretful of the bad character elements revealed by my act and my choice, and I will make sincere efforts to correct that problem."

Of course—as a practicing moral responsibility abolitionist—Alice recognizes that it is no good beating herself up. She doesn't deserve to suffer for her misdeeds or her own character flaws; furthermore, she may recognize that such self-flagellation is not an effective means of improving her own character. But she can be genuinely sorry that her own character and acts caused Barbara harm and sincerely sorry to discover such flaws in her own character. I fear that had I been recruited for Milgram's notorious obedience experiment, I would have continued to "administer shocks" even when the supposed victim screamed for mercy, and even though no one was actually harmed by my behavior—no real shocks were administered—I would have genuinely regretted such an "obedience to authority" character flaw deep in myself. But recognizing the profound influence of the authoritarian culture and religion in which I grew up, I would not *blame* myself for such a character flaw, though I deeply regret it, and blaming myself for the character flaw would not be a positive step in reshaping my character; instead, paying careful attention to the factors that shaped my character might lead to discovering effective ways to *change* my flawed character. Had I participated in an experiment with genuine shocks, and caused harm to some other experimental subject, I would be sincerely sorry for the harm and for the character weakness that generated the harm. But nothing in this regret would require that I believe myself to be morally responsible for my character or my acts.

Sincere apology requires that I recognize I am at fault (though I need not believe that I am to blame for my genuine fault), and perhaps it requires that I have take-charge responsibility for the harmful act that stemmed from my own flaw (but not that I have moral responsibility). Sincere apology (at least in most cases) requires that one resolve not to continue doing such wrongs and a desire to set the wrongs right (to the degree possible). All of this is possible for the moral responsibility abolitionist, and it is important to recognize the consistency of moral responsibility denial with sincere apology. Sincere apology has great moral importance, and if those who deny moral responsibility could not sincerely apologize, it would reveal a severe moral deficiency in moral responsibility abolitionists. First, sincere apology involves genuine acknowledgment of wrongful behavior and a resolve to reform. One lacking those capacities can hardly count as a moral being at all and certainly would not count as a moral being who is capable of moral improvement. As Jennifer Roback Morse notes, "If a person is not repentant, then we suspect that he is either justifying his offense, or indifferent to it" (2005, 206). Neither attitude is likely to result in moral reform.

Second, if the moral responsibility abolitionist could not sincerely apologize, that lack of apology could easily be taken to indicate extreme arrogance among moral responsibility abolitionists. If I go to great trouble to meet you for a luncheon engagement and you simply fail to show up, I want you to apologize. If in your haste you run through a door and flatten me, scattering my books and papers and scraping my knee, I want an apology. If I greet you with a cheery good morning and you tell me to go to hell, I want an apology. If you refuse to apologize, you "add insult to injury." Why so? Because the clear implication is that I can be ignored, mistreated, harmed, and insulted—and it doesn't matter. I want an apology, because I want you to acknowledge that I am a person whose welfare and feelings are important. Harms and insults to me are not insignificant, because I am not insignificant. As Govier and Verwoerd point out, a sincere apology involves "acknowledgment of the *human dignity and moral worth of victims*" (2002, 69).

It is notoriously true that members of the "elite" feel that it is beneath their dignity to apologize to the "lower classes." A nobleman might feel some regret at harming a peasant, and might even make some payment to mitigate the peasant's suffering, but the nobleman will not apologize to the peasant, because that would acknowledge the peasant's right to be recognized as a person—as someone who matters. Thus if it is assumed that those who deny moral responsibility must reject sincere apology, that assumption perhaps accounts for some of the hostility often directed at moral responsibility abolitionists. When I deny all moral responsibility, it is mistakenly assumed that I could never sincerely apologize to anyone. And if I can never sincerely apologize, that implies incredible arrogance: when I wrong you it doesn't matter, I can harm you and not be sorry for it, because you are beneath my consideration. When the compatibility of sincere apology with moral responsibility denial is recognized, and the denial of moral responsibility is not mistakenly linked with the contemptuous arrogance that refuses to apologize, then perhaps we moral responsibility abolitionists will be looked upon more kindly.

Openness about mistakes—which is encouraged by eliminating blame—is a natural partner to apology, because apology for unacknowledged mistakes is impossible. Furthermore, sincere apology normally must include a genuine desire to reform and to prevent recurrence of the wrong. If I am genuinely sorry that I did some act or was involved in some wrong, then I must be honestly eager to avoid any recurrence of the act. "I'm sorry I cheated you and I can't wait to do it again" is not a sincere apology. The best way of avoiding mistakes and harms in the future—the errors and mistakes I am genuinely sorry for and for which I sincerely apologize—is to focus on what caused the mistake, rather than focusing on "who is to blame." Blaming the unfortunate individual in whom the flawed process reached its fulfillment fails to fix the deeper systemic causes and does nothing to prevent other persons from developing similar flaws and making the same mistakes.

Turning away from individual blame does not undercut sincere apology for wrongs and mistakes; to the contrary, it lays an important foundation for sincere apology. Sincere apology requires that we honestly acknowledge that a mistake was made, and eliminating blame facilitates that open acknowledgment. Second, sincere apology implies that we do not want the mistake to be repeated, and abolishing the culture of blame is the best way to promote effective systemic and individual reform. Third, sincere apology requires that we strive to correct the error, so far as possible, and hiding mistakes (as the blame culture encourages) precludes effective measures to correct mistakes or reduce their harmful effects.

Gratitude without Moral Responsibility

Rejecting moral responsibility does not prevent sincere apology, but what about the flip side: the sincere and legitimate expression of *gratitude*? P. F. Strawson counted gratitude as one of the reactive attitudes that would be lost if moral responsibility were eliminated, and Galen Strawson agrees:

Clearly, our more positive attitudes to other people are the best cases to consider. For when we consider these attitudes, the idea that people can be true originators of their actions in such a way as to be truly responsible for them emerges as integral to some of our strongest beliefs about what is valuable (and therefore worth wanting) in human life and interaction. It seems that we very much want people to be proper objects of gratitude, for example. And they cannot be proper objects of gratitude unless they can be truly responsible for what they do. (1986, 308)

Apparently Galen Strawson finds that result so obvious that it need only be stated, as he offers no further grounds for that claim. But in fact, the claim seems obviously false. Donna is a good and loyal friend who is kind and considerate and generous to her friends because she is deeply devoted to them. Donna considers it her moral duty to help her friends, and even if she were tired, she would quickly come to a friend's aid. However, Donna rarely requires the promptings of duty, for she takes great pleasure in doing kindnesses for her friends. Donna is not an automaton, but an intelligent and reflective person who places great value on friendship and on the welfare of her friends, and who purposefully and intentionally acts generously and supportively toward her friends. When Donna brings me books and flowers and a warm smile and a cheerful comforting presence during my hospital stay, she does so out of sincere friendship and care and affection. I believe that Donna—like all of us—is not morally responsible for her splendid character and kind behavior; rather, she is fortunate to have been raised in a loving family and a supportive community that shaped Donna to be a warm and wonderful person who is capable of sincere and deep friendships. That does not change the fact that Donna *is* a very good person, and it in no way prevents me from feeling deeply grateful for her sincere friendship and her many acts of genuine kindness. I don't believe that Donna deserves any special reward: she is not morally responsible for her kind acts or the consistently kind character from which her behavior flows. But out of the kindness of her heart, Donna has brought special cheer to my drab and depressing hospital room; why would I not feel special affection and special gratitude toward my good friend Donna? My feeling of gratitude is an appropriate response to Donna, just as my resentment is an appropriate response to Matthew when he gratuitously insults me (if I did not resent it, that would indicate a very poor self-image). Neither Matthew nor Donna is morally responsible, and neither justly deserve reward or punishment, but that fact—and my recognition of it—does not preclude reactive feelings of resentment and gratitude.

The possibility and the legitimacy of reactive gratitude among moral responsibility abolitionists becomes even clearer when we consider our gratitude and affection toward dear old Mom. My mother loves me dearly, and not only treats me with deep affection and attentive care (and did so when I was most vulnerable), but also is fiercely protective of me in the face of threat or danger. Her affectionate and protective attitude toward me is rooted in a profound maternal instinct, which she certainly did not choose nor construct, and thus (though some might not agree) it seems particularly clear to me that Mom is not morally responsible for her deep and genuine affection and care toward her son, but recognizing and believing that does not reduce in any way the deep gratitude I feel for my mother's profound affection and diligent care.

Consider one more example. You are deeply distressed, sitting in a corner of the couch feeling desolate. Your dog, who is quite fond of you, comes up and quietly rests her head on your arm, licks your hand, and shows sympathy at your distress. (Anyone who doubts the plausibility of this account obviously has never lived with an affectionate dog.) Certainly, you do not consider your faithful dog to be morally responsible, but you have no trouble feeling gratitude for your canine friend's genuine affection. So (like your friend and your mom), your dog is a "proper object of gratitude" even though dogs are not "truly responsible for what they do" (Strawson 1986, 308).

A full, rich ethical system—one that includes moral judgments and admonitions, strong efforts for reform and improvement, profound ethical commitments, sincere apology, and heartfelt gratitude—is fully consistent with the abolition of moral responsibility. Unless one regards blame and punishment (and praise and reward) as the key elements of ethics, ethics has little to lose and much to gain from the rejection of moral responsibility.

11   The Moral Responsibility System

Moral responsibility has a powerful hold on our intuitions, our common sense, our legal system, and our philosophical reflections. The moral responsibility system is locked in place by our retributive emotions, our central institutions, and our philosophical axioms. It is celebrated in song and story, from Shakespeare's dramas to Western movies. Small wonder, then, that many people find it almost impossible to contemplate its rejection, and many philosophers believe that no one can actually deny moral responsibility: Peter van Inwagen (1983) states that although he knows some philosophers who claim to deny moral responsibility, he has "a hard time taking them seriously"; Saul Smilansky (2000) acknowledges that moral responsibility is philosophically indefensible, but insists that the illusion of moral responsibility is essential; P. F. Strawson (1962) treats the dispute over moral responsibility as an empty exercise because it is so deeply embedded in our conceptual system that it cannot be dislodged by argument.

So strong and pervasive is the belief in moral responsibility that it is hardly surprising when some of its supporters slide into question-begging arguments when they defend moral responsibility. In particular, advocates of moral responsibility often work from *within* the moral responsibility framework and assume that anyone who questions moral responsibility must also be starting from the basic principle of that framework: the principle that people are morally responsible unless they meet a special excusing condition. Under that assumption, there are only two ways to deny moral responsibility: people are either excused in a specific case because of some special impediment—the person was drugged, suffered temporary insanity, was overcome by grief or justified rage, was acting on false information—or they are permanently excused because of insanity or senility or some other cause of severe incompetence. Thus—if operating from within the assumptions of the moral responsibility system—when one proposes a *universal* denial of moral responsibility, that proposal must be based on the belief that all people are permanently deranged or otherwise permanently incompetent. P. F. Strawson sees that as an implication of the hard determinist denial of moral responsibility, and rejects it as absurd: "For it is not a consequence of any general thesis of determinism which might be true that nobody knows what he's doing or that everybody's behavior is unintelligible in terms of conscious purposes or that everybody lives in a world of delusion or that nobody has a moral sense, i.e. is susceptible of self-reactive attitudes, etc." (1962, 74).

Universal derangement is a consequence of universal rejection of moral responsibility from within the moral responsibility system, because the system bases the special exemption from moral responsibility on deep delusion and insanity. And from within the system of moral responsibility, the universal denial of moral responsibility does generate absurdities, which is hardly surprising: within a system that treats moral responsibility as a basic assumption, the denial of that assumption results in fundamental inconsistencies. But those absurdities disappear when the question is whether the moral responsibility *system* itself is a fair and beneficial system, or whether some alternative system—that rejects moral responsibility altogether—might be better.

Arguments like Strawson's are not simple circular arguments, but rather arguments that draw upon basic elements of the moral responsibility system. Such arguments work by showing that—given the system of moral responsibility—various challenges to that system result in absurdity or cruelty; or that from within the moral responsibility system, objections to moral responsibility border on incoherence; or that from the moral responsibility perspective, giving up moral responsibility would produce a cold and morally desolate world.

Some of Strawson's claims have been examined and critiqued in earlier chapters. It was argued that renouncing claims and ascriptions of moral responsibility would not undercut moral judgments (except judgments of blame), would not eliminate important moral evaluations, and that although blame-fault would be eliminated, we could get along quite nicely without it (we could continue to make judgments of character-fault). But it is time to look more closely at Strawson's arguments, and examine the systemic argument that he offers against the abandonment of moral responsibility.

Arguments for Moral Responsibility from within the Moral Responsibility System

The key problem in Strawson's argument is that Strawson is so deeply immersed in the moral responsibility system that he cannot genuinely consider alternatives to that system; rather, he imagines what it would be like to stay within the moral responsibility system while making a universal rejection of moral responsibility. And from within that system, it is easy to paint a very dark picture of what would be involved in the total elimination of moral responsibility. When are you not morally responsible? Under what circumstances do we conclude that a malefactor does not deserve punishment and should not be held responsible? Who is excused from blame? We excuse small children, of course, and generally we excuse the insane. We often decide that one who acted in ignorance or under dire threat or extreme duress does not justly deserve blame. We may quibble about the details, but the basic pattern is clear enough: people are excused from moral responsibility when they are insane, incompetent, or ignorant. Specific acts are excused when the actor is temporarily impaired (suffers a seizure, is under coercion, has been drugged, acts inadvertently or ignorantly), and people are completely exempted when they are permanently debilitated (by insanity or incompetence).

Philosophers who attempt to enlarge—and ultimately universalize—the denial of moral responsibility sometimes start from the same assumption. In contemporary philosophy, the classic universal denial of moral responsibility is found in the work of John Hospers (1952, 1958). Hospers starts with examples of individuals gripped by neurotic compulsions that they can neither understand nor control, and from there he extends excusing conditions far beyond a few modest exceptions: "Psychiatrists began to realize, though philosophers did not, that the domination of the conscious by the unconscious extended, not merely to a few exceptional individuals, but to all human beings" (1952, 572). Thus excuses are extended to cover all, because we are universally afflicted by a tyrannical unconscious that deprives us of rational control along with moral responsibility. The "generalization strategy" proposed by R. Jay Wallace (1994) is a more recent attempt to start from recognized excuses and ultimately to enlarge those excuses (on the basis of determinism) until excuses swallow up all of moral responsibility. This model of denying moral responsibility might be called the *excuse-extensionist model*.

P. F. Strawson (1962) appears to be fundamentally opposed to Hospers. Hospers champions universal denial of moral responsibility, and Strawson argues that all of us—at least all of us who count as persons—are morally responsible; the exceptions are those who are so severely defective that we must regard them with objective detachment (and exclude them from our moral community). But looking below the surface differences, we find that Strawson's brief in *support* of moral responsibility rests on the same excuse foundation that Hospers uses to *attack* moral responsibility.

Strawson makes an impressive study of the situations in which we suspend the "participant reactive attitudes" of resentment and gratitude and blame (the ordinary attitudes of our interpersonal relationships) and instead employ the "objective attitude" of clinical detachment (in which we regard someone "as a subject for . . . treatment; as something . . . to be managed or handled or cured or trained") (1962, 66). The most important context for the objective attitude is when we say such things as, "He's only a child," "He's a hopeless schizophrenic," "His mind has been systematically perverted." As Strawson summarizes, "Seeing someone, then, as warped or deranged or compulsive in behaviour or peculiarly unfortunate in his formative circumstances—seeing someone so tends, at least to some extent, to set him apart from normal participant reactive attitudes on the part of one who sees him, tends to promote, at least in the civilized, objective attitudes" (1962, 66).

So when do we exempt someone from resentment or blame, adopting the objective attitude and excusing from moral responsibility? We do so when we regard someone as "warped or deranged or compulsive." Thus a universal exemption from moral responsibility must be based on the judgment that *everyone* is "warped or deranged or compulsive": precisely what Hospers offers as grounds for the universal denial of moral responsibility.

Steven Pinker pursues the same line of thought, to the same dreadful conclusion:

A biology of human nature would seem to admit more and more people into the ranks of the blameless. A murderer may not literally be a raving lunatic, but our newfangled tools might pick up a shrunken amygdala or a hypometabolism in his frontal lobes or a defective gene for MAO oxidase, which renders him just as out of control. Or perhaps a test from the cognitive psychology lab will show that he has chronically limited foresight, rendering him oblivious to consequences, or that he has a defective theory of mind, making him incapable of appreciating the suffering of others. After all, if there is no ghost in the machine, *something* in the criminal's hardware must set him apart from the majority of people, those who would not hurt or kill in the same circumstances. Pretty soon we will find this something, and, it is feared, murderers will be excused from criminal punishment as surely as we now excuse madmen and small children.

Even worse, biology may show that we are *all* blameless. Evolutionary theory says that the ultimate rationale for our motives is that they perpetuated our ancestors' genes in the environment in which we evolved. Since none of us are aware of that rationale, none of us can be blamed for pursuing it, any more than we blame the mental patient who thinks he is subduing a mad dog but really is attacking a nurse. (2008, 312–313)

Thus as the range of excuses is extended to cover all of us, it drowns our rationality and self-control: we are excused because we are merely pawns, incapable of choice or control, ultimately indistinguishable from madmen and small children. This excuse-extensionist model of the universal denial of moral responsibility has implications as dreadful as they are implausible.

The same underlying pattern can be traced in the arguments of Daniel Dennett (1984). Hospers, Strawson, and Pinker exempt people from blame and moral responsibility when they are "warped or deranged or compulsive" and not really in control of their own behavior; thus universal denial of moral responsibility is based on universal compulsion or derangement. From the other direction, but using the same reasoning, Dennett withholds credit and responsibility from someone whose success was merely a matter of luck and not the result of their own exercise of skill: the person who draws the winning lottery ticket, the incompetent basketball player whose wild heave at the basket careens in for the winning points. Generalizing from such cases, Dennett concludes that those who deny that we are ever due credit for our success (deny that we are ever morally responsible) must be basing that denial on a universal repudiation of skill: we are always merely lucky (or unlucky), and when we race or shoot or live successfully, it is never the result of our own skillful control. Dennett describes the position of those who deny all responsibility thus: "There is a tendency to treat 'lucky' and 'unlucky' as complementary and exhaustive, leaving no room for skill at all. On this view nothing in principle could count as skill or the result of skill. This is a mistake. Once one recognizes that there is elbow room for skill in between lucky success and unlucky failure, the troubling argument that seems to show that no one could ever be responsible evaporates" (1984, 97). That is, luck is an *exception* that exempts one from the standard situation of credit and moral responsibility, and the universal exemption from moral responsibility must be based on the universal extension of luck and incompetence. So what are the alternatives? Either we are morally responsible or we are helpless and incompetent, warped and deranged, compulsive and controlled.

When universal denial of moral responsibility is thought to entail universal helplessness, compulsion, and derangement (as in excuse-extensionism), then it is a simple matter to derive odious consequences from the denial of moral responsibility. As helpless, deranged, incompetent pawns with no control over ourselves or anything else, we obviously cannot employ reason or make plans or act morally. With such severe impairments, how could we ever confidently claim to know anything at all, much less to know that there is no moral responsibility? It is little wonder, then, that many philosophers have regarded the denial of moral responsibility as ludicrous and self-defeating.

From the excuse-extensionist perspective (which denies moral responsibility from *within* the basic assumptions of the moral responsibility system), it is obvious that those who lack moral responsibility are helpless incompetent deluded creatures who do not qualify as moral beings. When viewed from within the perspective of the moral responsibility system, the universal denial of moral responsibility implies that *everyone* is incompetent and *no one* qualifies as a moral being capable of skillful reflective purposeful principled behavior; as Strawson phrases it, such a universal denial of moral responsibility (based on universal flaws) would imply "that nobody knows what he's doing or that everybody's behaviour is unintelligible in terms of conscious purposes or that everybody lives in a world of delusion or that nobody has a moral sense" (1962, 74). So within the moral responsibility system—in which moral responsibility is the default setting, and the operating assumption is that you are morally responsible unless you are profoundly incompetent and irrational—the universal denial of moral responsibility would wreak havoc: it would imply the denial of rationality, morality, reflective choice, skillful behavior, and (as

Strawson notes) all the personal reactive attitudes of gratitude, resentment, and reciprocated adult love.

Though the views of Hospers, Strawson, Pinker, and Dennett differ in many respects, they share an important assumption: moral responsibility is the given, and exceptions to moral responsibility require special excusing conditions. This assumption wedges those who deny moral responsibility into a destructive dilemma. Either it is not the case that all our behavior is impaired by delusion or insanity or incompetence, and the denial of moral responsibility fails; or it is the case that we are universally impaired, and the destruction of moral responsibility carries in its wake the destruction of all our participant reactive attitudes, the elimination of all genuine skill and self-control, the loss of all moral evaluation, the demise of rational deliberation, *and* it makes all attempts to rationally argue against moral responsibility self-defeating.

This sad dilemma applies only to those who reject moral responsibility from within the moral responsibility system. When Hospers attempts to undercut moral responsibility by enlarging the realm of excuses, he makes a fatal concession: he concedes that in the right natural circumstances—no damaging or constricting or constraining special impediments—we can make sense of holding people morally responsible. Under that assumption, the denial of moral responsibility requires special justification, and those who deny moral responsibility bear the burden of proof. And a heavy burden it is, because to the degree that we lift the burden of moral responsibility, we are crushed under the weight of insanity or incompetence.

Rejecting the Moral Responsibility System

The path to the universal denial of moral responsibility does not start from the assumption of natural moral responsibility and then chip away at the responsibility edifice by enlarging and extending excuses. Instead, it challenges moral responsibility at its foundation and proposes an alternative system in which moral responsibility has no place. The universal denial of moral responsibility rests on the same premise that libertarians propose: genuine moral responsibility requires that the morally responsible person be the ultimate author of her behavior and that the person genuinely could have been and acted otherwise. As Roderick Chisholm states, "If we are responsible . . . then we have a prerogative which some would attribute only to God: each of us, when we really act, is a prime mover unmoved. In doing what we do, we cause certain events to happen, and nothing and no one, except we ourselves, causes us to cause those events to happen" (1982, 32). The difference is that libertarians suppose that we have such godlike powers, and those naturalists who deny moral responsibility reject such powers. Obviously, the claim that miraculous powers are necessary for moral responsibility does not settle the question of moral responsibility. Maybe the libertarians are right, and we do have such special powers. Or maybe there is some naturalist version of libertarian free will—such as Robert Kane's (1985, 1996, 2007)—that will allow us to be the ultimate authors of our open choices without the need for godlike powers. Or perhaps the compatibilists are right, and moral responsibility has more modest requirements: moral responsibility does not require alternative possibilities or ultimate authorship. Obviously, I reject all such efforts to establish moral responsibility, both those that approach the problem from the front door of libertarian miracles and those that try the back door of natural compatibilism. But this denial of moral responsibility is not based on eroding away the moral responsibility structure by extending excuses; rather, it is based on the claim that when we make a careful naturalistic study of how characters and behavior were shaped, such a detailed examination leaves no room for the sort of special control and special powers that would be required to make moral responsibility—and punishment and reward—genuinely *fair*. We differ in our strengths and weaknesses, our choices and hesitations, our virtues and our vices, but whatever our capacities and characters, our basic differences in starting points and racing luck and situations and formative influences make "just deserts" fundamentally unfair. No one deserves punishment or reward, whatever their good or bad qualities, their rationality or irrationality, or their vicious or virtuous acts. Moral responsibility cannot be justified within the naturalistic system.

An argument by Stephen J. Morse helps mark the line between the traditional system that starts from the assumption of moral responsibility (and then considers excuses within that system) and on the other hand the moral responsibility abolitionism that rejects the moral responsibility system root and branch—rejects it as incompatible with scientific naturalism and as fundamentally unfair. Morse writes:

Our characters and our opportunities are in large measure the product of luck, and if luck excused, no one would be responsible. A brain tumor or other neuropathology that enhances the probability of the sufferer engaging in antisocial behavior is surely an example of dreadful bad luck. But unless the agent is irrational or the behavior is compelled, there is no reason to excuse the agent simply because bad luck in the form of biological pathology played a causal role. A cause is just a cause. It is not per se an excuse. (1996, 537)

Luck does not excuse; rather, when we recognize that "our characters and our opportunities are in large measure the product of luck" and are ultimately the complete product of our good or bad fortune, then the fundamental unfairness of the moral responsibility system is plain. Morse is both wrong and right on a very important point: "If luck excused, no one would be responsible." He is wrong in thinking that the basic objection to moral responsibility lies in excuses and their expansion, for excuses are part of the rejected moral responsibility system; but he is right in thinking that if we fully recognize that all elements of our characters and all details of our behavior are ultimately the product of luck, then we also recognize that "no one would be responsible."

Excuse-Extensionism

The goal of moral responsibility abolitionists is not to broaden the range of excuses, nor to make punishments less severe, nor to lessen the gap between the rewarded and the denied, nor even to approach more closely to equality of opportunity (though all of these are worthy goals, at least for the interim). Rather, the goal is to abolish the moral responsibility system and replace it with a very different system that rejects all claims and ascriptions of moral responsibility; analogously, the goal is not to devise more humane execution methods for witches, but to abolish belief in witchcraft altogether and replace it with a system that eliminates magic in favor of a thoroughgoing naturalism.

Dennett refers with approval to what he calls the *default responsibility principle*: "If no one *else* is responsible for your being in state A, you are" (2003, 281).[1] Such a principle implies that those who wish to deny their own moral responsibility are trying to shift the blame to others. But that assumes that someone must be to blame, someone must be morally responsible, and the only way I can avoid blame is by placing the burden on someone else. Such a shifting of blame—refusing to acknowledge your own moral responsibility—is craven and cowardly and unjust. But the basic assumption is false; it comes from within the system of moral responsibility, in which someone must be to blame. The opposing view does not shift blame to someone else, but denies blame and moral responsibility altogether.

The grip of the moral responsibility system is powerful, and thus it is hard to break away from the idea that denial of moral responsibility must be based on enlarging and extending excuses until those excuses swallow up reason and self-control and reflective powers. Even those who know perfectly well that universal denial of moral responsibility is not based on excuse-extensionism can be pulled back into that false assumption by the gravitational force of the moral responsibility system. Thus Saul Smilansky objects to the universal denial of moral responsibility on the following grounds: "Well-meaning extensions of the valid compatibilist excuses in the direction of blanket universal application threaten rather than serve the careful and humane consideration of individual circumstances, and hinder self-betterment and social progress" (2000, 89). And a little later in the same work, Smilansky expands on the doleful effects of the excuse-extensionist denial of moral responsibility:

The universal application of excuses along hard determinist lines is not a further extension of the compatibilist excuses so much as it is the wholesale elimination of any distinctions. It may seem that there are benefits to the hard determinist perspective, say, in mitigating the harsh judgement of the lazy, but this misses the central point: the idea that a person deserves not to be discriminated against for factors beyond his control, such as race or sex, is toppled from its currently high moral standing. (156)

Such effects might follow from the *excuse-extensionist* model that Smilansky suggests as the basis for universal denial of moral responsibility, but Smilansky knows well enough—when he is not enmeshed in the moral responsibility web—that the universal denial of moral responsibility is not based on extending and enlarging excuses. As Smilansky stated earlier, "From the ultimate perspective, the injustice follows from not taking into account the moral arbitrariness of a person's being whoever she is, with her character, reasons and the like" (77). One might conclude that "the ultimate perspective" is not the optimum perspective, and that we ought to find a way of preserving moral responsibility at all costs (even at the cost of approving and fostering illusion, as Smilansky recommends), but whatever one concludes about that conclusion, it does not change the fact that the denial of moral responsibility on the basis of taking a longer and more detailed perspective on character development is very different from denying moral responsibility on the basis of excuse-extensionism.

In contrast to the excuse-extensionist model for universal denial of moral responsibility, consider (what we might call) the *miracle-requisite model*: moral responsibility requires a miraculous self-creation that is not compatible with naturalism. The miracle-requisite grounds for denying moral responsibility allow room for important distinctions. We are complex animals, thoroughly the product of our short-term (conditioning) and long-term (genetic) environments, with no miraculous powers of first cause free will. But this framework leaves open a wide range of abilities and disabilities. Some of us are severely damaged, woefully lacking in powers of rational deliberation and self-control. Others enjoy marvelous powers of rational planning, careful thought, effective self-control, and iron fortitude (they are wonderfully *skilled*, as Dennett would say, in all these areas). But they are no more morally responsible for their skills and the successes that flow from exercising those skills than are the incompetents: they are fortunate—lucky—to have been shaped by environments that gave them such powers. Most of us are somewhere in-between: neither brilliant nor incompetent, neither iron-willed nor hopelessly wishy-washy. We may have the skills to undertake self-improvement projects: to eat fewer sweets, think more carefully and avoid rash decisions, and gain better control of our tempers; we may carry those projects out successfully, and become better— and more deliberative and self-controlled—persons. But that we have (or lack) the inclination to undertake such self-reform, and the self-control and fortitude and planning capacities to succeed in such self-development are a matter of our good (or bad) environmental fortune, not something for which we deserve credit or blame.

The person who employs her skills to successfully overcome a nicotine addiction has indeed accomplished something important, and she accomplished it herself, by means of her own skills and capacities. She did it, true enough, but supposing that she is morally responsible is another matter altogether. The person who undertakes a similar project but fails (due to weaker resolve, or less self-control, or inadequate planning powers) is likewise not morally responsible for her failure. Again, the failure is due to her own—in this case, inadequate—capacities, but there is no suggestion that she is so severely flawed that she can never exercise self-control or employ reason and certainly no suggestion that she can never exercise genuine skill or be the appropriate subject of Strawson's participant reactive attitudes.

By carefully planning and deliberating we *can* make things happen, and the effective plans we sometimes make and execute are genuinely our own. We *do* have skills, and our successes are often the result of our own skills. We are not helpless puppets of unconscious forces that thwart our plans and distort our thoughts. But neither is rational planning a power that transcends our environmental history. Some people are much better at reasoning than others; some have a greater sense of cognitive self-efficacy; some people (the "chronic cognizers") have impressive cognitive fortitude, just as "cognitive misers" find it difficult or impossible to engage in extensive deliberation. Even as a rather dull cognitive miser, I am still capable of some deliberative choices and of exercising control and making my own decisions. But I do not deserve blame for making worse decisions than the chronic cognizer of greater mental ability. It's not luck that the latter deliberates more successfully and makes wiser decisions than I do, but it is ultimately luck that he has greater cognitive skills than I do, and thus it is not fair to reward him for his better decisions or to punish me for my flawed and badly deliberated choices. Neither chronic cognizers nor cognitive misers justly deserve credit or blame for their judicious or impetuous decisions (their respective capacities for sustained thought were shaped by their early conditioning), but cognitive misers are not lunatics, not hopelessly impaired, not objects to be managed by others. Reflective Monica may be more reliable, but impetuous Patricia is not beyond the pale of friendship and affection. Neither is morally responsible for her character or deliberative powers or the results that flow from them.

I am rather impetuous, not terribly bright, and sorely lacking in fortitude; thus I often do what I should not, and fail to do what I should—and given the fact that I was shaped to have such characteristics by environmental forces far beyond my control, I deserve no blame for my failings. But my friends (and enemies) have no reason to banish me to the realm of cold "objective attitudes." Perhaps I can improve, as I often try, but if I should manage to develop an improved version of myself, the capacity to make such changes will be the product of my history, not something that justifies attributions or claims of moral responsibility.

Of course, both libertarians and compatibilists will reject this conclusion, but the present point is to make clear what the miracle-requisite universal rejection of moral responsibility actually involves, and what it does not involve: it does not involve universal excuses based on universal incompetence. Moral responsibility abolitionists are not operating *within* the system of moral responsibility and extending incompetence excuses to everyone. Rather, the universal denial of moral responsibility involves a different system altogether: a system that rejects moral responsibility as a remnant of a shallow prescientific understanding of human psychology that endeavors to keep humans in a special unique moral status, apart from the natural world.

Strawson offers a false dilemma. We do not have to choose between being helpless objects of pity, excluded from normal participant reactive relations, or, on the other hand, being proper subjects of blame and punishment and moral responsibility. Another possibility is that I am at fault, the fault is genuinely my own, and my bad behavior stems from my own fault, but that I am not morally responsible for either the fault or the behavior. That is, there is the possibility that my flaw is a character-fault, but not a blame-fault. Such a possibility opens space for recognizing vices and virtues without holding their possessors morally responsible. Joan is genuinely bad—she is dishonest, and this trait is her own, and she purposefully acts on it—but she does not deserve blame (we do not consider it fair to blame her, or punish her, when—for example—we understand the history that shaped her flawed character). Also, there are no grounds for excluding her from the moral community: she remains eligible for a wide range of participant reactive attitudes (excluding blame, but including love, affection, and friendship), and we can reason with her and respect her (though we recognize and regret her flaws). Of course, some will want to insist that Joan really is morally responsible. That's not the point. Strawson's position turns on showing what a cold, cheerless world we would inhabit if we dropped moral responsibility and turned instead to purely objective attitudes. But Strawson's argument fails to consider the alternative of not morally responsible, yet not helpless or incompetent or insane. Strawson demands a choice between accepting moral responsibility or being excluded from the reactive warmth of the moral community on grounds of radical incompetence; rejecting moral responsibility on grounds *other than* the excuse-extensionist grounds (which are the only ones allowed within the moral responsibility system) opens a broad passage between the horns of that false dilemma.

Benefits of Rejecting Excuse-Extensionism

Recognizing that universal denial of moral responsibility is not based on universal incompetence has several important implications. First, the denial of all moral responsibility does not exclude everyone from Strawson's "participant reactive attitudes" (of course, the denial of moral responsibility will undercut the justification of such reactive attitudes as vengeance, but will not undermine attitudes of affection, gratitude, love, and friendship). And along with that, there is no reason to suppose that denying all moral responsibility entails treating everyone as an incompetent who can be managed and "treated" by others without his consent.

Second, the rejection of excuse-extensionism means there is no reason to suppose that the absence of moral responsibility would undercut all morality. Rafia is a profoundly virtuous person. She holds deep moral principles to which she is reflectively and emotionally committed, she is resolute in her virtuous efforts, and she is courageous in the face of opposition. She deserves no reward for her virtuous character and generous behavior: her fortunate early environment shaped her enduring character traits, including her reflectiveness, her principled commitments, and her generous spirit. She is lucky to be such a good person, and she is not morally responsible for her character and behavior, but she is nonetheless a paragon of virtue; her principled virtuous behavior is not merely luck, and it is morally good that we nurture our children to be more like Rafia (though neither we nor they will deserve blame if we fall short).

Third, arguing against moral responsibility is not self-defeating. If the denial of moral responsibility were based on the claim that we are all imbeciles or demented or otherwise severely defective, then it would be silly to suppose that such severely defective individuals could intelligently argue against anything, including against moral responsibility. In fact, it would be doubly self-defeating: we could not be moral beings, making moral claims about whether punishment and reward are fair or justly deserved, and even if we were somehow moral, we couldn't intelligently argue about morality. But when we reject excuse-extensionist grounds for denying moral responsibility, there is no reason to suppose that in the absence of moral responsibility we could not make moral claims, follow moral principles, argue for moral conclusions, and consistently campaign for the conclusion that "just deserts" are unfair. Of course, we deserve no special praise for following moral principles, or blame for violating them, but not deserving these responses does not imply that we can never follow such principles, find them meaningful, and regard them as true. The basic claim of this book is that the moral responsibility system is morally wrong because it is fundamentally *unfair*, and that there are good reasons for that claim. Those claims may be false, but when they are made outside the moral responsibility system, at least they are not self-defeating.

The previous argument is designed to show the coherence and consistency of a system that *starts* with the abolition of moral responsibility (rather than, implausibly, assuming moral responsibility and trying to eliminate it through excuse-extensionism). There is a shorter argument to the same end. What is the basis for the universal denial of moral responsibility? It is basically that in order to establish moral responsibility, we need miracles: the power to be an unmoved mover, the power of contra-causal free will, the miraculous ability to make yourself ab initio. (So far, this argument agrees with the standard libertarian argument of Chisholm and Campbell; at the next step, we part company.) But we do not have such miraculous powers (we may still have free will, but not the miracle-working libertarian free will that is required for moral responsibility). Therefore, we do not have moral responsibility. Obviously, the strength of that argument is a vexed issue, and there are two standard lines of attack: first, the libertarian line, which attacks the second premise and asserts that we do have such special powers; and second, the compatibilist line, which attacks the first premise and denies that miracle-working powers are necessary for moral responsibility. The strength or vulnerability of that argument against moral responsibility is not the current question. The point is instead a simple one: denying the existence of the requisite miraculous powers is not denying the existence of moderate (nonmiraculous) levels of rationality, self-control, and moral commitment. In sum: representing the denial of moral responsibility as based on universal irrationality, amorality, and imbecility is a *strawman* representation.

Arguing without Excuse-Extensionism

Eliminating the excuse-extensionist strawman does not resolve the issue of moral responsibility. It does, however, have very important implications for that issue. First, it shifts the burden of proof away from those who deny all moral responsibility (we are not attempting to establish excuses) and places it squarely on those who are claiming justification for treating individuals in special harmful (punitive) or beneficial (rewarding) ways. This is an important shift. After all, we rightly judge people competent unless proven otherwise: if I wish to count someone as so severely defective that she cannot function in at least the minimal way necessary to live as a free and self-governing member of society, then I must prove beyond a reasonable doubt that she is very severely flawed. And if I wish to prove such severe defects in everyone, then the burden of proof become crushing. With the burden shifted, those who deny just deserts and moral responsibility do not have to prove incompetence; instead, the burden of proof rests on those who claim that it is fair to blame or punish the person whose environment shaped him as a "cognitive miser" with weak self-confidence and minimum fortitude.

So the first important consequence of rejecting excuse-extensionism is that the burden of proof shifts, and falls upon those who support moral responsibility. There is a second important result from eliminating the excuse-extensionist strawman: it destroys the foundation of a very popular style of argument in support of moral responsibility. This is such a common form of argument for moral responsibility that we might christen it the *Modus Tollens* Proof of Moral Responsibility, or MTPMR for short. A good example of MTPMR can be found in a passage from van Inwagen that was mentioned in the previous chapter:

I have listened to philosophers who deny the existence of moral responsibility. I cannot take them seriously. I know a philosopher who has written a paper in which he denies the reality of moral responsibility. And yet this same philosopher, when certain of his books were stolen, said, "That was a *shoddy* thing to do!" But no one can consistently say that a certain act was a shoddy thing to do *and* say that its agent was not morally responsible when he performed it. (1983, 207)

How does this argument actually work? When we unpack it, the form is simply *modus tollens*:

If there is no moral responsibility, then there can be no moral judgments.
But we certainly do make moral judgments.
Therefore there must be moral responsibility.

But this perfectly valid argument depends for its first premise on the excuse-extensionist model of the denial of moral responsibility: that is, it depends on the assumption that we are denying moral responsibility on the basis of characteristics that make one incompetent (and thus excused) as a moral being. That may well be an implication of excuse-extensionism, but it is not an implication of the more plausible (miracle-requisite) denial of moral responsibility.

MTPMR comes in several varieties, but they all have the same basic structure. The variation occurs in the predicate of the initial premise: if there is no moral responsibility, then there can be no moral judgments (or no rationality, or no argument, or no exercise of skill, or no legitimate emotions or friendship or gratitude, or no self-control). But the second premise is that we do make moral judgments (we are sometimes rational, we are capable of argument, we do exercise skill, the emotions that accompany friendship are legitimate, we are not manipulated by a hideous hypnotist). The second premise is true, and the conclusion does follow. But the first premise is built on a foundation of excuse-extensionism, and that is a foundation of straw.

When it is recognized that excuse-extensionism is a misinterpretation of the case against moral responsibility, that recognition opens the way to critically examining a third argument concerning moral judgment and the denial of moral responsibility. The claim that denying moral responsibility entails denial of all moral judgments is popular, and two arguments for that claim were considered in chapters 9 and 10. The first argument ignored the distinction between blame-fault and character-fault; the second argument was built on the venerable but shaky foundation of "ought implies can." There is also a third argument, which is based on the excuse-extensionist distortion of the case against moral responsibility. If universal denial of moral responsibility were based on universal extension of excuses—everyone is excused from moral responsibility because everyone is permanently deranged, irrational, incapable of reasoning, or unfit for deliberation—that would imply, a fortiori, that everyone is incapable of moral reasoning and moral judgment. Thus it is not surprising that when denial of moral responsibility is firmly implanted within the moral responsibility system, it seems obvious that such denial would leave no room for moral judgment. But when the *system* of moral responsibility is rejected, there is no suggestion that everyone is irrational and inept; rather, the claim is that a coherent case for moral responsibility cannot be made within the naturalistic model, that moral responsibility cannot be squared with the naturalistic worldview, and that *no one*—no matter how splendidly rational or deeply reflective or psychologically sound—can legitimately and fairly be held morally responsible. That denial of moral responsibility is consistent with the recognition and celebration of all the splendid cognitive and deliberative capacities that flourish in our natural world, and there is nothing whatsoever in such a systemic denial of moral responsibility that casts doubt on full, rich moral judgment.

12   Begging the Question for Moral Responsibility

The previous chapter examined systemic arguments against the rejection of moral responsibility: the universal rejection of moral responsibility (as seen from within the moral responsibility system) must be based on universal incompetence or "excuse-extensionism," which generates absurdities. But there are also systemic moral responsibility arguments that *start* from the assumption that normally we are morally responsible and then argue that because in our natural nonmiraculous world people can meet the requirements for moral responsibility, the system itself is therefore naturalistically justified. That type of argument goes like this: we have in place a system for holding people morally responsible, with specific conditions for when people are morally responsible (they can deliberate, they can respond to reasons, they are not under coercion); those specific conditions can be met within the naturalistic world (they do not require miracles or mysteries), and therefore holding people morally responsible is naturalistically legitimate.

The powerful temptation of such arguments—and their strong persuasiveness—can be seen in one of the most famous arguments of that type: Harry Frankfurt's argument against the alternate possibilities requirement for moral responsibility. Frankfurt argues, "The principle of alternate possibilities is false. A person may well be morally responsible for what he has done even though he could not have done otherwise" (1969, 832). His argument for that conclusion is based on the story of the murderous villain, Jones, and the nefarious (but idle) neuroscientist, Black. Black wants Jones to commit a murder, and is prepared to manipulate Jones's brain to cause Jones to commit the murder if Jones hesitates. Jones, therefore, will commit the murder (either with or without Black's manipulation): there are no alternate possibilities. But in fact Jones never hesitates, and Black never intervenes. Jones commits murder of his own volition, with no interference, and thus is morally responsible; the fact that Black was standing by ready to intervene if Jones faltered—but in fact never intervenes in any way—obviously has no influence on the action that Jones performs or the moral responsibility that Jones bears for that action. So Jones is morally responsible, though he has no genuine alternate possibilities open to him, and therefore moral responsibility does not require alternate possibilities, and compatibilist moral responsibility is vindicated.

This is a fascinating argument, and it has generated fascinating responses, including the many variations of the "flicker of freedom" reply. But for all its charms and insights—and Frankfurt's work is invariably insightful—the argument is grounded in the assumption of the moral responsibility system and uses the basic principles of that system to lift itself by its own bootstraps. As an elaboration of what the moral responsibility system implies it is quite effective; as an argument *for* the moral responsibility system— and against moral responsibility abolitionism—it is a nonstarter. Frankfurt's argument is built on the assumption that Jones (as long as he acts on his own volition, with no outside compulsion) is morally responsible. Within the system that assumes moral responsibility as a default setting, obviously Jones is a fitting candidate for moral responsibility, but the moral responsibility abolitionist—who rejects the *system* of moral responsibility, and does not base denial of moral responsibility on finding excuses for every act—would not start from the assumption that Jones, acting without interference and on his own volition, is morally responsible.

If we start from the assumption of moral responsibility for all competent persons who do not suffer special coercion or interference with their behavior, then Jones does not lose his moral responsibility just because a potential intervener has arranged things so that Jones has no genuine alternate courses of behavior: the act is Jones's own act, done from his own motives, his own choice, his own character. We might say that it is *authentically* Jones's own act (perhaps Jones even reflectively approves at a higher order level of his murderous desires), and according to the compatibilist moral responsibility system, that makes Jones morally responsible. This argument is very effective in bringing out the nature of the compatibilist account of moral responsibility and its distance from libertarian insistence on open alternate possibilities. But it is not an effective argument *for* that compatibilist system because it assumes as a systemic premise the very issue that is at stake. The moral responsibility abolitionist does not deny that Jones is now acting from his own genuine volition; rather, the moral responsibility abolitionist rejects the claim that Jones is morally responsible for his acts, or for the volitions and character traits from which they flow, because ultimately Jones was shaped by forces that were not of his own making or choosing. If Jones is morally responsible, then almost all of us are morally responsible—lack of alternate possibilities notwithstanding—but the pivotal systemic assumption that Jones is morally responsible cannot be used to prove the plausibility of the moral responsibility system that generates that assumption. This is a point brought out very effectively by Mark Bernstein:

> If we are inclined to agree with Frankfurt's assessment of his cases and believe it justified to assess the agents as morally responsible, we are assuming that, in fact, the agent freely decided to act as she did. We hold Judy morally responsible for killing Bill, despite the fact that an inactive mad scientist would have intervened to ensure her murderous decision had she wavered, because we believe that Judy's will was "her own." . . . Frankfurt yields no help in countering the Strawsonian [Galen Strawson] insight that in the formation of our original natures by events foreign to our control we are . . . forever distanced from buck-stopping responsibility. Free will deniers impute the lack of ultimate responsibility not to the fact that an agent has no alternative original character from which to choose . . . but rather to the fact that no agent can be in control of what constitutes his original nature. (2005, 9)

The Moral Responsibility Plateau

Belief in moral responsibility is so pervasive—and thus the assumption of moral responsibility so easily made—that systemic arguments for moral responsibility are very tempting. Another argument of this type is the plateau or threshold argument: significant differences in our capacities and abilities and histories are largely irrelevant to moral responsibility, because moral responsibility is not a matter of degree. Instead, those who have reached a minimum level of competence—those who have reached the *plateau* or crossed the *threshold* of moral responsibility—are all morally responsible, and for purposes of moral responsibility, we need not worry about any remaining differences. Moral responsibility is a wonderfully *egalitarian* doctrine: Maria had all the advantages of a superb early education, a supportive family, top tutoring; while Wanda grew up in a dysfunctional family, attended poor schools, and received little support and less encouragement, but both have reached the level of minimum competence, so both are now completely equal in moral responsibility; thus, when assigning subsequent just deserts, we need not worry over differences in history or ability or skill. This line of argument might be christened the *plateau argument*, after one of Daniel Dennett's charming metaphors:

Moral development is not a race at all, with a single winner and everyone else ranked behind, but a process that apparently brings people sooner or later to a sort of plateau of development—not unlike the process of learning your native language, for instance. Some people reach the plateau swiftly and easily, while others need compensatory effort to overcome initial disadvantages in one way or another.

But everyone comes out more or less in the same league. When people are deemed "good enough" their moral education is over, and except for those who are singled out as defective . . . the citizenry is held to be composed of individuals of roughly equivalent talents, insofar as the demands of such citizenship are concerned. (1984, 96)

This model of a "general level" of competence that qualifies all at that level for moral responsibility is not a passing fancy; the same idea shows up in Dennett's *Freedom Evolves*, though the image of a plateau has been replaced by a threshold:

It is . . . not in any way your own doing that you were born into a specific milieu, rich or poor, pampered or abused, given a head start or held back at the starting line. And these differences, which are striking, are also diverse in their effects—some inevitable and some evitable, some leaving life-long scars and others evanescent in effect. Many of the differences that survive are, in any event, of negligible importance to what concerns us here: a second threshold, the threshold of moral responsibility—as contrasted, say, with artistic genius. (2003, 274)

Once you have reached that moral responsibility plateau—the threshold of moral responsibility competence—it doesn't matter what path you took. Whether you cruised up by limousine or struggled up hand over bleeding hand, if you meet the qualifications for moral responsibility, you are morally responsible: you justly deserve credit and blame, reward and punishment. Exactly what qualifies you for moral responsibility is a subject of some disagreement: Dennett focuses on capacity for rational and purposeful deliberation, Harry G. Frankfurt (1971) and Gerald Dworkin (1988) insist on the capacity for hierarchical reflection on one's values and goals, George Sher (1987) on investment of your efforts and abilities, John Martin

Fischer (2006a) on rational guidance control, Thaddeus Metz (2006) on reflective control, and Angela M. Smith (2008) on judgmental activity. However, plateau advocates share a common principle: don't look back; how you became morally responsible doesn't matter; it is your current ability that makes you morally responsible. Angela M. Smith gives a very clear statement of the basic distinction that underlies the plateau account of moral responsibility:

I think we would do well to distinguish two different questions: the question of one's responsibility for becoming a certain sort of person, and the question of one's responsibility for the judgments expressed in one's actions and attitudes. It will be a complex story, for each and every one of us, how we became the sorts of people we are, with the particular values, interests, cares and concerns that we hold, and very few, if any, of us can plausibly claim to bear full or even substantial responsibility for how we became the particular people we are. Even so, I submit, we cannot help but regard ourselves as responsible and answerable for the particular judgments expressed in our actions and attitudes, regardless of what circumstances may have shaped these assessments. (2008, 389)

Plateau theorists see moral responsibility abolitionists as obsessing about how you *became* morally responsible when the question is simply this: do you meet the minimum requirements for being morally responsible? Thaddeus Metz, in his recent version of the plateau argument for moral responsibility, offers this account of that supposed mistake:

One must cash out responsibility of the sort warranting imposition of a burden in terms of an agent who is, in some naturalistic sense, in control of his behaviour. Control is, roughly, a matter of one's actions being determined by one's reflection, where one's reflection is of course determined in turn by antecedent natural causes. . . . [Control is] sufficient for responsibility . . . ; being an unmoved mover is not necessary. With regard to people who have control over their behaviour, institutions ought to place burdens on those who have chosen wrongly, even at substantial cost to the general welfare.

I think the deep mistake that leads Tabensky [and other moral responsibility abolitionists] astray is the common one of thinking that, for us to be responsible for having performed an act in such a way as to warrant the imposition of a burden [to be morally responsible and justly deserving of retributive punishment], we must have been in control of the conditions that have put us in control of our behavior. (2006, 233)

Daniel Dennett developed the most philosophically famous version of the plateau argument for moral responsibility, explicitly rejecting the notion that moral responsibility requires that one be morally responsible for being morally responsible: "We are not totally responsible for being responsible, or course. . . . After all, a mugger might leap out of an alley and brain me tomorrow. I would then be unlucky enough to lose my status as a responsible citizen through no fault or error of my own" (1984, 98). So we are not responsible for being responsible, we aren't ab initio creators of our own moral responsibility, but (as noted earlier) Dennett insists that such a requirement sets the moral responsibility bar much too high: "Skepticism about the very possibility of culpability arises from a misplaced reverence for an absolutist ideal: the concept of total, before-the-eyes-of-God Guilt. That fact that *that* condition is never to be met in this world should not mislead us into skepticism about the integrity of our institution of moral responsibility" (165).

Although the condition of being responsible for being responsible may not be viable, neither is it necessary. No one, Dennett states, has such "before-the-eyes-of-God Guilt," but that does not preclude genuine moral responsibility that justifies reward and retributive punishment. We "lucky ones" are morally responsible, and our fortunate histories do not alter the fact that we are morally responsible. Those who deny moral responsibility get it confused, and demand an unconditional ground-up, self-made moral responsibility that does not exist and is not required. A good basketball player—one of Dennett's favorite examples—may owe some of her genuine skill at playing basketball to good fortune, such as genetically generated quick reflexes and good early coaching. Those influences do not change the fact that the player really is skillful. Likewise, those of us who are morally responsible may be fortunate to have such a capacity, but that doesn't change the fact that we justly deserve reward and punishment for our choices and acts.

Moral responsibility advocates who favor a plateau of moral responsibility insist that those who reach the level of moral responsibility competence are morally responsible for their choices and behavior and that how they reached that level of moral responsibility is irrelevant. The question of moral responsibility is about the present, not the past: your present capacity (to deliberate, or to reflectively evaluate your own desires, or to exercise reflective control) makes you morally responsible. That is a good account of the moral responsibility system, which obviously does not require that all who are morally responsible must be precisely equal in abilities and opportunities. Sam is brighter, more energetic, and has greater fortitude than Tom, but as long as both meet the minimum competence standard, both are morally responsible for their behavior. The moral responsibility system must ascribe the same moral responsibility to persons having significant differences in characters, capacities, and abilities; after all, it is quite clear that such differences exist, and if those differences invalidated claims and ascriptions of moral responsibility, there would be no room left for moral responsibility. Of course, one could avoid the problem by insisting that we are not different in our special capacity of libertarian miracle-working free will: each of us has the power to choose virtue or vice because our wondrous free will power can transcend all differences in wisdom, fortitude, or deliberative powers. But naturalist advocates of moral responsibility cannot make such appeals to miracle-working wills, so significant individual differences must be acknowledged and treated as compatible with moral responsibility.

Challenging the Moral Responsibility Plateau

The plateau argument brings into sharp focus the key issue that divides moral responsibility advocates from abolitionists. That question is not about being morally responsible for being morally responsible: the abolitionist concurs with the plateau advocate that the important question concerns current capacities rather than individual history. For the abolitionist, the issue is one of current *fairness*. Ann and Barbara are competent adults; both deliberate about what they should do, and then Ann acts badly and Barbara acts virtuously. Is it fair to blame or punish Ann and reward Barbara? Do they justly deserve such significant differences in treatment? Ann and Barbara obviously have different histories and different genetic endowments, but (from the abolitionist perspective) that is not what makes moral responsibility practices unjust. It is not fair to blame Ann and reward Barbara (the abolitionist insists) because the resources and capacities they bring to their deliberating and choosing are significantly unequal. Moral responsibility abolitionists find it helpful to look closely at the developmental history because differences in history are often the clearest indicator of important differences in current capacities: we can see the differences in current capacities writ large in individual formative histories. However, it is not the differences in histories but the differences in current capacities that are critical. Plateau advocates of moral responsibility insist that there is a general level of moral responsibility, and beyond that level, the individual differences have no effect on moral responsibility. Moral responsibility abolitionists reply that even very small differences in capacities invalidate claims and ascriptions of moral responsibility.

The importance of small but significant differences can be seen when we look more carefully at the details of the deliberation by Ann and Barbara, who must choose between a desired weekend at the beach and a promised commitment to help a friend move to a new apartment. Ann deliberates, considers her options, thinks of the delightful smell of the sunny sweep of sand and ocean, then considers the fact that Carol and Dave will also be around to help with the move—and at that point she stops deliberating and proceeds beachward. Barbara likewise deliberates, considers the marvelous aroma and warmth of the beach, remembers that Carol and Dave will be available to assist the apartment move, and then *continues* to deliberate, now taking into consideration how kind her friend has been in the past; Barbara goes still further and asks whether she really wants to be the sort of person who would skip out on a promise to a friend, and she then chooses to honor her commitment. *Why* does Ann deliberate briefly and ineffectually (had she continued deliberating, as Barbara did, she would have remembered the relevant facts Barbara brings to the equation and would have chosen and acted as Barbara did), while Barbara deliberates more thoroughly and effectively? *Why*—within a natural scientific explanatory system—does one deliberate well and the other poorly? Plateau advocates of moral responsibility counsel that we need not look more closely: both Ann and Barbara have reached the plateau of moral responsibility, both are capable of deliberation and choice, and both are morally responsible for their choices. In contrast, moral responsibility abolitionists insist on seeking an explanation for why Ann and Barbara chose differently.

As noted in earlier chapters, there are solid psychological answers for such questions. Perhaps Barbara was shaped—as a child and adolescent— as a chronic cognizer, with great cognitive fortitude; perhaps Ann (who can and does reason) was discouraged from careful lengthy deliberation and instead became a cognitive miser. Perhaps Barbara was given progressively more difficult cognitive challenges that she successfully met and now has a stronger sense of cognitive self-efficacy; perhaps Ann's cognitive confidence was sapped by a long history of cognitive failure as she consistently faced intellectual tasks for which she was ill-equipped. Or possibly Barbara found herself in a situation or setting that facilitated careful deliberation, and Ann's situation (without her awareness of its powerful influence) prompted a quick shallow response. The point is that when we look closely at the causes of different outcomes from Barbara and Ann—both of whom are competent creatures who can and do use reason, though to very different degrees—we quickly discover that their different capacities are the source of their different choices. Given who she is and the situation she is in, Ann could not make the choice that Barbara made; Ann could not make a better choice than she made. Of course, she could have chosen differently if she had been shaped with greater cognitive self-efficacy, or if she were in a different situation, or if she had different capacities—or if she were a deity not limited by natural causes and conditions. But given a naturalistic framework and the character she has and the situation she was in, she could not have made the better choice that Barbara made. Those considerations do not imply that it was not Ann's own faulty choice, or that she should be deprived of all future opportunities to make choices, or that she is an incompetent who should be excluded from our moral community, but it does mean that it is unfair to blame Ann for a choice she could not avoid making. In stark contrast stands the moral responsibility *system*, in which Ann has reached the plateau of competence, and therefore she is morally responsible: no questions asked, no inquiries allowed.

That *is* how the moral responsibility system works: Ann and Barbara have both reached the plateau of moral responsibility, and now the differences in their capacities are irrelevant. Barbara (with stronger abilities) makes good choices, and deserves reward; Ann (with weaker abilities but above the minimum competence level) makes bad choices and justly deserves blame. But that is a description of how the moral responsibility system works, not an argument to show that it is fair. And its fairness— which is the question at issue—is very doubtful. Calvin grows up in poverty, attends terrible schools, suffers childhood abuse and a low degree of lead poisoning, finds little support in his community and less in his dysfunctional family; he can reason (though he has little confidence in his ability to use reason effectively and his cognitive fortitude is very limited) and make his own choices, and he squeaks under the competence wire. Donald's loving and supportive family makes sure that he goes to the best schools and gets top tutoring, and his family and community and school offer abundant encouragement to think long and carefully. Donald is also competent, and he has great cognitive fortitude as well as strong cognitive self-confidence. Rewarding Donald for his good choices and punishing Calvin for his bad ones is just as fair—or just as unfair—as saying that, having reached adulthood, they can "compete equally" for desirable positions and that as long as the position goes to the most qualified individual, everything is fair and just: We don't care what your history is: right now the playing field is level, and may the best person win. That is indeed how moral responsibility works in the moral responsibility system, but that marks the deep flaws in that system, not its justification.

In our society, some have enormous advantages of birth, and others have enormous disadvantages. Some go to elite prep schools, receive extensive tutoring, take expensive prep courses for the SAT, and have access to a wide range of advanced courses, and others go to schools that are plagued with violence, have inadequate materials, often have the weakest teachers with overwhelming burdens, receive no tutoring, and certainly take no expensive courses for the SAT—now we say, "Okay, everyone halfway through your senior year of high school, let's compete evenly, and the best get the elite colleges and the worst get (maybe) trade school." If we complain, the answer is that this is how the game is played and how the system works. The reply is that yes, this is how the game is played, but the game is fundamentally unfair, and the rules are wrong. When people start with differing advantages and burdens that shape their subsequent ability and capacities, you can't "make things fair" by offering "equal opportunity" at some later date when the special advantages and cruel disadvantages have already left deep marks on one's strengths and weaknesses. Likewise, we can say of moral responsibility: that's just how the game is played; we don't care what your childhood was, or what differences there are in your abilities. As long as you squeak past the competence threshold, everyone is regarded as equal: it's what you do now that counts. And the response is: yes, that is how the game is played—in our courts and elsewhere in our society—but the game and its rules are unfair.

The challenge to moral responsibility is not over whether this individual happens to fit under this *given* system of rules in these circumstances, but rather, whether the whole *system* of moral responsibility is a fair and worthwhile system. It is not. It is neither fair nor productive, and we should junk it for an alternative. That claim may be wrong, but the reply that "these are the rules of our system" begs the question. Thus even if Dennett is right about the moral responsibility system being a plateau, he is wrong in offering that response to the challenge of those who find this entire system fundamentally unfair.

As noted earlier, even small differences—such as the difference in cognitive fortitude between Ann and Barbara—can result in strikingly different behavior. One might hypothesize that it is fair and just to reward Barbara and punish Ann only if they have equal resources (including equal fortitude and equal cognitive ability), but in the absence of miraculous godlike powers or significantly different circumstances, those equal resources will yield equal behavior and thus can offer no grounds for differing treatment. So rather than asking why abolitionists cannot recognize the plateau of moral responsibility, the question becomes: what is it about the plateau model that misleads people into supposing that uneven resources are compatible with just deserts and moral responsibility?

The moral responsibility system treats everyone on the competence plateau as morally responsible and justly deserving of punishment and reward. Thus the moral responsibility plateau of competence serves a very useful function in preserving the moral responsibility system: by postulating that all on the plateau are equally moral responsible—any differences in their capacities or background are irrelevant because all have reached the plateau of competence—it blocks any scrutiny of the actual capacities and abilities of those judged morally responsible and of the historical circumstances that shaped their differences. Preventing such careful scrutiny is essential to the survival and functioning of the system of moral responsibility.

Of course, even plateau advocates must acknowledge that there are important differences among those on the moral responsibility plateau, and they are willing to consider those differences as *mitigating* factors: because of Calvin's cognitive miserliness, we punish him less severely. (At least that's the way it is supposed to work; in practice, those who are most disadvantaged are often those—like Robert Harris—who seem most dangerous and who are thus punished more severely.) But the key point is that when we look carefully at *all* of the details, then those details undercut *all* claims of moral responsibility. "Mitigation" does not fix the flaws in the moral responsibility system; instead, it prevents us from looking closely at the full causal spectrum and thus mitigates concerns about the unfairness of the moral responsibility system.

The Plateau of Take-Charge Responsibility

The moral responsibility plateau is an important means of preserving moral responsibility from inquiries that would reveal its unfairness. That is not to suggest that moral responsibility advocates have purposefully employed the plateau model to protect moral responsibility from embarrassing inquiries. Rather, moral responsibility advocates (as discussed in chapter 6) confuse *moral* responsibility with *take-charge* responsibility; although it is difficult to justify holding people morally responsible even though they have significant differences in capacities and abilities, it is quite reasonable to insist that all those who have minimum competence should have the opportunity to exercise take-charge responsibility, their significant differences in abilities notwithstanding. Dennett emphasizes that responsibility does not require even starting points, equal capacities, or a precisely level playing field. Rather, Dennett's responsibility is a plateau, and everyone who manages to clamber up—even though there may be significant variations in elevation across that plateau—has full moral responsibility. As already noted, such differences undercut claims of moral responsibility; however, they are a perfect fit for take-charge responsibility. If Ann is a cognitive miser and Barbara is a chronic cognizer (or Barbara enjoys a stronger sense of self-efficacy, or greater fortitude), then it is unfair to punish Ann and reward Barbara for the different outcomes yielded by those different capacities (capacities not of their making or choosing), but both can claim—and benefit from claiming—take-charge responsibility for their own lives and decisions. For those who enjoy at least a minimal level of sense of self-efficacy (who have adequate confidence in their ability to manage their own lives and make their own decisions), the opportunity to exercise take-charge responsibility for their own lives and choices is both inherently satisfying and developmentally sound, and those deprived of this opportunity are likely to suffer severe depression and a sense of profound helplessness. With the right support, even those weak in sense of self-efficacy can learn to make their own choices, do so with some effectiveness, and gradually enhance both their sense of self-efficacy and their skill at exercising their own take-charge responsibility.

A precisely "level playing field" of even starts or equal investment resources is not required in order to receive those take-charge responsibility benefits. I am not as good at taking responsibility for my life as you are, but that is no reason to deny me equal opportunity to exercise take-charge responsibility for my life and my projects. Our unequal capacities undercut claims of moral responsibility, but such unequal resources are compatible with a full measure of take-charge responsibility. In short, there *is* a take-charge responsibility plateau, and those who reach that general level of competence—though they have significant differences in talents and capacities—can take, exercise, and benefit from take-charge responsibility. But a plateau of moral responsibility is a different matter altogether, and establishing the benefits of the former offers no evidence for the legitimacy of the latter.

When people reach a plateau of adequate cognitive ability and sufficient sense of self-efficacy, then—significant differences among them notwithstanding—they can take responsibility and benefit from doing so. Plateau advocates give excellent arguments in support of responsibility, but the responsibility they support is take-charge responsibility, not moral responsibility. When take-charge responsibility is distinguished from moral responsibility, then the benefits of take-charge responsibility are clear. Furthermore, when moral responsibility stands alone—distinguished from take-charge responsibility—then we gain a clearer perspective on moral responsibility: the supposed benefits of moral responsibility are illusory, its actual harms are real, and its incompatibility with naturalism is plain. Whether valley, mountain, or plateau, there is no natural habitat for moral responsibility.

Make Them an Offer They Can't Refuse: The Moral Responsibility Contract

When we recognize that the denial of moral responsibility is not based on excuse-extensionism, then the flaw in the false dilemma proposed by Strawson becomes obvious: we do not have to choose between accepting moral responsibility and being classified as deranged and incompetent and "excused" from connections with the human social and moral community. There is a third alternative, namely, that we are generally competent and reflective and purposeful but we are *not* morally responsible, and we are not excluded from the human community because *no one* in that community is morally responsible (moral responsibility is not the price of admission). However, if we accept the Strawsonian dichotomy, then advocates of moral responsibility make a very demanding offer: either accept moral responsibility or be banished from the human moral and social community. If you choose the second option, you are incompetent and an outcast (and the best that incompetent outcasts can hope for is pity). So the offer is: sign on to the moral responsibility contract, or else. It is hardly surprising that when faced with such an offer, hardly anyone declines.

The opportunity to exercise take-charge responsibility is very appealing, and the prospect of being treated as an object and ostracized from the human community is deeply appalling. That stark contrast, based on Strawson's false dichotomy, is at the heart of Dennett's *contractual* argument for moral responsibility:

People *want* to be held accountable. The benefits that accrue to one who is a citizen in good standing in a free society are so widely and deeply appreciated that there is always a potent presumption in favor of inclusion. Blame is the price we pay for credit, and we pay it gladly under most circumstances. We pay dearly, accepting punishment and public humiliation for a chance to get back in the game after we have been caught out in some transgression. And so the best strategy for holding the line against creeping exculpation is clear: Protect and enhance the value of the game one gets to play if one is a citizen in good standing. . . .

Since there will always be strong temptations to make yourself really small, to externalize the causes of your actions and deny responsibility, the way to counteract these is to make people an offer they can't refuse: If you want to be free, you must *take* responsibility. (2003, 292)

This is indeed an offer hard to refuse: either you are morally responsible and justly deserving of blame and punishment, or you are a deranged incompetent who is banished from the protection of our social contract and excluded from human moral and social relations. When that is the choice, even those who have suffered the most and will benefit the least are eager to claim moral responsibility in preference to being banished from the human community (and its warm reactive attitudes) and classified as deranged and incompetent.

Dennett claims that "many a murderer has no doubt of his own culpability" (1984, 65). And certainly many murderers do insist on such moral responsibility. After describing the brutalizing childhood of executed murderer Robert Harris (hated by his mother, abused by his alcoholic father, teased at school for a speech defect, and repeatedly raped at age fourteen in a federal detention center), Gary Watson states, "It is noteworthy that Harris himself seems to accept responsibility for his life," quoting someone with whom Harris talked: "He told me he had his chance, he took the road to hell and there's nothing more to say" (1987b, 281n). John Spenkelink (the first person executed in Florida after the resumption of capital punishment in that state) at age eleven found the body of the father he idolized (a suicide victim) and began a series of petty crimes that led to the murder of a fellow drifter. Shortly before his execution, Spenkelink asserted, "Man is what he chooses to be. He chooses that for himself" (At issue: Crime and punishment 1979, 14). But it is hardly surprising that those most brutally shaped for failure are insistent on their own moral responsibility. They have been taught that moral responsibility distinguishes humans from subhumans, that moral responsibility is the condition for membership in the human community. Offenders most severely damaged by their conditioning histories (deprived of any freedom or human dignity, and brutally excluded from the social community) are pitifully eager to claim full moral responsibility and accept whatever scraps of community recognition they can find, even if those scraps are retributive punishment. If even Harris and Spenkelink are willing to make such a bargain, it is no surprise that philosophers jump at the deal. In stark contrast to the deprivations and abuses suffered by Harris and Spenkelink, philosophers are typically the privileged beneficiaries of great advantages: loving and supportive families, stable communities and surroundings, and superb educational opportunities. We fortunate ones have been shaped as chronic cognizers with robust self-confidence—why else would we arrogantly offer our own answers and solutions to such ancient problems as free will and moral responsibility? And so we choose between social isolation, loss of free choice, and treatment as an incompetent, or potential blame and punishment for our wrongs (which given our fortunate backgrounds we are unlikely to commit) and reward for all our accomplishments and successes (that flow from our favored histories). It is not a difficult choice for *us*, but we may wonder if it's a fair deal for everyone.

James Lenman makes a similar contractual case for moral responsibility. Though he starts with idealized "Human Beings" who are somewhat more stable and rational and self-controlled than the ordinary run of humans, Lenman's basic approach echoes Dennett and Strawson: if the condition

for gaining respect as a valued member of the human community is accepting moral responsibility, then most will prefer to be counted as morally
responsible:

> Worries about fairness arise because responsibility can be a burden to Human Beings.
> When Human Beings are caught with their fingers in the till and held responsible
> for this, it can be extremely unpleasant for them. But this coin has two sides. For
> my idealized Human Beings, let us suppose, tend to value being held responsible
> for their actions just because to hold them responsible for their actions is itself to
> accord them a form of respect, a form of respect they see as desirable and choice-
> worthy. Like us, Human Beings like being treated like grown-ups and not like chil-
> dren. (2006, 20)

So given that "choice," we accept the contract, but Lenman takes a further
step, to make the contractual choice considerably more palatable:

> What is crucial here is the focus we put not, in the first place, on the perspective
> of other people trying to figure out whether it is fair to hold some agent responsible
> but, in a distinctively contractualist spirit, on the agent's own perspective in trying
> to figure out whether this is something she would be willing to take the gamble of
> having them—and herself—do. From this perspective, it is important that she has
> a set of values and principles, that she has these wholeheartedly, and that she has
> a strong but not complete (otherwise the gamble would be no gamble) confidence
> that she can govern her future behavior by their lights. It is these factors that do
> the work. The c-autonomous agent [who has "a stable and coherent set of highest-
> order desires, values, and principles" and "a high degree of self-control"] is, in these
> respects at least, someone who likes and trusts herself, and there's no reason this
> liking should be, in any deep or general way, conditional on where that self comes
> from. For her to be willing to take responsibility for acting in the light of her values,
> it matters only that they are *her* values. She may reasonably, where this question is
> concerned, not give much of a stuff how she came by them. (2006, 24)

So for those of us who have strong value commitments, who are deeply
reflective, have strong self-control, are chronic cognizers, and are powerfully self-efficacious (that is, for us philosophers who have the benefits of
a very positive history and a superb education): would *we* accept moral
responsibility (with, for us, the very small attendant risk of changing into
weak and vile persons and deserving blame for our bad behavior, which is
greatly overbalanced by the great likelihood of substantive success for
which we can justly claim credit and reward)? Well, yes—where do I sign?
The moral responsibility contract seems like a wonderful deal. And it's easy
to forget that those who don't enjoy our tremendous advantages will also
sign up, because their only alternative is to be ostracized from the human

social and moral community and treated as unworthy of respect, affection, and consideration.

If I agree to play a game, it does not follow that the game is *fair*. You *agree* to a tennis match, but you are required to wear oversize combat boots that weigh 10 pounds each, while your opponent plays in perfectly fitted, well-designed tennis shoes. The match will be unfair, your agreement to play notwithstanding. And if that is the only way you will be allowed to play, and the alternative to not agreeing to play is to be ostracized from the community and treated as an incompetent who is fit only to be managed by others, then it's not surprising that you *choose* to play. Both of you agreed to play, but when you lose and your opponent wins, there remains the question of whether you deserve blame for your poor performance and she deserves special credit for her superior play.

In the Soviet "show trials" of the Stalin era, many defendants eagerly accepted blame for terrible crimes; it does not follow that they *deserved* blame. Contractual models of moral responsibility run aground on one fundamental problem: the question of whether it is *fair* to hold people responsible cannot be decided by whether people acquiesce in such claims and ascriptions of moral responsibility, especially when the only escape from moral responsibility is by way of insanity, incompetence, and isolation.

13 Does Moral Responsibility Promote Respect?

In addition to the arguments discussed in the previous two chapters, there are other arguments that stem from the systemic assumption of moral responsibility. The *elitism* argument is also based on the assumption—made within the moral responsibility system—that anyone not held morally responsible must be categorized as profoundly *flawed* and thus *excused*. The most impressive version of the elitism argument is offered by the legal theorist and philosopher Michael Moore, as part of his argument against the moral legitimacy of feeling sympathy for those who commit criminal acts. According to Moore, those who feel sympathy for the disadvantaged criminal are motivated by an elitist view that the criminal is not worthy of being held to the same moral standards we set for ourselves:

In the case of those feelings of sympathy on which the causal theorist relies, one aspect of their psychology should make us hesitate to honour them as sources of moral insight. There is an elitism and a condescension often (and perhaps invariably) connected with such feelings. To stand back and to refuse to judge because one understands the causes of criminal behavior is to elevate one's self over the unhappy deviant. The elevation of self takes place because these causal theorists typically maintain high moral standards for themselves, yet refuse to judge others by those same standards. This discrimination betokens a refusal to acknowledge the equal moral dignity of others. It betokens a sense about one's self—as the seat of subjective will and responsibility—that one refuses to acknowledge in others. (1997, 545–546)

Moore makes the same argument in an earlier chapter, using the example of Richard Herrin, a Latino student at Yale, who grew up in the barrios of Los Angeles and who murdered his wealthy girlfriend (a fellow Yale student) when she wished to end their romance. Moore offers an impassioned criticism of those who would deny that Herrin deserves severe retributive punishment:

We are probably not persons who grew up in the barrio of East Los Angeles, or who found Yale an alien and disconcerting culture. In any case, we certainly have never been subject to the exact same stresses and motivations as Richard Herrin. Therefore, it may be tempting to withhold from Richard the benefit each of us gives himself or herself: the benefit of being the subjective seat of a will that, although caused, is nonetheless capable of both choice and responsibility.

Such discrimination is a temptation to be resisted, because it is no virtue. It is elitist and condescending toward others not to grant them the same responsibility and desert you grant to yourself. Admittedly, there are excuses the benefit of which others as well as you may avail themselves. Yet that is not the distinction invoked here. Herrin had no excuses the rest of us could not come up with in terms of various causes for our choices. To refuse to grant him the same responsibility and desert as you would grant yourself is thus an instance of what Sartre would call bad faith, the treating of a free, subjective will as an object. It is a refusal to admit that the rest of humanity shares with us that which makes us most distinctively human, our capacity to will and reason—and thus to be and do evil. Far from evincing fellow-feeling and the allowing of others to participate in our moral life, it excludes them as less than persons.

Rather than succumbing to this elitism masquerading as egalitarianism, we should ask ourselves what Herrin deserves by asking what *we* would deserve had we done such an act. In answering this question we should listen to our guilt feelings. (1997, 148–149)

The crux of Moore's argument is well-known: wrongdoers have a *right* to be punished because subjecting them to deserved punishment recognizes them as members of the human moral community and excusing them from punishment excludes and demeans them. C. S. Lewis offers a clear statement of this view:

To be "cured" against one's will and cured of states which we may not regard as disease is to be put on a level with those who have not yet reached the age of reason or those who never will; to be classed with infants, imbeciles, and domestic animals. But to be punished, however severely, because we have deserved it, because we "ought to have known better," is to be treated as a human person made in God's image. (1971, 246)

And Herbert Morris develops the philosophically best known version of this argument:

The primary reason for preferring the system of punishment as against the system of therapy might have been expressed in terms of the one system treating one as a person and the other not. . . . When we talk of not treating a human being as a person or "showing no respect for one as a person," what we imply by our words is a contrast between the manner in which one acceptably responds to human beings and the manner in which one acceptably responds to animals and inanimate objects. When we treat a human being merely as an animal or some inanimate object our responses to the human being are determined, not by his choices, but ours in disregard of or with indifference to his. And when we "look upon" a person as less than a person or not a person, we consider the person as incapable of rational choice. (1968, 490)

Thus, according to Morris and Lewis and Moore, punishment respects the person as a rational being and a member of the human moral community who is capable of free rational choice and who thus has the right to enjoy or suffer the consequences of those choices. Rejecting the retributive model treats humans as so flawed that they fall outside the moral realm—as individuals who are incapable of reason and are thus fit only for coercive treatment. If we regard disadvantaged others as *not* deserving retribution, then we treat them as so defective that they cannot be held to the same standards we apply to ourselves. Such a view is based on an ugly elitism; in contrast, the retributivist view is wonderfully egalitarian: *everyone* who is minimally rational deserves punishment for their misdeeds, whether they grew up with the social and cultural and environmental advantages we enjoyed or suffered the stress and harsh treatment meted out by poverty and discrimination. A refusal to hold Herrin and others morally responsible and deserving of retributive punishment is, according to Moore, "a refusal to admit that the rest of humanity shares with us that which makes us most distinctively human, our capacity to will and reason—and thus to be and do evil. Far from evincing fellow-feeling and the allowing of others to participate in our moral life, it excludes them as less than persons" (1997, 149).

But that argument misconstrues the nonretributivist (the moral responsibility abolitionist) denial of justly deserved retributive punishment. It is not a question of excusing Herrin because he is flawed (he is flawed, like all of us, though more severely than most, but he is still a rational person, and the nonretributivist regards Herrin as a full member of the human moral community). It is not a question of excuses at all. The nonretributivist does not selectively excuse particularly damaged individuals from retributive punishment; rather, the nonretributivist-abolitionist denies that *anyone* ever justly deserves retributive punishment. The entire system of retributive justice is rejected: *no one*—no matter how flawed, talented, or generically "average"—justly deserves special reward or punishment. Thus there is no elitism in this denial that Herrin justly deserves retributive punishment; to the contrary, Herrin and other malefactors are fully included—along with all of us—in the category of persons who do not justly deserve punishment.

Moore's misinterpretation is common. Believers in retributivism and just deserts assume a universal starting point in which people are morally responsible for their behavior and therefore justly deserving of special reward or punishment. Starting from that assumption, the denial that Richard Herrin justly deserves retributive punishment must imply that Herrin is a *special case*: one who is so severely defective that he falls outside the boundaries of the human moral community. That might well be an elitist position, but it is not the position occupied by nonretributivists who deny moral responsibility; rather, it is the position often mistakenly *attributed* to those who deny all moral responsibility and "just deserts." The basic problem is revealed when Moore insists that "Herrin has no excuse the rest of us could not come up with in terms of various causes for our choices" (1997, 149). The issue is not excuses, but causes. Herrin obviously experienced causes the rest of us did not, for each of us has a unique causal history, and ultimately none of us chose or controlled the causes that shaped us. When people perform different acts, make different choices, and have different characters, then there are different causes in their histories that shaped those different results. The rejection of moral responsibility and retributive punishment is based on universal causes rather than universal excuses. As described in chapter 11, the universal denial of moral responsibility is based on a miracle-requisite model rather than an excuse-extensionist model.

Rejecting Moral Responsibility and Promoting Inclusiveness

The rejection of moral responsibility and retributivism is based on the view that *all* of us, whether vicious or virtuous, are shaped by forces outside of our control, so *none* of us justly deserve special reward or punishment. Of course, we all have "various causes for our choices," but (as Moore acknowledges) most of us did not have the experiences of growing up in a Los Angeles barrio; being dropped from there into the wealthy and privileged world of prep school–educated, world-traveled, socially polished Yale undergraduates; feeling like an inadequate alien in that rich and fascinating new environment; gaining special admission to its wonders through the affection of a beautiful young woman; and finally having that affection and amazing opportunity for acceptance withdrawn. If we are naturalists and believe that all events and all human behavior are explicable by *natural* nonmiraculous causes, then we must accept that if we had experienced exactly the same causes and circumstances that Herrin experienced, we would have committed the same horrible deeds. Obviously none of that justifies (or excuses) Herrin's act of murder: Herrin's choices and act were profoundly wrong. But the question is not whether Herrin did wrong, and was in fact a very bad person (he did and he was), but rather, whether he is morally responsible for his bad act and choice and for the character from which his choices stem. The claim of those who reject moral responsibility and retributive just deserts is that Richard Herrin—like *all* of us—was crucially shaped by forces he neither chose nor controlled. Unless we are willing to embrace godlike self-making mysteries—and Moore insists that he is not (1997, 522)—then there are causes for those choices that undercut any claims that the choosers are morally responsible for their choices. We make different choices because of our different capacities and abilities, and those different capacities were shaped by forces and factors that we neither chose not controlled.

Some of us are strong-willed, others weak; some have a robust sense of self-efficacy, and others lack self-confidence; some are chronic cognizers, others cognitive misers; some have a healthy internal locus-of-control, and others view themselves as manipulated by external powers. Those are important differences, but they are not differences that we controlled or chose. A weak-willed cognitive miser can still make free choices, but his moral responsibility for those (frequently bad) choices is another question altogether (just as industrious chronic cognizers are not morally responsible for more often making good choices). We do not "make ourselves," as the existentialists imagine (thus we are not morally responsible), but we do make choices and exert (varying powers of) deliberation, and making such choices is something we generally enjoy. Moral responsibility abolitionism does not reject free choices; to the contrary, it examines *why* some people are more effective and self-efficacious and self-controlled in their choice-making (and therefore better at exercising their valuable freedom), and thus it encourages the improvement of free behavior and free choices, and the strengthening of free will. Rather than treating free behavior as a given, or as some inexplicable miraculous power, or as something that we should not examine too closely, freedom should be understood as a desirable feature that can be nurtured. If an adequate level of careful cognitive reflection enhances our free choice-making (and it does), then we can study and strengthen the causal factors that shape the development of chronic cognizers, while avoiding conditions that lead people to become cognitive misers.

I am lethargic, and you are industrious; I give up when facing obstacles, and you have courage and fortitude; I act capriciously and thoughtlessly, and you are carefully deliberative. From the *non*retributivist-abolitionist perspective, ultimately you were lucky and I was unlucky (in our formative influences). We are not radically different, but were simply shaped by different contingencies, and you do not deserve greater rewards and privileges and benefits than I do, nor do I deserve penalties and hardships and deprivations from which you are exempt. It is not the *non*retributive rejection of moral responsibility that promotes elitism; rather, elitism is nurtured by the strong belief in moral responsibility and just deserts that forms the retributivist foundation. From the retributivist and just deserts perspective, you justly deserve the "fruits of your labor" and the higher status and the special benefits you receive on the basis of your wonderful abilities and wise choices, and I justly deserve the meager portion that falls my way and the deprivations I suffer and the punishments I receive. And because we wind up with such radically different portions—you get the lion's share of the wealth, I get the crumbs; you get the rewards, I suffer the punishments—we must be radically different. You are a paragon of virtue, and I am almost worthless (or even worse than worthless). Elitism does not emerge from "but for the grace of environmental contingencies, there go I"; rather, it comes from "*I* deserve reward, *they* deserve punishment; I'm special, because I rose to duty; they had the same opportunity, and failed."

Elitist Retributivism

Contrary to the myth that harsh punishment is respectful and inclusive, careful examination shows that it is the punitive/retributive/moral responsibility model that fosters elitism and exclusion. That conclusion is best shown through empirical observation of those societies and cultures that insist on harsh retributive punishment and contrasting them with societies that move in the other direction. Cavadino and Dignan note that in "neo-liberal" societies (such as the United States):

Economic failure is seen as being the fault of the atomized, free-willed individual, not any responsibility of society. . . . Crime is likewise seen as entirely the responsibility of the offending individual. . . . And as neo-liberal societies have become even more neo-liberal in recent decades, so they have become more punitive. . . . [In] the United States . . . the toughening of criminal justice and penal policies during the Reagan and Bush (senior) presidencies . . . accompanied a systematic reversal of various "incorporative" social policy initiatives in other spheres. . . .

On the other hand, corporatist societies like Germany—and to an even greater extent, social democratic ones like Sweden . . . tend to pursue more inclusionary economic and social policies that offer their citizens a far greater degree of protection against the vicissitudes of market forces, binding citizens to the state via national interest groups and ensuring the provision of welfare benefits and care of various kinds to ensure that all citizens are looked after. The communitarian ethos which gives rise to these policies—and which is in return shaped by them—also finds expression in a less individualistic attitude toward the offender, who is regarded not as an isolated culpable individual who must be rejected and excluded from law-abiding society, but as a social being who should still be included in society but who needs rehabilitation and *resocialization*, which is the responsibility of the community as a whole. The corporate citizen, unlike the neo-liberal, is much more his brother's keeper—even if he has done wrong—with a stronger sense that "there but for the grace of God go I"—in terms of both economic failure and criminal activity. (2006a, 448)

As a simple but powerful indication of whether retributivism really goes along with social inclusiveness (or whether to the contrary, as Cavadino and Dignan argue, inclusiveness wanes as punitive policy waxes), consider which societies tend to exclude wrongdoers from the most basic right of participating in elections as voting citizens. In the United States, convicted felons are routinely excluded from the right to vote (in most states, suggesting that imprisoned felons should be given the opportunity to vote would be committing political suicide); in Sweden, Denmark, Finland, France, Germany, Netherlands, Canada, New Zealand, Australia, and a number of less harshly punitive countries, even the imprisoned are included in the basic voting rights of citizens. Within the United States (where convicted felons are routinely denied the right to vote until they have completed their imprisonment and their supervised parole), some of the most harshly and enthusiastically retributive states (such as Virginia and Mississippi) permanently deny convicted felons (including those who have long since served their prison terms) the rights of voting citizens; those states that are the least harshly retributive are also the most inclusive of wrongdoers: Vermont and Maine are the only states that allow prisoners to vote. By almost any measure of empirical reality, the more retributive the society, the less inclusive the society toward wrongdoers. That result is not a strange accident that goes contrary to the logic of retributive moral responsibility; rather, it is the clear social manifestation of the individual-istic ostracism that moral responsibility/retributivism fosters.

Sustaining the retributivist/just deserts perspective requires that differ-ences in our histories must be hidden or dramatically understated. My privileged position is justly deserved, so it cannot be based on good luck in our starting points or formative histories, and that props up the belief that my special benefits and rewards are purely my own doing, with any help from my history being insignificant. This suppressing of attention to formative history plays a major role in Michael Moore's defense of retributivism:

In the most famous recent example [of brainwashing], the Patty Hearst case, we were certain of a causal connection between the conditioning Hearst received and her criminal behaviour. That certainty, however, was irrelevant to the issue of whether her behaviour was an action. She robbed the bank; it was her act, whether or not a situation that was not of her making implanted in her the beliefs that caused her to act. One might have allowed her some affirmative defence if she had not had adequate time between the conditioning and the criminal act in which to reject or integrate her new beliefs into her character. Such an affirmative defence is irrelevant to the issue of action. She plainly acted, whether or not her act was caused. (1997, 533–534)

Of course Patty Hearst acted: she chose to engage in criminal behavior with the members of the Symbionese Liberation Army (SLA). But it is incredible to suggest that her history of being kidnapped and brainwashed is not relevant to her just deserts. Patty Hearst endured terrifying weeks of com-plete helplessness and dependence during which she lost all sense of controlling the events around her; in short, she was reduced to a state of severe "learned helplessness" (Seligman 1975) in which the subject loses all confidence in her own abilities to make things happen and becomes profoundly dependent and passive. While in this state, she chose—in accordance with the values and character that had been shaped—to follow the lead of the powerful confident persons who guided her; indeed, she did "integrate her new beliefs into her [new] character." But to suppose that her history of brainwashing—which left her in a state of extreme emotional dependence and learned helplessness—is *irrelevant* is a supposition that could only be made under a just deserts–inspired blindness to the importance of conditioning history.[1]

Patty Hearst was imprisoned for her competent choice to join in the activities of the SLA. Some people were outraged at that verdict, but by moral responsibility standards, it was the only verdict possible. Patty Hearst's psychological capacities were severely compromised by her captivity, but she was still competent. Robert Harris's psychological capacities were severely compromised by a lifetime of brutal abusive treatment, but he was also able to reason and plan and choose, so he also was competent. If we look closely at Patty Hearst's diminished psychological resources and decide that she does not justly deserve punishment, then the case against Robert Harris's "justly deserved punishment" will be even more obvious. And if we scrutinize Hearst and Harris, that may open the door to looking carefully at the actual psychological strengths and weaknesses of everyone, and then—unless we are miracle-believing libertarians—we must conclude that differences in behavior are the product of differences in capacities (if there is a difference in outcome, then—barring miracles or chance—such a difference must result from a difference in capacities), that those differences were ultimately a product of good or bad luck (which shaped the personal resources from which we developed and which were available to foster subsequent self-development), and that there is no room for judgments of moral responsibility.

The Clockwork Orange Specter

Treating moral responsibility abolitionism as an excuse-extensionist project *within* the system of moral responsibility is the source of many flawed arguments against those who reject moral responsibility. But of all that multitude of flawed arguments, one stands out for its popularity, its inflammatory claims, and its transparent absurdity: the "Clockwork Orange" argument, which claims that those who reject moral responsibility (and the retributive punishment that is its common cohort) want to replace it with "Clockwork Orange therapy" that is cruel and demeaning to those so "treated." The charge is so obviously false that it would not be worth discussing if it were not so common and so closely related to the foregoing "elitism" argument. There are four fundamental mistakes in the Clockwork Orange accusation. First, there is erroneous assumption that denial of retributive just deserts is based on a system of excuses: that people are excused from retributive punishment because they are so severely flawed that they cannot be considered rational competent persons. From there, it is an easy step to the conclusion that because criminals are considered subhuman, there can be no moral restraints against brutal techniques that shape these subhuman monsters in any way and by any means. But that is a distortion of the grounds on which nonretributivists reject retributive punishments. The actual grounds emphasize the close similarities between those who commit criminal acts and those who live lives of virtue and restraint: their differences are in fortunate or unfortunate causal histories that were not of their own making. Such a view blocks any justification of harsh treatment for those who—but for the bad luck of their conditioning histories—are no different from the rest of us, and it certainly blocks any slide toward treating criminals as profoundly flawed individuals who are proper objects for abusive "therapy." In contrast, the retributivist—who refuses to look carefully at the causes that shape both virtuous and vicious characters and behavior—finds it tempting to embrace a view that the *bad* people are "radically different" from you and me and the rest of our virtuous community, so it becomes much easier to treat these criminals (who are, after all, nothing like *us* and our loved ones) in harsh and demeaning ways. Peter French, in his celebration of rough retributive "justice," is a case in point: "The defenders of the moral virtues of vengeance endorse the view that recommends itself in even a cursory study of human history, literature, popular culture, or the daily newspapers: that there is an unbridgeable moral chasm between people who regularly do wicked deeds and those who typically do good deeds" (2001, 89). On two points, French may be correct: first, this might well be "the view that recommends itself in even a cursory study," but it is not a view that can withstand careful detailed study of the factors that shaped both the lucky virtuous and the unlucky vicious; second, this might indeed be the view of "popular culture," but it is not a view that passes reflective scrutiny.

There is a second reason why moral responsibility abolitionists reject Clockwork Orange brutality: abolitionists are keenly aware that such brutal methods (and such contemporary manifestations as punitive "boot camps" or "shock incarceration") are not good ways of shaping positive character traits. A harsh, discouraging childhood and adolescence cannot be offset by a "shock" program of brutal boot-camp humiliation. Such harsh treatment—whether doled out in the form of Clockwork Orange therapy or "boot camps" for youthful offenders or Supermax prisons for adults—is not an effective means of shaping the self-control and self-confidence needed for living successfully and cooperatively. When Seligman's dogs—that had been subjected to repeated episodes of painful inescapable shock and thus conditioned to a state of deep learned helplessness—were placed in a shuttle box and subjected to additional shock, they did not recover; to the contrary, they sank even more deeply into profound learned helplessness. Shock "treatments" are no more promising for adolescent humans than for abused dogs.

Third, it is not the *non*believer in moral responsibility who is tempted by harsh Clockwork Orange coercive therapy, but the believing retributivist: the harsh boot camp programs for youthful offenders appeal to those who believe that youthful offenders should "suffer the consequences" of their behavior—notwithstanding the fact that we clearly can't shock, bully, or demean people into being self-confident, socially responsible, emotionally healthy citizens. Retributive insistence that the individual offender justly deserves punishment legitimizes ignoring how an enormously wealthy society indulges in luxuries while allowing children to grow up in brutal conditions with substandard physical and mental health care, grossly deficient educational resources, and few opportunities for success; when crimes result, we blame it on the children who have suffered such treatment and pretend that a few weeks of on-the-cheap "boot-camp discipline" can change them into good (or at least acquiescent and passive) citizens or that they justly deserve sentencing to harsh adult facilities. Moral responsibility abolitionists focus on the detailed causal histories that shape both the vicious and the virtuous, and they recognize that neither harsh early environments nor brutal coercive "therapy" can shape self-confident and self-controlled individuals.

There is a fourth reason that the Clockwork Orange brutality charge against moral responsibility abolitionists is false, and it is the most basic. The assumption behind that charge is that we must focus on the *individual* who commits the wrong: the retributivists want to subject this person to ennobling retributive punishment, and their opponents would demean that individual with enforced therapy. But that false assumption of radical individualism produces a false dichotomy between retributive punishment and coerced psychological "treatment." It is not only Moore and Lewis and Morris who make this false assumption; in fact, it is such a common error that psychologists have named it the *fundamental attribution error* (Ross 1977)—because it is as fundamental as it is common. This is the error of overestimating the importance of individual characteristics or character or dispositions in explaining behavior, and neglecting the importance of the larger environment or "situation" in accounting for how people behave. Psychologists have examined the willingness of subjects to inflict severe shocks (Milgram 1963); the high rate of cruelty when acting as a prison guard (Haney, Banks, and Zimbardo 1973; Haney and Zimbardo 1977); the willingness of theology students to help a distressed stranger (Darley and Batson 1973); and the likelihood of stopping to help a fellow student pick up dropped papers (Isen and Levin 1972). In these experiments (and many others), psychologists have found that the *situation* (rather than individual character traits) is the key determinant of behavior. I am not here arguing for the accuracy of this situationist psychological account, though it is backed by an enormous body of empirical research. The point here is that there does exist an alternative to the "elitist" coercive individual therapy position that is often depicted as the only option to retributive punishment. Rather than concentrating on "therapy" for the individual malefactor, a better alternative is focusing on how to change the system so that situations eliciting positive behavior replace those that generate harmful behavior. We must still shape positive behavior in individuals (while recognizing that the situation in which they find themselves may override individual characteristics), which requires fostering strong individual self-efficacy and paying close attention to the social environment and its influences on individual character. But the key to such reform is reforming the *systems* that produce brutalized individuals and that will cause even "reformed" individuals to revert if they are returned to flawed environments (Haney and Zimbardo 1998).

In sum, universal denial of moral responsibility does not have the harmful effects generally thought—the effects that follow only if denial of moral responsibility is based on universalizing and exaggerating excuses. When moral responsibility is denied on miracle-requisite grounds (as part of a naturalistic system that rejects the assumption that all competent persons are morally responsible), then moral responsibility denial leaves ample room for competence and skill, reason and morality, affection and revulsion. And the denial of moral responsibility does not ostracize one from the human moral community: after all, if no one has moral responsibility, then lack of moral responsibility does not set one apart. It certainly does not encourage brutal treatment of malefactors in the guise of "therapy"; to the contrary, it blocks such programs and opens the way to ending the cruel and counterproductive policies of retribution. It does not promote an "elitist" attitude among the more fortunate, but instead challenges such attitudes at their roots.

Distinctions that Are and Are Not Lost When Moral Responsibility Is Rejected

Along the same lines as P. F. Strawson, Saul Smilansky maintains that if we deny moral responsibility, then we must also abolish two very valuable moral distinctions: the distinction between the guilty and the innocent, and the distinction between discriminating on the basis of race or gender and discriminating (legitimately) on the basis of laziness or fortitude. Concerning the first distinction, Smilansky notes with approval Elizabeth Anscombe's sentiment that someone who thinks it is an open question whether we should sometimes judicially execute the innocent "shows a corrupt mind," and Smilansky argues, "Surely, if a moral system, which seeks to preserve and guard vigilantly the common conception of innocence, is to function well, such a sentiment should be prevalent, almost instinctive. But if this is to be so, the worst thing one could do would be to point out that, ultimately, none of this makes sense—because the 'guilty' are, ultimately, no more guilty than others" (2000, 152).

First, if we abolish moral responsibility, there does remain an important distinction between those who commit wrongs and those who do not: as noted earlier, rejecting blame-fault does not imply rejection of character-fault. Robert Harris does not deserve blame, but it is important to recognize that he has a profoundly flawed character that results in horrific acts: important, because we must protect others from the effects of those flaws, we must carefully examine the possibility and means of reforming Harris's flawed character, and we must examine the causal history that shaped such a profoundly flawed person in order to prevent others from developing the same flaws.

Second, *within* the moral responsibility system, the "innocent/guilty" distinction offers vital protections to the innocent: it is the only thing that protects the innocent from harsh treatment in the form of retributive punishment. But that protection comes at a terrible price: the guilty are different, they are in a radically different category, and we innocent ones can sanction and tolerate the brutal treatment of the guilty (dragging them into execution chambers, subjecting them to the psychological damage of long-term solitary confinement in Supermax prisons, sentencing them to long terms in brutal prison conditions) precisely because the guilty are very different from we innocent ones who are *protected* from such treatment. When we step outside the constraints of the moral responsibility system, then the radical difference between the "innocent" and the "guilty" disappears. Robert Harris remains a brutal man with terrible character-faults, but when we remove the moral responsibility blinders and look closely and carefully, we recognize that Robert Harris is a human being, just as you and I are, and that the difference between Robert Harris and ourselves is that we were raised in a nurturing caring environment and strongly encouraged to avoid violence and study hard and gain and enjoy the benefits of careful deliberation and academic achievement, but Robert Harris was subjected to brutal treatment and harsh parental rejection and schoolyard belittlement. Denying a radical difference between the innocent and the guilty obviously does not imply approval of the judicial execution of the innocent, which is still recognized as a terrible wrong, but it does mean that we would come to recognize that judicial execution—or other forms of mistreatment—of the "guilty" (those with deep character-faults) is also wrong. Understanding the basic similarity between those who enjoy character-virtues and those who suffer from character-flaws is perfectly consistent with recognizing the existence of character-flaws, striving to reform those flawed characters, protecting others from the harms that flow from them, and working to change the conditions that shape such flawed characters. Within the moral responsibility system, the deep chasm separating us innocents from those guilty is our only protection against the brutal treatment meted out to those on the other side of the chasm; as Smilansky acknowledges, the price for that protective chasm is acceptance of the illusion of ultimate moral responsibility (an illusion that blocks the careful detailed study of the causes that shape both the innocent and the guilty). When we liberate ourselves from the moral responsibility system, then the need for the illusion disappears along with the radical distance between the guilty and the innocent, and the illusion is replaced by careful clear scrutiny of the causes for our characters and our behavior, resulting in deep concern for the well-being of *both* the virtuous and the vicious. In short, the radical difference between the guilty and the innocent is a vital element of the moral responsibility system, but when taken out of that system and examined closely on its own account, it can be seen for what it is: an ugly artifact from an ugly system.

Starting from the mistaken assumption that denial of moral responsibility is an excuse-extensionist assertion of universal incompetence, Peter Strawson paints a very dark picture of moral responsibility abolitionism. As noted earlier, Saul Smilansky is—usually—well aware that universal denial of moral responsibility is not based on universal flaws and excuses, yet when he draws his own picture of the second problem that would be generated by universal rejection of moral responsibility, he nonetheless slides back within the moral responsibility system and assumes that universal rejection of moral responsibility requires universal incompetence. That assumption can be seen in the following passage, and it is the key to the second important moral distinction that Smilansky believes would be lost if we abandoned moral responsibility. The first distinction—the radical divide between the innocent and the guilty—plays an important role *within* the moral responsibility system, but can be happily discarded along with the moral responsibility system itself: character-fault (as opposed to blame-fault) considerations will of course remain very important. Smilansky's second distinction—between discriminating on the grounds of character flaws such as laziness and discriminating on the grounds of race or gender—is a distinction that is well worth preserving, but when the rejection of moral responsibility is properly understood, there is no danger of losing that distinction. Smilansky notes that on the "common view," there is an important distinction between discriminating on the basis of effort or laziness and discriminating on the basis of race or gender:

From the ultimate hard determinist perspective the common view does not make normative sense. If a person is worse off due to laziness, this is no different from his being worse off because of his skin pigment—ultimately one is equally lacking in responsibility for both traits. The idea that everyone should be given an opportunity to show what he can do may have pragmatic merits, but from the ultimate perspective it lacks the moral basis that the common view attributes to it.

Discriminating on grounds of race or sex is no different, for the hard determinist, from discriminating on grounds of intelligence or of a disposition to hard work. Ultimately, only the outcome counts. On hard determinist assumptions, such racist or sexist discrimination does not morally legitimize particular resentment by those who suffer from it, or general moral indignation at the wrong, by others! Just as the privileged, positive position of the innocent is undermined by universal inno-cence or blamelessness, so the privileged position of work-related conditions which are within people's control, such as hard work, loses its intrinsic value. The univer-sal application of excuses along hard determinist lines is not a further extension of the compatibilist excuses so much as it is the wholesale elimination of any distinc-tions. It may seem that there are benefits to the hard determinist perspective, say, in mitigating the harsh judgement of the lazy, but this misses the central point: the idea that a person deserves not to be discriminated against for factors beyond his control, such as race or sex, is toppled from its currently high moral standing. (2000, 156)

There is an important element of truth in Smilansky's claim: from the ultimate perspective (the "hard determinist" perspective that denies all claims and ascriptions of moral responsibility), there *is* a basic similarity between blaming someone for skin color or gender (or the color of their eyes) and blaming someone for being lazy. That similarity does not make it any less wrong to blame someone for gender or skin color; rather, it emphasizes how wrong it is to blame for laziness (or any other serious character fault): when we look carefully and deeply, and without the illu-sion of moral responsibility, we recognize (as Smilansky himself acknowl-edges) that we ultimately had no more control over our laziness or our industriousness than we had over our race or gender. It is an important comparison, because it brings out the fundamental moral wrongness of moral responsibility practices, but it in no way diminishes the wrongness of racial and gender discrimination. From the ultimate perspective of moral responsibility denial, blaming for race or gender is analogous to blaming for laziness, but there remain very important reasons why blaming on the basis of race or gender is especially damaging.

First, and most obviously, being lazy is a genuine character flaw (it is a character-fault, not a blame-fault); in contrast, being a member of a race or gender or ethnic group is not a character flaw—the problem is that it is often treated as one. One fundamental problem with racial/gender/ethnic discrimination is that it treats race and gender and ethnic group as moral categories: one is a morally inferior person because of one's race or gender or ethnic group. Women are classed as "sinks of iniquity" or "naturally subservient," blacks as "mud people" or "God's rejected tribe," Jews as "Christ-killers" or "greedy and treacherous," Native Americans as lazy, Irish as drunkards, and Poles as stupid. Such vicious prejudices are significantly worse than judging an individual lazy, because no matter how industrious one is, if one lives in a culture that brands all members of one's group as lazy, then one is helpless to overcome that prejudiced judgment. If I am individually judged to be lazy, I can through my own efforts overcome that judgment: if I am genuinely lazy, then perhaps I can change by following a program that gradually develops my fortitude; if I am mistakenly perceived to be lazy, I can overcome that judgment through demonstration of my sustained hard work (whether I have the capacity or the support necessary for such a program of fortitude-development or fortitude-exhibition is my good or bad fortune, not something for which I am morally responsible). But if I am invariably judged by society as lazy because of my ethnic identity, then all my efforts to change that perception must be futile, and such futile efforts and total lack of control over outcome is a path to learned helplessness and deep hopelessness. It entrenches helplessness and despair in huge groups of people—a terrible wrong. Little girls once learned that they could never be doctors (and never hold any position of high prestige and authority) and must never aspire to be more than nurses who unquestioningly follow "doctors' orders." In past years, young African-Americans learned that no matter how hard they worked, they could never hold positions of authority, they could never be recognized for their own worth, and they could never be treated with dignity and respect. Such prejudices are profoundly harmful, and the sense of futility they engender often make them into brutally self-fulfilling traps. From the "ultimate" perspective that denies all moral responsibility, neither the lazy person nor the victim of prejudice justly deserves to be worse off, but acknowledging that fact does not preclude recognizing the special wrong and great harm of social prejudice. You do not justly deserve more because you were fortunate enough to develop the vitally important character-virtue of fortitude and industriousness; however, industriousness is still a very desirable character trait, and laziness is a serious character flaw. Prejudice blinds us to the character flaws of the privileged and blocks recognition of the character virtues of the prejudice victims, obstructs effective measures for promoting virtue and preventing vice, and fosters helplessness and despair, all of which is more than sufficient to establish the particularly vile nature of prejudice (notwithstanding the fact that *any* program that "makes one worse off" than another is morally wrong, whether that program is based on vile prejudice or on spurious claims of just deserts and moral responsibility).

Smilansky claims that "the universal application of excuses along hard determinist lines is not a further extension of the compatibilist excuses so much as it is the wholesale elimination of any distinctions" (2000, 156), but as already noted, Smilansky knows that the universal denial of moral responsibility is not based on excuse-extensionism (it is a mark of how powerful this temptation is that it inveigles even such a clear thinker as Smilansky). Thus the universal denial of moral responsibility does not eliminate important moral distinctions, such as the distinction between being genuinely lazy and being a victim of prejudice that wrongly judges one to be lazy. If everyone were so severely flawed as to be excused from moral responsibility (if denial of moral responsibility were based on excuse-extensionism), then no one would be sufficiently competent to be judged either lazy or industrious, and the distinction between prejudiced judgments of fault and genuine judgments of fault would be useless. That is, if severe fault is universal, such distinctions make no sense. But when we universally deny moral responsibility by rejecting the moral responsibility system (thus rejecting the idea that moral responsibility can be denied only on the basis of excuses), then there is plenty of room for the moral judgment that the victim of prejudice does not have character faults and the lazy person does.

14 Creative Authorship without Ultimate Responsibility

When we give up belief in moral responsibility, we must give up the belief that blame and punishment can be justly deserved, which is a great benefit—or so I claim in the following chapters. But even if one is convinced that rejection of justly deserved blame and punishment is a gain, a strong sense may remain that loss of *ultimate responsibility* is a grievous loss. Two philosophers who are among the most profound and insightful proponents of moral responsibility—Robert Kane and Saul Smilansky—would certainly feel the loss. They might respond, "Set aside the whole question of blame and punishment; we think it's valuable, you think it's harmful, but ignore that for the moment; concentrate on what *else* would be lost if we lose the ultimate responsibility that underpins just deserts." Kane insists that the loss would be significant: "If I am ultimately responsible for certain occurrences in the universe, if the only explanation for their occurring rather than not is to be found in my rational will, then my choices and my life take on an importance that is missing if I do not have such responsibility" (1985, 178). Smilansky warns:

Illusion is a buffer from threats to our self-conceptions and family relationships on the level of the meaning of our lives. If the ultimate perspective [of moral responsibility denial] is allowed to poison the *appreciation* of past concern and effort, or the *acknowledgment* of fault for past deeds or omissions, it is not only our functioning within families which can be harmed, but the very significance of our relationships and the value we achieve for ourselves within them. . . . Awareness of the ultimate inevitability of any level of functioning . . . *darkens* our fundamental ways of appreciating ourselves and others. (2000, 177; see also Smilansky 2005)

The sense of loss that is of genuine concern to Kane and Smilansky (and many others) is not one that I share, so I am tempted to be dismissive: *get over it*. We're not gods, we didn't make ourselves, we're not ultimately responsible, and I didn't fulfill my youthful dream of being the starting quarterback for the Dallas Cowboys, but I learned to deal with that reality, and it's not so bad. I might (in my arrogance) be tempted to go further: you are suffering from an unwillingness to give up the autarchic fiction described by Freudian psychoanalysts. Infants initially believe that they are omnipotent (or at the very least, totally self-sufficient); this *autarchic fiction* is shattered by the discovery that they are *dependent*—that is, not in total control. That loss of the autarchic fiction is a traumatic experience that we must struggle to repair. Most of us make the repairs and move on, but some philosophers never cease their quest to recover omnipotence and ultimate responsibility. But even if I found Freud plausible (and I don't), the discovery of a psychological cause for this ultimate responsibility quest would do nothing to prove its illegitimacy. In any case, such a dismissive attitude is hardly justified. After all, the concern raised by Kane and Smilansky is profound and important. Neither is motivated by a deep desire for retributive justice; they are not moved by desire for personal glory (if they are, then they stumbled into the wrong career path); and certainly, neither harbors a megalomaniacal passion to be apotheosized into deity status. Yet they are committed to the claim of and need for ultimate responsibility (even if Smilansky believes that the need can be fulfilled only through the embrace of illusion). The fundamental longing seems to be something like this: a desire to make a special unique impact on the world, a desire to contribute something more than the sum product of one's causal history, a wish to be someone who is—for better or worse—something other than what is ground out by the wheels of one's causal destiny.

What We Accomplish

Some of the great souls of history—King Solomon, Fyodor Dostoyevsky, William James, Albert Camus—have felt the force of this fundamental longing to accomplish something that transcends the causal powers that shaped us; that I do not reveals the poverty of my imagination rather than my superior insight. So this is a concern that should be addressed, however inadequately. We do not have the ultimate responsibility that is a necessary condition for moral responsibility, and the itch that troubles Kane and Smilansky cannot be scratched; nonetheless, it may be that from a slightly different perspective the loss will not seem so disturbing.

John Lewis was a pianist and composer who made enormous contributions to American music throughout the second half of the twentieth century. No one did more to bring together the best of European classical music with the most innovative American jazz, and this extraordinary synthesis reached its heights in the exquisite creations of the Modern Jazz Quartet, for which Lewis was the primary composer as well as the musical director. What Lewis produced was unique and wonderful, and without Lewis, those wonderful creations would never have come into existence. But nothing in that requires that Lewis have ultimate responsibility for those creations—indeed, Lewis would have been the first to affirm that he was not their ultimate source. His work was shaped by the influences of Duke Ellington and Lester Young, the "free jazz" of Ornette Coleman and the more traditional Kansas City blues, together with his studies at the Manhattan School of Music and his work with colleagues in the Lenox School of Jazz and the City College of New York. All of these factors—and many, many more—came together in John Lewis, and the result was splendid. And if Laplace's demon could trace all of the elements that shaped every line Lewis composed and every note Lewis played, that would in no way lessen Lewis's accomplishment or authorship or the uniqueness of John Lewis and his work. Though the factors that shaped Kane and Smilansky have taken them along very different paths from the one traveled by John Lewis, those factors have resulted in significant accomplishments by wonderfully unique individuals.

Trevor Pisciotta is another who fears the baleful effects of finding that our choices and behavior and accomplishments were ultimately the result of causes beyond our control: "a robust sense of meaningfulness in lives requires 'up to usness' of a sort incompatible with the truth of determinism" (2008, 81). To show the valuable element that is missing from the determinist picture, Pisciotta imagines an agent, Tom, who is manipulated by neuroscientists who subtly control his thinking processes. Tom still thinks, and has values on which he acts, but his values as well as his thought processes and evaluations are manipulated by the neuroscientists. What would be the effect on Tom? "Tom would, I contend, be shattered to hear the news about the true nature of his life and of his commitment to the fight against poverty [one of Tom's deep values]. What was once for Tom a source of pride and satisfaction would cease to be so" (83).

Pisciotta may well be correct about this. After all, suppose that the wonderful creations of John Lewis were the guided effects of subtle brain manipulations by these devious neuroscientists; in that case, Lewis would be merely an instrument playing out the music that the neuroscientists actually composed. But that is a very different scenario from the actual determined one, in which Lewis is the person in which all of the special influences came together and produced something *new*. Furthermore, the darkest element in this picture is the manipulation by the neuroscientists: we have good reason to fear such manipulation, for bitter experience shows that manipulators rarely manipulate us for any benefit other than their own. The covert nature of the manipulation heightens the horror: Kane is particularly concerned to block control by *covert* nonconstraining controllers (1985, 34–35; 1996, 64–71). But determinism in the natural world—a world devoid of nefarious neurosurgeons and manipulative gods—is a very different matter. Obviously, the natural contingencies of our world do not always provide the most beneficial influences and outcomes, but we evolved in response to such influences, so it would be surprising if we were not moderately well adapted to benefit from them—and certainly they do not shape us for devious ulterior motives.

Pisciotta's case of the mind-controlling neuroscientists is important in bringing into the open a concern—a legitimate and important concern—that disturbs those who are troubled by determinism and its effects on creativity and originality and genuine accomplishment. When the neuroscientists manipulate Tom's brain, they are *implanting* in Tom the thoughts and ideas he had foolishly *imagined* that he himself had authored: ideas that he did not work out for himself, ideas that the neuroscientists worked out and then gave to (implanted in) Tom. One of the common themes among those most deeply disturbed by determinism's threat to originality and creativity is the idea that—if determinism is true—there is nothing genuinely new, nothing original, nothing that we really create. Whatever we imagine to be our own creative thoughts or ideas are actually ideas and theories and solutions and creations that were already there: someone (some god or neuroscientist or covert controller) is pushing the buttons and guiding us along paths and to "discoveries" that the guide/god/controller had already made. Kane struggles mightily to banish any possibility of a "covert nonconstraining controller" who *knows in advance* the path we will take and the ideas we will have and the discoveries we will make;

William Barrett (1958) detests the notion of someone "knowing in advance" when Poincaré will make his great mathematical discovery, because the prescient knower would also have to know—before Poincaré—the solution to Poincaré's problem, and thus Poincaré's "discovery" would be second-hand. For Pisciotta, the great fear of determinism—and the source of discontent—is the possibility of neuroscientists who *insert* thoughts and ideas into the mind: Tom imagines he has made a new discovery, but it was in fact just a prepackaged idea that the neuroscientists had previously discovered and inserted into Tom.

"Vanity of vanities, saith the Preacher, vanity of vanities; all is vanity. . . . The thing that hath been, it is that which shall be; and that which is done is that which shall be done: and there is no new thing under the sun. Is there any thing whereof it may be said, See, this is new? It hath been already of old time, which was before us" (Eccl. 1:2, 9–10). That was a depressing thought to wise King Solomon, and two millennia later it depressed William James (1890, 1897). William Barrett (1958) has a similar reaction to the idea of a determinism in which everything is known in advance: it would stifle us with boredom. But Barrett notes only the half of it: it would stifle us not only with boredom, but also with a sense of deep helplessness, leading typically to severe depression. To see why this is so, consider more carefully one of Barrett's favorite examples: Poincaré, stepping onto a bus at Coutances while thinking of something else altogether and suddenly finding the key to a mathematical quandary that had long puzzled him. Barrett regards this as evidence against determinism: no one knew or could predict exactly *when* Poincaré would solve the problem, because the predictor would have to know the solution to the problem, but no one was as close to the solution as Poincaré himself, so prediction was impossible. Barrett's argument is a nonstarter against naturalistic non-deity determinism, which (in agreement with Barrett) denies that anyone (mortal or divine) is miraculously prescient. But Barrett's failed argument is very revealing of the way Barrett thinks about determinism and of why he—and perhaps others—find it so disturbing.

Under Barrett's conception, determinism implies that everything is worked out in advance—that if determinism is true, then it must make sense to think of someone knowing the solution to Poincaré's problem before Poincaré discovered it. Poincaré is just "writing the answer off the board," writing down a solution already found by forces outside of him.

It is not surprising that this picture arises when people consider determinism; after all, for many centuries—and probably still, for most people—the great source for belief in determinism was belief in God's omniscience and thus in God's foreknowledge. An omniscient God must know the answer before Poincaré does, so Poincaré is not doing anything original or genuinely creative. That idea is depressing in itself, but it is even more depressing than our immediate reaction can explain. The presence of a god or neuroscientist who gives us our "discoveries" implies not only that we did not make the discoveries by our own powers, but that we were not capable of such accomplishments on our own.

There are disturbing psychological studies of the debilitating effects of believing that—rather than being able to accomplish tasks on one's own—one must be helped or guided by someone who already knows the answer. In one study (Avorn and Langer 1982), elderly persons were divided into two groups, and both groups were given puzzles to complete. In one group, the subjects were left entirely on their own to complete the puzzle; in the other group, helpers gave hints and help in completing the puzzle ("try this piece in the corner," "what about this piece?") when the subjects were trying to select the most promising next step in the puzzle. A few days later, the same groups tried the same puzzles again with a third group that had never seen the puzzles or seen them solved. This time, the researchers did not help any of the groups. The people in the group that had worked the puzzle before with no help finished the puzzle in the shortest time, and members of the group that had never seen the puzzle were next in puzzle-solving effectiveness. But the subjects who had done the same puzzle before while getting tips and coaching finished slower even than those who had never seen the puzzle at all, and were more likely to give up without completing the puzzle. At first glance, that is a very surprising result; after all, shouldn't the people who had worked the puzzle before (with some help) be faster at solving the puzzle than people who had never seen the puzzle at all? But that result is not so surprising when we consider what the coached puzzle-solvers had learned from their aided efforts: they had learned that they needed help, that they were incapable of solving the puzzle on their own through their own abilities. If the image of determinism is of someone or some power knowing the answer in advance, and guiding us to that answer, that gives us a strong sense that we couldn't reach that end by our own powers and resources, that we need outside help; such an underlying sense of helplessness is a very debilitating result that often leads to profound depression (Seligman 1975).

In this case, Dennett's (1984) counsel is wise: if you are worried about some covert controller or nefarious neuroscientist or manipulative deity, your fears are groundless. When you solve a problem or work out a new theory or develop a new musical form, you are not merely writing out a discovery or insight that was previously known and that someone has coached or directed you to find; rather, *you* did the work, made the discovery, solved the problem, developed the style. It is true—as John Lewis acknowledged, in his own case—that there are causal factors that contributed to your accomplishment and shaped your abilities; that does not make them any less your own abilities, or the accomplishments any less your own original work. You are—from my perspective—*lucky* that all of these forces combined to make you such a successful and creative musician or mathematician (so you do not deserve special reward, and those who were shaped in less fortunate ways do not deserve punishment for their failures), but that does not make your accomplishments (or your misdeeds) any less your *own*. The person in whom all those forces came together was John Lewis, and without him, the marvelous musical creations that he wrote would not exist.

Original Authorship and Moral Responsibility

Carlos Moya uses a similar case in his effort to establish that we *can* be morally responsible, though his case is a great physicist (Isaac Newton) rather than a great musician. According to Moya (and contrary to my claim concerning the brilliant and productive John Lewis), Newton is a person who "truly deserves praise":

Let us now reflect on a particular example, Newton's *Philosophiae Naturalis Principia Mathematica*, in order to discern some aspects of our notion of authorship or source in relation to cognitive achievements. We agree, I hope, that provided he wrote it, Newton truly deserves our unrestricted praise and gratitude for producing such a great scientific work. . . . We are grateful to him not only for his strenuous effort he expended in producing his work, not only for the careful cognitive activity he carried out in order to produce it, but also for the result itself. . . . He has genuine merit and truly deserves praise for his great intellectual achievement. (2006, 177)

Like John Lewis, Newton produced something great, and like Lewis, Newton "has genuine merit," but it does not follow that "Newton truly deserves our unrestricted praise." Consider in comparison Oldton, a contemporary of Newton. You have never heard of Oldton, because he was rather lazy, avoided lengthy or "careful cognitive activity," and produced no great or even modest intellectual achievements. Newton had genuine merit, and Oldton had significant flaws; as a result, Newton accomplished much, and Oldton accomplished little. But although Newton certainly did accomplish much and has genuine merit, and his accomplishments were the result of his own genuine abilities and efforts (they were not just luck, like hitting the lottery); still, Newton was *fortunate* to have been shaped to have great fortitude along with remarkable mathematical abilities and to have been in a situation in which he could gain a superb education and become aware of the earlier scientific work on which he built his own magnificent accomplishment. And Oldton was unfortunate to have fewer resources and worse abilities and less drive. When we look at the details, the genuine accomplishments of Newton and the genuine failures of Oldton remain, but the legitimacy of praise and blame for the successes and failures becomes doubtful.

Moya sometimes inadvertently slides between a work being "praiseworthy" in the sense of being *excellent* and "praiseworthy" in the very different sense that the author of the work *justly deserves praise* for his excellent work. But even if one supposes that typically the author of a "praiseworthy" work genuinely deserves praise for that work, it is clear that these are two separate questions. Suppose that God capriciously, miraculously, and instantaneously transforms me from someone devoid of literary talent into a wonderful poet; my excellent poems would then be praiseworthy (excellent), but there would remain serious questions about whether I justly deserved praise for those wonderful poems.

Moya emphasizes that Newton's work could not have happened without many other contributions, such as those from Kepler and Galileo, just as Lewis could not have accomplished his work without the contributions of many other earlier musicians and composers. Indeed, both Newton and Lewis generously acknowledged how much they had gained from the work of their predecessors and contemporaries (as in Newton's famous statement, "If I have seen further than others, it is because I have stood on the shoulders of giants"). And in both cases, the fact that the work of others was essential to their accomplishments does not change the fact that both Newton and Lewis themselves accomplished marvelous work: work that was distinctively their own. So it is acknowledged that the work was their own, and that it resulted from their own efforts and abilities, but the question of whether Lewis and Newton are *morally responsible* for those accomplishments is not settled by those acknowledgments. Newton and Lewis were ultimately lucky to have become such industrious and brilliant creators of superb work; their work is wonderful, but it does not follow that they justly deserve praise for their wonderful accomplishments. Similarly, Robert Harris did horrific things, and those acts were the result of his own vicious character, but because that character was the product of forces that were ultimately not under his control or selected by his choice, it is unfair to hold Robert Harris morally responsible for his bad character and bad acts. Perhaps those claims are false, and Harris, Newton, and Lewis are morally responsible and justly deserve punishment or reward. But all sides acknowledge that Newton and Lewis had wonderful qualities and did wonderful works and that Harris was vicious and did horrific things. This acknowledgment is the starting point for the question of their moral responsibility, rather than justification for moral responsibility.

In short, the fact that Newton's work built on the work of others and that his culture, education, and society contributed to his accomplishments in no way lessens his genuine accomplishments. As Moya correctly notes, "It is hard to see . . . how the *Principia Mathematica* could have been produced without the contributions of such thinkers as Copernicus, Galilei, or Kepler, whose work is in turn indebted to prior scientists and philosophers. And something similar can be said about many methodological and mathematical instruments and empirical data that Newton did not discover or create himself, but found already there" (2006, 177). Moya goes on to say, "Nevertheless, this does not incline us to question Newton's full authorship, merit, and responsibility for his work" (177). And again, Moya is correct. It is not the fact that Newton drew on the discoveries of his predecessors that raises questions about Newton's moral responsibility for his work, but rather the fortunate factors that equipped Newton (and the unfortunate factors that disqualified Oldton) to be able to fit all this material together into his magnificent work: a splendid work of which he is the author, but for which he is not morally responsible and for which he does not justly deserve special reward or praise. The fact that guns were available that Robert Harris did not create for himself and that certainly facilitated his vicious murder of two young men does not change the fact that he was a bad person who did a terrible deed, but the brutal background and history that shaped Harris into a brutal and callous killer—and that Harris did not control—do call into question his moral responsibility. If Newton were not the genuine author of something good, and Harris the genuine perpetrator of something bad, then the whole question of their moral responsibility would not arise. Their genuine authorship is the motivation for the question of whether they are morally responsible, not an answer to that question.

When it comes to actually answering the question of whether Newton is morally responsible and justly deserves praise for his acknowledged accomplishments, Moya falls back on intuitions:

If a particular theoretical construal of the sort of control required for true desert, such as Kane's or [Galen] Strawson's notion of ultimate control, leads to rejecting the subjects' [such as Newton] praiseworthiness . . . we should conclude that, at least in the cognitive field, that theoretical construal is not correct, not that our subjects are not praiseworthy, for our intuitive judgement about their praiseworthiness is much firmer than our confidence in such theoretical constructions. They do indeed have all the control over their beliefs that is required for them to truly deserve praise for having them. And if we call all the control required for true desert "ultimate control," they certainly have ultimate control over their beliefs. (2006, 178)

But that is not an argument for moral responsibility and just deserts; rather, it is a statement of unswerving *commitment* to moral responsibility: if ultimate control is required for moral responsibility, then we must have ultimate control (no matter what evidence there is to the contrary) because we are committed to moral responsibility and thus to all the necessary conditions for moral responsibility. And to base this firm belief in an intuition of moral responsibility and just deserts is to close the curtain on the argument at precisely the point when the show should start. There is no question that we *have* such an intuition; the question is whether we should take the intuition as a reliable guide. As noted earlier, there have been many powerful "intuitions" that we now regard as very poor guides indeed, and the more we learn about the dark strike-back roots of this moral responsibility intuition, the less plausible it seems as a legitimate moral guide. There has never been any doubt that we have such an intuition, whether we are moral responsibility abolitionists or moral responsibility advocates. The serious philosophical questions arise *because* we have such an intuition, but (I claim) we can find no rational justification for that deep intuition and strong arguments against its legitimacy as a moral guide.

Conscious Reason and Moral Responsibility

It is not only an intuition of just deserts that is behind Moya's belief in moral responsibility. Like many other philosophers, Moya regards reason as the best basis for moral responsibility. In fact, he holds that there has been too much emphasis on will and choices made by the power of willing; instead, the basis of the ultimate control required for moral responsibility must be found in our rational rather than our volitional powers, and Moya regards rational evaluative beliefs as the best grounds for avoiding skepticism about moral responsibility:

We have suggested that such scepticism may arise out of a conative or volitive perspective on moral responsibility, as centrally grounded in choices or acts of will. So, as applied to our evaluative beliefs, the requirement of alternative possibilities should not be understood in terms of choice. We should not require that, in order to be morally responsible for her evaluative views, and for the actions that she performs in the light of them, a subject could have *chosen* to have different beliefs. . . .

In focusing on evaluative beliefs, rather than choices and willings, as the root of moral responsibility, we are trying to show that moral responsibility is indeed possible, even if its presence and degree may be hard to assess in many or even most cases. (2006, 189, 194)

Moya illustrates his claim with a comparison of two slave holders: Meno, an Athenian landowner living in Greece in the fourth century BC, and Timothy, a landowner in South Carolina during the middle of the nineteenth century. Moya claims that Meno "did something morally wrong in buying the slave, but he is not morally blameworthy for doing so" (191), because although Meno "was the author of his evaluative beliefs," and he "had alternative possibilities of decision and action," Meno "did not have relevant alternative possibilities concerning his evaluative belief that buying slaves is not morally wrong" (191). The idea that slavery is wrong did not develop until several centuries later, and so "given his historical and social circumstances, the true belief that buying slaves is morally wrong was not within his possible cognitive landscape; it was not available to him" (191).

In contrast, Moya claims that Timothy, the South Carolina slave holder of the nineteenth century, *is* morally responsible for his bad beliefs and the bad behavior that results from them:

> Assume, as before, that buying slaves is morally wrong and that Timothy thinks, like his Ancient Greek counterpart, that buying slaves is not morally wrong. Timothy thinks so, we may suppose, owing to his upbringing in a slave state and environment. Now, though an accurate judgement about his moral responsibility would require filling in more details, I think that, with the elements at hand, the correct verdict in this case is that he is morally blameworthy for buying the slave. He does not think he is doing something morally wrong, but in this case he could, and should, have had a different belief. The truth that slavery is a morally wrong institution, and so that buying a slave is not morally permissible, was within his possible cognitive landscape. He, unlike Meno, his Greek counterpart, could have believed the truth. For Meno, this moral truth lay four centuries ahead, but for Timothy, it was eighteen centuries behind. Moreover, he lived in a Christian environment, in which such a truth could be found relatively easily. And, for an educated man, the arguments against it, concerning for example the inferiority of black people, could easily be seen as fallacious. Therefore Timothy is morally blameworthy for buying the slave, given that this action comes from a belief over which he had ultimate regulative control. (2006, 191–192)

But if Meno does not deserve blame because he could not have embraced the belief that slavery is morally wrong, then Timothy likewise deserves no blame, for he also could not have embraced that belief. Recognizing that will require "filling in more details," as Moya notes, but the details are not difficult to find. In the first place, it would certainly *not* be "relatively easy" for a South Carolina slave holder to recognize the basic moral wrongness of slavery. After all, this slave holder has been taught from childhood that slavery is morally good (indeed, that it is part of God's righteous plan), that it is an essential pillar of the society and the economy, and that chaos would result from changing it. Furthermore, his family and friends and the most respected members of his community—the large plantation owners—are firm in their belief that slavery is just, and that it has God's stamp of approval. To suppose that it would be "relatively easy" for Timothy to recognize the evil of slavery would be like supposing that it would be "relatively easy" for one deeply immersed in an insular fundamentalist Christian community—and taught those beliefs at home, in school, and in church—to renounce belief in God: After all, she lives in a *scientific* environment "in which such a truth could be found relatively easily," and the arguments for such fundamentalist beliefs "could easily be seen as fallacious." But it is not just the influence of pervasive belief *systems* that Moya ignores, but also the important details about Timothy himself and his capacities.

The comparison of Meno and Timothy is interesting and insightful, but in order to get a clearer picture of whether Timothy genuinely deserves blame—whether he is morally responsible—for his morally repulsive belief in slaveholding (or for the acts stemming from that belief), it is more useful to consider a comparison between Tim and one of his South Carolina landowning contemporaries, Jim, who rightly rejects belief in the legitimacy of slavery. *Could* Tim, like Jim, have rejected belief in slavery? Yes, he could have; *if* he had a different developmental history, and different influences, and (as a result of those developmental differences) different capacities, then Tim could have also recognized and embraced the belief that slavery is a terrible wrong. But it does not follow that because one of Tim's contemporaries—in a roughly similar situation and with a roughly similar environmental history to Tim's—was able to reject belief in slavery, Tim also could reject belief in slavery, because the key is not in rough general comparisons, but in the detailed differences.

Recall the case of Betty and Benji from chapter 2. Betty and Benji grow up in the same family and in the same racist social system and are enculturated into the same set of racist beliefs, but Betty recognizes the wrongness of racism and renounces it and Benji quietly acquiesces in the racist values that dominate his community and friends. Benji's beliefs and behavior are morally bad, but does he deserve blame for them? When we look closely at the details of Benji's developed character—his much weaker sense of self-efficacy, his external locus-of-control, his much lower capacity for cognitive fortitude—and compare them with Betty's, it is clear that Benji does not have the same resources for renouncing the deep value system in which he is immersed.

Betty can and does become strongly cognizant of the moral ugliness of racism, and she has the cognitive strength and self-confidence and effective internal locus-of-control to reject the comfortable system in which she has long believed and the authority figures in whom she has trusted and to forge her own path based on her confidence in her own value judgments. Betty's character is rich with virtue, and Benji's is rife with flaws; as a result, Betty embraces a new and better value system, and Benji cannot break the hold of the vile racist system. But when we look carefully at the details of their characters and their character formation (and the fact that neither exercised ultimate control in that formation or its results), then it is much less plausible to conclude that Benji *could* have recognized the wrongness of his value system and rejected it. To the contrary, Benji did not embrace a new value system because (absent miracles) he *could not*: he lacked the resources to do so.

If the power of reason—whether robust like Betty's, or relatively weak like Benji's—is always sufficient to transcend the many detailed differences among the forces that shaped our different characters and capacities, then indeed anyone who has this amazing rational power is morally responsible for the full range of both accurate and inaccurate, virtuous and vicious beliefs. But that sort of miracle-working rational power is not compatible with naturalism, and it is not compatible with careful scrutiny of the many forces and factors that shape us to be better or worse at thinking—at challenging tradition and authority, at recognizing flaws in our own beliefs, at drawing our own conclusions. Blaming Benji for his racist beliefs may make us feel better, but it blocks rather than facilitates our understanding of *why* Benji is a racist and of what must be done to prevent others from embracing such a vile and twisted thought system.

Moya claims that we believe that Tim could have recognized the wrongness of slavery, and could have adopted other values: "In saying that Timothy, the American landowner, could have had a different evaluative belief, we are not simply saying that he could have carried out an appropriate and more careful cognitive activity, though we may also mean this. We are also saying he could (and ought to) have *seen* what was there to be seen" (2006, 192). And Moya is correct: we *are* inclined to say and believe that, as long as we do not look in depth and in detail. When we don't look closely, all we notice is that both Tim and Jim have rational powers, and we are tempted to suppose that those rational powers could and should overcome differences (maybe not the differences in history between one born in ancient Greece and one who lived in nineteenth-century South Carolina, or maybe not the differences between one living in the virulently racist culture of nineteenth-century South Carolina and the more tolerant and open-minded culture of twenty-first-century Toronto, but certainly enough to overcome differences in details, so those details can be ignored). But when we *do* look closely—at subtle but vitally important differences in cognitive fortitude, degree of self-efficacy, sense of locus-of-control, and the many other details of their characters and development, which they did not ultimately control—then it is clear that those differing cognitive and evaluative results followed from different cognitive and evaluative abilities.

Fear of Nonconscious Reason

Daniel Wegner recently proposed an account of conscious willing and deliberating that many people find disturbing. Rather than conscious willing and reasoning being special transcendent powers, the consciousness of willing and deliberating is epiphenomenal: the real work of deliberation and willing occurs in brain machinations of which we are not conscious; the conscious thought is a side effect that serves to inform us that the willed decision or act was our own (my hand moved because *I* nonconsciously decided to move it, rather than it being moved by some external force). Wegner's theory was discussed in chapter 5, along with some objections to it. But the present concern is not the strengths or weaknesses of Wegner's epiphenomenalism, but rather this question: why do many people find this theory of the epiphenomenal nature of conscious thought so disturbing?

When we are consciously thinking, it seems to us that we think almost without limits: that we could think almost anything, reason our way to the most difficult conclusion, think without limits or constraints, reject any false belief, overthrow systems, and launch our reasoned thoughts into hidden corners and remote discoveries. Conscious deliberation continues to seem that way to us even when we realize that our thoughts and our reasoning capacities are shaped and limited by biases (those of which we are blissfully unaware being the most dangerous and controlling), by the systems of belief that are so pervasive that we cannot gauge and often cannot even recognize their ubiquitous influence, by our conditioned powers as chronic cognizers or our shaped impediments as cognitive misers, by the "intuitions" embedded in us by nature and/or culture, by our degree of self-confidence (or sense of self-efficacy) in our reasoning abilities for this particular sphere (my arrogant sense of self-efficacy for thinking about philosophy is quite different from my severe insecurity when the thoughts turn to advanced calculus), by our deep sense of internal or external locus-of-control, and by the powerful but unrecognized influence of our immediate situations. No doubt our powers of conscious reasoning will continue to *feel* unlimited even if we come to believe that all conscious deliberation is the epiphenomenal side effect of nonconscious deliberation, but the difference would be significant because if we came to believe such an idea, it would then be much more difficult to believe that our conscious reason and reflection can support just deserts and moral responsibility. One may still be thoughtful, reflective, insightful, and creative and still be the author of significant discoveries: the fact that Poincaré's mathematical discovery was made *non*consciously does not alter the facts that the discovery was made by Poincaré and that it was a remarkable discovery. But if we came to believe that our thinking and willing were ultimately carried on by brain processes of which we were not conscious (the consciousness arriving only to inform us that the deliberation and the actions flowing from that deliberation are our own), then the illusion of unconstrained and unlimited cognitive powers would be much more difficult to sustain.

Why is the prospect of discovering that conscious thought is epiphenomenal so widely disturbing—so that even Libet (1999) takes refuge in the hope of a bare moment of conscious veto power? After all, we have long known the power and benefits of nonconscious thought processes (or perhaps it would be better to speak of cognitive brain processes that occur without our consciousness of them). I consciously "rack my brain" trying to think of a name, with no success—and an hour later, when my conscious thoughts are dealing with something else entirely, the name "pops up," retrieved by the ongoing brain operations that occurred without my being conscious of them. This is a common but mundane example, but there are also some very special and uncommon examples, such as Poincaré's nonconsciously discovered mathematical solution. The deep concern over the idea of conscious thought being epiphenomenal is not because it would deprive us of a sense of ownership of our own thoughts or undercut our claims to creativity and originality and authorship. (Poincaré's nonconsciously derived mathematical discovery remains his own original creative work.) My guess is that the epiphenomenal account of conscious thought is disturbing because the special power of conscious deliberation is often the unacknowledged source of belief in a special power of ultimate control that can justify belief in moral responsibility. If one believes that such rational conscious deliberative power *is* godlike and unlimited—or at least that it is godlike and unlimited within a special sphere of choice—then perhaps such belief suffices for ultimate control and moral responsibility, but it also suffices to move the position well beyond the natural realm. As noted before, Charles Taylor maintains that at least in the realm of our basic evaluations, it is always within our power to scrutinize and reevaluate them:

> The question can always be posed: ought I to re-evaluate my most basic evaluations? . . .
>
> Because this self-resolution is something we do, when we do it, we can be called responsible for ourselves, and because it is within limits always up to us to do it, even when we don't—indeed, the nature of our deepest evaluations constantly raises the question whether we have them right—we can be called responsible in another sense for ourselves whether we undertake this radical evaluation or not. (1976, 221, 224)

But if it is *always* up to us to think deeper—if this is a power independent of any conditioning or situational constraints—then it is not a power that is part of our natural world. When we look carefully, we realize that such boundless rational powers are not plausible, especially given what we now know about the development and limits of cognitive fortitude, sense of self-efficacy, situational influences, and many other factors. Belief in slavery may well be one of Timothy's deepest and most basic values, but that in itself makes it one of the hardest to expose to genuine scrutiny because rejecting that value would mean rejecting the entire system of thought that held that belief in place. For Timothy, it would mean that the values he learned at his slaveholding father's knee were wrong, that the teachings of his minister regarding slavery were wrong, that his beliefs regarding "natural aristocracy" were wrong, that his own behavior—perhaps his whole life—has been in the service of a terrible moral wrong, not to mention that it would mean ostracism from his friends and family and indeed from his entire culture. It will take enormous powers of self-confidence and courage to probe hard at that deeply held value. Fortunately, some people—even some slave holders—did have such powers of radical value evaluation. But to suppose that it is "always up to us" to engage in such radical evaluation, that any competent person can always do so, is to greatly underestimate the powers of the culture and conditioning and influences which shape our deepest beliefs, or—perhaps more likely—to greatly *over*estimate the powers of rational reflection, making them into a miracle-working power that rises above all conditioning and cultural constraints. The power of reason is a wonderful thing, but it is not unlimited, it is not an ultimate power that transcends our developmental histories, and it is not miraculous. If a substantial part—or perhaps *all*—of our conscious deliberation is epiphenomenal as the real work goes on nonconsciously, it is even more obvious that our *sense* of what is happening in conscious deliberation is mistaken, and thus it is even more difficult to suppose that deliberative processes are a source of unlimited ultimate control. Belief that we actually have an important range of effective control and that we can use our cognitive powers skillfully to make wise choices is important to our psychological well-being and a vital protection against the sense of helplessness that leads to severe depression. And in fact this healthy psychological belief is often true. But belief in a transnatural power of super reason is neither helpful, nor necessary, nor conducive to better understanding of the key factors that can impede or enhance effective self-confident exercise of rational control.

The power of reason is a wonderful thing. If I think of my role as a teacher of philosophy and what I hope to accomplish in my many hours with my students, at the top of the list would be my hope that my students learn to reason more precisely, systematically, and logically and that they learn to avoid falling for the tricks and fallacies with which hucksters and advertisers, charlatans and tricksters, politicians and lobbyists will attempt to deceive them. Among our worst fears are diseases and accidents that would deprive us of our power of reason. But this wonderful power of reason is a power that evolved through natural processes and that has strong parallels with the cognitive abilities of other primates. It is a power that is natural and limited and imperfect, and it is shaped by both our genetic and our environmental histories; it is not a miraculous power that breaks all bounds, knows no limits, and transcends all causes. As naturalists, this is something we know and acknowledge; as defenders of moral responsibility, it is something we are tempted to forget. And when we consider the glories of conscious reasoning, the temptation to attribute to it special powers that can transcend the forces that shaped us becomes very powerful indeed. If conscious reasoning is epiphenomenal and the real cognitive work is going on in our material brains without our being conscious of it, then the lingering belief in reason as a miracle-working power becomes painfully implausible.

Perhaps conscious thought is epiphenomenal; perhaps it is not. Research into this question is in its infancy. Frankly, I suspect that consciousness plays a larger role than just alerting us that thoughts and movements are our own; after all, if that is the function of conscious thought, then it doesn't do a very good job: too many people have too much trouble distinguishing their own thoughts from thoughts inserted by God or by aliens. But that is another issue: the immediate question is why the epiphenomenal hypothesis seems so disturbing to so many people, including those who consider themselves naturalists. The fear that reason might then be securely tethered to the natural world and incapable of providing sufficient support for moral responsibility is at least one possible explanation. But although the epiphenomenal theory casts doubt on the moral responsibility of Betty and Benji, Tim and Jim, Isaac Newton and Henri Poincaré, it does not change the fact that it was Jim who saw through and rejected the moral system of slavery, Betty who was able to courageously and insightfully recognize the wrongness of racism, Poincaré who originally discovered the proof, and Lewis who brought together the many influences that resulted in his wonderful compositions.

15 A World without Moral Responsibility

Many are reluctant to contemplate the abolition of moral responsibility, and one source of that reluctance may be fear of the unknown. For better or worse, we have been wedded to the moral responsibility system for a very long time. It is frightening to consider a world without the practices and institutions of moral responsibility. This chapter is an effort to allay some of those fears.

What Is Left When Moral Responsibility Is Eliminated?

What would our world look like without moral responsibility? In many respects, not so different: certainly not as disastrously different as many have supposed. We would still make free choices, moral judgments, and sincere apologies; still feel affection and gratitude; still recognize our faults and strive (more effectively) to correct them. We could retain and strengthen our self-respect and our sense of individual worth, though Smilansky (among others) thinks otherwise: "We can hardly continue to respect ourselves in the same way if we really internalize the belief that all action and achievement is ultimately down to luck and not ultimately attributable to us" (2000, 228). Smilansky's concern is an echo of the fear that we could not be worthy of self-respect if we were not the center of the universe, but were instead circling through space in orbit around a small star in a vast galaxy, and an echo of those who worried that we would lose our self-respect if we were not special beings, distinct from evolved animals, and made in the glorious image of God. Smilansky himself has a very clear view of the fact that his considerable achievements are "ultimately down to luck," but that view does not undermine his own self-respect—nor should it. He has written a marvelous book that takes a fascinating new angle on a question on which new angles are rare. It is the unique accomplishment of a unique individual. It is not the work of a god who makes himself from scratch; rather, it is the accomplishment of a person who brings together a vast array of shaping influences—family, school, community, culture—that made him who he is. Nothing in that diminishes his accomplishments or his person. We need not be self-making gods or rugged self-sufficient Wild West individuals to accomplish things and sustain self-respect. To the contrary, to the degree that we think of ourselves as "ultimately self-creating," we cannot look closely (for fear of destroying the illusion), we cannot examine the factors that shaped Smilansky into a highly accomplished individual, and we cannot learn how to provide such opportunities for others.

Furthermore, a world devoid of moral responsibility would not lack all individual responsibility; it would leave ample room for take-charge responsibility and increase the likelihood of exercising it well, and when we look closely (and distinguish take-charge from moral responsibility), take-charge responsibility is the responsibility most of us really want. It enables us to exercise effective control, make our own decisions and choices, reflect carefully on what we deeply value, and manage our own lives. Indeed, the demise of moral responsibility opens more space for effective exercise of take-charge responsibility and for the development and enhancement of the capacities and opportunities essential for optimum take-charge responsibility.

The elimination of moral responsibility would not open a Pandora's Box of Clockwork Orange brutality. Instead it would promote stronger self-control and nurture genuine self-respect. Rather than a brutalizing tendency to regard offenders as being of a radically different nature and justly deserving to suffer for their wrongdoing, we could recognize that such wrongdoing is the result of larger systemic causes: the failure to shape persons who can make a positive social contribution is a failure shared by all of us.

Finally, the denial of moral responsibility would not mean the loss of freedom or natural free will, but would instead lead to a better understanding of the sort of freedom human animals value; why we value it; and how it can be protected, expanded, and strengthened. Divorcing free will from the burden of moral responsibility enables us to understand human freedom as a natural and naturally valuable phenomenon with no taint of mystery and open to scientific investigation and effective methods of improvement.

All of these claims are made and argued for in the earlier chapters of this book: the denial of moral responsibility does not have the catastrophic implications often supposed (unless one makes that denial from *within* the moral responsibility system and thus bases the universal denial of moral responsibility on universal incompetence and insanity). But if those disastrous consequences do not follow from the denial of moral responsibility, what consequences *would* follow? Before going into detail on that question, there is one other supposed implication of denying moral responsibility that must be examined. Some researchers have suggested that even if it might theoretically be possible for people to live morally in the absence of moral responsibility, the empirical research indicates that in fact the denial of moral responsibility (and the embracing of determinism/naturalism) results in an increase in immoral behavior.

Does Belief in Determinism (and Rejection of Moral Responsibility) Cause Moral Decay?

Experiments conducted by Vohs and Schooler (2008) have drawn significant attention from psychologists, philosophers, and the popular media. The experiments purport to show that belief in determinism undermines moral character and increases the likelihood of immoral behavior. (Because the authors of the study assume incompatibilism, they equate belief in determinism with rejection of free will and moral responsibility; thus the resulting moral depravity might equally be attributed to belief in determinism or nonbelief in free will and moral responsibility). This result is certainly surprising, whether one's frame of reference is individual anecdotal observations or more systematic comparisons. In the world of academia, I have known many libertarians who reject determinism in favor of a very special power of free will, compatibilists who accept determinism as well as free will and moral responsibility, and a variety of incompatibilists who accept determinism or naturalism and reject free will or moral responsibility or both. Although I would not suggest that the determinists are noteworthy for their virtue, neither do they seem less virtuous or more vicious than nondeterminists. David Hume was probably the Enlightenment Period's most articulate and influential proponent of determinism, yet he was widely acclaimed for his generous, gracious, and virtuous character. In France, he was known as "le bon David," and his Scottish friends referred to him as "Saint David"; Adam Smith (in a letter to William Strachan) said of Hume:

Even in the lowest state of his fortune, his great and necessary frugality never hindered him from exercising, upon proper occasions, acts both of charity and generosity. . . . The gentleness of his nature never weakened either the firmness of his mind or the steadiness of his resolutions. His constant pleasantry was the genuine effusion of good nature and good humor, tempered with delicacy and modesty, and without even the slightest tincture of malignity. . . . Upon the whole, I have always considered him, both in his lifetime and since his death, as approaching as nearly to the idea of a perfectly wise and virtuous man, as perhaps the nature of human frailty will permit. (1776/1854, xxix)

In contrast, the era's great champion of libertarian free will was Jean-Jacques Rousseau, who was arrogant, self-centered, deeply suspicious of everyone, and abandoned his children to poverty and an early death. Looking more broadly, the Puritans were fervently committed to not only determinism but also a fatalistic doctrine of predestination, and though they are regarded as a trifle too straitlaced for contemporary tastes, they have never been accused of moral laxity. In contemporary terms, U.S. culture—with its fierce commitment to the Horatio Alger myth of every person having the power of free will to lift him or herself from poverty to wealth and its deep-rooted Western frontier belief in rugged individualism—is also the most warlike of contemporary western countries, the most neglectful of the welfare of its children (leaving many in poverty, in inadequate and dangerous living conditions, and without health care), and also the most crime-ridden. So it is surprising to discover empirical research demonstrating that determinism encourages immorality; if anything (and were I not acquainted with many virtuous libertarians), I might have suspected that belief in libertarian free will is the more likely path to moral turpitude. But psychological experiments often yield surprising results that run counter to our anecdotal experience, so these experimental results deserve attention.

In their studies, Vohs and Schooler (2008) first exposed the experimental group to strongly affirmative statements about determinism and had the control group read a neutral passage, then gave both groups opportunities to "cheat" on a task: in one study, the experimental subjects were given small problems to work out on a computer and were told that due to a glitch in the program, the answers would show up on the screen: the subjects were supposed to press the space bar to prevent that from happening and thus avoid "cheating." The experimental group—primed with determinist doctrines—were more likely to cheat than were the nondeterminists.

Obviously, students who have grown up with video games and searching for "secret codes" that enable them to "cheat" the game may have a very different concept of "cheating" at a computer task than do the researchers; whether such "cheating" has any implications for real cheating and dishonesty is a serious question. The second study had the experimental group cheating—slightly more often than the control group—in order to gain a few extra dollars in the course of the experiment, but whether they regarded their behavior as "cheating" or as shrewd play within the experimental game is open to question.

Even if we accept that those in the experimental groups were more likely to genuinely cheat, the problems with the experiments run much deeper. The experimenters started from the assumption that determinism equals helplessness: belief in determinism means that you have no control, you can't make things happen, your efforts make no difference. They seemed to take their ideas about determinism almost entirely from traditional libertarians such as William James and William Barrett, and according to Barrett, determinism frustrates "the desire for freshness, novelty, genuine creation—in short, an open rather than a closed universe" (1958, 46). But that is, at the very least, a controversial starting point. Few contemporary writers—whether philosophers or psychologists—take such a view of determinism. Determinism does not imply some powerful manipulator or coercive force that constrains our movements and thoughts, blocks our efforts, and stifles our creativity. William James regarded determinism as a very pessimistic doctrine, precisely because he saw it in that manner. In contrast, most determinists have regarded determinism as a profoundly optimistic view: we can understand causes (whether for disease, or crop failure, or human behavior) and then change things for the better. That we have such understanding and motivation is a product of our determined history, but it is a history in which we are actors, not passive spectators. When a scientist discovers the cause of a disease and ways to treat that disease, then her motivation and her abilities were determined by earlier factors, but she herself and her abilities and her desire play an essential role in making progress in finding an effective treatment. Rather than causing loss of control, it is the understanding that there are determining factors and causal processes—and that they are determined rather than wildly random—that pushes us to believe that there are causes that can be discovered, understood, and controlled.

The researchers primed their experimental group not toward belief in determinism, but rather in the direction of a diminished sense of self-efficacy (Bandura 1997), to acceptance of helplessness (Seligman 1975), and toward an external locus-of-control (Rotter 1966). A weakened sense of control has a powerful negative psychological effect (Rodin 1986) that might well result in weakening of moral resolve. But many believers in determinism have a very strong internal locus-of-control, and many believers in libertarian free will actually have an external locus-of-control (many Christian fundamentalists believe that through their own magical libertarian choice they chose salvation, but that everything is now in the hands of God—the ultimate "powerful other" [Rotter 1966]—and now they must only "trust and obey"). Furthermore, it is clear that many of the most fervent advocates of determinism embrace determinism precisely because they see it as promising stronger and more effective control; consider, for example, the exhortations of B. F. Skinner, perhaps the most famous defender of determinism in the second half of the twentieth century:

If the position I have presented here is correct, he [mankind] can remedy these mistakes and at the same time build a world in which he will feel freer than ever before and achieve greater things.

He can do this only if he recognizes himself for what he is. He has failed to solve his problems because he has looked in the wrong place for solutions. The extraordinary role of the environment opens the prospect of a much more successful future, in which he will be most human and humane, and in which he will manage himself skillfully because he will know himself accurately. (1974, 240)

This is a determinist clarion call to build a new and better future, not a retreat into helplessness. The research of Vohs and Schooler may be useful in indicating yet another unfortunate effect of a sense of diminished control, but it offers no evidence whatsoever that belief in determinism—or rejection of belief in libertarian free will and moral responsibility—increases the likelihood of immoral behavior.

What Would the World Look Like without Moral Responsibility?

The previous points examine what would not follow from the denial of moral responsibility. But what can be said about the positive differences in a world without moral responsibility? How would the world look different if we did not view it through the lens of moral responsibility?

First, it would look a lot clearer. When we see through the glass of moral responsibility, we see through a glass darkly. Perhaps the greatest harm caused by adherence to moral responsibility is the severe limits it places on our inquiries and understanding. Erin Kelly (while defending the legitimacy and justice of criminal punishment) acknowledges the inimical effect that retributive attitudes and commitment to moral responsibility can have on the understanding: "Because the moral breaches of criminal activity can be so egregious, they may provoke reactive sentiments with the moral depth and urgency more characteristic of involved relationships and the morally principled basis of self-criticism and guilt. The higher the moral stakes, the more judgmental and less understanding we may become" (2009, 443).

As British prime minister, John Major called for harsher criminal justice measures, especially against juveniles: "Society needs to condemn a little more and understand a little less" (1993, 8). That line generated considerable criticism, but in one sense the Prime Minister was exactly right: *less understanding* is the price we pay for moral responsibility. If we look carefully into causal histories, we cannot make sense of holding people morally responsible. That is why those who wish to support moral responsibility—whether in law or philosophy—must block such inquiries, or insist they are irrelevant. Thus Michael Moore, a contemporary champion of the retributivist approach to criminal justice, insists that when we know that someone acted from his or her own desires, then it is irrelevant how those desires were developed or implanted, even if they were the result of brainwashing. Recall his comments on the case of Patty Hearst:

In the most famous recent example [of brainwashing], the Patty Hearst case, we were certain of a causal connection between the conditioning Hearst received and her criminal behavior. That certainty, however, was irrelevant to the issue of whether her behaviour was an action. She robbed the bank; it was her act, whether or not a situation that was not of her making implanted in her the beliefs that caused her to act. One might have allowed her some affirmative defence if she had not had adequate time between the conditioning and the criminal act in which to reject or integrate her new beliefs into her character. Such an affirmative defence is irrelevant to the issue of action. She plainly acted, whether or not her act was caused. (Moore 1997, 533–534)

Along similar lines, the *plateau* defenders of moral responsibility insist that once people have reached the plateau of moral responsibility—they can deliberate and can act from their own value preferences—it doesn't matter how they reached that level or what differences (as a result of their developmental journey) in deliberative skills or cognitive fortitude or values they might have, and all considerations of their conditioning history should be ignored. Such blindness to different histories and different capacities is essential because deeper detailed understanding of how character and behavior were shaped (and the differing abilities that resulted) undermines claims of moral responsibility.

Saul Smilansky faces this problem unflinchingly. Smilansky acknowledges the essential role of illusion in preserving belief in moral responsibility: illusion that cannot be scrutinized too closely for fear of revealing its illusory nature. But the illusion of moral responsibility is not a harmless feel-good illusion (like my relatively harmless illusion that I am good-looking); it blocks better alternatives discovered through careful inquiry, prevents scrutiny of deep systemic causes, and results in great harm through blaming and punishing.

Although Smilansky is the most straightforward, he is certainly not the only defender of moral responsibility to seek refuge in not looking too closely. You could have tried harder, so you are morally responsible for your failure, but don't look closely at how fortitude and lassitude were shaped. You could have thought more carefully, but don't look hard at why some are chronic cognizers and others become cognitive misers. Everyone gets a fair start because luck evens out, but don't examine the actual cases in which initial advantages and disadvantages are cumulative. Weaknesses in one area are balanced by talents in another, so the person with weaker skills can offset that disadvantage by harder practice, but don't look closely at how superior skills and confidence and fortitude tend to group together, rather than being distributed evenly. You could have practiced more effectively, but don't inquire about degrees of self-efficacy that underlie our efforts. You could have resisted that authority, but don't look at the situation that powerfully influenced the behavior. You could have considered alternatives, but don't look at the deep universal tendency to decide on the basis of immediate intuition and then rationalize. You could have exerted willpower, but don't scrutinize the nonconscious process that triggers acts of will. John Major was right: if you insist on retributive moral responsibility, then less understanding is the price you must pay.

Thus the most salient feature of a world without moral responsibility is its openness to inquiry: its openness to recognizing and reporting and dealing with problems and flaws and mistakes. Because there is no push to assign blame to individuals (and to not look deeper for fear of finding causes that undercut the legitimacy of such blaming practices), there is greater opportunity to seek the deeper systemic causes of problems, rather than stopping with surface observations.

The second positive feature of a world without moral responsibility is that it shifts the focus to systems and away from individuals. Psychologists are familiar with the "fundamental attribution error" (Ross 1977) that causes most people to exaggerate the influence of formed character and underestimate the influence of specific situations on behavior. But belief in moral responsibility has contributed to an even deeper version of this mistake: a commitment to a rugged individualism that blinds us to the ways in which our character traits and abilities (as well as our immediate behavior) are shaped by our culture and our history. Of course, most philosophers who champion moral responsibility know that the rugged individualism model is implausible, but when entranced by moral responsibility, they fall into the strong individualistic perspective and forget that we are profoundly social animals shaped by our culture, our social groups, our families, and our biological heritage. But it is not surprising that commitment to moral responsibility results in a slide into rugged individualism, for they are two sides of the same coin: to believe that you are a morally responsible individual—who justly deserves special credit and blame for your own behavior, and for your own accomplishments and failures—you must ignore or deny the fact that you did not make yourself but are instead the complex product of your social history. Michael Cavadino and James Dignan make clear the connection between moral responsibility and rugged individualism, as well as the consequences of that connection:

The neo-liberal society [such as the United States] tends to exclude both those who fail in the economic marketplace and those who fail to abide by the law—in the latter case by means of imprisonment, or even more radically by execution. This is no coincidence. Both types of exclusion are associated with a highly *individualistic* social ethos. This individualistic ethos leads a society to adopt a neo-liberal economy in the first place, but conversely the existence of such an economy in return fosters the social belief that individuals are solely responsible for looking after themselves. In neo-liberal society, economic failure is seen as being the fault of the atomized, free-willed individual, not any responsibility of society—hence the minimal, safety-net welfare state. Crime is likewise seen as entirely the responsibility of the offending individual. The social soil is fertile ground for a harsh "law and order ideology." (2006a, 448)

In the absence of moral responsibility, it is possible to look more deeply at the influences of social systems and situations and to move away from both the fundamental attribution error and the individualistic blindness that hides the forces that shaped our qualities of character (qualities of character that do influence behavior, even if not as much as we had supposed).

"Rugged individualism" is generally a term of derision among philosophers. Ayn Rand and John Wayne and Ronald Reagan may find it plausible, but the evidence from psychology and sociology and from our own experience makes it plain that we are not and never were self-created, but are instead the wonderfully complex result of the culture, the family, the community, and the evolutionary history that shaped us. Yet it is precisely that common knowledge that is driven out of our memory by the siren song of moral responsibility. Robert Harris is the individual who is morally responsible, and all the brutal forces that shaped his violent character are irrelevant. John Major, in a speech to the 1992 Conservative Party Conference, stated, "Crime wrecks lives, spreads fear, corrupts society. It is the fault of the individual, and no one else." Philosophers, psychologists, and sociologists know better—that is, until commitment to moral responsibility induces forgetfulness. Rugged individual forgetfulness is an essential element of the illusion required by moral responsibility: Robert Harris, like all of us, is the master of his fate and the captain of his soul, and nothing in the circumstances that shaped him or the situation in which he lived had any significant impact on who he is or what he does; for if it did, if he were not a rugged independent individual, rather than the complex product of his social and biological history, then it would make no sense to single him out for blame and punishment. In contrast, the rejection of moral responsibility means that the focus is less on the individual, and more on the *system* and the environment and the situation that shape both character and behavior.

None of this implies that the individual is insignificant or that the individual and individual rights are less important. We *are* individuals, and our individual values, plans, and taken responsibilities are vitally important and worthy of respect. But individuals require nurture and support: a good education, genuine opportunities to exercise take-charge responsibility, the opportunity to develop a strong and resilient sense of self-efficacy. John Stuart Mill's *On Liberty* (1869) lays out a compelling case for why our individual freedoms are valuable—a case that psychologists such as Bandura have strengthened and deepened. But the importance of individual capacities should remind us of how important it is to nurture and support such abilities; it is not grounds for blaming those whose developmental history did not foster positive character traits. Individual liberties—including the liberty of exercising take-charge responsibility—are vitally important for psychological development of strengths such as confident self-efficacy and fortitude and cognitive capacity. But that one has the opportunity and history to develop (or not) such powers is a matter of one's good fortune—one's good fortune in developing within a supportive system of positive influences—and is not a basis for claiming or ascribing moral responsibility.

Programs that Move Beyond Blame and Shame

A world without moral responsibility is a world in which we can look more clearly at causes and more deeply into the systems that shape individuals and their behavior. Although such a world may seem difficult to imagine for those locked within the moral responsibility perspective, there already exist some programs and places where we can observe the incipient benefits of systems that reject moral responsibility and blame and punishment. One of the first areas to demonstrate such benefits was the manufacturing industry, in which concern with production flaws and faulty products led to a change from blaming problems on individual workers to a policy of treating mistakes as systemic problems for which no individual should be blamed (Shingo 1986; Nikkan Kogyo Shimbun 1988). Such programs have two very important advantages. First, because individuals are not blamed for problems and mistakes (when a mistake or error occurs, that is treated as symptomatic of bad structural design, with the *individual* worker being only the point at which the larger systemic failure became manifest), workers are willing and even eager to report not only serious mistakes, but also the "harmless" mistakes and "near-misses," and armed with this information on where problems are occurring, the production system can be modified and improved to eliminate such mistakes and to correct problems that could eventually result in mistakes. Second, because the individual is not blamed when mistakes occur, there is no need to avoid looking deeper at more systemic causes of the mistake (such an inquiry undercuts ascriptions of individual blame), and thus the scrutiny of problems tracks deeper than the surface level symptom down into the root cause of the problems. The underlying problems can then be corrected (whether that root problem is in design of the production process, or inadequate training of workers, or the deadening and error-inducing effects of repetitive assembly line tasks).

Learning from the success of the nonblame systemic approach to manufacturing processes, the aviation industry adopted similar programs with similar success (Sabatini 2008; Harris and Muir 2005). The air traffic control system was plagued by mistakes: mistakes that led to tragic accidents and terrifying near-misses. As long as errors were regarded as the mistakes of an individual controller who would be singled out for blame, controllers struggled to keep their errors hidden; unsurprisingly, the errors were repeated. When the focus was shifted to problems and flaws in the air traffic control *system*, controllers were no longer blamed for errors. Workers were instead encouraged to bring errors and potential sources of error into the light, where people could work together to correct the problem, procedures could be devised to prevent errors, and small errors could be fixed before becoming tragedies. If an individual controller could not function successfully—including cases when a once-competent controller wore down under the physical and emotional stress of a trying job—the individual could report the problem, and rather than being condemned as incompetent, the individual would be recognized as taking responsibility for air safety, treated as a valuable contributor to a safer system, and reassigned to a more appropriate position with no hint of blame. Rather than concealing their own problems and their own close calls and errors—or striving to shift the blame—controllers worked cooperatively to find the source of problems and correct them. Rather than seeking nonexistent infallible air traffic controllers and then blaming them when they made mistakes, reformers successfully found and corrected the problems in the system. The Commercial Aviation Safety Team, founded in 1998, adopted the systems approach in its efforts to improve commercial airline safety in the United States; using that methodology, it implemented policies that reduced commercial air traffic fatalities by 83 percent over the next decade.

The success of no-blame systemic approaches to fixing problems in manufacturing processes led to the successful adoption of the same approach to improve air traffic safety. Though changing the blame culture in medical practice is obviously a much bigger and more difficult process—medical practices and attitudes are, after all, deeply entrenched—the clear success of the nonblame systemic approach in other areas has led to limited adoption of the same model in medicine, and where adopted, it has led to similar improvements, with the promise of much greater benefits as the culture slowly shifts from a "name, blame, and shame" approach to a blame-free model that encourages the open reporting and examination of problems and potential problems and seeks solutions through deep examination of the flawed systemic structure (Reason 2000; Spath 2000). There is currently well-justified concern about the high rate of medical error. In the United States, deaths due to medical error are estimated at between forty thousand and one hundred thousand annually (Kohn, Corrigan, and Donaldson 2000). Although there are many causes, a central element of the problem is that medical caregivers—especially doctors—are assumed to have full responsibility (both take-charge responsibility and moral responsibility) for their individual treatment decisions and acts. Of course, no one suggests that a doctor can control all medical outcomes: some diseases and injuries are beyond contemporary medicine's healing powers. Furthermore, doctors don't make all the decisions: patients have the right to make choices concerning their own medical treatment. But in the current model, doctors are responsible for making the most accurate possible diagnosis, recommending the optimum treatment, and carrying out the agreed-upon treatment process in the most effective manner. If mistakes are made, the doctor is morally responsible and deserves blame (unless the doctor can shift the blame to a nurse, a technician, or the patient). A physician, Lucian L. Leape, describes the unfortunate effects of this model:

Physicians are socialized in medical school and residency to strive for error-free practice. There is a powerful emphasis on perfection, both in diagnosis and treatment. In everyday hospital practice, the message is equally clear: mistakes are unacceptable. Physicians are expected to function without error, an expectation that physicians translated into the need to be infallible. One result is that physicians, not unlike test pilots, come to view an error as a failure of character—you weren't careful enough, you didn't try hard enough. This kind of thinking lies behind a common reaction by physicians: "How can there be an error without negligence?" . . .

This need to be infallible creates a strong pressure to intellectual dishonesty, to cover up mistakes rather than to admit them. The organization of medical practice, particularly in the hospital, perpetuates these norms. Errors are rarely admitted or discussed among physicians in private practice. Physicians typically feel, not without reason, that admission of error will lead to censure or increased surveillance or, worse, that their colleagues will regard them as incompetent or careless. Far better to conceal a mistake or, if that is impossible, to try to shift the blame to another, even the patient. (1994, 1851–1852)

This model of individual moral responsibility results in significant harms. First, when there are problems and mistakes, the focus is on the individual who made a mistake and deserves blame. Attention is deflected from the systemic problems that are the root cause of individual errors: inadequate training of physicians, confusing practices for naming and abbreviating medications, exhausting schedules, understaffing and resultant pressure, failure to employ available computerized diagnostic aids as a check on physician observations and memories, lack of scanning devices to double check all medications, absence of multiple safeguard levels so that errors are detected before harm results, and the sleep-deprived working conditions of interns. When the focus is narrowed to finding and blaming an individual, the systemic causes of individual errors are left in place to produce repeated failure.

The second problem with the system of individual blame fits closely with and exacerbates the first. When blame is focused on the individual who was the last link in the chain that produced the mistake, then individuals who make errors are reluctant to admit their mistakes, striving instead to hide the problem. This problem is particularly severe in medicine, for two reasons: medical errors often have tragic consequences (a mistaken diagnosis results in death, an anesthesiologist's error leaves a child severely brain damaged, a mixup in medications causes severe injury and suffering). The miscalculation of an exam grade is easily reversed; the miscalculation of a medication may be fatal. Furthermore, the medical culture operates under the assumption of medical infallibility: good doctors and good nurses simply don't make mistakes, so those who do make mistakes are obviously incompetent. But when medical errors are denied and hidden, the causes of those errors go unexamined; errors continue to flow from the same systemic flaws, and nothing is done to correct the system.

A crucial step in reforming the system and reducing the error rate is eliminating the "blame culture"; that is, first we must stop blaming individuals for mistakes and instead focus on what caused the mistake and how to correct it. The British National Health Service and the government of the United Kingdom recently recognized the importance of that step in a document designed to launch the development of a better medical system with fewer errors. *A Commitment to Quality, a Quest for Excellence*—a 2001 joint statement by the National Health Service and the UK government—pledges "to recognise that honest failure should not be responded to primarily by blame and retribution, but by learning and a drive to reduce risk for future patients" (National Health Service 2001, 7). A similar approach is recommended by the 2000 Institute of Medicine report entitled "To Err Is Human" (Kohn, Corrigan, and Donaldson 2000). That study rejects the traditional medical culture of "naming, shaming, and blaming," promoting instead examination of the larger systemic causes of mistakes in order to design a safer medical system.

Blaming individuals and holding people morally responsible—air traffic controllers, doctors, nurses, or anyone else—is not an effective way of making either systems or people better; instead, it is a design for hiding small problems until they grow into larger ones and a design for concealing system shortcomings by blaming problems on individual failure. If we want to promote effective attention to the causes and correction of mistakes and the development of more effective behavior and more reliable systems, then we must move away from the model of individual blame and instead encourage an open inquiry into mistakes and their causes and into how a system can be devised to prevent such mistakes and improve individual behavior.

Of course, some mistakes do not indicate moral flaws in the physician. A smudge on an X-ray leads to a mistaken diagnosis, a hand slips in surgery: these are errors, and physicians may be profoundly troubled by them, but they don't reveal moral faults in the physician's character. Some mistakes, however, may well stem from serious character flaws: I was in a hurry to make my tee time, and I neglected to check as carefully as I should have before performing the surgery; I was arrogant, and thought I could successfully perform the surgery without proper training. If the medical community is shaping some physicians to develop such hazardous arrogance, that is a dangerous systemic *moral* problem that should be acknowledged and corrected, but blame will impede such positive reform efforts.

Jeanne L. Steiner favors a model that combines the systems approach with moral responsibility: some faulty individual behavior—such as the behavior of those "who knowingly disregard safe practices or policies in high-risk situations" (2006, 97)—justly deserve blame and punishment. From Steiner's perspective, the "systems approach" is valuable in its focus on detecting the systematic causes of error, but it must be balanced with the understanding that "there may be situations in which personnel and/ or legal sanctions are entirely warranted" (98). But there are serious disadvantages to adding an individual blame component. The systems approach has proved its worth in reducing mistakes and correcting problems; it seems more plausible to extend it further, rather than stopping short because of a commitment to an individual retributive moral responsibility model that is a well-established failure. One could adopt a limited systems approach, combined with individual moral responsibility at some limiting points, but the result seems likely to limit the effectiveness of the systems model. The question is not whether such a mixed system is possible, but rather why anyone would wish to adopt it.

Steiner maintains that when practitioners "knowingly disregard safe practices or policies in high-risk situations," this is a clear example of when it is best to suspend the systems (nonblame) model and switch to the punitive perspective of moral responsibility. Unfortunately, Steiner's type of case is all too common in medical practice: a physician fails to take proper precautions to avoid high-risk infection during surgery, or fails to follow guidelines in checking for potentially deadly conditions during an examination, or rushes to a diagnosis without considering all the relevant factors. When this happens, the physician has made a terrible mistake that may have terrible consequences for patient care, and the fault can be traced to the flawed character of the physician who failed to take sufficient care and exercise proper concern. If we adopt the individual moral responsibility model, the physician is disciplined, and the problem is regarded as "solved": we have found and punished the morally responsible individual. But the problem continues to occur as other physicians make the same sort of mistake—and make every effort to hide their mistakes to avoid blame and punishment. In fact, the medical community can and does conspire to hide such mistakes, with physicians cooperating in the cover-up in hopes that their colleagues will return the favor when their own rushed mistakes occur.

Under a systems approach, physicians can openly acknowledge that they rushed (when they should have exercised greater caution), the extent and nature of the problem can be critically examined, the causes can be discovered (perhaps in understaffing, or in administrative pressure to increase speed and "efficiency," or inadequate medical school training, or—in the worst scenario—in the licensing of physicians who are so greedy that they rush patient care in order to maximize their own earnings). The individual physician who rushes through a treatment process and thus places the patient at greater risk is certainly a *flawed* physician, whatever the causes of that serious character flaw. But the best way of discovering and changing such flaws and preventing their development in new physicians is by adopting policies that make it easier to detect the flaw, understand its nature and causes, and implement programs for correcting it. A policy of individual moral responsibility blocks that process, and rejection of moral responsibility facilitates it.

A Clearer Look at Crime

The no-blame systems approach to manufacturing, air safety, and medicine sketches a possible world without moral responsibility, but the greatest challenge to imagining a future without moral responsibility concerns the criminal justice system. How could it function without moral responsibility? What it would *not* be has already been examined: it would not be some brutal Clockwork Orange system, it would not treat people as objects for manipulation, it would not ratchet up the harsh cruelty of the current retributive system, and it would not treat offenders as alien creatures to be disposed of in the most expeditious manner. But can one give a positive outline of a criminal justice system that rejects moral responsibility and just deserts?

Changing the deeply traditional medical culture of individual blame for medical errors is a great challenge, though we have at least made a solid start. But shifting the medical culture away from blame and shame is a trivial task compared to shaking the vast machinery and moribund traditions of retributive justice. What programs work for rehabilitating those who have been shaped toward criminal behavior? That is a matter for empirical discovery that will be advanced by removing the moral responsibility blinders and looking clearly. One of the dominant views in the mid-twentieth century concerning reform of criminal behavior was a simple one: *nothing works*. In other words, there was a facile claim that we have made great efforts to find effective means of reforming criminals, and that nothing works, so we should simply warehouse them and thus protect society from these evil people. This was a very convenient conclusion. First, it made the satisfying claim that we had tried everything and invested enormous energy and resources in reforming miscreants and still nothing works. It was obviously false, as we had invested very little indeed in trying to find and develop effective rehabilitative programs (consider that there were hardly any drug or alcohol rehabilitation programs and that there was very little in the way of prison education programs and almost nothing in the way of psychological counseling for prisoners), but it was pleasant to pretend that we had made a tremendous effort. Second, it conveniently kept the focus on the prisoners: the problem was changing *them*; we could deny or ignore systemic problems of racism, inadequate educational facilities, job discrimination, lack of employment opportunities, lack of medical care, and lack of respect. Because the focus was on the bad individual, no attention need be given to the bad system that shaped such individuals— before they offended, during imprisonment, and after prison release. Finally, "nothing works" indicated that "those people" were independent of their conditions: we gave them every opportunity for reform in prison, and it had no effect; of course, the corollary is that they are not shaped by any conditions (inside or outside of prison), they are inherently bad—so the fault cannot lie with the social system that shaped them, and we need not examine that system nor consider its reform. Not surprisingly, when genuine efforts were made to develop effective rehabilitation programs, some achieved considerable success; it also became clear that those effective programs start with the careful examination of the systemic negative influences that shaped violent antisocial character.

"Reform" programs that shame—a popular desire for those driven by moral responsibility belief in retribution—are very satisfying: they satisfy the desire to cause retributive suffering, they feed on our self-righteous assumptions, and they protect us from looking closely at the causes of the flawed character and flawed behavior. But they are profoundly counterproductive. They further damage those on whom the shame is inflicted, and they more deeply blind those who inflict the shame. Dan M. Kahan notes with approval that "jurisdictions throughout the United States are rediscovering public humiliation as a criminal punishment. . . . These punishments gratify rather than disappoint the public demand for condemnation" (1998a, 706). Kahan even celebrates the degrading aspect of prison as an effective means of shaming the imprisoned: "By inflicting countless . . . indignities—from exposure to the view of others when urinating and defecating to rape at the hand of other inmates—prison unambiguously marks the lowness of those we consign to it" (1998b, 1642). But as James Gilligan (2001)—unimpeded by a commitment to moral responsibility and just deserts—makes clear, it is precisely such disrespect and consignment to "lowness" that is a major factor in causing violence. The indignities of such treatment may satisfy the retributive demands of a public obsessed with moral responsibility, but at the price of not only ignoring the real causes of the problems but also severely exacerbating prisoners' tendencies toward violent crime. Successful reform programs start with recognition of the assault on dignity and pride and self-respect that our society makes against those who lack the opportunity to "get ahead" in education, status, and wealth. We have a choice between an approach that systematically obscures the causes of our basic problems and a system that facilitates deeper understanding of the causes of those problems. Understanding seems the more promising path.

It is curious that the system of retributive justice should be the last ditch defense of moral responsibility, because it would seem to be a very weak defense indeed. It is difficult to look closely at our dominant retributive system of "justice" and judge it worth defending and even more difficult to regard it as strong grounds for the defense of moral responsibility (on the grounds that moral responsibility is the essential foundation for this retributive system). The flaws in the retributive system are as pervasive as they are obvious. In the West, the deepest commitment to retributive justice can be found in the United States, and it is in the United States that the ugly elements in the retributive justice system can be seen writ large. As crime increases, we ratchet up the retribution against the morally responsible individual who committed the crime. When the crime is really severe, we execute the criminal—and pretend that the problem is solved. And we're not overly careful about it: jailhouse informants are offered bribes—in the form of reduced sentences or reduced charges—to swear that the defendant confessed to the crime during lunch or in the exercise yard, and everyone involved, from the judge to the district attorney, knows that these witnesses are being paid for their perjured testimony. The severe problems with eyewitness testimony are well-known to psychologists; indeed, they are now well-known to almost any student who has taken a course in introductory psychology. But those problems do not deter prosecutors from basing cases on that shaky support or juries from convicting on that flimsy evidence. A wrong has been done, so someone must suffer; if it happens to be the person who committed the crime, so much the better, but obviously that is not essential: the number of innocent people freed from prison—many from death row—on the basis of DNA evidence has become so large that it no longer prompts press coverage, much less outrage. The much larger number of wrongly convicted—in cases in which DNA evidence is not available or has been destroyed or the prisoner lacks the resources to have it tested—does not seem to trouble those who champion our system of retributive "justice." To the contrary, those who are most deeply committed to severe retributive justice are often eager to block any process that might reveal that the wrong person was convicted; states pass laws restricting appeals and limiting access to evidence that might exculpate those who have been wrongly convicted. The retributive justice system is designed to strike back: the poor, the powerless, the minorities are the easiest targets, and meticulous concern over whether they actually committed a crime gets in the way of the retributive strike-back response. We spend enormous resources on retribution and deprive ourselves of the resources that could fix the problems: the problems that we easily discover—when we study the system rather than blame the individual—cause crime. The retributive system makes it impossible for us to look closely at those problems; if we look closely at causes, the moral responsibility foundation for retribution collapses. Looking closely at the problem is hard: it's not *them*, it's *us*. Perhaps recognizing that we do not deserve *blame* for those problems will make it easier to recognize and examine and fix the systemic flaws.

Moral responsibility advocates might grant that reforms are needed in our system of retributive justice, but also insist that rather than junking the system, we should reform the moral responsibility system of retributive justice and make it work better. The problem is that the flaws are inherent in the system of retributive justice. First, the retributive system insists we must have someone to punish; thus, when advances in DNA testing make the number of mistaken convictions too great to ignore, champions of retributive "justice" are undeterred, insisting that we must accept such mistakes as a minor by-product of the glorious retributive process. As Ernest van den Haag, a dedicated proponent of capital punishment, writes:

> Miscarriages of justice are rare, but do occur. [Van den Haag's article was written before DNA testing had made clear the frightening regularity with which the innocent are wrongly convicted.] Over a long enough time they lead to execution of some innocents. Does this make irrevocable punishments morally wrong? Hardly. Our government employs trucks. They run over innocent bystanders more frequently than courts sentence innocents to death. We do not give up trucks because the benefits they produce outweigh the harm, including the death of innocents. Many human activities, even quite trivial ones, foreseeably cause wrongful deaths. Courts may cause fewer wrongful deaths than golf. Whether one sees the benefit of doing justice by imposing capital punishment as moral, or as material, or both, it outweighs the loss of innocent lives through miscarriages, which are as unintended as traffic accidents. (1985, 967)

The important thing is retribution, not justice; the execution of "some innocents" should not trouble us. And it doesn't—not because retribution has overriding benefits, but because the basic nature of strike-back retribution precludes any great delicacy about its target. But the second problem that makes reforming the retributive system impossible is even more severe: in order to retain the retributive system, we *cannot* scrutinize the real problems that need reform because careful scrutiny is death to the moral responsibility beliefs that prop up retribution.

There are promising programs that offer clear indications of what form a criminal justice system might take in a world without moral responsibility. The restorative justice movement (particularly in juvenile justice and in special community courts for "first-nation" Canadians and aboriginal New Zealanders) is a promising possibility. In contrast to the traditional retributive justice model, restorative justice (Braithewaite 1999, 2002; Johnstone 2003; Morris, 2002) focuses on restoring to wholeness or health the community where the crime occurred and the crime victims (so far as possible), as well as restoring the perpetrator to the community. Restorative justice programs vary widely, but there are some important common features. First, it is important that the person committing a crime—who harmed the community and individuals within the community—acknowledge the wrongdoing, recognize that others were hurt by the wrongdoing, recognize her own fault, and sincerely apologize for the wrong done (and, as was argued earlier, rejecting moral responsibility promotes rather than precludes sincere apology). Second, the community emphasizes restoring the wrongdoer to the community and examines what went wrong to cause this community member to become seriously flawed in her character and what can be done to change the causal forces to correct such flaws and prevent their development in others. Thus the restorative justice model combines a strong commitment to sincere apology with an equal commitment to finding and understanding and correcting the causes for flawed character (including causes within the community itself) and deemphasis of punitive measures and individual blame and punishment.

Restorative justice programs are still in their infancy. Perhaps they will grow up to be the ideal alternative to the retributive system; more likely, they will suggest other and better programs. But one feature will certainly be part of any system without moral responsibility, and it is of greatest importance: without moral responsibility, we can look more carefully and clearly at the actual causes of criminal behavior and criminal character and start taking effective steps to change those causal conditions (rather than obsessing with the individual criminal behavior symptoms).

When we look carefully at the systemic causes for violent behavior—and enlarge the narrow focus on the *individual* whom we blame and punish— then the systemic problems are not difficult to discover. James Gilligan was the medical director of the Bridgewater State Hospital for the criminally insane and director of mental health for the Massachusetts prison system; he also directed the Center for the Study of Violence at Harvard Medical School. From his extensive research on the causes of violence, he concluded that the basic factor triggering violent behavior is a deep sense of shame or disrespect, and he discovered several key systemic factors that cause such a violence-provoking sense of shame:

There is a great deal of evidence . . . that shame is spread via the social and economic system. This happens . . . through what we might call the "vertical" division of the population into a hierarchical ranking of upper and lower status groups, chiefly classes, castes, and age groups, but also other means by which people are divided into in-groups and out-groups, the accepted and the rejected, the powerful and the weak, the rich and the poor, the honored and the dishonored. For people are shamed on a systematic, wholesale basis, and their vulnerability to feelings of humiliation is increased when they are assigned an inferior social or economic status; and the more inferior and humble it is, the more frequent and intense the feelings of shame, and the more frequent and intense the acts of violence. (Gilligan 2001, 38)

Following this lead, Gilligan notes:

The most powerful predictor of the homicide rate in comparisons of the different nations of the world, the different states of the United States, different counties, and different cities and census tracts, is the size of the disparities in income and wealth between the rich and the poor. Some three dozen studies, at least, have found statistically significant correlations between the degree of absolute as well as relative poverty and the incidence of homicide. Hsieh and Pugh in 1993 did a meta-analysis of thirty-four such studies and found strong statistical support for these finds, as have several other reviews of this literature. (2001, 39; see also Wilkinson 2004)

And Gilligan notes that the high rate of violence in the United States can be traced to some clear systemic factors:

In fact, the social and economic system of the United States combines almost every characteristic that maximizes shame and hence violence. First, there is the "Horatio Alger" myth that everyone can get rich if they are smart and work hard (which means that if they are not rich, they must be stupid or lazy, or both). Second, we are not only told that we can get rich, we are also stimulated to want to get rich. For the whole economic system of mass production depends on whetting people's appetites to consume the flood of goods that are being produced (hence the flood of advertisements). Third, the social and economic reality is the opposite of the Horatio Alger myth, since social mobility is actually less likely in the U.S. than in the supposedly more rigid social structures of Europe and the U.K. As Mishel, Bernstein, and Schmitt [2001] have noted: "Contrary to widely held perceptions, the U.S. offers less economic mobility than other rich countries. . . ." Fourth, as they also mention, "the U. S. has the most unequal income distribution and the highest poverty rates among all the advanced economies in the world. . . ." The net effect of all these features of U.S. society is to maximize the gap between aspiration and attainment, which maximizes the frequency and intensity of feelings of shame, which maximizes the rates of violent crimes. (2001, 44–45)

Helen Epstein (2009) notes that a recent study found that between 60 percent and 75 percent of African-American teenagers in Baltimore and New York reported frequent and routine police harassment. Even if one doubts those numbers, it is clear that young urban blacks *feel* that they are being singled out for harassment and disrespect—and systematic shaming. These are obviously not all the factors, but the point is that when we shift the focus from blaming the individual to examining the systemic causes of violent behavior, then we can make swift progress in finding the causes of the problems. It will be more difficult to *correct* those problems, especially in a system in which privilege and wealth have become so deeply entrenched. But at least we can focus our attention and efforts in the right direction and treat the causes rather than the behavioral symptoms.

The Last Challenge

When all else fails, the final challenge to a system that rejects retribution and moral responsibility is: what do you propose we do with the violent criminals (shaped by our society)? What do we do with Robert Harris? That is a serious challenge. Obviously, we will not set him loose, wish him well, and allow him to continue murdering people. Perhaps we could lock him in a cage, eventually drag him out and kill him, and ignore the rampant problems of child abuse, inadequate schools (especially for children with special needs), and the brutal juvenile detention centers that shaped Harris and are even now shaping others to follow in his footsteps. That is the policy currently in place in our moral responsibility system and that many think is worth preserving; possibly *without* moral responsibility, we can think of something better. Whatever new proposal is put forward, it is difficult to imagine that it will not be an improvement.

For specifics, first of all, the focus would be on discovering and changing the causes that shaped Harris's brutal character and vicious behavior; rather than neglecting those causes or even denying—in order to preserve belief in moral responsibility—that they played a significant role in shaping who Harris became. In this new approach, we would regard the continued existence of such horrific conditions as a national emergency requiring serious investments in reform. What would we do with Harris himself? Obviously, we won't send him on his way: he *is* (or was, until his execution) a violent man, and others must be protected from that violence. We would not subject him to Clockwork Orange brutality or any other form of brutality: it was brutal treatment—at home, at school, and in juvenile detention centers—that shaped this brutal man, and rejection of moral responsibility removes the temptation to suppose that he *deserves* brutal treatment for his brutal behavior. And we would be very reluctant to "give up" on Robert Harris: we recognize that had we been subjected to similar horrors, we might well have become similarly horrific; further, we recognize that Robert Harris is a frightening mark of some profound societal failures in which we fortunate ones played a role. We enjoyed luxuries while children like Robert Harris were subjected to almost unimaginably brutal conditions year after year, and we—with our privileged positions and significant influence—did not make sufficient efforts to bring about the needed changes. The resources were available to deal with or at least mitigate the enormous problem of child and spousal abuse, to improve schools and provide special speech education for all children with speech problems (not just those in affluent neighborhoods), and to fix the brutal conditions in juvenile facilities (which were widely known); we failed to do so, and Robert Harris is a product of that failure. It make no sense, and it is not productive, to *blame* either Robert Harris or ourselves, but that understanding will prevent us from regarding Harris as some alien moral monster who is not our concern. His failure is our failure, and giving up on Robert Harris means giving up on ourselves and giving up on correcting the wrongs to which we contributed by our privileged neglect and our privileged consumption of a disproportionate share of resources that could have prevented the problem. Believers in individual moral responsibility may justify executing Harris or locking him out of sight and out of mind in some brutal Supermax prison, but that easy "solution" is not available to moral responsibility abolitionists.

Is it possible to rehabilitate persons like Robert Harris? I don't know. Our society has invested billions in punishment, harsh incarceration facilities, and executions, but very little in trying to find effective programs for reclaiming those who have been shaped to be brutal social misfits. The claim that "nothing works" in rehabilitation of violent criminals was always a way of avoiding any real efforts or substantial investment in helping those whom our society shaped for brutality and rationalizing our ratcheting up of extreme retributive policies of long-term mandatory incarceration in ever-harsher prison environments (culminating in Supermax prisons, with their psychologically devastating isolation policies). But even with the meager resources that have been devoted to this effort, some humane and promising programs have been developed. And rather than brutalizing and demeaning "Clockwork Orange" programs, they involve respect for prisoners and respect for the prisoners' own resilient powers to improve themselves. One salient example is the work of James Gilligan, who developed strategies that greatly reduced both in-prison violence and recidivism in Massachusetts and later in San Francisco. As Gilligan makes clear, the first step involves stopping the harshly punitive measures that are supposedly justified by moral responsibility:

The criminal justice and penal systems have been operating on the basis of a huge mistake, namely, the belief that punishment will deter, prevent, or inhibit violence, when in fact it is the most powerful stimulus of violence that we have yet discovered. . . . I am not suggesting that it would make sense to let those who are actively raping and murdering others free to walk the streets. Physical *restraint* of those who are currently and actively physically violent, including confining or "quarantining" them in a locked facility, is at times the only way, in our ignorance, we have yet discovered to prevent further violence. But to *punish* people—that is, to deliberately cause them pain—above and beyond the degree that is unavoidable in the act of *restraining* them, only *constitutes* further violence (on our part), and only *causes* further violence (on the part of the "criminals" we punish). . . .

Prisons themselves could actually start preventing violence, rather than stimulating it, if we took everyone out of them, demolished the buildings, and replaced them with a new and different kind of institution—namely, a locked, secure residential college, whose purpose and functions would be educational and therapeutic, not punitive. It would make sense to organize such a facility as a therapeutic community, with a full range of treatments for substance abuse and any other medical and mental health services needed to help the individual heal the damage that deformed his character and stunted his humanity. (2001, 116–117)

It is noteworthy that Gilligan's impetus for developing such programs was his rejection of the deep assumption of individual blame that is inherent in our contemporary criminal justice system. Though Gilligan's proposals are promising and his programs have proven their effectiveness, they are certainly not the final word on reforming violent offenders (as Gilligan himself acknowledges). But the point is that once we turn away from the model of moral responsibility and individual blame and punishment, we can effectively examine not only the causes that shape violent criminal behavior, but also the best means of working with those who have been shaped in that manner.

The moral responsibility obsession with blaming and punishing the offender makes it impossible to look closely at how such offenders were shaped and very difficult to objectively consider the most effective means of reforming their character and behavior. Brutal Clockwork Orange "therapy" is not the solution (it would appeal only to those who regard the offenders as less than human and as deserving of such ignominious treatment: the same extreme advocates of individual moral responsibility who are drawn to harsh "boot camp" treatment of prisoners and to shaming punishments). The commitment to treating prisoners as deserving to suffer, deserving to be "put in their place," and deserving humiliation ("shaming" punishments are as popular with moral responsibility advocates as they are profoundly counterproductive) is a severe obstruction to developing effective respectful noncoercive means of improving the character and behavior of offenders. Though Gilligan has done marvelous work in making clear the problems commonly afflicting violent offenders, in fact it is not difficult to recognize that prominent among those problems are the deep threat of shame and vulnerability and feelings of inadequacy—not difficult to recognize, that is, unless they are obscured by belief in moral responsibility. The illusion of moral responsibility is not benign.

And what do we do with Bernie Madoff: a gentle person of marvelous talents, who is extremely competent and apparently quite self-confident and who steals billions of dollars? That's not an easy question. But in a system that rejects moral responsibility, we will not give him a lengthy prison sentence and suppose that the problem is solved without examining carefully how to put in place safeguards that will catch such wrongs before they become massive and without even *trying* to understand why someone with such talents and opportunities would follow a path that he obviously knew would end in personal disaster. A system that rejects moral responsibility and just deserts does not have all the answers, but at least it is willing to address the right questions and start the hard work of trying to make reforms and find solutions. The moral responsibility system, in contrast, must insist that the problem begins and ends with Bernie Madoff and in order to sustain that illusion, it must scrupulously avoid understanding any deeper systemic causes: a culture of greed that judges people harshly if their accumulative prowess lessens and a culture of deregulation that promotes irresponsible and greedy practices and places people in pressured situations to conform to acquisitive and immoral practices. The response is, "Blame him; don't make excuses." But these are not excuses; rather, they are explanations that the blame culture insists we must not examine. The blame culture responds angrily if anyone brings them up: you are treating him as a nonperson, you are making excuses for evil, you are taking the side of the criminals and forgetting about the victims, you are "soft on crime," you are too concerned with *understanding* when the goal is *condemnation*.

Rejecting our moral responsibility–based system of retributive justice means rejecting a system that blocks deeper inquiries into the causes of criminal behavior; that prevents reforms that would reduce crime; that condones the infliction of enormous suffering, humiliation, and psycho-logical damage on people who do not deserve such treatment. In short, it means rejecting a system of profound *in*justice. In the United States, our moral responsibility system of criminal justice keeps millions of men and women locked in cages and steadfastly refuses to look hard at the real causes of crime; our moral responsibility–based system of distributive justice has resulted in the greatest disparity of wealth of any western country and a system in which many live in poverty with no health care and little opportunity for themselves or their children, while others live in profligate luxury (an unjust distributive system that is also a major cause of our high crime rate). When we reject moral responsibility and consider carefully, it is clear that we can do better.

There are great advantages to a world without moral responsibility. Not only can we look squarely and in depth at faults in our system, but we can also look more carefully at the causes of individual bad behavior and how to change it. Doing so will require looking carefully at how our flawed society shaped flawed individuals, which means getting beyond the vis-ceral desire to blame, punish, and shame. It means carefully studying the problem, not relying on our retributive impulses for guidance. There are programs that show great promise, but they are not the programs endorsed by those who are blinded by desire for vengeful retribution, by the desire to inflict suffering, and by the desire to blame and shame. If we want to develop effective means of shaping free and productive people and reshap-ing bad behavior, then we must learn how to move beyond blame. How do we move beyond that natural punitive motive? Educating and develop-ing understanding is a vital step. By calling into question the moral respon-sibility model, rather than being its champions, philosophers can make a positive contribution.

16 Is It Possible to Eliminate Moral Responsibility?

Champions of moral responsibility can hardly survey the current scene with satisfaction. If Lakatos's (1970) notion of a "degenerative research program" has any application in philosophy, then the defense of moral responsibility must be its poster child. The sense of desperation in the efforts to shore up moral responsibility is almost palpable, and the enormous variety of distinctly different and conflicting proposals for supporting moral responsibility is powerful evidence of that desperation. The existentialists invoke magical phrases—we responsible persons are "being-for-itself"—to proudly insist that we make wondrous choices independent of all constraints and conditions. More cautious libertarians offer a similar account, with some trepidation. Roderick Chisholm (1982) affirms that the choices required for moral responsibility are mysterious and godlike, and Richard Taylor (1963) is driven to the same conclusion—which "one can hardly affirm . . . without embarrassment"—concerning the unique and mysterious powers of human choice. Robert Kane is a contemporary libertarian who rejects mystery and relies on quantum indeterminism amplified by chaos; Timothy O'Connor embraces mystery and divine powers. Peter van Inwagen finds libertarian free will inexplicable, but is confident that we have it. Compatibilists are united in their rejection of miracles but divided on almost everything else. Moral responsibility is on a plateau (Harry G. Frankfurt, George Sher, Thaddeus Metz, and Angela M. Smith), and equality is not required. Moral responsibility rests on a foundation of roughly equal talents (Sher) or roughly equal luck (Dennett). Moral responsibility comes when we follow the True and Good (Susan Wolf). We are morally responsible because we make ourselves (Dennett). We are morally responsible because we can always choose to remake ourselves (Charles Taylor). Moral responsibility comes from higher-order reflective self-approval (Frankfurt, Gerald Dworkin). We *take* moral responsibility (Frankfurt, Dennett). Moral responsibility requires only guidance control (Fischer)—and not much of it. Belief in moral responsibility is inevitable (P. F. Strawson). These are wonderfully creative theories, but their sheer number indicates their problems.

Why Do Philosophers Believe in Moral Responsibility?

Its state of philosophical crisis notwithstanding, the moral responsibility system is deeply embedded in our common sense as well as our legal system and deeply entrenched in our natural strike-back emotions. Philosophers are subject to this powerful pull as much as others are, and probably more so, because there are factors that enhance (or from my perspective, exacerbate) our strong natural feeling that we *are* morally responsible. As psychologists Jonathan Haidt and Fredrik Bjorklund note, philosophers are highly trained in considering alternatives: "If you are able to honestly examine the moral arguments in favor of slavery and genocide (along with the much stronger arguments against them), then you are likely to be either a psychopath or a philosopher. Philosophers are one of the only groups that have been found spontaneously to look for reasons on both sides of a question" (2008, 196).

Thus philosophers have a strong sense of choosing among open alternatives, even when their intuitive inclinations settle their *actual* choice prior to their deliberation. As Robert Wright notes: "The . . . human brain is a machine for winning arguments, a machine for convincing others that its owner is in the right—and thus a machine for convincing its owner of the same thing. The brain is like a good lawyer: given any set of interests to defend, it sets about convincing the world of their moral and logical worth, regardless of whether they in fact have any of either. Like a lawyer, the human brain wants victory, not truth" (1994, 280). If Haidt and his fellow social intuitionists are correct, our basic moral stances (including our reciprocity/retributive inclinations) are set by strong emotional (or "intuitive") commitments, and our deliberative processes are called into play to defend our intuitive decisions. Although almost everyone enjoys considerable facility at developing deliberative justifications for moral stances taken prior to deliberation, philosophers are polished pros at that task.

There are other factors promoting philosophical allegiance to moral responsibility. Philosophers are chronic cognizers, moving in packs of chronic cognizers. Although I have seen no empirical data on this, my decades of mingling with philosophers convinces me that almost all have a robust sense of *internal* locus-of-control. Philosophers have a remarkably strong—perhaps even overdeveloped—sense of self-efficacy: why else would we believe (mea culpa) that we can and sometimes have found the answer to philosophical quandaries that have troubled humankind for centuries, if not millennia. Our sublime confidence in our capacities to tackle almost any question is strong evidence of our healthy sense of self-efficacy. All of this gives philosophers a robust sense of being in control, which is good; as argued in earlier chapters, it is also accurate. But it has an unfortunate side effect: given our natural tendency to believe in retributive moral responsibility and the powerful cultural reinforcement of that tendency, this strong sense of being in control also promotes a strong sense of moral responsibility (because as noted in chapter 3 we assume that if we are free— which we are—then we *must* be morally responsible). Add the fact that as highly educated academics we hold privileged and very comfortable positions in society, and we like to think we justly deserve those special benefits; we've accomplished much, and we are delighted to claim credit for it.

Yet for all our powerful inclination and desire to believe in moral responsibility, we also recognize that moral responsibility and the claims on which it rests are threatened on every side. Neither luck nor talents average out. Our capacity to continue deliberating is a product of our history (Cacioppo et al. 1996). Our deliberations function more to prop up beliefs already intuitively established than to rationally examine them (Haidt 2001). Our abilities to choose are limited by our locus-of-control (Rotter 1966) and sense of self-efficacy (Bandura 1997), which are a product of our fortunate or unfortunate conditioning histories and of which we are only dimly aware. Situations control our choices more than we ever imagined (Doris 2002). Our basic moral stances are given by our history, genetic and cultural, not our choice. Our willpower is epiphenomenal (Wegner 2002). Decisions are made nonconsciously (Libet et al. 1983). Philosophers such as Smilansky (2000) who look straight and hard at the problems confronting the justification of moral responsibility find themselves clinging to the illusion of moral responsibility, floating amid the wreckage of moral responsibility arguments.

Without moral responsibility—and with the naturalistic account of free will—we can happily accommodate most of the concerns that people have: we can make moral judgments, we can be creative, we can apologize, we can work to change things for the better. We can have all the freedom that human animals genuinely need, and we can pay closer attention to the factors that inhibit and promote that freedom and work effectively to enhance individual freedom. One thing is lost: the ultimate responsibility that is craved by Kane, Smilansky, Pico della Mirandola, and others. We are not God's special creation or our own special godlike creation; we are not gods, or demigods, or the specially favored of the gods. We did not make ourselves from scratch; indeed, to the degree that we made ourselves at all, we were dependent on the tools and materials already at our disposal. We can accomplish much, and by understanding the causal factors that shaped our abilities, we can accomplish more. But we cannot claim special credit or ultimate responsibility for our accomplishments, which deters many from accepting the demise of moral responsibility. This is a familiar story. Copernicus can't be right, because we are no longer center stage; circulation of the blood can't be right, because we are not machines; the mind can't be just the brain, because we have the special power of reason and our special soul; we can't have evolved like all the other species, because we are special and separate and distinct. Such views have their charms, but they cause more trouble than they are worth. They block better understanding, and they make it impossible to take effective measures. And just as we have learned that it's really not so bad being an evolved little animal occupying a small planet in orbit around an insignificant star on the outer reaches of a rather ordinary spiral galaxy among billions of galaxies, so we can learn to live without the special distinct glory of being morally responsible; indeed, we can learn to live better.

Getting Over Moral Responsibility

It is not surprising that philosophers have tried so desperately to prop up moral responsibility: If Haidt (2001) is right, we feel its intuitive pull, from a visceral strike-back inclination, and although everyone is good at using reason to find rationalizations for moral conclusions that we draw intuitively (Haidt and Bjorklund 2008), philosophers are the masters. But on reflection, this is an inclination that we need to control and mitigate—or at least not celebrate. If all else fails, we can sustain it through illusion, but it's a bad policy. Smilansky (2000) thinks that libertarian free will belief is a necessary illusion for justice, but keeping the illusion means that we keep belief in moral responsibility, which he acknowledges is not legitimate. He worries that we will lose the distinction between punishing the guilty and punishing the innocent, and I have given reasons for thinking that is not so. But whatever one concludes about this issue, it is quite clear that by keeping the belief in moral responsibility—though we know it is illegitimate—we punish those who do not deserve punishment. This situation is not a risk, but a reality; not a possible if unlikely wrong, but an actual and egregious injustice: We knowingly and purposefully punish those who *do not deserve* punishment. Furthermore, by keeping the focus on the individual who did wrong and "deserves punishment" (end of inquiry), we block careful attention to the *causes* of wrongdoing—the deeper sources of violent behavior. Thus we draw attention away from the root causes in poverty and social neglect. This destructive system of moral responsibility harms those who are punished and hides the problems that we could start to solve; instead of seeking to justify it, we should focus on controlling this deep inclination and pushing society to look harder at real causes and how they could be corrected. That is a better occupation for philosophers than propping up a belief in moral responsibility and just retribution that serves as the philosophical underpinning for a profoundly unjust system.

Is Belief in Moral Responsibility Unshakable?

Even if we acknowledge that moral responsibility is a harmful doctrine, that it is battered by scientific advances in our understanding of human behavior, that it has no rational justification, and that it cannot withstand close scrutiny; even if we acknowledge all that, can we actually consider renouncing moral responsibility? Is it an illusion we cannot live without (Smilansky 2000) or even consistently see through? Is the case against moral responsibility merely an abstract philosophical exercise, as P. F. Strawson (1962) would insist? Is belief in moral responsibility so deeply entrenched in our culture, our belief system, and our psyches that there is no real possibility of renouncing it? In concurrence with Strawson, that appears to be van Inwagen's view. He rejects compatibilism as being implausible and as not being a legitimate way of supporting moral responsibility.

But he insists that he would nonetheless embrace compatibilism rather than give up moral responsibility: he knows that he is morally responsible, and he knows it with greater confidence and conviction that he could ever have toward any evidence or argument to the contrary:

> If incompatibilism is true, then either determinism or the free-will thesis is false. To deny the free-will thesis is to deny the existence of moral responsibility, which would be absurd. Moreover, there seems to be no good reason to accept determinism. . . . Therefore we should reject determinism.
>
> This conclusion is, at least in principle, open to scientific refutation, since it is conceivable that science will one day present us with compelling reasons for believing in determinism. Then, and only then, I think, should we become compatibilists. (van Inwagen 1983, 223)

The tenacity of philosophers in hanging on to our cherished beliefs is comparable to the tenacity of a Scottish Terrier with its teeth in a favorite bedroom slipper. The fixed Earth, the immaterial mind, the fixity of species: all have had their immovable and often very imaginative philosophical champions. If moral responsibility joins that list of philosophical lost causes, there is no reason to suppose that philosophers will be any less dogged or creative in its defense. But in the case of moral responsibility, there is an additional concern: might it be—for reasons quite distinct from those given by Strawson—that giving up moral responsibility is a *psychological* impossibility?

It was noted earlier that the deep commitment to strike-back retributivism is rooted in motives that are not rational, and one of the points made against this motive is its nondiscriminating nature. This point may count against rational grounds for moral responsibility, but on the other hand, it may make rational grounding for moral responsibility irrelevant. Perhaps belief in moral responsibility runs so deep that no rational argument can unseat it, though no argument can be given to support it. In that case, philosophers are doomed to eternally push the great boulder of moral responsibility toward the peak of rational justification, only to have it roll back down again. But even with all the resources of philosophical ingenuity, once we squarely recognize that moral responsibility is fundamentally unjustifiable, we cannot continue to believe that it is somehow justified.

Or perhaps we can. Perhaps we must. Doing so would certainly be uncomfortable: we must believe in something we know is false. That is precisely the depressing burden that Saul Smilansky (2000) has recently shouldered.

So is it possible to adopt a system that genuinely rejects all moral responsibility? Not one that rejects all deliberation, or all moral judgments, or all *take-charge* responsibility, but one that fully rejects all *moral responsibility*? That is an empirical question, and neither philosophical argument nor armchair psychology can resolve it. Philosophers have, of course, weighed in on that issue: P. F. Strawson (1962) maintains that we could never actually do so, given our psychological nature; Galen Strawson (1986) thinks it might be possible, though at terrible psychological costs, and Saul Smilansky (2000) thinks it might be possible for a few very remarkable people, but not for many. But those philosophical conclusions are heavily weighted (as earlier chapters have attempted to show) by profoundly mistaken views of what else would be lost in losing moral responsibility: free will, moral evaluation, moral judgment, deliberation, competence. Philosophical concerns aside, there are significant psychological studies that pose a serious challenge for the campaign to abolish moral responsibility. Specifically, there are psychologists who hold that commitment to reciprocity/retributivism is such a deeply entrenched element of human nature (an element we share with a number of other species) that any attempt to eliminate moral responsibility must fail. Two psychologists who offer powerful support for that view are Jonathan Haidt and Fredrik Bjorklund, who maintain that endeavoring to modify or resist strong deep natural preferences—such as the desire to strike back—is futile:

It is just not very easy to shape children, unless one is going with the flow of what they already like. It takes little or no work to get 8 year old children to prefer candy to broccoli, to prefer being liked by their peers to being approved of by adults, or to prefer hitting back to loving their enemies. Socializing the reverse preferences would be difficult or impossible. The resistance of children to arbitrary or unusual socialization has been the downfall of many utopian efforts. Even if a charismatic leader can recruit a group of unusual adults able to believe in universal love while opposing all forms of hatred and jealousy, nobody has ever been able to raise the next generation of children to take on such unnatural beliefs. (2008, 201–202)

So if retributivism/reciprocity/just deserts is so deeply entrenched, perhaps speculation about a system that rejects it is idle. Were I charismatic, I might persuade a few "unusual adults" to adopt it temporarily, but the system would soon collapse under its unnatural weight. And according to Haidt and Bjorklund, fairness/reciprocity ("a set of emotional responses related to playing tit-for-tat" [2008, 203]) is one of five basic moral intuitions, along with harm/care ("a sensitivity to or dislike of signs of pain and suffering in others, particularly in the young and vulnerable" [203]), authority/respect ("about navigating status hierarchies" [203]), purity/sanctity (related to the emotions of disgust, necessary for explaining why so many moral rules relate to food, sex, menstruation, and the handling of corpses), and "concerns about boundaries between ingroup and out-group" (203). Haidt and Bjorklund "believe these five sets of intuitions should be seen as the foundations of intuitive ethics" (203); because reci-procity is a clear element among those sets of intuitions, it appears to be a "foundation" that cannot be shaken.

Rejecting the Moral Responsibility System

Haidt and his fellow researchers have made important discoveries about our moral decision-making processes, particularly discoveries regarding the strength of our "intuitive" reactions in comparison to the lesser role for rational deliberation. But there are several reasons for doubting that the reciprocity/retributive intuition is as unshakable as might be supposed or that it is impossible to control it. There is no doubt that the strike-back retributive "intuition"—which is the fundamental source for our belief in moral responsibility—is very powerful. Its strength and depth have already been noted, and there is no one who has not felt that powerful impulse well up in response to being harmed, as well as in response to witnessing harm. My deep visceral response to the torture at Abu Ghraib is the desire to see the torturers tortured—and a deep feeling that justice demands it. The views of Jonathan Haidt and the contemporary social intuitionists sound like an echo from Adam Smith: "As every man doth, so shall it be done to him, and retaliation seems to be the great law which is dictated to us by Nature" (1759/1976, 82).

As Haidt and his colleagues note, however, there is also a powerful feeling of the importance of *fairness*. The reciprocity/retributive/responsi-bility intuition does not have the field to itself, for it can be opposed by a strong sense of fairness. And this brings us to the basic reason for doubting the overwhelming power of the retributive "intuition": our fairness incli-nations have made significant inroads in modifying and mitigating the strike-back response. If you harm me, whether purposefully or inadver-tently, my impulse is to strike back, but over many centuries, we have seen the sense of fairness effectively counter at least some of this strong retributive impulse. If the harm was accidental, or the result of a seizure, or caused by someone insane or a child, then the strong sense that it would be unfair to reciprocate can mitigate or even neutralize the powerful retributive intuition. It doesn't work as effectively as we might wish: following Hinckley's attack on Ronald Reagan and Hinckley's subsequent acquittal on grounds of insanity, many states—at the demand of outraged citizens who desired retribution against Hinckley, his insanity notwithstanding—passed laws allowing for severe punishment of the criminally insane. Indeed, as Joel Feinberg points out, in the United States, the current tendency seems to be swinging back toward blaming and punishing those whom we had come to understand were not morally responsible: "Instead of being a kind of softening excuse, mental illness has become in some quarters a kind of hardening aggravation. Instead of saying, 'He is mentally disordered, poor fellow, go easy on him,' now some say, 'He is a damned sicko, so draw and quarter him'" (2003, 141).

Perhaps we have made some progress since the days when large crowds gathered in London to watch children being hanged for their petty crimes, but the widespread public enthusiasm for harsh "boot camps" for juvenile offenders (together with the public eagerness to charge children with crimes and punish them as if they were adults) indicates that progress has been slow. Still, there is this fairness impulse that can oppose the reciprocity inclination, and feelings of fairness have had some success in limiting and sometimes overcoming the retributive intuition.

Unfortunately, activating the fairness intuition is not as easy as firing up the retributive impulse. We immediately feel a strong desire for revenge against Robert Harris for his brutal murders. The feeling that such revenge might be unfair must await knowledge of his brutalizing childhood. On the other hand, that slower response may be grounds for hope: Our understanding of the conditions and circumstances that shape character and behavior has been very slow in coming and is certainly not widespread. As that knowledge grows and spreads, the space for effective deployment of the fairness intuition may well increase.

As understanding increases and our sense of fairness comes up against our sense of retributive rightness, we are more likely to get what Haidt calls the phenomenon of "moral dumbfounding" (Haidt and Hersh 2001; Haidt and Bjorklund 2008, 197): we have conflicting moral inclinations that leave us "dumbfounded"; that is, they leave us temporarily in a state of indecision. Under those circumstances (according to Haidt and other social intuitionists), our powers of rational deliberation (which usually operate only for rationalization or justification of choices made on the basis of immediate "intuition") can actually have a powerful effect. Because deeper understanding is on the side of rejecting moral responsibility, there is a significant opening for genuine deliberation to push us out of our moral responsibility myopia and toward the acceptance of an alternative perspective.

There is evidence that our sense of fairness *can* sometimes overcome our sense of righteous retribution. That evidence can be seen more clearly in a comparison between, on the one hand, cultures in which retributive impulses are considered suspect (and are carefully controlled), and on the other, cultures in which retributive impulses are celebrated (and exploited by politicians and tabloids). Consider two horrible cases in which children murdered other children, one in Great Britain and the other in Norway. In 1993, two ten-year-old boys abducted and murdered a two-year-old child, James Bulger, near Liverpool. The British media went into a feeding frenzy, with each tabloid trying to top the others with headlines about "Evil Freaks of Human Nature." British politicians pandered to the retributive fervor, demanding that the two be tried as adults and expressing enthusiastic approval when the ten-year-old children received life sentences with a minimum fifteen years of imprisonment. A year later, in Norway, five-year-old Silje Marie Redergård was killed by three six-year-old boys. Though horrified at this brutal act, the response in Norway was very different. As David Green notes, the Norwegian media took an alternative approach to that of the British tabloids:

In contrast, the dominant theme used to explain the Redergård homicide in the Norwegian press is the tragic accident or the "all victims" theme, which holds fast to the notion that all parties in this case were victims, including the killers themselves. Silje, of course, is a victim of violent abuse at the hands of three playmates, but the perpetrators as well are constructed as victims of their own innocence (innocent of the knowledge of what damage their violent behaviour could bring and innocent victims of violent television). One is a victim of child welfare services that failed to intervene properly when his mother asked for help with his aggressive behaviour in the past. (2008, 202–203)

Furthermore, politicians did not suggest and the public did not demand that children be subjected to harsh punishment. Indeed, as Green states,

"Norwegians seem culturally incapable of accepting that children under 15 should be prosecuted as adults or that any child should be in prison" (2008, 209). That is not to suggest that Norwegians do not feel a desire for retributive punishment or that they have abolished moral responsibility and eliminated prisons. But it does make clear that cultural forces can have a profound effect on the retributive "intuitive" response, either reducing its strength, or holding it in check, or both.

As Green—drawing on the research of Cavadino and Dignan (2006a, 2006b)—notes, "Appetites for punitive responses to crime are highest in those countries where *neo-liberalism* dominates" (2008, 214). Cavadino and Dignan contrast *neoliberal* societies (such as Margaret Thatcher's Great Britain and Ronald Reagan's United States) with *social democratic corporatism*, found in Sweden and Finland. The former are fiercely individualistic:

The general ethos is one of *individualism* rather than communitarianism or collectivism. Under neo-liberalism, the welfare state is minimalist and residual, consisting mainly of means-tested welfare benefits, entitlement to which is often heavily stigmatized. Consequently, the status and economic well-being of citizens is heavily dependent on how well they can succeed in the (free) marketplace of the economy.

Although social relationships in neo-liberal societies are formally egalitarian, this economic system results in extremely marked (and currently still widening) income differentials. This material inequality, combined with a lack of social entitlements afforded to individuals as of right, results in the *social exclusion* of many who find themselves marginalized by the markets in which they cannot compete effectively or afford to operate, particularly the labour and housing markets. . . . The term "social exclusion" is not merely a synonym for poverty, but is used to refer to the denial of full *effective* rights of citizenship and participation in civil, political, and social life. (Cavadino and Dignan 2006a, 440, 442)

One advantage of getting past moral responsibility is the opening it affords for getting past "neoliberalism," with its emphasis on individualism and its reliance on harsh punishment. It is no accident that these go together: moral responsibility requires that we hold the individual responsible and that we largely ignore the systemic causal factors that shape character and conduct, so the only means available of social control—because the real causes are off limits—is severe punishment, which causes more social damage (by damaging those punished, pulling apart families and communities, and neglecting social problems), ratcheting the problem higher and harsher. Prison sentences become longer and prisons become larger. Fewer resources remain to correct the underlying problems

(problems that are studiously ignored, in any case). I am not suggesting that those who advocate for moral responsibility are law-and-order zealots or that they are unconcerned with social programs and social inequities. But moral responsibility carries with it baggage that its proponents may not have considered. For example, if almost everyone—from very privileged to severely disadvantaged—can ultimately arrive at the plateau of moral responsibility (at which remaining differences in developed abilities are ruled irrelevant), then obviously our society offers everyone a fair opportunity for success, and problems of substandard education, hazardous living conditions, and lack of adequate nutrition and health care can be ignored. And if everyone has miraculous powers of self-transformation that can triumph over any personal history—as standard libertarian theories insist—then brutal childhood social conditions are irrelevant.

The Norwegian experience demonstrates that it is possible to develop a culture in which fairness can make significant progress against retribution: retributive impulses can be modified and controlled by cultural forces. Empirical study can discover the key cultural factors that inhibit retributive responses (including means of fostering the deeper understanding that checks retributive inclinations). We can, after all, learn impulse control, and if we take seriously the need to control our retributive impulses—which we have learned to control, though they are still felt when someone accidentally harms us—then there is no reason that such impulses cannot be effectively mastered, especially in a culture that promotes such mastery (as opposed to an *honor culture* in which small slights demand murderous revenge). This is not to suggest that in order to gain better control of retributive impulses we *merely* need to change our culture from "neoliberal" to "social democratic corporatist"; the point is rather that the retributive impulse or intuition is not immutable, that it is subject to modification by cultural forces, and that the idea of changing our retributive/moral responsibility system is not mere philosophical musing. Changing from the moral responsibility system will not be easy, but—as the British-Norwegian study indicates—not all cultures are locked into the retributive impulse. If the strike-back intuition cannot be eliminated, it can at least be held in check, and we can learn to view it and react to it quite differently.

Finally, there is evidence that the grip of Haidt's moral "intuitions" can loosen. In some of his most interesting work, Haidt describes the contrast between those cultures (and sometimes between different people within the same culture) that have differing sets of moral intuitions: some cultures (and some people) downgrade particular "moral intuitions" into nonmoral preferences. Specifically, the "moral intuitions" associated with purity/sanctity and ingroup/outgroup vary widely, with some cultures and people demoting them from moral obligations to the status of personal preferences. As Haidt and Bjorklund note:

American liberals in particular seem quite uncomfortable with virtues and institutions built on these foundations, because they often lead to jingoistic patriotism (ingroup), legitimization of inequality (authority), and rules or practices that treat certain ethnic groups as contagious (purity, as in the segregation laws of the American South). Liberals value tolerance and diversity, and generally want moral regulation limited to rules that protect individuals, particularly the poor and vulnerable, and that safeguard justice, fairness, and equal rights. Conservatives, on the other hand, want a thicker moral world in which many aspects of behavior, including interpersonal relations, sexual relations, and life-or-death decisions are subject to rules that go beyond direct harm and legal rights. Liberals are horrified by what they see as a repressive, hierarchical theocracy that conservatives want to impose on them. Conservatives are horrified by what they see as the "anything goes" moral chaos that liberals have created, which many see as a violation of the will of God, and as a threat to their efforts to instill virtues in their children. (2008, 209–210; see also Haidt 2008)

Failing to honor God (*my* God) was a moral wrong for most cultures and still is for some, but in many cultures the moral pendulum has swung so far that religious tolerance is the virtue and religious bigotry the vice. Not so long ago in our culture, homosexual relations were a crime, and the crime was punished severely as an abominable moral wrong. Now (at least in large sections of our culture), homosexuality is a matter of easy acceptance or even a cheerful recognition of the cultural enrichment diversity brings, and although there are no doubt those who still feel a deep aversion, it is likely that they are on their way to considering it personally offensive but not a question of morality. The same pattern occurred with the profound moral wrong of interracial marriage; once criminalized and regarded as a horrific moral offense, the change in only a few decades has been remarkable: in much of our culture, one is more likely to face moral censure for expressing disapproval of interracial marriage than for marrying interracially. Oral sex was once a serious moral wrong in American culture, and although it may not have joined the catalog of virtues, it has certainly left the category of vices. In fact, it is not only specific cases within the "clean/unclean" intuition that can change; the basic intuitive category of clean/unclean can change from a moral judgment to a matter of nonmoral preference (for many—if not most—people in Europe and North America, sexual practices and preferences are no longer moral issues because that entire clean/unclean category is no longer a moral category). Whether the reciprocity/retributive intuition is as malleable as some others is not clear, but because it is somewhat counterbalanced by the intuition of fairness, and considering the fact that at least some modifications in our retributive impulses *have* occurred (especially responses to accidental harms), the possibility of significantly altering our moral responsibility orientation is not foreclosed by deep psychological commitments. Clearly, we can remove some of these basic impulses from the moral realm: we may still feel them, but we feel less inclined to count them as moral reactions. Indeed, we can even *reverse* them: racial and ethnic prejudice is now widely recognized as a moral flaw rather than regarded as a virtue.

The retributive impulse will not go away, but it may be held in check and strongly counterbalanced by cultural forces and the counterweight of the sense of fairness that develops and strengthens along with knowledge. As we overcome ignorance of how our characters and behavior are shaped, we gain strength in the struggle to master our powerful retributive impulses. The goal is to recognize the retributive impulse—and the moral responsibility system that celebrates it—as a problem rather than a solution. Righteous retribution is generated by our darkest (but not necessarily deepest) visceral impulses and fostered by our ignorance. Certainly, we will continue to feel the strike-back response; it does not follow that we must continue to feel it as a basic *moral* impulse.

Conclusion

When Gary Watson (1987b) shows us the brutal murders that Robert Harris committed, we feel a strong sense that Harris deserves retribution. When Watson turns to show us the dreadful conditions that shaped Harris, we feel that punishment is unfair, and we are brought to a stop: we are dumbfounded, Haidt would say. Under those conditions, we can stop and deliberate, genuinely deliberate, and consider both sides. And that is the opening for defeating our powerful retributive "intuition": look carefully at the causes, and the powerful feeling can be neutralized. This neutralization is why Dennett refuses to look carefully—we are on the plateau, it doesn't matter how we got there, and why Moore refuses to look *carefully* at Herrin (many others had "similar" backgrounds and did not murder), why the courts cannot look carefully at Patricia Hearst, and why Smilansky (2000) insists on an illusion that blocks such scrutiny. I am not suggesting intellectual dishonesty; rather, astute philosophers sense (and Smilansky clearly recognizes) that if moral responsibility is to survive, we must block careful study of deeper causes. But it is that study which gives us hope for dealing with this problem and effecting change. The answer is in deeper scrutiny and better education and broader understanding, not in illusion. One side wants deeper understanding, and the other requires myopic illusion; is it really difficult to decide which is more promising?

Even if it is accepted that moral responsibility is a lot more trouble than its very dubious worth, it is tempting to counsel: go slow. Trying to change something this deep and important must be a gradual process. In fact, as already noted, there has been a slow chipping away at moral responsibility: we are less inclined to blame and punish children or the insane or for accidents. So perhaps we might take it slowly and allow the gradual increase and dissemination of knowledge to bring about the steady curtailment of moral responsibility, until at last it withers away entirely. The denial of moral responsibility requires a dramatic change in perspective, and such dramatic changes have often gone slowly. The Copernican Revolution was initially embraced by only a few, and they were brutally persecuted by both Catholics and Protestants; rather than jumping all the way to belief in the motion of the Earth, Tycho Brahe's system—with the Earth stationary at the center of the universe, the Sun in orbit around the Earth, and all the other planets in orbit around the Sun—became the dominant view, until finally the Copernican theory gained general acceptance. Darwin's views were widely condemned, and compromise positions—humans evolved, but as part of God's purposeful plan; God created different species during different eras, saving the best for last—helped pave the way for its wider acceptance. But though the mitigation of the worst moral responsibility abuses (such as the hanging of children) is certainly welcome, it is doubtful that a gradualist approach to the abolition of moral responsibility is a plausible path. As already noted, "excuse-extensionism" (decreasing the scope of moral responsibility judgments by increasing the scope of insanity

and incompetence excuses)—though a legitimate path to *mitigation*—is a
failed path to moral responsibility *abolition*, for it plays into the worst fears
of those who resist the rejection of all moral responsibility: the fear that
denying moral responsibility is based on excusing those who are severely
flawed. Thus *universal* denial of moral responsibility entails the universal
denial of rationality, moral judgments, deliberation, legitimate reactive
attitudes. Dennett's (2003) fear of "creeping exculpation" is fear that
extending excuses will lead to denial of all significant human rational
capacities and to the universal attribution of incompetence.

From the perspective of the moral responsibility system, the abolition
of moral responsibility means universal ascription of derangement. Thus
the *universal* rejection of moral responsibility cannot be accomplished
through internal reform, but only by adopting a different system altogether. The Copernican Revolution ultimately required recognizing that
the Earth moves, and without that recognition, the benefits of the Copernican system could not emerge. The abolition of moral responsibility
ultimately requires adopting a different system of thought in which moral
responsibility claims and ascriptions make no sense, and the advantages
of that system—in opening the way to clearer and deeper scrutiny of
human behavior—cannot occur as long as the moral responsibility obscu-
rity remains in place. The sun still appears to rise for a Copernican, and
the hand still appears designed to a Darwinian, and the feeling of moral
responsibility is still felt by a moral responsibility abolitionist, but all of
those are phenomena to be explained away by the new perspective, not
basic facts that control our inquiries.

Saul Smilansky acknowledges that overcoming illusions is an important
step in developing better ways of seeing and living in and gaining understanding of our world: "In a way, much of the story of the growth of
human knowledge, and possibly of human progress, can be told in terms
of the overcoming of comfortable illusions—from Copernicus to Darwin
and to Freud, many of our pleasant illusions about ourselves and the world
have been realized as such" (2000, 295). But unlike those rejected illusions,
Smilansky regards the illusion of moral responsibility (and of the libertarian power of free will which he acknowledges as essential for moral responsibility) as indispensable: "A striking outcome of shattering the illusions
in the free will case is the very realization of our inability to live without
substantial illusion. Important illusions have been successfully confronted

before, but perhaps here we have reached bedrock, where the scope of our illusions defies us: we confront here the illusoriness of the belief that we can live, in practice, totally without illusion" (296).

It is a mark of the deep embeddedness of our belief in moral responsibility that a very clear-sighted philosopher like Saul Smilansky can honestly recognize that moral responsibility is fundamentally incompatible with our naturalistic view (*and* is fundamentally unjust), yet still conclude that belief in libertarian-supported moral responsibility is a belief—an illusion—that we cannot live without. We can give up the illusion that we are the fixed point around which the world revolves, and we can give up the illusion that we are God's special creation, but we cannot give up the illusion of moral responsibility. That claim makes it a special illusion indeed.

As already noted (chapter 13), Smilansky's fears of what would be lost with the demise of moral responsibility are very similar to Strawson's: we could not make moral judgments, we would lose the reactive attitudes toward one another, we would lose all sense of self-respect, we would make no distinction between the innocent and the guilty, we would lose all belief in the power of reason and inquiry, we would regard ourselves and others as mere objects. Those claims have already been examined, and—I hope—those concerns have been eliminated or at least allayed. The current concern is the nature of the moral responsibility illusion, its strength, the forces that hold it in place, and what is actually involved in retaining or rejecting it.

First and foremost, Smilansky believes that rejecting the illusion of moral responsibility poses severe hazards: "Serious harm to the recognition of moral requirements and to moral motivation can be envisaged here" (2000, 287). That the demise of moral responsibility should be celebrated rather than feared has already been argued, but set aside the success or failure of those arguments; the current point is what Smilansky correctly acknowledges to be the awful price to be paid for keeping that supposed threat at bay: the price of continuing to maintain the illusion of moral responsibility with its profoundly unjust practices, and the necessity of accepting that deep absurdity: "What could be more absurd than the moral necessity of belief in the justness of deeply unjust practices, practices that ought largely to continue and flourish?" (279). Smilansky suggests that we must maintain belief in moral responsibility because there are "fundamentals of morality, justice, and human self-respect at stake" (267). But maintaining the moral responsibility illusion is not a means of preserving justice, but of preserving *in*justice. The deep truth that the moral responsibility illusion hides is that *no one justly deserves* punishment.

The moral responsibility illusion is purchased at the price of blocking deeper inquiry into causes of both good and bad behavior: the price of not discovering ways to enlarge and enhance the genuine free behavior of human animals. What do we buy at that price? We get an illusion that locks in place a system in which those who receive the advantages—of a supportive family and community, of excellent educational opportunities, perhaps genetic advantages—believe that they justly deserve their special benefits and privileges (their large share of the goods handed out by distributive justice) and in which those who suffer the disadvantages (of less educational opportunity, a less supportive early environment, fewer advantageous connections) and who wind up with significantly less in the "justice" distribution and significantly more in criminal justice retribution are forced to accept their "just deserts" (or suffer ostracism from the human community). No doubt this illusion offers some benefits to the privileged, but broader benefits are more doubtful. And even for those who are on the privileged side of the criminal and distributive justice systems, the benefits of the moral responsibility system are outweighed by the costs. After all, living with illusion is not easy; furthermore, the myopia that holds the moral responsibility system in place blocks all of us from clearer understanding of human behavior and of ways to expand and strengthen our own natural freedom and forces us to live in a culture that employs grossly inefficient and ill-informed means of dealing with the threat of criminal behavior. In short, we pay a high price for maintaining an illusion of moral responsibility that is of little benefit for anyone, a profound harm to many, and a considerable detriment to all.

Clearly, there are those—like van Inwagen ("to deny the existence of moral responsibility . . . would be absurd")—who would not give up belief in moral responsibility under any circumstances. But although some would never enter a system that denies moral responsibility, such a system is not a philosophical fantasy. The struggle to eliminate moral responsibility will be an uphill slog, but it is not the philosophical pipe dream that P. F. Strawson imagined it to be. Strawson considered the possibility of shrinking the range of moral responsibility until it disappeared while remaining *within* the basic assumptions of the moral responsibility system. Such a system *would* be cold and dreadful—devoid of rich reactive attitudes and deprived of competent control—and we could not live intelligent emotionally satisfying human lives in such an austere environment. But the interesting question is whether a competing naturalistic *system* that rejects the moral responsibility axiom is possible. Such a system would not have the stark cold "objective perspective" that Strawson foretold, but the question remains: is it a genuine possibility? In such a system of moral responsibility abolition, we would not eliminate the strike back attitude, but like racism, we would treat it as a problem, rather than celebrate it as a virtue; we could learn to control retributive impulses and lessen the harm they cause, and we could gain a deeper understanding of how our characters are shaped and our behavior elicited. That understanding is both the greatest threat to belief in moral responsibility and the greatest benefit of its abolition.

Notes

1 Moral Responsibility

1. Susan Wolf makes a similar distinction between the questions asked in "everyday contexts" (such as in the criminal courts) when moral responsibility is assumed and the questions philosophers ask concerning "whether, and if so why, any of us are ever responsible for anything at all" (1987, 47).

2. Richard Double (1991) explores this issue in great depth and detail.

2 The Basic Argument against Moral Responsibility

1. The psychological literature on self-efficacy is enormous; a good guide to the literature can be found in a book by a researcher, Albert Bandura (1997), who has been at the forefront of the research into self-efficacy (and it should be noted that Bandura would not concur with my conclusion concerning moral responsibility). Research on self-efficacy ranges across many cultures and focuses on a wide range of capacities. Some of the studies can become very narrowly defined: for example, self-efficacy of patients in managing diabetes (Rosenstock 1985). But these are nonetheless very important studies, for a patient's sense of self-efficacy for managing a chronic illness such as diabetes may be quite different from sense of self-efficacy for managing a short-term illness; if the diabetic patient is weak in sense of self-efficacy, that is a serious impediment to effective treatment and management of the disease and should be addressed by the medical team (Aljasem et al. 2001).

3 Rescuing Free Will from Moral Responsibility

1. There are rare exceptions to this consensus. Saul Smilansky agrees that "the free will problem" is not essentially connected to moral responsibility, though on somewhat different grounds: "A person may well also wonder whether, given determinism, his actions, his achievements, and indeed his life have any meaning, even if he cares very little about morality. Hence the free will problem is not essentially

about morality, let alone moral responsibility" (2005, 248). Bernard Williams seems to agree that even if we must "revise our ethical practices"—in particular blaming and holding morally responsible—that depend on a libertarian concept of free will, we could still have a workable concept of free will: "If the Plurality Principle [of open alternatives] fails for metaphysical reasons, we may have to revise our ethical practices, but we could still be left with functioning psychological concepts of choice and intentional action" (1995, 9).

2. The research into sensation-seeking—and into the strong inclination of humans and many other species for finding, exploring, and preserving open alternatives— stretches back into the early twentieth century, and it remains an area of vigorous biological and psychological study. A small sample of this fascinating literature might include Tolman 1925; Glanzer 1953; Sackett 1972; Suomi and Harlow 1976; Catania and Sagvolden 1980; Zuckerman 1983, 2007; Mason 1993.

4   Hierarchical Free Will and Natural Authenticity

1. Gary Watson develops "brave new world" cases to challenge Frankfurt's claim that the willing addict has free will, noting ways in which free will can be impaired even though one identifies with and approves of the impairment, and he emphasizes an important point: "It is a mistake to think that it matters whether this impairment has a natural or human origin" (1987a, 152). It is also worth noting just how mundane such a shaping process can be.

2. B. F. Skinner (1971, 39) warns of the danger of "happy slaves" who are so deeply conditioned to slavery that they embrace slavery and make no efforts to escape and also suggests methods of making people more aware of such powerful and dangerous covert control, of encouraging them to escape such forces, and of helping them gain greater freedom. Some may find it strange to think of Skinner—the arch enemy of "free will"—promoting individual freedom. But in fact the "free will" that Skinner argues against is libertarian free will; he is committed to the protection and enhancement of natural compatibilist free will.

6   Taking Responsibility

1. Virginia A. Sharpe draws a somewhat similar distinction in her work on medical ethics, and it is interesting to note that—although she does not cite Hart—she also finds the concept of "roles" important in drawing the distinction:

Moral responsibility can be taken in a retrospective or a prospective sense. The backward-looking or retrospective sense is linked to practices of praising and blaming and is the basis for theories of moral assessment. It is typically captured in expressions such as . . . , "He made a mistake and should be held responsible for it." The forward-looking or prospective sense of responsibility, by contrast, is linked to theories and practices of goal setting and moral deliberation and as such is central to theories of moral reasoning. It may be expressed in phrases such as, "As a parent, I am responsible for the welfare of my child." . . . . In distinguishing these two senses of responsibility, it is also important to note that the backward-looking sense tends to have an individual as its object, while the forward-looking sense contextualizes responsibility as it relates to the particular roles a person may occupy. (2000, 183–184)

2. There is an enormous literature documenting the psychological benefits of a sense of control. Key contributions to this research are described in Bandura 1997, Rodin 1986, and Wallston 1993. There is a summary of the relevant research in Waller 2004.

3. Perhaps the clearest evidence of the harmful effects of loss of a sense of control was discovered inadvertently, in the follow-up to a study conducted in a long-term-care facility. In the original study (Schulz 1976), residents gained significant benefits from exercising control over when visits from area students would occur. In a follow-up to that study (Schulz and Hanusa 1978), it was discovered that when the original study ended (and residents no longer had any control over student visits), residents soon felt a severe sense of loss of effective control, coupled with (when compared with a control group) significant decline in both health status and zest for life.

10 What Does Not Follow from the Denial of Moral Responsibility

1. Additional examples of the assumption that denial of moral responsibility entails denial of genuine morality can be found in Hospers 1958, Hintz 1958, and Rychlak 1979. Recent dissenters include Lawrence Blum (1980, 189), Judith Andre (1983), and Michael Otsuka (1998, 695–698).

11 The Moral Responsibility System

1. Dennett attributes the principle to Alfred Mele, but Mele (2005, 422) denies ever championing such a principle—indeed, he rejects it—but whatever the source of the principle, clearly Dennett embraces it.

13 Does Moral Responsibility Promote Respect?

1. Hannah Arendt recognizes that criminal courts must steadfastly refuse to look deeply at the causes that shaped character and behavior, but regards that refusal as one of the virtues of the system:

The simple fact of courtroom procedure in criminal cases, the sequence of accusation-defense-judgment that persists in all the varieties of legal systems and is as old as recorded history, defies all scruples and doubts—not, to be sure, in the sense that it can put them to rest, but in the sense that this particular institution rests on the assumption of personal responsibility and guilt, on the one hand, and on a belief in the functioning of conscience, on the other. . . .

It is the undeniable greatness of the judiciary that it must focus its attention on the individual person . . . even in the age of mass society where everybody is tempted to regard himself as a mere cog in some kind of machinery—be it the well-oiled machinery of some huge bureaucratic enterprise, social, political, or professional, or the chaotic, ill-adjusted chance pattern of circumstances under which we all somehow spend our lives. . . . No matter what the scientific fashions of the time may say, no matter how much they may have penetrated public opinion and hence also influenced the practitioners of the law, the institution itself defies, and must defy, them all or pass out of existence. (2003, 57–58)

References

Aljasem, Layla I., Mark Peyrot, Larry Wissow, and Richard R. Rubin. 2001. The impact of barriers and self-efficacy on self-care behaviors in type 2 diabetes. *Diabetes Educator* 27:393–404.

Andre, Judith. 1983. Nagel, Williams, and moral luck. *Analysis* 43:202–207.

Arendt, Hannah. 2003. *Responsibility and judgment*, ed. Jerome Kohn. New York: Schocken Books.

Aristotle. 350 BC/1925. *Ethica Nicomachea. The works of Aristotle*, trans. W. D. Ross, vol. 9. Oxford: Clarendon Press.

At issue: Crime and punishment. 1979. *Time*, June 4, 14–16.

Avorn, J., and E. Langer. 1982. Induced disability in nursing home patients. *Journal of the American Geriatrics Society* 30:397–400.

Bandura, Albert. 1997. *Self-efficacy: The exercise of control*. New York: W. H. Freeman.

Banziger, George, and Sharon Roush. 1983. Nursing homes for the birds: A control-relevant intervention with bird feeders. *Gerontologist* 23:527–531.

Barash, David P. 2005. Redirected aggression. CPS Working Papers No. 8:1–12.

Bargh, John A. 2008. Free will is un-natural. In *Are we free? Psychology and free will*, ed. John Baer, James C. Kaufman, and Roy F. Baumeister, 128–154. New York: Oxford University Press.

Bargh, John A., and T. L. Chartrand. 1999. The unbearable automaticity of being. *American Psychologist* 54:462–479.

Bargh, John A., and Melissa J. Ferguson. 2000. Beyond behaviorism: On the automaticity of higher mental processes. *Psychological Bulletin* 126:925–945.

Baron, R. A. 1997. The sweet smell of . . . helping: Effects of pleasant ambient fragrance on prosocial behavior in shopping malls. *Personality and Social Psychology Bulletin* 23:498–503.

Baron, R. A., and M. I. Bronfen. 1994. A whiff of reality: Empirical evidence concerning the effects of pleasant fragrances on work-related behavior. *Journal of Applied Social Psychology* 24:1179–1203.

Barrett, William. 1958. Determinism and novelty. In *Determinism and freedom in the age of modern science*, ed. Sidney Hook, 46–54. New York: New York University Press.

Beauvoir, Simone de. 1947/1948. *The ethics of ambiguity*, trans. Bernard Frechtman. New York: Philosophical Library.

Bennett, Jonathan. 1980. Accountability. In *Philosophical subjects*, ed. Zak van Stratten, 14–47. Oxford: Clarendon Press.

Bernstein, Mark. 2005. Can we ever be really, truly, ultimately, free? *Midwest Studies in Philosophy* 29:1–12.

Berzonsky, M. D., and C. Sullivan. 1992. Social-cognitive aspects of identity style: Need for cognition, experiential openness, and introspection. *Journal of Adolescent Research* 7:140–155.

Blum, Lawrence A. 1980. *Friendship, altruism and morality*. London: Routledge & Kegan Paul.

Bowers, K. S. 1968. Pain, anxiety, and perceived control. *Journal of Consulting and Clinical Psychology* 32:596–602.

Braithwaite, John. 1999. Restorative justice: Assessing optimistic and pessimistic accounts. *Crime and Justice: A Review of Research* 25:1–110.

Braithwaite, John. 2002. *Restorative justice and response regulation*. Oxford: Oxford University Press.

Brasil-Neto, J. P., A. Pascual-Leone, J. Valls-Solé, L. G. Cohen, and M. Hallett. 1992. Focal transcranial magnet stimulation and response bias in a forced choice task. *Journal of Neurology, Neurosurgery, and Psychiatry* 55:964–966.

Brown, Marshall. 1899. *Wit and humor of bench and bar*. Chicago: T. H. Flood.

Butler, Samuel. 1872. *Erewhon, or, Over the range*. London: Trubner & Co.

Cacioppo, J. T., and R. E. Petty. 1982. The need for cognition. *Journal of Personality and Social Psychology* 42:116–131.

Cacioppo, J. T., R. E. Petty, J. A. Feinstein, and W. B. G. Jarvis. 1996. Dispositional differences in cognitive motivation: The life and times of individuals varying in need for cognition. *Psychological Bulletin* 119:197–253.

Campbell, C. A. 1957. *On selfhood and godhood*. London: George Allen & Unwin, Ltd.

Catania, Charles A., and Terje Sagvolden. 1980. Preference for free choice over forced choice in pigeons. *Journal of the Experimental Analysis of Behavior* 34:77–86.

Cavadino, Michael, and James Dignan. 2006a. Penal policy and political economy. *Criminology & Criminal Justice* 6:435–456.

Cavadino, Michael, and James Dignan. 2006b. *Penal systems: A comparative approach.* London: Sage Publications.

Chisholm, Roderick M. 1982. Human freedom and the self. In *Free will*, ed. Gary Watson, 24–35. New York: Oxford University Press.

Cicero, Marcus Tullius. 44 BCE/1923. On *divination*, trans. W. A. Falconer. In *On old age, On friendship, On divination.* Cambridge, MA: Loeb Classical Library of Harvard University Press.

Clarke, Randolph. 2005. On an argument for the impossibility of moral responsibility. *Midwest Studies in Philosophy* 29:13–24.

Cohen, A. R., E. Stotland, and D. M. Wolfe. 1955. An experimental investigation of need for cognition. *Journal of Abnormal and Social Psychology* 51:291–294.

Copleston, F. C. 1965. The existence of God: A debate. In *A modern introduction to philosophy*, rev. ed., ed. Paul Edwards and Arthur Pap. New York: Free Press.

Copp, David. 2003. "Ought" implies "can," blameworthiness, and the principle of alternate possibilities. In *Moral responsibility and alternative possibilities: Essays on the importance of alternative possibilities*, ed. David Widerker and Michael McKenna, 265–299. Burlington, VT: Ashgate.

Corlett, J. Angelo. 2006. *Responsibility and punishment*, 3rd ed. Dordrecht, The Netherlands: Springer.

Damasio, Antonio R. 1994. *Descartes' error: Emotion, reason, and the human brain.* New York: G. P. Putnam's Sons.

Darley, J. M., and C. D. Batson. 1973. From Jerusalem to Jericho: A study of situational and dispositional variables in helping behavior. *Journal of Personality and Social Psychology* 267:100–108.

Davis, Paul. 2002. On apologies. *Journal of Applied Philosophy* 19:169–173.

Delgado, José M. R. 1969. *Physical control of the mind: Toward a psychocivilized society.* New York: Harper and Row.

Dennett, Daniel. 1978. *Brainstorms.* Montgomery, VT: Bradford Books.

Dennett, Daniel. 1984. *Elbow room.* Cambridge, MA: MIT Press.

Dennett, Daniel. 2003. *Freedom evolves.* New York: Viking.

Dennett, Daniel. 2008. Some observations on the psychology of thinking about free will. In *Are we free? Psychology and free will*, ed. John Baer, James C. Kaufman, and Roy F. Baumeister, 248–259. New York: Oxford University Press.

Devins, G. M., Y. M. Binik, D. J. Hollomy, P. E. Barre, and R. D. Guttmann. 1981. Helplessness and depression in end-stage renal disease. *Journal of Abnormal Psychology* 90:531–545.

Devins, G. M., Y. M. Binik, T. A. Hutchinson, D. J. Hollomby, P. E. Barre, and R. D. Guttmann. 1984. The emotional impact of end-stage renal disease: Importance of patients' perception of intrusiveness and control. *International Journal of Psychiatry in Medicine* 13:327–343.

de Waal, Frans. 1982. *Chimpanzee politics: Power and sex among apes*. Baltimore: Johns Hopkins University Press.

de Waal, Frans. 1996. *Good natured: The origins of right and wrong in humans and other animals*. Cambridge, MA: Harvard University Press.

Dickens, Charles. 1843. *A Christmas Carol*. London: Chapman and Hall.

Doris, John M. 2002. *Lack of character: Personality and moral behavior*. Cambridge, UK: Cambridge University Press.

Dostoyevsky, F. 1864/1961. *Notes from Underground*, trans. Andrew R. MacAndrew. New York: New American Library.

Double, Richard. 1991. *The non-reality of free will*. New York: Oxford University Press.

Double, Richard. 2002. The moral hardness of libertarianism. *Philo* 5:226–234.

Dworkin, Gerald. 1988. *The theory and practice of autonomy*. Cambridge, UK: Cambridge University Press.

Eliot, T. S. 1943. *Four quartets*. New York: Harcourt.

Epictetus. 107/1865. *The works of Epictetus*, trans. Thomas Wentworth Higginson. Boston: Little, Brown.

Epstein, Helen. 2009. America's prisons: Is there hope? *New York Review of Books* 11 (June):30–32.

Feinberg, Joel. 2003. Evil. In *Problems at the roots of law: Essays in legal and political theory*, 125–192. New York: Oxford University Press.

Fischer, John Martin. 1994. *The metaphysics of free will: An essay on control*. Oxford: Blackwell.

Fischer, John Martin. 2006a. *My Way: Essays on moral responsibility*. New York: Oxford University Press.

Fischer, John Martin. 2006b. The cards that are dealt you. *Journal of Ethics* 10: 107–129.

Fletcher, F. J. O., P. Danilovics, G. Fernandez, D. Peterson, and G. D. Reeder. 1986. Attributional complexity: An individual difference measure. *Journal of Personality and Social Psychology* 51:875–884.

Frankfurt, Harry G. 1969. Alternate possibilities and moral responsibility. *Journal of Philosophy* 66:829–839.

Frankfurt, Harry G. 1971. Freedom of the will and the concept of a person. *Journal of Philosophy* 68:5–20.

Frankfurt, Harry G. 1973. Coercion and moral responsibility. In *Essays on freedom of action*, ed. Ted Honderich, 65–86. London: Routledge & Kegan Paul.

Frankfurt, Harry G. 1975. Three concepts of free action. *Aristotelian Society Proceedings Supplementary* 49:113–125.

French, Peter. 2001. *The virtues of vengeance*. Lawrence, KS: University of Kansas Press.

Gaylin, Willard. 1982. *The killing of Bonnie Garland*. New York: Simon and Schuster.

Gill, Kathleen. 2000. The moral functions of an apology. *Philosophical Forum* 31: 11–27.

Gilligan, James. 2001. *Preventing violence*. New York: Thames & Hudson.

Ginet, Carl. 1990. *On action*. Cambridge, UK: Cambridge University Press.

Ginet, Carl. 1997. Freedom, responsibility and agency. *Journal of Ethics* 1:374–380.

Glannon, Walter. 1998. Responsibility, alcoholism and liver transplantation. *Journal of Medicine and Philosophy* 23:31–49.

Glanzer, M. 1953. Stimulus satiation: An exploration of spontaneous alteration and related phenomena. *Psychological Review* 60:257–268.

Golding, Martin. 1984–1985. Forgiveness and regret. *Philosophical Forum* 16: 121–137.

Gomberg, P. 1978. Free will as ultimate responsibility. *American Philosophical Quarterly* 15:205–211.

Govier, Trudy, and Wilhelm Verwoerd. 2002. The promise and pitfalls of apology. *Journal of Social Philosophy* 33:67–82.

Green, David A. 2008. Suitable vehicles: Framing blame and justice when children kill a child. *Crime Media Culture* 4:197–220.

Haidt, Jonathan. 2001. The emotional dog and its rational tail: A social intuitionist approach to moral judgment. *Psychological Review* 108:814–834.

Haidt, Jonathan. 2008. Morality. *Perspectives on Psychological Science* 3:65–72.

Haidt, Jonathan, and Fredrik Bjorklund. 2008. Social intuitionists answer six questions about morality. In *Moral psychology*. Vol. 2, *The cognitive science of morality*, ed. W. Sinnott-Armstrong, 181–217. Cambridge, MA: MIT Press.

Haidt, Jonathan, and M. A. Hersh. 2001. Sexual morality: The cultures and reasons of liberals and conservatives. *Journal of Applied Social Psychology* 31:191–221.

Haji, Ishtiyaque. 2000a. Control requirements for moral appraisals: An asymmetry. *Journal of Ethics* 4:351–356.

Haji, Ishtiyaque. 2000b. Excerpts from Ishtiyaque Haji's discussion with members of the audience. *Journal of Ethics* 4:368–381.

Hammar, N., L. Alfredsson, and J. V. Johnson. 1998. Job strain, social support at work, and incidence of myocardial infarction. *Occupational and Environmental Medicine* 55:548–553.

Haney, C., W. Banks, and P. Zimbardo. 1973. Interpersonal dynamics of a simulated prison. *International Journal of Criminology and Penology* 1:69–97.

Haney, Craig, and Philip Zimbardo. 1977. The socialization into criminality: On becoming a prisoner and a guard. In *Law, justice, and the individual in society: Psychological and legal issues*, ed. J. Tapp and F. Levine, 198–223. New York: Holt, Rinehart, and Winston.

Haney, Craig, and Philip Zimbardo. 1998. The past and future of U.S. prison policy: Twenty-five years after the Stanford prison experiment. *American Psychologist* 53:709–727.

Harris, Don, and Helen C. Muir, eds. 2005. *Contemporary issues in human factors and aviation safety*. Aldershot: Ashgate.

Hart, H. L. A. 1968. *Punishment and responsibility*. Oxford: Clarendon Press.

Hieronymi, Pamela. 2004. The force and fairness of blame. *Philosophical Perspectives* 18:115–148.

Hill, H. F., C. R. Chapman, J. A. Kornell, L. C. Saeger, and C. Benedetti. 1990. Self-administration of morphine in bone marrow transplant patients reduces drug requirement. *Pain* 40:121–129.

Hintz, Howard. 1958. Some further reflections on moral responsibility. In *Determinism and freedom in the age of modern science*, ed. Sidney Hook, 176–179. New York: New York University Press.

Hocutt, Max. 1992. A review of Bruce Waller's *Freedom without Responsibility*. *Behaviorism* 20:71–76.

Holbach, Paul Henri Thiry, Baron de. 1770/1970. *The system of nature*, trans. H. D. Robinson. New York: Burt Franklin.

Hospers, John. 1952. Free will and psychoanalysis. In *Readings in ethical theory*, ed. Wilfrid Sellars and John Hospers, 560–575. New York: Appleton-Century-Crofts.

Hospers, John. 1958. What means this freedom? In *Determinism and freedom in the age of modern science*, ed. Sidney Hook, 126–142. New York: New York University Press.

Hsieh, Chang-Chi, and M. D. Pugh. 1993. Poverty, income inequality, and violent crime: A meta-analysis of recent aggregate data studies. *Criminal Justice Review* 18:182–202.

Hume, David. 1748/2000. *An enquiry concerning human understanding*. Oxford: Clarendon Press.

Isen, A. M., and P. F. Levin. 1972. Effect of feeling good on helping: Cookies and kindness. *Journal of Personality and Social Psychology* 21:384–388.

Jacobs, Jonathan. 2001. *Choosing character: Responsibility for virtue and vice*. Ithaca, NY: Cornell University Press.

Jacobson, J. W., J. A. Mulick, and A. A. Schwartz. 1995. A history of facilitated communication: Science, pseudoscience, and anti-science. *American Psychologist* 50:750–765.

James, William. 1890. *Principles of psychology*. Boston: Henry Holt.

James, William. 1897. The dilemma of determinism. In *The will to believe and other essays in popular philosophy*, 145–183. New York: Longmans, Green & Co.

Johnstone, Gerry, ed. 2003. *A restorative justice reader*. Cullompton, Devon, UK: Willan Publishing.

Kahan, Dan M. 1998a. Punishment incommensurability. *Buffalo Criminal Law Review* 1:691–709.

Kahan, Dan M. 1998b. The anatomy of disgust in criminal law. *Michigan Law Review* 96:1621–1657.

Kane, Robert. 1985. *Free will and values*. Albany: State University of New York Press.

Kane, Robert. 1996. *The significance of free will*. New York: Oxford University Press.

Kane, Robert. 2002. Free will: New directions for an ancient problem. In *Free Will*, ed. Robert Kane, 222–248. Malden, MA: Blackwell.

Kane, Robert. 2007. Libertarianism. In *Four views on free will*, ed. John Martin Fischer, Robert Kane, Derk Pereboom, and Manuel Vargas, 5–43. Oxford: Blackwell Publishing.

Kant, Immanuel. 1793/1960. *Religion within the limits of reason alone*, trans. T. M. Greene, Hoyt H. Hudson, and J. R. Silber. New York: Harper & Row.

Karasek, Robert. 1979. Job decision latitude, job demands, and mental strain: Implications for job redesign. *Administrative Science Quarterly* 24:285–308.

Karasek, Robert. 1990. Lower health risk with increased job control among white collar workers. *Journal of Organizational Behavior* 11:171–185.

Karasek, R., D. Baker, F. Marxer, A. Ahlbom, and T. Theorell. 1981. Job decision latitude, job demands, and cardiovascular disease: A prospective study of Swedish men. *American Journal of Public Health* 71:694–705.

Kavanau, J. Lee. 1963. Compulsory regime and control of environment in animal behavior I. Wheel-running. *Behaviour* 20:251–281.

Kavanau, J. Lee. 1967. Behavior of captive white-footed mice. *Science* 155:1623–1639.

Kawamura, S. 1967. Aggression as studied in troops of Japanese monkeys. In *Aggression and defense, brain function*, ed. C. Clemente and D. Lindsley, 195–224. Berkeley: University of California Press.

Kelly, Erin I. 2009. Criminal justice without retribution. *Journal of Philosophy* 106:440–462.

Kohn, Linda T., Janet M. Corrigan, and Molla S. Donaldson. 2000. *To err is human: Building a safer health system*. Washington, DC: National Academy Press.

Kort, Louis F. 1975. What is an apology? *Philosophy Research Archives* 1:80–87.

Lakatos, Imré. 1970. Falsification and the methodology of scientific research programmes. In *Criticism and the growth of knowledge*, ed. Imré Lakatos and Alan Musgrave, 91–96. Cambridge, UK: Cambridge University Press.

Langer, Ellen J., and Judith Rodin. 1976. The effects of choice and enhanced personal responsibility for the aged: A field experiment in an institutional setting. *Journal of Personality and Social Psychology* 34:191–198.

Leape, Lucian L. 1994. Error in medicine. *Journal of the American Medical Association* 272:1851–1857.

Lenman, James. 2006. Compatibilism and contractualism: The possibility of moral responsibility. *Ethics* 111:7–31.

Lewis, C. S. 1971. The humanitarian theory of punishment. In *Undeceptions: Essays on theology and ethics*, 238–249. London: Curtis Brown.

Libet, Benjamin. 1999. Do we have free will? *Journal of Consciousness Studies* 6:47–57.

Libet, Benjamin, C. A. Gleason, E. W. Wright, and D. K. Pearl. 1983. Time of conscious intention to act in relation to onset of cerebral activity (readiness-potential): The unconscious initiation of a freely voluntary act. *Brain* 106:623–642.

Luther, Martin. 1525/1823. *The bondage of the will*, trans. Henry P. Cole. London: W. Simpkin and R. Marshall.

Major, John. 1992. Speech to the 1992 Conservative Party Conference, October 9. http://www.johnmajor.co.uk/page1208.html (accessed June 6, 2011).

Major, John. 1993. Interview with the editor of the *Mail* (London), Jonathan Holbrow, February 21, 8.

Marmot, M. G., G. Rose, M. Shipley, and P. J. S. Hamilton. 1978. Employment grade and coronary heart disease in British civil servants. *Journal of Epidemiology and Community Health* 32:244–249.

Mason, William A. 1993. The nature of social conflict: A psycho-ethological perspective. In *Primate social conflict*, ed. William A. Mason and Sally P. Mendoza, 13–47. Albany: State University of New York Press.

McKenna, Michael. 1998. The limits of evil and the role of moral address: A defense of Strawsonian compatibilism. *Journal of Ethics* 2:123–142.

McKenna, Michael. 2005. Where Frankfurt and Strawson meet. *Midwest Studies in Philosophy* 29:163–180.

McKenna, Michael. 2008. Ultimacy and Sweet Jane. In *Essays on free will and moral responsibility*, ed. Nick Trakakis and Daniel Cohen. Newcastle upon Tyne, UK: Cambridge Scholars Publishing.

McKenna, Michael. 2009. Compatibilism and desert: Critical comments on *Four Views on Free Will*. *Philosophical Studies* 144:3–13.

Mele, Alfred R. 1995. *Autonomous agents*. New York: Oxford University Press.

Mele, Alfred R. 2005. Dennett on freedom. *Metaphilosophy* 36:414–426.

Mele, Alfred R. 2006. *Free will and luck*. New York: Oxford University Press.

Mele, Alfred R. 2009. *Effective intentions: The power of conscious will*. New York: Oxford University Press.

Metz, Thaddeus. 2006. Judging because understanding: A defence of retributive censure. In *Judging and understanding: Essays on free will, narrative, meaning, and the ethical limits of condemnation*, ed. Pedro Alexis Tabensky, 221–240. Burlington, VT: Ashgate.

Milgram, Stanley. 1963. Behavioral study of obedience. *Journal of Abnormal and Social Psychology* 67:371–378.

Mill, John Stuart. 1865/1979. On freedom of the will. In *The collected works of John Stuart Mill*. Vol. 9, An examination of Sir William Hamilton's philosophy. Toronto: University of Toronto Press.

Mill, John Stuart. 1869. *On liberty*. London: Longman, Roberts & Green.

Miller, William Ian. 2006. *Eye for an eye*. Cambridge, UK: Cambridge University Press.

Mishel, Lawrence, Jared Bernstein, and John Schmitt. 2001. *The state of working: America 2000–2001*. Ithaca, NY: Economic Policy Institute Report.

Moore, Michael S. 1997. *Placing blame: A general theory of the criminal law*. Oxford: Oxford University Press.

Mostert, Mark P. 2001. Facilitated communication since 1995: A review of published studies. *Journal of Autism and Developmental Disorders* 31:287–313.

Morris, Allison. 2002. Critiquing the critics: A brief response to critics of restorative justice. *British Journal of Criminology* 42:596–615.

Morris, Herbert. 1968. Persons and punishment. *Monist* 52:475–501.

Morris, J., and G. T. Royale. 1988. Offering patients a choice of surgery for early breast cancer: A reduction in anxiety and depression in patients and their husbands. *Social Science & Medicine* 26:583–585.

Morse, Jennifer Roback. 2005. Rationality means being willing to say you're sorry. *Social Philosophy & Policy* 22:204–225.

Morse, Stephen J. 1996. Brain and blame. *Georgetown Law Journal* 84:527–549.

Moya, Carlos. 2006. *Moral responsibility: The ways of skepticism*. New York: Routledge.

Murphy, Jeffrie G. 1988. Hatred: A qualified defense. In *Forgiveness and Mercy*, ed. Jeffrie G. Murphy and Jean Hampton. Cambridge, UK: Cambridge University Press.

Murphy, Nancey, and Warren S. Brown. 2007. *Did my neurons make me do it? Philosophical and neurobiological perspectives on moral responsibility and free will*. New York: Oxford University Press.

Nagel, Thomas. 1979. Moral Luck. In *Mortal questions*, 24–38. Cambridge, UK: Cambridge University Press.

Nair, K. Unnikrishnan, and S. Ramnarayan. 2000. Individual differences in need for cognition and complex problem solving. *Journal of Research in Personality* 34:305–328.

National Health Service. 2001. A commitment to quality, a quest for excellence: A statement on behalf of the government, the medical profession, and the NHS. Report. London: Department of Health.

Netterstrom, B., F. E. Nielsen, T. S. Krisfensen, E. Bach, and L. Moller. 1999. Relation between job strain and myocardial infarction: A case-control study. *Occupational and Environmental Medicine* 56:339–342.

Nikkan Kogyo Shimbun. 1988. *Poka-yoke: Improving product quality by preventing defects*. Portland, OR: Productivity Press.

Nowell-Smith, P. 1948. Free will and moral responsibility. *Mind* 57:45–61.

Nozick, Robert. 1981. *Philosophical explanations*. Cambridge, MA: Harvard University Press.

O'Connor, Timothy. 2005. Freedom with a human face. *Midwest Studies in Philosophy* 29:207–227.

Olson, K., C. Camp, and D. Fuller. 1984. Curiosity and need for cognition. *Psychological Reports* 54:71–74.

Osberg, T. 1987. The convergent and discriminant validity of need for cognition scale. *Journal of Personality Assessment* 51:441–450.

Otsuka, Michael. 1998. Incompatibilism and the avoidability of blame. *Ethics* 108:685–701.

Pereboom, Derk. 2001. *Living without free will*. New York: Cambridge University Press.

Pereboom, Derk. 2007. Hard incompatibilism. In *Four views on free will*, ed. John Martin Fischer, Robert Kane, Derk Pereboom, and Manuel Vargas, 85–124. Oxford: Blackwell Publishing.

Perlmuter, L. C., R. A. Monty, and F. Chan. 1986. Choice, control, and cognitive functioning. In *The psychology of control and aging*, ed. M. M. Baltes and P. B. Baltes, 91–118. Hillsdale, NJ: Lawrence Erlbaum.

Petty, R. E., and B. G. Jarvis. 1986. An individual difference perspective on assessing cognitive processes. In *Answering questions: Methodology for determining cognitive and communicative processes in survey research*, ed. N. Schwarz and S. Sudman, 221–257. San Francisco: Jossey-Bass.

Pico della Mirandola, Giovanni. 1496/1948. Oration on the dignity of man, trans. Paul O. Kristeller. In *The Renaissance philosophy of man*, ed. Ernst Cassirer, Paul O. Kristeller, and John H. Randall, 223–254. Chicago: University of Chicago Press.

Pinker, Steven. 2008. The Fear of Determinism. In *Are we free? Psychology and free will*, ed. John Baer, James C. Kaufman, and Roy F. Baumeister, 311–324. New York: Oxford University Press.

Pisciotta, Trevor. 2008. Meaningfulness, hard determinism and objectivity. In *Essays on free will and moral responsibility*, ed. Nick Trakakis and Daniel Cohen, 71–89. Newcastle upon Tyne, UK: Cambridge Scholars Publishing.

Popper, Karl. 1959. *The logic of scientific discovery*. London: Hutchinson.

Popper, Karl. 1963. *Conjectures and refutations*. London: Routledge.

Popper, Karl. 1977. Natural selection and the emergence of mind. Lecture delivered at Darwin College, Cambridge, UK, Nov. 8, 1977.

Potegal, Michael. 1994. Aggressive arousal: The amygdala connection. In *The dynamics of aggression: Biological and social processes in dyads and groups*, ed. Michael Potegal and John F. Knutson, 73–106. Hillsdale, NJ: Lawrence Erlbaum Associates.

Quine, Willard Van Orman. 1951. Two dogmas of empiricism. *Philosophical Review* 60:20–43.

Reason, James. 2000. Human error: Models and management. *BMJ* 320:768–770.

Reesor, K. A., and K. P. Craig. 1987. Medically incongruent chronic back pain: Physical limitations, suffering, and ineffective coping. *Pain* 32:35–45.

Richards, Janet Radcliffe. 2000. *Human nature after Darwin: A philosophical introduction*. New York: Routledge.

Richter, Daniel K. 1983. War and culture: The Iroquois experience. *William and Mary Quarterly* 40:528–559.

Rodin, Judith. 1982. Patient-practitioner relationships: A Process of Social Influence. In *Contemporary health services: Social science perspectives*, ed. A. W. Johnson, O. Grusky, and B. H. Raven. Boston: Auburn House.

Rodin, Judith. 1986. Aging and health: Effects of the sense of control. *Science* 233:1271–1276.

Rodin, Judith, and E. J. Langer. 1978. Long-term effects of a control-relevant intervention with the institutionalized aged. *Journal of Personality and Social Psychology* 35:897–903.

Rodin, Judith, K. Rennert, and S. K. Solomon. 1980. Intrinsic motivation for control: Fact or fiction? In *Advances in environmental psychology*. Vol. 2, *Applications of personal control*, ed. A. Baum and J. E. Singer, 131–148. Hillsdale, NJ: Erlbaum.

Rosenstock, I. M. 1985. Understanding and enhancing patient compliance with diabetic regimes. *Diabetes Care* 8:610–616.

Ross, L. 1977. The intuitive psychologist and his shortcomings: Distortions in the attribution process. In *Advances in experimental social psychology 10*, ed. L. Berkowitz, 174–221. New York: Academic Press.

Rotter, Julian B. 1966. Generalized expectancies for internal versus external control of reinforcement. *Psychological Monographs* 80 (609): 1–28.

Rotter, Julian B. 1975. Some problems and misconceptions related to the construct of internal vs. external control of reinforcement. *Journal of Consulting and Clinical Psychology* 43:56–67.

Rotter, Julian B. 1979. Individual differences and perceived control. In *Choice and perceived control*, ed. L. C. Perlmuter and R. A. Monty, 263–269. Mahwah, NJ: Lawrence Erlbaum Associates.

Rotter, Julian B. 1989. Internal versus external control of reinforcement. *American Psychologist* 45:489–493.

Ruse, Michael. 1986. *Taking Darwin seriously*. Oxford: Basil Blackwell.

Rychlak, Joseph F. 1979. *Discovering free will and personal responsibility*. New York: Oxford University Press.

Sabatini, Nicholas. 2008. Reaching the next level of aviation safety. *FAASTeam News* (Federal Aviation Administration—FAASTeam—FAASafety.gov).

Sackett, G. P. 1972. Exploratory behavior of rhesus monkeys as a function of rearing experiences and sex. *Developmental Psychology* 6:266–270.

Sartre, Jean-Paul. 1946/1989. Existentialism is a humanism, trans. Philip Mairet. In *Existentialism from Dostoyevsky to Sartre*, ed. Walter Kaufmann, 345–368. New York: Meridian.

Schlick, Moritz. 1939. When is a man responsible? trans. David Rynin. In *Problems of ethics*, 141–158. New York: Prentice-Hall.

Schneider, C. E. 1994. Bioethics with a human face. *Indiana Law Journal* 69: 1075–1104.

Schneider, C. E. 1995. From consumer choice to consumer welfare. *Hastings Center Report* 25:S25–S27.

Schopenhauer, Arthur. 1841/1960. *Essay on the freedom of the will*, trans. Konstantin Kolenda. Indianapolis: Bobbs-Merrill.

Schulz, Richard. 1976. The effects of control and predictability on the psychological and physical well-being of the institutionalized aged. *Journal of Personality and Social Psychology* 33:563–573.

Schulz, Richard, and Barbara Hartman Hanusa. 1978. Long-term effects of control and predictability-enhancing interventions: Findings and ethical issues. *Journal of Personality and Social Psychology* 36:1194–1201.

Searle, John R. 2007. *Freedom and neurobiology: Reflections on free will, language, and political power*. New York: Columbia University Press.

Seligman, Martin E. P. 1975. *Helplessness: On depression, development, and death*. New York: W. H. Freeman.

Shakespeare, William. 1596–1598/1993. *The merchant of Venice*, ed. Jay L. Hightower. Oxford: Oxford World's Classics, Oxford University Press.

Shakespeare, William. 1599/1998. *The tragedy of Julius Caesar*, ed. Arthur Humphreys. Oxford: Oxford World's Classics, Oxford University Press.

Sharpe, Virginia A. 2000. Taking responsibility for medical mistakes. In *Margin of error: The ethics of mistakes in the practice of medicine*, ed. Susan B. Rubin and Laurie Zoloth, 183–192. Hagerstown, MD: University Publishing Group.

Sher, George. 1987. *Desert*. Princeton, NJ: Princeton University Press.

Sher, George. 2006. *In praise of blame*. Oxford: Oxford University Press.

Shingo, Shigeo. 1986. *Zero quality control: Source inspection and the poka-yoke system*. Portland, OR: Productivity Press.

Skinner, B. F. 1971. *Beyond freedom and dignity*. New York: Alfred A. Knopf.

Skinner, B. F. 1974. *About behaviorism*. New York: Alfred A. Knopf.

Smart, J. J. C. 1961. Free will, praise, and blame. *Mind* 70:291–306.

Smilansky, Saul. 2000. *Free will and illusion*. Oxford: Clarendon Press.

Smilansky, Saul. 2005. Free will and respect for persons. *Midwest Studies in Philosophy* 29:248–261.

Smith, Adam. 1759/1976. *The theory of the moral sentiments*, ed. D. D. Raphael and A. L. Macfie. Oxford: Clarendon Press.

Smith, Adam. 1776/1854. Letter from Adam Smith, LL.D. to William Strachan, Esq. In *The philosophical works of David Hume*, vol. 1, xxiii–xxix. Edinburgh: Adam and Charles Black.

Smith, Angela M. 2008. Control, responsibility, and moral assessment. *Philosophical Studies* 138:367–382.

Smith, Marcia Datlow, Pamela J. Haas, and Ronald G. Belcher. 1994. Facilitated communication: The effects of facilitator knowledge and level of assistance on output. *Journal of Autism and Developmental Disorders* 24:357–367.

Smith, Nick. 2005. The categorical apology. *Journal of Social Philosophy* 36: 473–496.

Solomon, Robert C. 2004. *In defense of sentimentality*. New York: Oxford University Press.

Spath, Patrice L., ed. 2000. *Error reduction in health care: A systems approach to improving patient safety*. San Francisco: Jossey-Bass.

Spector, Paul E. 1986. Perceived control by employees: A meta-analysis of studies concerning autonomy and participation at work. *Human Relations* 39:1005–1016.

Spinoza, Baruch. 1677/1985. Ethics, trans. Edwin Curley. *The collected writings of Spinoza*, vol. 1. Princeton: Princeton University Press.

Steiner, Jeanne L. 2006. Managing risk: Systems approach versus personal responsibility for hospital accidents. *Journal of the American Academy of Psychiatry and the Law* 34:96–98.

Stern, Robert. 2004. Does "ought" imply "can"? And did Kant think it does? *Utilitas* 16:42–61.

Strawson, Galen. 1986. *Freedom and belief*. Oxford: Clarendon Press.

Strawson, Galen. 2002. The bounds of freedom. In *The Oxford handbook of free will*, ed. Robert Kane, 441–460. New York: Oxford University Press.

Strawson, Galen. 2010. Your move: The maze of free will. *New York Times Opinionator*, July 22, http://opinionator.blogs.nytimes.com/2010/07/22/your-move-the-maze-of-free-will (accessed July 22, 2010).

Strawson, P. F. 1962. Freedom and Resentment. *Proceedings of the British Academy* 36. Page references as reprinted in *Free Will*, ed. Gary Watson. New York: Oxford University Press, 1982.

Suomi, S. J., and H. F. Harlow. 1976. The facts and functions of fear. In *Emotions and anxiety: New concepts, methods, and applications*, ed. M. Zuckerman and C. D. Speilberger, 3–34. Hillsdale, NJ: Lawrence Erlbaum Associates.

Taylor, Charles. 1976. Responsibility for self. In *Identities of persons*, ed. Amelie Rorty. Berkeley: University of California Press.

Taylor, Richard. 1963. *Metaphysics*. Englewood Cliffs, NJ: Prentice-Hall.

Taylor, Shelley E. 1983. Adjustment to threatening events: A theory of cognitive adaptation. *American Psychologist* 38:1161–1173.

Taylor, Shelley E., V. S. Helgeson, G. M. Reed, and L. A. Skokan. 1991. Self-generated feelings of control and adjustment to physical illness. *Journal of Social Issues* 47:91–109.

Thompson, S. C., A. Sobolew-Shubin, M. E. Galbraith, L. Schwankovsky, and D. Cruzen. 1993. Maintaining perceptions of control: Finding perceived control in low-control circumstances. *Journal of Personality and Social Psychology* 64:293–304.

Tolman, E. C. 1925. Purpose and cognition: The determiners of animal learning. *Psychological Review* 32:285–297.

Trakakis, Nick, and Daniel Cohen. 2008. Introduction. In *Essays on free will and moral responsibility*, ed. Nick Trakakis and Daniel Cohen, ix–xxii. Newcastle upon Tyne, UK: Cambridge Scholars Publishing.

Ulrich, R. E., and N. H. Azrin. 1962. Reflexive fighting in response to aversive stimulation. *Journal of the Experimental Analysis of Behavior* 5:511–520.

Valla, Lorenzo. 1443/1948. Dialogue on Free Will, trans. Charles Edward Trinkaus, Jr. In *The Renaissance philosophy of man*, ed. Ernst Cassirer, Paul O. Kristeller, and John H. Randall, 155–182. Chicago: University of Chicago Press.

van den Haag, Ernest. 1985. The death penalty once more. *University of California Davis Law Review* 18:957–972.

van Inwagen, Peter. 1983. *An essay on free will*. Oxford: Clarendon Press.

Vargas, Manuel. 2007. Revisionism. In *Four views on free will*, John Martin Fischer, Robert Kane, Derk Pereboom, and Manuel Vargas, 126–165. Oxford: Blackwell Publishing.

Venkatraman, M. P., D. Marlino, F. R. Kardes, and K. B. Sklar. 1990. Effects of individual difference variables on response to factual and evaluative ads. *Advances in Consumer Research* 17:761–765.

Venkatraman, M. P., and L. L. Price. 1990. Differentiating between cognitive and sensory innovativeness. *Journal of Business Research* 20:293–315.

Virgin, Charles E., and Robert Sapolsky. 1997. Styles of male social behavior and their endocrine correlates among low-ranking baboons. *American Journal of Primatology* 42:25–39.

Vohs, K. D., and J. W. Schooler. 2008. The value of believing in free will: Encouraging a belief in determinism increases cheating. *Psychological Science* 19:49–54.

Wallace, R. Jay. 1994. *Responsibility and the moral sentiments*. Cambridge, MA: Harvard University Press.

Waller, Bruce N. 1989. Denying responsibility: The difference it makes. *Analysis* 49:44–47.

Waller, Bruce N. 1990. *Freedom without responsibility*. Philadelphia: Temple University Press.

Waller, Bruce N. 1998. *The natural selection of autonomy*. Albany: State University of New York Press.

Waller, Bruce N. 1999. Deep thinkers, cognitive misers, and moral responsibility. *Analysis* 59:44–47.

Waller, Bruce N. 2001. Patient autonomy naturalized. *Perspectives in Biology and Medicine* 44:584–593.

Waller, Bruce N. 2002. The psychological structure of patient autonomy. *Cambridge Quarterly of Healthcare Ethics* 11:257–265.

Waller, Bruce N. 2004. Neglected psychological elements of free will. *Philosophy, Psychiatry, & Psychology* 11:111–118.

Waller, Bruce N. 2006. Denying responsibility without making excuses. *American Philosophical Quarterly* 43:81–89.

Wallhagen, Margaret I., and Meryl Brod. 1997. Perceived control and well-being in Parkinson's disease. *Western Journal of Nursing Research* 17:467–483.

Wallston, K. A. 1993. Psychological control and its impact in the management of rheumatological disorders. *Bailliere's Clinical Rheumatology* 7:281–295.

Watson, Gary. 1987a. Free action and free will. *Mind* 96:145–172.

Watson, Gary. 1987b. Responsibility and the limits of evil. In *Responsibility, character, and the emotions*, ed. Ferdinand Schoeman, 256–286. Cambridge, UK: Cambridge University Press.

Webster, D. M., and A. W. Kruglanski. 1994. Individual differences in need for cognitive closure. *Journal of Personality and Social Psychology* 67:1049–1062.

Wegner, Daniel. 2002. *The illusion of conscious will*. Cambridge, MA: MIT Press.

Wegner, Daniel, and T. Wheatley. 1999. Apparent mental causation: Sources of the experience of will. *American Psychologist* 54:480–491.

White, Stephen L. 1991. *The unity of the self*. Cambridge, MA: MIT Press.

Wiedenfeld, S. A., A. O'Leary, A. Bandura, S. Brown, S. Levine, and K. Raska. 1990. Impact of perceived self-efficacy in coping with stressors on components of the immune system. *Journal of Personality and Social Psychology* 59:1082–1094.

Wilkinson, Richard. 2004. Why is violence more common where inequality is greater? *Annals of the New York Academy of Sciences* 1036:1–12.

Williams, Bernard. 1995. How free does the will need to be? In *Making sense of humanity*, 3–21. Cambridge, UK: Cambridge University Press.

Wilson, T. D. 2002. *Strangers to ourselves: Discovering the adaptive unconscious*. Cambridge, MA: Belknap Press of Harvard University Press.

Wolf, Susan. 1980. Asymmetrical freedom. *Journal of Philosophy* 77:151–166.

Wolf, Susan. 1981. The importance of free will. *Mind* 90:386–405.

Wolf, Susan. 1987. Sanity and the metaphysics of responsibility. In *Responsibility, character, and the emotions*, ed. Ferdinand Schoeman, 46–62. Cambridge, UK: Cambridge University Press.

Wolf, Susan. 1990. *Freedom within reason*. Oxford, UK: Oxford University Press.

Woodward, N. J., and B. S. Wallston. 1987. Age and health care beliefs: Self-efficacy as a mediator of low desire for control. *Psychology and Aging* 2:3–8.

Wright, Robert. 1994. *The moral animal.* New York: Pantheon.

Zuckerman, Marvin. 1983. A biological theory of sensation seeking. In *Biological bases of sensation seeking, impulsivity, and anxiety,* ed. Marvin Zuckerman, 37–76. Hillsdale, NJ: Lawrence Erlbaum Associates.

Zuckerman, Marvin. 2007. *Sensation seeking and risky behavior.* Washington, DC: American Psychological Association.

Index